Environmental Law and Policy in India

This book focuses on administrative regulation in environmental law. It also focuses on climate change, and the push for sustainability.

Covering the regulation on forest conservation, wildlife protection, water pollution, air pollution, and noise pollution, the book looks into the practical application of environmental legislation. This includes responses to international environmental agreements within India and the economic impact. It also discusses historical jurisprudence, and the administrative frameworks existing as a result of this.

Focusing on contemporary issues within the legal landscape, the book aims to provide a solid foundation for researchers, legal practitioners, and scholars in the field of environmental law and policymaking.

Sairam Bhat is a Professor of Law at NLSIU and provides training and advisory to various Government and Non-governmental entities engaged in Start-up incubation and funding, public tender, RTI, corporate law compliance, etc. He is a recipient of numerous fellowships including the Fulbright-Nehru Fellowship in 2010 at the University of Georgetown, Washington, and the Linnaeus-Palme Academic Exchange Fellow at the Royal Institute of Technology, Stockholm in 2013, and received the 'Young India Environmental Law Fellowship' in 2003. His research contributions on various legal aspects include those published with *inter alia* Sage Publications, Bloomsbury, and Eastern Book House.

The **Centre for Environmental Law, Education, Research, and Advocacy (CEERA)**, established in 1997, is a leading research centre within NLSIU that primarily focuses on research, policy advocacy, and training in environmental law. Over the years, CEERA, through its environmental law database, has undertaken training and capacity-building, and provided consultancy, by effectively networking among all stakeholders towards an environmental law fraternity. CEERA works closely with the UNDP, Ministry of Environment and Forest, National Biodiversity Authority, Ministry of Jal Shakti, ICSSR, and the Department of Justice on various policy research projects.

Routledge Research in International Environmental Law

Compensation for Environmental Damage Under International Law
Jason Rudall

International Environmental Law Compliance in Context
Mechanisms and Case Studies
Belen Olmos Giupponi

Sustainable Fisheries Management and International Law
Marine Fisheries in Bangladesh and the Bay of Bengal
Abdullah Al Arif

Marine Conservation and International Law
Legal Instruments for Biodiversity Beyond National Jurisdiction
Sarah Louise Lothian

Nature Law and Policy in Europe
Edited by Andrew L.R. Jackson

Environmental Liability and the Interplay between EU Law and International Law
Dr Emanuela Orlando

Implementing International Environmental Law and Policy
An Interactive Approach to Environmental Regulation
Joanna Miller Smallwood

Environmental Law and Governance in India
Sairam Bhat and Centre for Environmental Law, Education, Research, and Advocacy (CEERA)

Environmental Law and Policy in India
Sairam Bhat and Centre for Environmental Law, Education, Research, and Advocacy (CEERA)

https://www.routledge.com/Routledge-Research-in-International-Environmental-Law/book-series/INTENVLAW

Environmental Law and Policy in India

Sairam Bhat and Centre for Environmental Law, Education, Research, and Advocacy (CEERA)

Routledge
Taylor & Francis Group
LONDON AND NEW YORK

First published 2025
by Routledge
4 Park Square, Milton Park, Abingdon, Oxon OX14 4RN

and by Routledge
605 Third Avenue, New York, NY 10158

Routledge is an imprint of the Taylor & Francis Group, an informa business

British Library Cataloguing-in-Publication Data
A catalogue record for this book is available from the British Library

ISBN: 978-1-032-69259-3 (hbk)
ISBN: 978-1-032-70388-6 (pbk)
ISBN: 978-1-032-70390-9 (ebk)

DOI: 10.4324/ 9781032703909

Typeset in Times New Roman
by Deanta Global Publishing Services, Chennai, India

Contents

Preface

In light of an ever-escalating environmental crisis, environmental law plays a pivotal role in safeguarding the environment. Since the landmark United Nations Conference on Human Environment (Stockholm Conference) in 1972, the corpus of environmental law has experienced exponential growth both internationally and domestically. Over the last five decades, environmental law has percolated through the 'greening' of Constitutions, the enactment and introduction of new legislations and policies, and the establishment of various dedicated institutional mechanisms for environmental protection. Further, the discipline of environmental law has emerged as a critical and integral tool for safeguarding our fragile ecosystems, protecting human health, and promoting sustainability. Another noteworthy and significant development in the discipline has been the paradigm shift from anthropocentric to an ecocentric approach for the conservation of nature. The ecocentric approach recognises the intrinsic value of nature itself and emphasises the importance of the conservation and protection of the environment and biodiversity for its own sake and independent of any immediate human benefit. Against the backdrop of these profound developments, there is a growing need for a comprehensive and contemporary resource on the subject of environmental law in India.

The purpose of the present work is not only to contribute to the existing pool of critical and analytical literature on environment law but also to further strengthen the working of the Centre for Environmental Law, Education, Research and Advocacy (CEERA), National Law School of India University (NLSIU), Bengaluru. Established in 1997, CEERA is the premier research centre in the field of environmental legal education in India. Over the course of more than 25 years, CEERA has carried out various projects for the Government of India, State Governments, and international agencies such as the World Bank and the United Nation Development Programme (UNDP). Some of the projects include a Global ABS project on capacity building in the implementation of the Biodiversity Act, 2002 (under the aegis of UNDP), a three-year research project on 'Collaborative Engagement for Research, Training and Development in Handling of Chemicals and Hazardous Waste' (under the aegis of MoEFCC), a five-year research project on 'Agricultural Water Governance and Policy' (under the aegis of ICAR-IIWM, Bhubaneshwar). Further, the centre has undertaken several training and capacity-building exercises in the field of environmental law for officers of various Government departments including Indian Forest Services Officers and Pollution

Control Boards. It has also been a part of various litigation and advocacy initiatives especially in the field of biodiversity and pollution control. Recently, CEERA prepared and published a Handbook on 'Prosecution of Offences under the Water Act, 1974 and Air Act, 1981' in pursuance of an order of the High Court of Karnataka. Further, the Centre also prepared the draft Climate (Protection) Bill, 2021, which is one of India's first dedicated laws on climate protection. The centre has published extensively in the field of environmental law and hosts a rich repository of material on its websites.

The previous publications of the Centre have primarily concentrated on specific areas in pursuance of the objectives and deliverables under research and other projects. These publications have contributed immensely towards enhancing the collective knowledge base of the Centre by providing in-depth sectoral experience and by fostering expertise. Further, they have been used by the Centre in providing research-based training and capacity-building to officers of both Government and non-government agencies, as well as for wider circulation and for the development of a knowledge repository in the discipline of environmental law. Although the previous sector-specific publications of the Centre have been well received and appreciated by various stakeholders, many of them have expressed a growing need for a comprehensive resource that addresses the broad spectrum of environment law in a single publication, a resource that not only encompasses theoretical knowledge but also its contextual application in practice, implementation, regulation, and adjudication which has been a hallmark of CEERA's activities. Recognising and appreciating this need, and acknowledging that CEERA as a premier research centre should contribute to the existing scholarship on environmental law with its unique stand point, the arduous endeavour of producing these two volumes was undertaken. The present work seeks to elucidate, examine, and evaluate the diverse facets of environmental law including governance, regulation, and policy in a comprehensive and holistic manner.

The present work, curated across two volumes and comprising ten chapters, traverses the rich and intricate tapestry of laws, regulation, principles, and policies that shape India's environmental legal landscape. The first volume, titled *Environmental Law and Governance in India*, comprises five chapters that provide a comprehensive understanding of the legal jurisprudence and governance structures designed to safeguard the environment in India. The topics covered include constitutional and common law principles of environmental protection, international environmental law, water governance and coastal regulation, and the National Green Tribunal. The second volume, titled *Environmental Law and Policy in India*, explores, examines, and evaluates the environmental regulatory landscape in India. It comprises five chapters that scrutinize the critical issues related to forest regulation and conservation, wildlife protection and prevention of cruelty to animals, and the regulatory framework for the prevention and control of water and air pollution. The various legal and policy dimensions discussed in the present work are central to mitigating the impact of environmental degradation and securing a better sustainable future.

The aim of these two volumes is to empower readers with the knowledge and insights required to engage and contribute to the ongoing discourse on environmental protection and sustainable development. It is curated for a diverse audience, it is intended be a textbook for law students, a comprehensive and rich source of contemporary environmental law literature for researchers, and a handbook that provides substantive and procedural clarity for officers, regulators, and legal professionals. It is my sincere wish that the discussion contained in these pages will prove beneficial and enrich the knowledge base of its readers.

The content of the present work was prepared by the collective working of the CEERA Team over the course of five years in the field of environmental law. It is a culmination and manifestation of our collective knowledge acquired through our various academic, research, litigation, advocacy, drafting, training, and capacity-building activities. In this regard, I would like to wholeheartedly convey my gratitude to each member of the CEERA Team who have contributed in this endeavour. I would like to thank Dr. Madhubanti Sadhya, Mr. Vikas Gahlot, Mr. Rohith Kamath, Mr. Jaibatruka Mohanta, Ms. Gayathri KK, Ms. Gayathri Gireesh, Mr. Raghav Parthasarathy, Mr. Divyanshu Privyadarshi, Ms. Geethanjali KV, Ms. Lianne D'Souza, and Ms. Aparna Sojan for their valuable contributions in the present work.

Prof. (Dr.) Sairam Bhat
Professor of Law & Coordinator CEERA-NLSIU

Acknowledgements

The present work is an outcome of the collective, collaborative, and continuous effort of all members of the Centre for Environmental Law, Education, Research and Advocacy, (CEERA) Team. It is an culmination and expression of our collective knowledge accumulated over the years through our various academic, teaching, research, litigation, advocacy, drafting, and capacity-building activities.

In this regard, I would like to express my sincere appreciation to all the members of the CEERA Team who dedicated themselves to the meticulous analysis of the vast array of legal precedents, statutes, and case studies which form the bedrock of this work.

I wholeheartedly thank **Mr. Vikas Gahlot, Mr. Rohith Kamath, Dr. Madhubanti Sadhya, Ms. Lianne D'Souza, Mr. Jaibatruka Mohanta, Ms. Gayathri KK, Ms. Gayathri Gireesh, Mr. Raghav Parthasarathy, Ms. Geethanjali KV, and Ms. Aparna Sojan** for their valuable contributions in the present work.

Lastly, in the spirit of collective responsibility for the future of environmental law, I pray and hope that this book serves as a reference material for deliberations, research, dialogue, and actions surrounding environmental law and policy in India.

List of Cases

A

- A Citizen v. District Collector R.R. District, 1998 (4) ALD 389 **[217]**
- A Rangaraj v. Union of India, W.P. 897 of 1996 **[87]**
- A Viswanathan v. State of Tamil Nadu, (2022) 6 Mad LJ 517 **[71]**
- A.P. Pollution Control Board v. Prof. M.V. Nayudu, 1999 (2) SCC 718 **[134,157]**
- Aam Janta v. State of M.P, 2014 SCC ONLINE NGT 6897 **[218]**
- Abdul Hamid v. The Gwalior Rayon Silk Mfg., 1989 Cri. LJ 2013 **[197]**
- Akhil Bhartiya Mengela Samaj Parishad v. Maharashtra Pollution Control Board, MANU/GT/0018/2022 **[158]**
- Alembic Pharmaceuticals Ltd. v. Rohit Prajapati, (2020)17 SCC 157 **[195]**
- Ambica Quarry Works v. State of Gujarat, (1987) 1 SCC 213 **[26]**
- Andhra Pradesh Pollution Control Board v. M.V. Nayudu (2001) 2 SCC 62 **[155]**
- Andreae v. Selfridge and Co. Ltd. (1938) Ch 1 **[240]**
- Animal Welfare Board of India v. People for Elimination of Stray Troubles and Ors., Special Leave to Appeal (C) 691/2009 clubbed with other SLPs and petitions decided on 17.11.2016 **[129]**
- Arjun Gopal v. Union of India, AIR 1996 SC 2231 **[226]**
- Arjun Gopal v. Union of India, AIR 2018 SC 5731 **[248]**
- Arjun Gopal v. Union of India, I.A. NO. 48692 OF 2022 and IA NO. 104836 OF 2023 IN WRIT PETITION (C) NO.728 OF 2015 **[227]**
- Attakoya Thangal v. Union of India, 1990 (1) K.L.T. 580 **[133]**
- Ayyappa Stone Crusher v. Mandal Revenue Officer, 2000 SCC OnLine AP 918 **[197]**

B

- Balram Kumawat v. Union of India, 2003 SCC OnLine SC 922 **[92]**
- Banwasi Seva Ashram v. State of U. P. (1987) 3 SCC 304 **[17]**
- Banwasi Seva Ashram v. State of U. P. (1992) 1 SCC 117 **[17]**
- Bengaluru Mahanagara Ganesh Utsav Samiti v. State of Karnataka (2017) Writ Petition Nos. 35047 and 35448 of 2017 (Kar HC) **[160]**

E

F

G

H

N

O

P

- State of Tripura v. Sudhir Ranjan Nath, (1997) 3 SCC 665 **[23]**
- State v. Salman Khan, S.B. C.A. No.53/2012 **[111]**
- Stella Silks v. State of Karnataka, AIR 2001 Kant 219 **[177]**
- Subhash Kumar v. State of Bihar AIR 1991 SC 420 **[218]**
- Suma Traders v. Karnataka State Pollution Control Board, AIR 1998 Kar 8. **[153]**
- Sunita Pandey v. Union of India (OA No. 384/2019) (NGT) **[198]**
- Suo Moto v. Union of India, (31.05.2019 - NGT): MANU/GT/0047/2019 **[213]**

T

- T. N. Godavarman Thirumulpad v. Union of India (1996) 9 SCR 982 **[23]**
- T. N. Godavarman Thirumulpad v. Union of India, W.P. 202/1995 **[27,40,68]**
- T. N. Godavarman v. Union of India, AIR 1997 SC 1228 **[16]**
- T. Narasimhamurthy v. State of Karnataka, W.P. No. 39682 of 2016 (Kar HC).**[165]**
- T.N. Godavarman Thirumulpad v. Union of India, WP (Civil) No. 202 of 1995, Order dated 26/09/2005 **[29,40]**
- T.N. Godavarman Thirumulpad v. Union of India, AIR 2014 SC 3614 **[38]**
- Tamil Nadu Pollution Control Board v. Sterlite Industries (I) Ltd., (2019) 19 SCC 479 **[155,157,171,193]**
- Tata Housing Development Company vs Aalok Jagga, 2019 SCC OnLine SC 1419 **[79]**
- Tata Tea Ltd. v. State of Kerala, 1983 SCC OnLine Ker 129 **[197]**
- Techi Tagi Tara v. Rajendra Singh Bhandari, Civil Appeal No. 1359 of 2017, decided on 22 September 2017 (Supreme Court of India) **[147,165]**
- Tirupur Dyeing Factory Owners Assn. v. Noyyal River Ayacutdars Protection Assn, (2009) 9 SCC 737 **[140]**

U

- U Khastia v. Range Officer, Jirimukh, AIR 1958 Manipur 31 **[19]**
- U.P. Pollution Control Board v. Dr. Bhupendra Kumar Modi, (2009) 2 SCC 147 **[182]**
- U.P. Pollution Control Board v. Mohan Meakins Ltd., (2000) 3 SCC 745 **[184]**
- U.P. Pollution Control Board v. Messrs Modi Distillery, (1987) 3 SCC 684 **[184]**
- Union of India v. Zavaray S. Poonawala, (2015) 7 SCC 347 **[113]**

V

- V. Sambasivam v. GoI, Ministry of Tribal Affairs, W.P. Np. 4533/2008 **[37]**

1 Introduction to Environmental Regulation

The environmental law and regulatory framework encompasses a diverse range of critical functions that are interwoven and unified by the common thread of the right to a clean and healthy environment as a fundamental and inalienable human right. The right to a clean and healthy environment underscores and emphasises that the quality of the environment is an essential determinant of quality of life.The broad aim of the discipline of environmental law is to define and delineate the various aspects of this inherent human right and to secure its effective realisation and uninterrupted enjoyment. However, the right over the environment is also the predominant focus of law governing the exploitation of natural resources. In this context, the rights of nature and the rights of other species to their natural environment are being increasingly advocated for and are being gradually recognised.

In light of this, one of the pivotal roles of environmental law is to oversee and regulate industrial and business activities, particularly their dependency and utilisation of earth's natural resources and their impact on the environment. However, this regulation should be in such a manner that balances the interests of the current generation without compromising the interests of future generations. Hence, through environmental law, it is necessary to strike a balance between conservation and protection of natural resources and ease of doing business. However, with rapidly growing public concerns related to a host of environmental issues, the demand and advocacy for the enactment of stringent and stricter regulations are increasingly gaining force. Therefore, it is crucial to remember that environmental justice is not about human-centric politics, but rather pertains to protecting nature's wealth. Thus, both over-protection and under-protection should be avoided. It is also critical to understand the difference between proactive environmental law and reactive environmental law. Proactive environmental law seeks to conserve, protect, and preserve nature whereas reactive environmental law seeks to impose strict sanctions and harsh penalties upon environmental violators. A balanced environmental regulatory regime is proactive but not reactive or overactive.

The Indian regulatory framework for environment protection is a combination of the spirit of international law, constitutional principles, and judicial pronouncements along with India's rich cultural heritage of living in harmony with nature, the principle of *Vasudhaiva Kutumbakam*, and the country's aspiration of fulfilling its local and developmental needs. Furthermore, the regulatory framework carefully

DOI: 10.4324/9781032703909-1

navigates the challenges of the wide geographical, topographical, and cultural landscape of the country.

1.1 Overview of Environmental Regulators in India

The evolution of the Ministry of Environment, Forests and Climate Change, from a small department to becoming one of the most prominent, proactive, and robust Government institutions is reflective of the growth of environmental law in India. The need for a separate department and thereafter as a distinct ministry was only felt during the Fourth Five-Year Plan.[1] The Constitution of India was amended in 1976, which laid the foundation for the establishment of a Department of Environment in 1980. In 1985, this department was turned into the Ministry of Environment and Forest. In 2014, the Ministry also incorporated within its ambit the issue of climate change, and was renamed the Ministry of Environment, Forests and Climate Change (MoEFCC). The various legal frameworks required the composition of a governance and regulatory framework. The Ministry of Environment at the Central level and the Ministry of Forests at the State level were in charge of monitoring and supervising the implementation of the Forest Act, 1927. The Forest Act, 1927, provided for the setting up of various authorities for settling claims, inquiry, and such other purposes as the Act specified. Apart from the authorities concerned with the forests, the Wild Life Protection Act, 1972, establishes various authorities including the Zoo Authorities,[2] National Board for Wildlife,[3] Crime Control Bureau,[4] and National Tiger Conservation Authority[5] across India. These authorities have been tasked with different responsibilities to ensure the implementation of the Wild Life (Protection) Act. As a result of the efforts of these authorities, the tiger and elephant species have seen gradual but marginal increases in numbers.

Furthermore, to implement the Water and Air Acts, the Central Pollution Control Board was established[6] at the Central level and the Pollution Control Committees in Union Territories. To implement the Water and Air Acts at the State level, the State Pollution Control Boards[7] were established. The functions of these boards are to advise their respective governments on the prevention and control of water and air pollution. The Boards have been vested with various powers to issue, grant, and revoke licences to industries. The Boards are also empowered to inspect and

1 Fourth Five-Year Plan 1969–1974.

2 The Central Zoo Authority was established in the year 1992 with the objective of conserving wildlife by housing, upkeep, health care, and overall management of animals in zoos.

3 The Wild Life (Protection) Act, 1972, § 5A.

4 The Wild Life (Protection) Act, 1972, § 38Y provides for the establishment of the Tiger and other Endangered Species Crime Control Bureau.

5 The National Tiger Conservation Authority was established in 2005 with the objective of increasing the tiger population, which was dwindling in numbers, in India.

6 The Water (Prevention and Control of Pollution) Act, 1974, § 3.

7 *Id.* § 5.

collect samples of trade effluents for testing purposes. Along with this, the Boards are also responsible for establishing laboratories, setting standards for effluents, and also investing in research and development for waste treatment and generally to spread awareness and prepare manuals, codes, and guidelines as prescribed under the Act.

1.2 Role of International Law in Environmental Regulation

International treaties have also been a source of environmental laws in India. For example, the Convention on International Trade in Endangered Species of Wild Fauna and Flora (CITES) was implemented by India's Wild Life (Protection) Act, 1972. The United Nations Conference on Environment and Development (UNCED), 1992, also known as the Earth Summit, aimed at promoting intergenerational equity and sustainable development. This led to actions compensating victims of pollution and environmental damages. Establishing adjudicatory bodies for handling environmental issues was the major outcome. In the past decade, India has spearheaded international action on environmental protection. Illustratively, India has played a pivotal role in supporting and implementing the Paris Agreement of 2015, a legally binding international treaty on climate change.

Despite the recent developments at the global level being inclined towards environmental protection and sustainable development, the contribution of international treaties to the growth of environmental regulation cannot be belittled. The UN Human Rights Council has recognised, for the first time, the right to a clean, safe, and sustainable environment as a human right. Further, the Trail Smelter case and the Corfu Channel case illustrate the doctrine of *sic utero tuoutalienum non laedas*, which became the guiding principle for the prevention of environmental pollution and damage between nations. The principle laid down in the Trail Smelter case became the binding principle which reflects the intentions of the Stockholm Declaration on Human Environment, 1972. The Action Plan developed under the Declaration emphasised national and international cooperation in the identification and appraisal of environmental damages of global importance. The Declaration resulted in amendments to the Constitution of India, which was reflected in several laws, viz., the Water Act, 1974, Air Act, 1981, Environment (Protection) Act, 1986, and Factories (Amendment) Act, 1987.

With the constant rise in industrial activities, several developed countries generating huge amounts of waste found it difficult to dump the waste in their backyard. Eventually, these wastes were dumped in poor countries in exchange for money. The Khian Sea Waste Disposal incident highlighted the need for a global treaty controlling the transboundary movement of hazardous wastes and their disposal in 1987. As a result of this, the Basel Convention took place. The Convention prevents the signatory countries from shipping hazardous wastes to non-parties. It lays down certain prescriptions for packaging and labelling wastes. Accordingly, India enacted the Hazardous Wastes (Management and Handling) Rules, 1989, and the Bio-Medical Wastes (Management and Handling) Rules, 1998.

1.3 Cross-Roads of Environmental Regulation

The growing consciousness of sustainability, technological advancements, and the climate crisis are paving the way to a regulatory framework that is dynamic and futuristic, moving beyond the rudimentary aspects. The challenges of the new era include greenwashing, property sinking, sustainability reporting, climate change, and green credit trading, amongst others. These do not strictly relate to environmental harms but are an off-shoot of environmental challenges.

1.3.1 Green Washing

The term 'greenwashing' was first introduced by Jay Westervelt, an environmental activist from New York, in 1986. Greenwashing refers to the practice of misleading consumers or investors about the environmental or social benefits of a product, service, or company.[8] As per Lyon and Maxwell, greenwashing refers to the 'Selective disclosure of positive information about a company's environmental or social performance, without full disclosure of negative information on these dimensions, so as to create an overly positive corporate image'.[9] Greenwashing can be seen as a form of marketing spin that exploits the growing demand for environmentally friendly and socially responsible products and practices. In the Indian context, evidence shows that there persists immense greenwashing in corporate claims of being environmentally friendly.[10] This is concerning because greenwashing can have negative consequences for consumers, investors, and the environment. Moreover, greenwashing diverts attention and resources away from addressing the real environmental and social challenges that we face.[11]

1.3.2 Green Financing, Green Deposits, and Green Credits

Green finance is also progressively gaining traction in India. The Reserve Bank of India (RBI), the central banking institution in India, unveiled its groundbreaking 'Framework for Acceptance of Green Deposits', an initiative of India's sustainable finance, establishing the commitment to promoting financial practices that are environmentally friendly. Noting that the financial sector can play a pivotal role in mobilising resources and the allocation thereof in green activities/projects, the framework was issued to the financial institutions in India. A remarkable feature of the regulations pertains to the 'use of proceeds' from green deposits. The

8 Béatrice Parguel, et al., *How Sustainability Ratings Might Deter "Greenwashing": A Closer Look at Ethical Corporate Communication*, 102 Journal of Business Ethics 15 (2011).

9 Thomas P. Lyon & John W. Maxwell, *Greenwash: Corporate Environmental Disclosure under Threat of Audit*, 20 Journal of Economics & Management Strategy 3 (2011).

10 Angeline Gautami Fernando, et al., *Nature of Green Advertisements in India: Are They Greenwashed?*, 24 Asian Journal of Communication 222 (2014).

11 Stephen J. Scanlan, *Framing Fracking: Scale-Shifting and Greenwashing Risk in the Oil and Gas Industry*, 22 The International Journal of Justice and Sustainability 1311–1337 (2017).

framework explicitly excludes investments related to fossil fuels, nuclear power, and waste incineration, offering a clear and concise definition of what qualifies as green. The 'use of proceeds' in the Green Deposit Framework presents numerous opportunities, including investments in renewable energy, electric mobility, and climate change adaptation.

Correspondingly, to promote environmentally positive actions, the Government of India has promulgated the Green Credit Rules, 2023, which is a pivotal step towards establishing a sustainable framework for a more ecologically sound future. With the implementation of these rules, companies and individuals are presented with incentives to embrace and incorporate eco-friendly practices into their operations and daily lives. The Rules provide for the setting up of the Green Credit Program, whereby a regime for trading of green credits is set up, bolstering the environmental conscientiousness of individuals and entities. These green credits are generated as a direct result of environmentally conscious initiatives undertaken by a wide array of participants. This innovative approach not only integrates environmental responsibility into economic participation but also establishes a tangible value for environmentally sustainable practices.

1.3.3 Rising Seas and Sinking Property

Environmental law plays a pivotal role in addressing and regulating issues related to property rights and environmental sustainability. One significant aspect of this field is the concept of 'property sinking' where property values deteriorate due to environmental degradation or contamination. Property sinking may be regarded as the 'diminution in property value,' whereby the economic worth of real property sinks on account of environmental factors, such as floods, droughts, landslides, etc. The floods in September 2022 in Bangalore, Karnataka, saw several properties including vehicles, land, apartments, shops, and other commercial establishments submerged due to the flooding of rainwater. The local municipal authorities identified over 696 encroachments, on probing the causes for such a devastation. A similar illustration is the Love Canal incident, which unfolded in the late 1970s in Niagara Falls, New York, wherein several properties lost value due to toxic waste contamination. This case had a profound impact on environmental law and the legal rights of property owners. Thousands of families residing in the Love Canal neighbourhood were exposed to hazardous chemicals, leading to a substantial decline in property values. Legal actions, ultimately, played a significant role in addressing this crisis, providing compensation to affected property owners and compelling the establishment of stricter regulations.[12]

12 Eckardt C. Beck, *The Love Canal Tragedy*, 5(1) EPA Journal 16 (1979).

1.3.4 Environment and Force Majeure

Environmental damage poses a significant challenge to the global community, necessitating a comprehensive legal framework to address the responsibility of individuals and entities for harm caused to the environment. The interface of *force majeure* and the environment mainly seeks redressal of two prime queries, viz. (i) does a *force majeure* event absolve one from environmental liability; and (ii) can environmental changes amount to *force majeure*? The term '*force majeure*' is a Latin term that translates to '*superior strength*', to mean anything that is beyond the control of the respective parties. The answers to both queries are complex and dependent on various factors. Domestic laws in many jurisdictions contain specific provisions for environmental liability and establish absolute liability on the owner/occupier of such operations amenable to liability in case of environmental harm.

In connection with environmental regulation and changes such as *force majeure* to the performance of contractual obligations, there seems to be a growing shift, as compliance with environmental regulations involves additional expenditure for the installation of needful technology. The courts have found themselves in a divide between economic hardship and the technological feasibility of the parties to the contract. Contractual agreements, particularly in the energy sector, have strict mandatory purchase clauses that are entered into to counter-balance the cost of the generator of energy. In *International Minerals & Chemical Corp v. Llano*, a court in the USA accepted that new emission limits imposed on the buyer's facilities excused the buyers' obligation to take delivery of gas.[13]

It is crucial to emphasise that *force majeure* typically applies to contractual obligations and not necessarily to statutory responsibilities under environmental laws.

1.3.5 SEBI-BSBR Guidelines

In May 2021, the Securities and Exchange Board of India (SEBI) issued a circular on Business Responsibility and Sustainability Reporting (BRSR) by listed entities. The BRSR is a new reporting framework that replaces the existing Business Responsibility Report (BRR) that was introduced by SEBI in 2012. The BRSR aims to capture the environmental, social, and governance (ESG) performance and impact of listed entities in a more comprehensive and standardised manner.[14]

It is designed to be integrated with SEBI's electronic filing system for listed entities and is expected to enhance the quality and comparability of ESG disclosures by listed entities in India. It will also enable investors and other stakeholders to make more informed decisions based on ESG factors. SEBI's recent update of ESG guidelines, starting from the 2023 financial reporting year, requires the top 1,000 companies in India, as ranked by market capitalisation, to include a BRSR

13 International Minerals and Chemical Corp v. Llano, Inc, 770 F2d 879, 886 (10th Cir 1985).

14 PTI, *SEBI's Proposed ESG Disclosure to Address Risk of "Green Washing": Experts*, The Economic Times, https://economictimes.indiatimes.com/mf/mf-news/sebis-proposed-esg-disclosure-to-address-risk-of-green-washing-experts/articleshow/87361687.cms (last updated Oct. 29, 2021).

with their annual submissions to stock exchanges. This underscores the increasing awareness and pressing importance of having a well-defined ESG policy.[15]

1.4 Summary of the Chapters

The first volume focussed on the law and governance aspects of environmental protection. Apart from introducing and elucidating the discipline of environmental law to its readers, it comprehensively dealt with a range of topics such as the principles of environmental protection, the constitutional and common law dimensions of environmental protection, and developments in international environmental law, amongst others.

The present volume is the continuation of the discussion that was initiated in the first volume. Titled *Environmental Law and Policy in India* this volume focusses on the regulatory aspects of environmental law and policy related to forest conservation, wildlife protection, water pollution, air pollution, noise pollution, and waste management. The discourse on these critical aspects is curated in the next five chapters as follows.

The second chapter, 'Forest Conservation: Law and Regulatory Framework', provides a comprehensive elucidation and analysis of the regulatory framework for forest conservation in India. It begins by examining the historical evolution of forest regulation from pre-independence to contemporary times, highlighting the shift in regulatory perspective from the regulation of forests for the exploitation of resources to the conservation of forests for their own intrinsic and critical value. Further, it provides an in-depth elucidation of the various legislative instruments, including the Indian Forest Act, 1927, the Compensatory Afforestation Act, 2016, etc. It also explores the concepts of protected areas, eco-sensitive zones, and best practices of forest conservation at the State level.

The third chapter, 'Laws on Wildlife Protection and Prevention of Cruelty to Animals in India', offers a thorough exploration of the legal regulatory framework concerning wildlife protection and the prevention of animal cruelty in India. Its primary emphasis is on the Wildlife (Protection) Act, 1972, which establishes the relevant authorities, lays down hunting regulations, makes provisions for protected areas and conservation initiatives, combating wildlife crimes, etc. Additionally, the chapter also outlines India's implementation of its international commitments under the Convention on International Trade in Endangered Species of Wildlife Fauna and Flora (CITES). A remarkable feature of this chapter is the comprehensive coverage of the Prevention of Cruelty to Animals Act, 1960.

The next two chapters, Chapters 4 and 5, provide an extensive examination of India's legal and regulatory framework related to pollution. Chapter 4 focusses

15 Vidushi Maheshwari & Ishaan Singh, *Examining ESG Regulation in India: Navigating the Path to Sustainable Corporate Practices*, Law School Policy Review & Kautilya Society (Oct 7, 2023), https://lawschoolpolicyreview.com/2023/10/07/examining-esg-regulation-in-india-navigating-the-path-to-sustainable-corporate-practices/.

on water pollution and offers a panoramic picture of the Water (Prevention and Control of Pollution) Act, 1974. It elucidates the provisions of Environment Impact Assessment (EIA), environmental clearance including the latest developments on *ex post facto* clearance, and other allied legislations. It also covers some of the landmark judgments related to the regulation of groundwater pollution. Complementing the discussion on water pollution, the fifth chapter delves into the regulatory regime for air and noise pollution, and the powers of the Pollution Control Boards in this regard. It also undertakes a sectoral analysis of air and noise pollution and focusses on India's international commitments in addressing air pollution.

Lastly, it is important to realise that environmental law is not pure law, it is intertwined with science, technology, engineering, and economics and they play a key role in the formulation and implementation of regulations. While these intricacies of environmental law may appear complex and technical, everyone must study and follow environmental regulations. There is an opportunity to become environment law specialists as companies race towards ESG compliance.

2 Forest Conservation

Law and Regulatory Framework

2.1 Introduction

India is an ecologically rich country with four major biological hotspots and approximately 24.6% of the area under forest cover.[1] The country supports 16 major forest types, varying from the alpine pastures in the Himalayas to temperate, sub-tropical forests and mangroves in the coastal areas.[2] Communities, both tribal and rural, have evolved and developed in and around forests in India. The economy as well as the culture and tradition find roots in the forested land. Tribes have included forests in their sacred religious practices and learnt that in order to survive, they must conserve forests and the produce procured from them. As forests attained a pivotal role in day-to-day activities, indigenous tribes took it as their conjoined responsibility to preserve forests and use as much as required for their sustenance. Forests thus became an integral part of the social and cultural ethos of the community.

Forest laws have a significant role to play in the management and regulation of forests. However, despite covering almost a quarter of the country's land area, forests and forest policy have been neglected in much of the existing literature on Indian development. The State has played a central role in forest management in India since the formal establishment of the Forest Department in 1864. This chapter seeks to address and examine these vital roles played by the State to conserve forests over the decades.

1 Ministry of Environment, Forest and Climate Change, *Forest Survey Report 2021 Released; Increase of 2,261 Sq Km in the Total Forest and Tree Cover of the Country in Last Two Years*, Press Information Bureau (Jan. 13, 2022), https://pib.gov.in/PressReleasePage.aspx?PRID=1789635.

2 Food and Agriculture Organization, Asia and the Pacific: National Forest Programmes Update No. 34, at 59 (2000).

DOI: 10.4324/9781032703909-2

2.2 Modern Evolution of Forest Conservation in India

2.2.1 Conservation of Forests in the Pre-Independence Era

The advent of the British in India marked the beginning of an era of massive destruction.[3] The vast forest cover and diversity of the country signified new commercial possibilities and possible economic development from the British perspective. In order to keep the rich forests to themselves, certain rules and regulations were framed in the form of the Indian Forest Act, 1878.[4] These laws were brought into force to reinforce the control of the British over the forest resources, to utilise Indian forests for the Crown's profit, and to keep the locals away from them. Conservation of the forests was not the main focus of these legislations. Vast areas of forests were ravaged by the British for the construction of railway lines. The introduction of railways created an insatiable demand for wood for wood fuel, sleepers, and carriage building and promoted greater consumption patterns for facilitating the ease of communication, thereby leading to indiscriminate felling of trees and even desolation.[5] A distinguished scientist and forest conservator, Hugh Cleghorn, noted that 'although there were several causes of deforestation, the timber requirements of the railways had the maximum negative impact on the forest'.[6] The advent of the British therefore marked a pronounced shift in the way in which forest resources were viewed. The rules, regulations, and legislations enacted by the colonial administration, under the command of the English sovereign, had transformed the concept of property rights, thereby redefining them contrary to established practices and local customs of indigenous communities. Contrary to the pre-established conception of individual private rights to forests and forest resources, the British colonial administration declared forests and access thereto to be the primary right of the State.[7]

While many Indians attempted to undertake initiatives for facilitating forest conservation, the presence of distinct ruling kingdoms led to localisation and a lack of uniform pan-India coordination between the aforementioned individuals. Inevitably, these attempts could not achieve great success. Nevertheless, as the British set foot on Indian soil, several policies and legislations came into existence.[8] Forest laws gradually developed in India, delving into various aspects of the utilisa-

3 V.R.S. Rawat J. Kishwan, *Forest Conservation-Based, Climate Change-Mitigation Approach for India*, 10 The International Forestry Review (Special issue) 269–280 (2008).

4 *The Forest Act of 1878*, Azadi ka Amrit Mahotsav (Oct. 10, 2023), https://amritmahotsav.nic.in/district-reopsitory-detail.htm?25146.

5 Aruna Awasthi, *Environmental Degradation: A Case Study of Railways and Deforestation in India in the Nineteenth and Twentieth Centuries*, 60 Proceedings of the Indian History Congress (1999).

6 Pallavi Das, *Hugh Cleghorn and Forest Conservancy in India*, 11 Environment and History 55–82 (2005).

7 Oliver Springate & Baginski Piers Blaikie, Forests People and Power: The Political Ecology of Reform in South Asia 33–34 (Earthscan London 2013).

8 Vaishali Arora et al., *Environmental Pollution in India: The Persisting Misery and Struggle*, SCC Online (2016) PL June 56.

tion of forest resources and, to some extent, their management and conservation. In order to bring in State control over the forests, the Forest Department was created in 1864. The first law on forests in the pre-unified country was passed in the year 1865. The enactment was brought in to establish rights for the British government to occupy all unoccupied areas or wasteland,[9] thereby depriving the owners of their customary or private rights over the land. The following were the laws introduced by the British to seemingly preclude the misappropriation of forest resources at the hands of private individuals, while ensuring the exploitation of resources by colonial authorities to fill State coffers.[10]

(1) The Charter of Indian Forestry [1855].
(2) The Indian Forest Act [1865], which was subsequently subjected to revision in 1878 and 1927.
(3) The Indian Forest Policy [1894].

The Act of 1865 brought in by the British curtailed community access to forests, through legislation that banned collectivist extraction. It was reserved solely for the extraction of timber 'earmarked most urgently for railway supplies'.[11] The next attempt to bring in legislation for forests was the Forest Act, 1878. This law allowed the British Raj to further tighten its grip over forest resources, without any changes or recognition of community rights. The next Act came much later in the year 1927,[12] a few decades before British rule ended. It was brought in once again with the object of exploiting resources. While some States have adopted the Forest Act of 1927, several States brought in their own legislation such as Karnataka,[13] Andhra Pradesh,[14] etc. Even though the objectives in those legislations are different, the spirit in those legislations manifests the principles of national law. Both the 1894 Policy and 1927 Act classified forests under the categories of 'commercial production', 'minor forests', 'protection', and 'pasture lands'.[15] The British utilised these legislative provisions to effectuate the ouster of forest dwellers, take the forests under their control, and thereafter commodify them. Insidious activities of this

9 The term 'wasteland' included all land covered by trees, brushwood, or jungle.

10 Vandana Swami, *Environmental History and British Colonialism in India: A Prime Political Agenda*, 3 The New Centennial Review 118 (2003).

11 Ramachandra Guha, *An Environmental Debate: The Making of the 1878 Act,* 27(1) Indian Economic and Social History Review 65 (1990).

12 The Indian Forest Act, 1927, was enacted with the objective to consolidate the law relating to forests, the transit of forest produce, and the duty leviable on timber and other forest produce.

13 The Karnataka Forest Act, 1963, was enacted with the objective of protecting the forests beyond the control of the Government from being razed. Apart from that, this law focusses on the cutting down of sandalwood and making it the property of the State, wherever the tree is grown, to prevent smuggling and other offences.

14 Andhra Pradesh Forest Act, 1967. The Andhra Pradesh Act was enacted for the protection and management of forests in the State of Andhra Pradesh.

15 The Indian Forest Act, 1927, §§ 11, 28, 29.

kind, including the extreme harvesting of timber from Indian forests in the early 1940s and the levelling of numerous trees for the construction of wooden sleepers and the continuous expansion of railways, culminated in large-scale deforestation and immense ecological degradation.[16] Thus, when India emerged as an independent nation-state from the oppressive British Raj in 1947, the need was felt to immediately re-conceptualise prevailing forest conservation laws.

2.2.2 Conservation of Forests in the Post-Independence Era

Although there was no legislation enacted immediately after securing independence, the law on forest conservation had begun to take shape through policies in independent India. In 1948, the State leaders conceptualised the idea of the **Central Board of Forestry (CBF)** which was later implemented in 1950.[17]

2.2.2.1 National Forest Policy, 1952

In 1952, the first 'National Forest Policy of Independent India' was introduced by the Central Government. This Policy was designed to balance the concern for ecology while meeting the economic demands of the country. The Policy provided a thrust for afforestation measures by pushing for the extension of forests beyond the traditional forest areas and invariably advocating for social forestry measures. The Policy postulated that 'India as whole, should aim at maintaining one-third of its total land area under forests'.[18] The significant highlights of the Policy include the functional categorisation of the forests under the four heads of 'protection' forests, 'national' forests, 'village or fuel' forests, and 'tree-lands or trees outside forests' (ToF).[19] Moreover, it emphasised the need for specialised research into the utilisation of forest products and the pertinent training of forest administration.[20]

Unfortunately, the 1952 Policy failed to see notable success. The disregard for ecological concerns, especially at the hands of the various State Governments, culminated in the rampant conversion of mixed forests into commercial plantations, which were low-value and high-value respectively. Thus, the Policy didn't bring about substantial improvement in forest preservation.

Further, in an attempt to combat an impending ecological disaster owing to rapid deforestation, the Central Government shifted the subject of forests to the concurrent list and, hence, empowered the Union Parliament to legislate on the

16 Jacques Pouchepadass, *Colonialism and Environment in India: Comparative Perspective*, 30 Economic & Political Weekly 2062 (1995).

17 Richard Haeuber, *Indian Forestry Policy in Two Eras: Continuity or Change?*, 17(1) Environmental History Review 49, 50 (1993).

18 National Forest Policy, 1952, para 19.

19 *Id.* at para 4.

20 *Id.* at para 25, 30.

same.[21] Subsequently, in 1976, the Central Government constituted the National Commission on Agriculture (NCA), members of which added suggestions concerning the utilisation of social forestry schemes in various States and making efforts to boost forest productivity.[22] Thereafter the Centre also enacted the Forest Conservation Act in 1980, which was aimed at preventing large-scale deforestation.[23] However, there still existed the need to review and update the utility-orientated approach as advocated by the 1952 Policy, owing to the continuation of forest depletion. This eventually led to the enactment of the revised National Forest Policy in 1988.

2.2.2.2 National Forest Policy, 1988

Unlike its predecessor, the Policy of 1988 placed ecological concerns in relation to forests on a higher pedestal. Emphasis was laid on giving due regard to the ecological balance while deriving benefits from forest produce. The principal aim of the Policy was to promote a people-centric model of forest conservation, which would give primacy to ecological concerns and the rights of traditional forest dwellers.

A significant contribution of the Policy of 1988 was strengthening of participatory forest management by the adoption of the 'Joint Forest Management' (JFM) system. The JFM comprised a partnership between local communities, NGOs, and the State Forest departments for the purpose of forest conservation. The concept of JFM recognised the claims of communities directly involved in protecting the forests, over the forest produce. The attempt to decentralise and hand over the management of natural resources was the primary intent of the Policy. While the beneficiaries of the Policy were the forest communities, their work had to be monitored closely by the forest department. The Government of India further elaborated upon JFM via the Joint Forest Management Guidelines in 1990, which were subsequently revised a decade later.[24] The JFM set specific targets for the forest dwellers to carry out certain works in a manner specified, based on a scheme of incentives.

Besides the initiative to promote participatory management of forests, besides aspects of wildlife conservation. The Policy advocated for the establishment of 'corridors' to ensure 'genetic continuity' between the artificially sequestered subsections of migrant wildlife.[25]

Most importantly, the Policy provided for rights to be given to bona fide forest dwellers, primarily tribals.[26] Consequently, the Scheduled Tribes and Other Traditional Forest Dwellers (Recognition of Forest Rights) Act was enacted in

21 India Const. sch. VII, list III, entry 17A.

22 Ministry of Agriculture and Irrigation, Government of India, Report of the National Commission on Agriculture 49 (1976).

23 The Forest (Conservation) Act, 1927, § 1.

24 Ministry of Environment & Forests, Joint Forest Management: A Handbook 1 (2024).

25 National Forest Policy, 1988, para 4.5.

26 *Id.* at para 4.3.4.3.

2006, to further strengthen the protection of the rights and concessions rendered to tribal communities.

2.2.2.3 Draft National Forest Policy, 2018

The Ministry of Environment, Forest and Climate Change (MoEFCC) brought out the draft National Forest Policy in 2018 to substitute its three decades old counterpart.[27] The underlying purpose of the draft Policy was to address the issues and challenges of forest conservation by focussing on specific goals. After the ratification of the Paris Agreement, the Indian Government and the MoEFCC adopted the strategies that were discussed on the global platform. India's Nationally Determined Contributions (NDCs) clearly stated that to battle climate change, one of the strategies would be to create a carbon sink through afforestation practices. One of the most important aspects reflected in the Draft Policy is the REDD+ strategy, which translates into 'Reducing Emissions from Deforestation and Forest Degradation'.[28]

The National Forest Policy, 2018, underlines forward thinking for addressing the aligned issues of strengthening wildlife protection and management and biodiversity conservation and management. However, one element of this Policy has stirred some concerns among conservationists, that of the intention to facilitate the 'forest – industry interface'.[29] The Policy states, 'Forest corporations and industrial units need to step up industrial plantations for meeting the demand of raw material'.[30] In addition, a platform for communication and cooperation between forestry institutions, interested parties, and forest-based industries would be established to generate demand for skilled workers in the industry.

The draft Policy has also come under fire from several environmentalists and experts for its apparent failure to adequately take into account the needs of local communities.[31] Furthermore, the 2018 Policy aims to utilise degraded land available with pertinent forest corporations for the extraction of high-quality timber and proposes the establishment of a 'public-private partnership (PPP)' model for facilitating afforestation.[32] When juxtaposed with its 1988 counterpart, this model raises concerns about the privatisation of forest resources in the near future. The 2018 Policy's emphasis on afforestation for ensuring water management and

27 S. Gopikrishna Warrier, *India's New Forest Policy Draft Draws Criticism for Emphasis on Industrial Timber*, MongaBay (Apr. 12, 2018), https://news.mongabay.com/2018/04/indias-new-forest-policy-draft-draws-criticism-for-emphasis-on-industrial-timber/.

28 Draft Forest Policy, 2018, para 2.13.

29 *Id.* at para 4.4.

30 *Id.* at para 4.4.

31 Sushant Agarwal, *National Forest Policy Draft 2018 Takes One Step Forward, Two Steps Back*, The Wire (Apr. 02, 2018), https://thewire.in/environment/national-forest-policy-draft-2018-takes-one-step-forward-two-steps-back.

32 Draft National Forest Policy, 2018, para 4.1.1 (d).

'preventing' frequent water shortages is also misplaced.[33] In a nutshell, the Centre seems to be attempting to fit a square peg into a round hole. Undoubtedly, the recent draft is a major setback to the progress made under the 1988 Policy.

2.3 Legislative Developments on Forest Conservation in India

The legislative framework governing forest management and conservation is broad and varied. As the Constitution recognises the forests as a subject matter for legislation both by the Parliament and the State legislatures,[34] there are a plethora of laws both at the Central and State levels that directly or indirectly provide for the conservation and protection of forests. Following are some of the notable central legislations that pertain to forest governance.

2.3.1 Indian Forest Act, 1927

The Indian Forest Act, 1927 (the Act), was enacted with the purpose of consolidating all the forest legislations in the country predating it. These legislations *inter alia* included the erstwhile Indian Forest Acts of 1865 and 1878, which were very limited in their scope and were primarily aimed at the commercialisation of forest produce. These legislations made the forests of India the property of the British Crown in order to secure timber for the expansion and development of railways in India, which invariably ended the ancient and traditional use of forests by communities and tribes dwelling in the forests.[35] Although the Indian Forest Act, 1927, was a step ahead of its predecessors, it was drafted to benefit the colonisers.

2.3.1.1 Definition of Forest

Section 2 of the Act provides for a list of definitions that *inter alia* include terms relevant to the interpretation of the Act, such as cattle, forest officer, forest offence, forest produce, owner, river, timber, and tree. Interestingly, though the Act is titled the Indian 'Forest' Act, it does not provide an express definition for the term 'forest' till date. However, the High Courts and the Supreme Court have stepped in to fill this gap by attempting to render an indicative definition of the term. The Allahabad High Court in the case of *Yashwant Stone Works v. State of U.P.*,[36] while defining the term, adopted the definition provided by the Food and Agriculture Organisation, according to which forest means

33 Mayank Aggarwal, *The National Policy That Governs India's Forests Has Not Been Updated Since 1988*, SCROLL (Jan. 11, 2020), https://scroll.in/article/949435/the-national-policy-that-governs-indias-forests-has-not-been-updated-since-1988.

34 India Const. sch. VII, list III, entry 17A.

35 Ramachandra Guha, *Forestry in British and Post-British India: A Historical Analysis*, 18(45/46) ECONOMIC & POLITICAL WEEKLY 1940 (1983).

36 Yashwant Stone Works v. State of UP, AIR 1988 All 121.

> all lands bearing vegetative association demarcated by trees of any size, exploited or not, capable of producing wood or other forest products or exerting an influence on the climate or on the water regime or providing shelter for livestock and wildlife.

While this was a positive attempt by the Court, the definition was not all-encompassing. Later in the year 1997, in the case of *T. N. Godavarman v. Union of India*, the Supreme Court also made an attempt to provide a definition. The Court stated that the term 'forest' must be understood according to its dictionary meaning. This description covers all statutorily recognised forests, whether designated as reserved, protected, or otherwise. Although the definition was phrased in the context of the Forest Conservation Act, 1980, the definition bears relevance to the Indian Forest Act, 1927, as both legislations are constructed in tandem. This definition of the Supreme Court rewrote the law by bringing into the ambit areas of forests not under the forest department but under tree cover.[37] The Court sought to give an expansive connotation to the term through its interpretation.

2.3.1.1.1 RESERVE FORESTS

'Reserve Forests' refer to any forest land or waste land over which the State Government has proprietary rights and which the State Government may declare to be a reserved forest through a Notification in pursuance of its power under Section 3 of the Act.[38] The Notification should clearly declare that the allotted land is constituted as a 'Reserve Forest' and it should also specify the limits of such land.[39] Such a notification extinguishes any previously recognised individual or community rights over the forests and access to any produce from such forests becomes a matter of privilege subject to the permission of forest officials. In the event any claims are made or any disputes arise in relation to the land notified as reserved forests, the forest settlement officer is the authority in charge of resolving disputes and settling claims.[40] Section 6 of the Act specifies details of the proclamation by the Forest Settlement Officer regarding the reserve forests in the local vernacular language in every town and village in the neighbourhood of the land comprising therein. If no claim is made to rights under Section 6, they shall be deemed to be extinguished, unless, before the notification under Section 20 is published, the person claiming them satisfies the Forest Settlement Officer that he had sufficient cause for not preferring such claim within the period fixed under Section 6. Since the State Government acquires proprietary interests in the forests and the forest produce, the rights or interests of any person in such forest/forest produce automatically lapses to the State Government.

37 T N Godavarman Thirumulpad v. Union of India, AIR 1997 SC 1228.
38 The Indian Forest Act, 1927, § 3.
39 *Id.* § 4.
40 *Id.* at § 4.

The case of *Banwasi Seva Ashram v. State of U. P.*[41] raised an important question relating to the right of the State to notify an area as 'Reserved Forest' and its effect on the *Adivasis* already living there. In this case, the State Government declared the area of Dudhi in Robertsganj tehsil to be a reserved forest under Section 20 of the Act. The validity of this notification was brought into question as, subsequent to the notification, criminal charges were recorded against the *adivasis* for encroaching upon the land. To this effect, the State pleaded that the forest land had been acquired to set up a thermal power station and provide cheaper electricity to the people. The Court ultimately upheld the validity of the notification while stating that the land could be utilised for running the power plant subject to fulfilment of the procedures under the Land Acquisition Act.

The main objective of declaring a particular forest area to be a 'Reserved Forest' is to prohibit certain activities that may amount to the destruction or degradation of the forest cover.

However, some of the activities can be permitted by obtaining permission of the Forest Officer in writing, or under any rule made by the State Governments. For instance, as most people are reliant on agricultural activities for their survival and cattle grazing being and essential part of it, the States have therefore enacted the Grazing of Cattle Rules[42] to regulate the grazing of cattle in reserved forests and other forests or lands that the Conservator of Forest of the State may direct. Under said Grazing Rules, areas that are open to grazing are earmarked.

In the case of *T. N. Godavarman v. Union of India*,[43] the Supreme Court categorically recognised certain activities that were to be expressly and strictly prohibited in reserve forests such as the felling of trees and their removal, removal of bamboo or grasses for any purpose whatsoever, removal of corals and other living forms from marine national parks/sanctuaries, construction of tourist complexes, hotels, and restaurants, zoos and safari parks, or any other building not for direct use for protection and management of wildlife and its habitat and other non-forest activities.

Further, in the case of *State of Maharashtra v. Arjun Tabadu Mahajan*,[44] the court held that the trial court is competent to forfeit the cattle used in committing any forest offence in addition to the compensation for damages under Section 55. It also held that the offence under Section 26(1)(d) is a 'forest offence'. The court also suggested that the complainant should adduce proper evidence and proper orders of compensation as well as forfeiture should be passed by the courts.

41 Banwasi Seva Ashram v. State of U. P. (1987) 3 SCC 304; Banwasi Seva Ashram v. State of U. P. (1992) 1 SCC 117; Banwasi Seva Ashram v. State of U. P., (1992) 2 SCC 202.

42 Odisha has enacted the Orissa Forest (Grazing of Cattle) Rules, 1980, providing for grazing in the forests without any permit except in those areas which are declared as closed. Orissa Rules came into effect in 1980.

43 T. N. Godavarman v. Union of India, AIR 1997 SC 122.

44 State of Maharashtra v. Arjun Tabadu Mahajan, (1987) SCC OnLine Bom 417.

In *Karna Laxman Gawali v. State of Maharashtra*,[45] the court held that any damage to forest wealth in any form is covered by Section 26 of the Act and there is no reason to draw a distinction between damage due to theft by carrying the property outside the forest and the damage due to eating or otherwise spoiling by the cattle on the spot itself.

In *Forest Development Corpn. of Maharashtra Ltd. v. Prakash Mallesh Cheraku*[46] the court held that the confiscation proceedings are separate and independent from the prosecution that may be instituted against the offender and that even if no prosecution has been initiated against the owner of the seized vehicle, the seized vehicle would be liable to confiscation.

In *Court on its own Motion v. State of H.P.*,[47] the court highlighted the impact of the felling of trees on the environment and ecology. The court said,

> to protect environment and ecology of the area from further deterioration, degradation, adverse impacts and to effectively implement the direction for afforestation, we injunct the seller, purchaser or any person or body claiming through them from raising any construction, temporary or permanent or from carrying on any commercial or non-forest activities, upon the land from where the 477 trees have been felled illegally and unauthorizedly. The land shall be used only for the purposes of afforestation.

The seller and buyer were made 60% and 40% liable respectively for the damages.

In *Orissa Mining Corporation Ltd. v. Ministry of Environment and Forest*[48] the Supreme Court issued the following direction in relation to Joint Forest Management: (a) the State Government should ensure that the forest rights under Section 3(1)(i) of the Act relating to protection, regeneration, or conservation or management of any community forest resource, which forest dwellers might have traditionally been protecting and conserving for sustainable use, are recognised in all villages and the titles are issued as soon as the prescribed Forms for claiming Rights to Community Forest Resource and the Form of Title for Community Forest Resources are incorporated in the Rules. Any restriction, such as a time limit, on the use of community forest resources other than what is imposed would be against the spirit of the Act; (b) in case no community forest resource rights are recognised in a village, the reasons for the same should be recorded. Reference can be made to existing records of community and joint forest management, van panchayats, etc., for this purpose; (c) the Gram Sabha would initially demarcate the boundaries of the community forest resource as defined in Section 2(a) of the Act for the purposes of filing claims for recognition of forest right under Section 3(1)(i) of the Act; (d) the Committees constituted under Rule 4(e) of the Forest Rights Rules,

45 Karna Laxman Gawali v. State of Maharashtra, (1989) SCC OnLine Bom 76.

46 Forest Development Corpn. of Maharashtra Ltd. v. Prakash Mallesh Cheraku, (2018) SCC OnLine Bom 72.

47 Court on its Own Motion v. State of H.P., (2017) SCC OnLine NGT 34.

48 Orissa Mining Corporation Ltd. v. Ministry of Environment and Forest, (2013) 6 SCC 476.

2008, would work under the control of Gram Sabha. The State Agencies should facilitate this process; (e) consequent upon the recognition of forest right in Section 3(i) of the Act to protect, regenerate, or conserve or manage any community forest resource, the powers of the Gram Sabha would be in consonance with the duties as defined in Section 5(d), wherein the Gram Sabha is empowered to regulate access to community forest resources and stop any activity that adversely affects the wild animals, forest, and biodiversity. Any activity that prejudicially affects the wildlife, forest, and biodiversity in forest areas would be dealt with under the provisions of the relevant Acts.

2.3.1.1.2 VILLAGE FORESTS

Village Forests[49] refer to those reserved forests that the State Government assigns to a particular village community with the concomitant rights and privileges of the Government vis-à-vis such forests. The State Government frames rules for specifying the rights of such village communities to access forest produce as well as the correlative duties of the community to protect and improve the forests. A careful perusal of Section 28 reveals that the State Governments have been given the ultimate authority in all matters pertaining to the handling of village forests. Further, all the provisions of the Act relating to reserved forests shall (so far as they are not inconsistent with the rules so made) apply to Village Forests.[50] Hence, the major difference between Village Forests and Reserved Forests is the aspect of rights assigned to the village community by the State Governments.

The case of *U. Khastia v. Range Officer, Jirimukh,* a landmark case, relates to who has the right to determine village forests and whether a Forest Range Officer can decide in this regard. In this case, 9 people settled upon a reserved forest land of about 220 *bighas*. About 20 *bighas* were used for residential purposes and the rest for cultivation. The Forest Range Officer issued a no-objection memo to the Petitioners on the payment of land revenue to cultivate Pan on the land. The contention of the Government was that the Range Officer had neither the authority nor was he competent under the law to permit any settlement in or upon any part of the reserved forest. The Manipur High Court ruled that only State Governments were empowered to make such pronouncements, and since the Manipur State Government had not granted the forest ranger any authority to provide settlement in that region, his actions were unlawful.[51]

2.3.1.1.3 PROTECTED FORESTS

Protected Forests are generally construed to be any forest land that does not squarely fall within the ambit of 'Reserve Forests'. The State Governments are

49 The Indian Forest Act, 1927, § 28.

50 *Id.* § 28(3).

51 U Khastia v. Range Officer, Jirimukh, AIR 1958 Manipur 31.

empowered to constitute any land other than reserved forests as Protected Forests over which the Governments have proprietary rights. Protected Forests,[52] therefore, refer to any forest land or waste land that does not form a part of the reserved forests but which is the property of the State Government and is declared via a notification by the respective State Government to be governed by the provisions of the Act. The Notification can be made only upon an inquiry into the nature and extent of the rights of the Government and of private persons in or over the forest-land or waste-land comprising therein in such other manner as the State Government thinks sufficient, after which a record is to be made. Every such record shall be presumed to be correct until the contrary is proved.[53] Under Section 32 of the Act, the State Government is empowered to make rules to regulate certain activities within the Protected Forests.[54]

Furthermore, under Section 30 of the Act, the State Governments are authorised to declare any trees or class of trees in a Protected Forest to be reserved from a date fixed by the notification, that any portion of such forest specified in the notification shall be closed for such term, not exceeding 30 years, as the State Government thinks fit.

2.3.1.1.4 PRIVATE FORESTS

The Act also briefly includes provisions related to Private Forests. As the name suggests, this category of forests is not the property of the Government, i.e., there is no proprietary right vested in the State Governments in respect of such forests. Nevertheless, the Act authorises the State Government to regulate certain activities on private forest land which includes timber cutting, cultivation, grazing, and burning or clearing of vegetation. The Act also authorises the State Government to acquire private forestland for public purposes under the Land Acquisition Act of 1894.[55]

The State Private Forests Act was enacted immediately after independence in most States to check the denudation of tree growth in 'private forests' due to extensive felling as a consequence of high prices of fuel. Private forests typically exclude (a) any land which is vested in the Government; (b) any land in respect of which notifications and orders issued under the Indian Forests Act, 1927, are in force. The State Private Forest Rules, enacted under the State Private Forest Act, prescribe the manner in which the notified area of private forest may be managed. It is provided under these Acts that the owner of Private Forests has to manage such forest in accordance with a working plan approved by a Forest Officer and in case the owner fails or refuses to manage the forest in accordance with the working plan,

52 The Indian Forest Act, 1927, § 29.
53 The Indian Forest Act, 1927, § 29(3).
54 *Id.* § 32.
55 *Id.* § 35.

the management of forest would be done by the Forest Officer in lieu of profits for such management.

2.3.1.2 Forest Settlement Officer: Duties, Powers, and Functions

The Forest Settlement Officer is an officer of the State appointed under the Act, who is primarily vested with powers concerning all forest-related business of the State. The officer so appointed to this post shall not hold any other forest office under this Act except that of the Forest Settlement Officer[56] and the number of members holding this post at a given time shall not be more than three.[57] He shall be the nodal agency for all settlement of claims, to inquire into and determine the existence, nature, and extent of any rights alleged to exist in favour of any person in or over any land comprised within such limits, or in or over any forest produce, and to deal with the same as provided in this chapter.

According to Section 6 of the Act, it is the duty of the Forest Settlement Officer to publish the Notification issued under Section 4 in the local vernacular daily in every town and village in the neighbourhood of the land comprised therein, a proclamation:

(a) specifying, as nearly as possible, the situation and limits of the proposed forest;
(b) explaining the consequences which, as hereinafter provided, will ensue on the reservation of such forest; and
(c) fixing a period of not less than three months from the date of such proclamation, and requiring every person claiming any right mentioned in Section 4 or Section 5 within such period either to present to the Forest Settlement Officer a written notice specifying or to appear before him and state the nature of such right and the amount and particulars of the compensation (if any) claimed in respect thereof.

Further the Forest Settlement Officer shall have the power to make an inquiry.[58] The Forest Settlement Officer shall take down in writing all statements made under Section 6, and shall at some convenient place inquire into all claims duly preferred under that section, and the existence of any rights mentioned in Section 4 or Section 5 and not claimed under Section 6 so far as the same may be ascertainable from the records of Government and the evidence of any persons likely to be acquainted with the same.[59] For the purposes of such an inquiry the Forest Settlement Officer may exercise all or any of the following powers:

56 *Id.* § 4(2).
57 *Id.* § 4(3).
58 The Indian Forest Act, 1927, § 7.
59 *Id.*

(a) power to enter, by himself or any officer authorised by him for the purpose, upon any land, and to survey, demarcate, and make a map of the same; and
(b) the powers of a Civil Court in the trial of suits. Here the power of a civil court shall include power to order production of evidence in support of claims, power of admissions, and inquiries normally assigned to civil courts in general.[60]

In case of practices of shifting cultivation, the Forest Settlement Officer shall record a statement setting forth the particulars of the claim and of any local rule or order under which the practice is allowed or regulated, and submit the statement to the State Government, together with his opinion as to whether the practice should be permitted or prohibited wholly or in part. Upon receiving this statement and opinion the State Government may permit the practice of shifting cultivation.[61]

Under Section 11 of the Act, the Forest Settlement Officer has the power to acquire land over which rights have been claimed. If land is proposed to be made a forest by the State Government, then the forest settlement officer shall pass an order admitting or rejecting the same in whole or in part. If such a claim is admitted in whole or in part, the Forest Settlement Officer shall either:

(a) exclude such land from the limits of the proposed forest; or
(b) come to an agreement with the owner thereof for the surrender of his rights; or
(c) proceed to acquire such land in the manner provided by the Land Acquisition Act, 1894.

Further, the court in the *Banwasi Seva Ashram*[62] case upheld the right of the Adivasi community, who were being evicted, to be heard of their claims by the Forest Officer. Further issues arose regarding the right to be heard of the forest-dwelling communities apart from SCs/STs/other recognised backward communities in the case of *Hari Prakash Shukla v. State of U.P.*[63] The court held that to enjoy possession of any land notified under Section 4 of the Indian Forest Act is not only limited to specific forest-dwelling communities but is also based on proof of residence, date of original possession, etc.

2.3.1.3 Powers of the Central and State Governments under the Act

The Central Government has been empowered through Sections 39 and 40 of the Act to levy duty on timber and other forest produce, in such a manner as it may declare by notification in the Official Gazette on all timber or other forest produce which is produced in the territories to which this Act extends, and in respect of

60 *Id.* § 8.
61 The Indian Forest Act, 1927, § 10.
62 Banwasi Seva Ashram v. State of U.P., (1992) 1 SCC 117.
63 Hari Prakash Shukla v. State of U.P., (2023) SCC OnLine SC 773.

which the Government has any right or which is brought from any place outside the territories to which this Act extends. Interestingly, the Act envisages no limit for purchase money or royalty.

The states have been granted the power to establish and regulate sawmills by way of rules. These rules typically provide that no person can establish or operate any sawmill or machinery for converting or cutting timber and wood without a licence from the concerned Divisional Forest Officer at the state level. By way of the *Godavarman* judgment, the Supreme Court directed the closure of all the illegal timber processing units operating in the country without requisite licences.[64]

Tendu leaf, used for wrapping tobacco, is grown extensively in several states across the country. Therefore, several states have enacted the State Tendu Patta (Vyapar Viniyaman) Adhiniyam.[65] These Acts restrict the sale, purchase, and transport of Tendu leaves to the State Government or an authorised officer of the State Government or an agent in respect of the unit in which the leaves have grown. The State Government is empowered to fix the price of the Tendu leaves and also register growers and manufacturers of bidis and exporters of Tendu leaves. The Rules under the above Act prescribe the manner in which agents are appointed, procedures for collecting Tendu leaves, the authority that can issue transport permits, etc.

The power of the State Governments to regulate the transit of timber and other forest produce provided under Section 42 was challenged in *State of Tripura v. Sudhir Ranjan Nath*,[66] as violative of freedom of trade and commerce. The Supreme Court declared that the Act is primarily enacted to preserve, protect, and promote the forest wealth of the country and collection of revenue is a regulatory measure to achieve this objective. Similarly, regulating the cutting, removal, transport, and possession of forest produce is in the interest of the State and its people. Therefore, control of the State over forests and over the collection of forest produce and the movement of drift and standing timber is in consonance with the provisions of the Constitution. Similarly, the Bihar High Court declared, in *Sarup Singh & Co. v. State of Bihar*,[67] that there cannot be any movement or transport of timber or other forest produce without any transit permit. Once the timber is brought to the State from another State, transit permit rules would apply.

Under Section 45 of the Act, the Government has the power to collect timber that is found adrift, beached, stranded, or sunk, or all wood or timber bearing marks that have not been registered in accordance with the rules made under Section 41. Public notice is given of the collected timber from time to time by the Forest Officer.[68] Any person claiming the timber to be their property is required to present

64 T. N. Godavarman Thirumulpad v. Union of India, (1996) 9 SCR 982.

65 State of Madhya Pradesh Tendu Patta (Vyapar Viniyaman) Adhiniyam, 1964.

66 State of Tripura v. Sudhir Ranjan Nath, (1997) 3 SCC 665.

67 Sarup Singh & Co. v. State of Bihar, AIR (2001) Pat 36.

68 The Indian Forest Act, 1927, § 46.

a written statement of such claim, within a period not less than two months from the date of such notice.

When any such statement is presented as aforesaid, the Forest Officer may, after making such inquiry as he thinks fit, either reject the claim after recording his reasons for doing so or deliver the timber to the claimant. If such timber is claimed by more than one person, the Forest Officer may either deliver the same to any of such persons whom he deems entitled thereto, or may refer the claimants to the civil courts, and retain the timber pending the receipt of an order from any such Court for its disposal. However, no person shall recover any compensation or costs against the Government, or against any Forest Officer, on account of such rejection, or the detention or removal of any timber, or the delivery thereof to any other person under this section.[69] No such timber shall be subject to process of any civil, criminal, or revenue court until it has been delivered, or a suit has been brought, as provided in this section.[70]

Additionally, the State Government also has the power to make rules and prescribe penalties under Section 51 of the Act. The State Government may, by notification in the Official Gazette, make rules in this regard.

The State Government may prescribe penalties for the contravention of any rules made under this section, imprisonment for a term which may extend to six months, or a fine which may extend to 500 rupees, or both. Such meagre punishment for those causing serious damage to the wealth of the nation is further evidence of the ineffectiveness of the Act.[71] Only Section 63 of the Act provides for a punishment of imprisonment which could extend to two years, or a fine, or both for counterfeiting or defacing marks on trees and timber and altering boundary marks of any forest or waste land.

An overview of the provisions of this Act creates an impression that the Act is steered towards the conservation of forests and green cover. But deeper scrutiny sheds light on the underlying reality that the Act was designed with the commercial motive of generating revenue[72] and forest produce, with the conservation of forests taking a backseat.[73]

2.3.1.4 The Jan Vishwas (Amendment of Provisions) Act, 2023

The Jan Vishwas (Amendment of Provisions) Act was recently passed by the Parliament with the intention of decriminalising and rationalising particular offences in order to improve the ease of living and doing business in India. The Act amended a total of 183 provisions across 42 statutes in India with the objective of

69 The Indian Forest Act, 1927, § 47(3).
70 *Id.* § 47(4).
71 *Id.* § 42.
72 *Id.* pmbl.
73 *Id.* § 41L (Power to make rules to regulate transit of forest produce).

reducing the gravity of the offence or a violation committed and the severity of the prescribed punishment, which would be phased out gradually.[74]

In the Indian Forest Act, 1927, the Amendment Act decriminalises the trespassing or pasturing of cattle or permitting cattle to trespass, and causing any damage by negligence in felling any tree or cutting or dragging any timber and provides the Forest Settlement Officer with the power to determine the compensation.

The Act also decriminalised leaving burning any fire kindled, felling any tree, or dragging any timber so as to damage any reserved tree, or permitting cattle to damage any such tree. The Act removed the imprisonment term and increased the fine to INR 5000. Further, these offences can also be compounded by the Forest Officer, and compensation for the damage done to the forest can be determined by him under Section 68 of the Forest Act, 1927.

2.3.2 Forest (Conservation) Act, 1980

The Forest (Conservation) Act, 1980, or the Van (Sanrakshan Evam Samvardhan) Adhiniyam [VSESA] is a cornerstone legislation in the field of social forestry and the conservation of forests. Despite being a very brief legislation with only five sections, the Act symbolises a positive shift to forest governance in the country as it was enacted with the main objective of combating deforestation and environmental deterioration.[75]

While the main purpose of the Indian Forest Act was to consolidate the law relating to forests in India, to regulate the transit of forest produce, and to create different categories of forests for effective administration, the primary aim of the Forest Conservation Act, 1980, was to restrict the de-reservation of forests and limit the use of forests for non-forest purposes in India with the ultimate aim of ensuring the conservation of forests. It expressly prohibits the use of forest land for non-forest purposes, the leasing of forest land to any private person, corporation, authority, or agency not owned or controlled by the Government, and the clearing of any forest land.[76] In doing so, the Act sought to introduce a control mechanism and place a check on the indiscriminate diversion of forest resources. It thus covers the aspects left out by the Indian Forest Act, 1927.

Though the Forest (Conservation) Act or the VSESA marked a positive step forward towards protecting forest cover, many legal issues arose, especially regarding the application of the Act. In the case of *State of Bihar v. Bansi Ram Modi*,[77] the Court was faced with the issue of whether Section 2 of the Forest Conservation Act, 1980, would be applicable to land already demarcated for non-forest purposes prior to the Act coming into force. The background of the case was such that the

74 Ashneet Hanspal & Guneet Mayall, *Analysis of the Jan Vishwas (Amendment of Provisions) Act, 2023*, Ahlawat & Associates (Sept. 12, 2023), https://www.ahlawatassociates.com/blog/analysis-of-the-jan-vishwas-amendment-of-provisions-act-2023.

75 The Forest (Conservation) Act, 1980, § 1.

76 *Id.* § 2.

77 State of Bihar v. Bansi Ram Modi, (1985) 3 SCC 643.

Appellants (State) had allotted 80 acres of land which were part of reserved forests to the Respondents for mining activity. This allotment was made prior to the enforcement of the 1980 Act, following which, the respondents undertook their mining activities. After the Act came into force, the State refused to renew the mining lease on the ground that permission of the Central Government as under Section 2 of the 1980 Act was not obtained. When the matter was raised in the High Court challenging the refusal of the Appellant State, the Court held that the provisions of the 1980 Act were not attracted as the land had been demarcated for mining before the enactment of the statute.[78] The same observation was reiterated by the Supreme Court on appeal.

Contrary to the above-mentioned case, the Supreme Court held a different view in the case of *Ambica Quarry Works v. State of Gujarat.*[79] In this case, the Apex Court was faced with the issue of determining the validity of the order of the Assistant Collector of the State of Gujarat, who had rejected the Appellant's request for renewal of the mining lease. The Court held that, in this case, the Appellants were asking for a renewal of the quarry leases which would lead to further deforestation or at least it would not help reclaim the areas where deforestation had taken place. The Court differentiated the facts of this case from that of the *Bansi Ram* case by stating that there was an existing lease where mining operation was being carried on for a particular mineral and the new lease merely permitted the applicant to collect other minerals in the allotted land. In that view of the matter, in the facts and circumstances of the case, the ratio of the decision in the *Bansi Ram* case cannot be made applicable to support the Appellants' demands in these cases because the facts are entirely different.[80] Furthermore, the Court held that if the State Government is of the opinion that it is not a case where the State Government should seek approval of the Central Government, the State Government cannot apparently seek such approval in a matter which it prima facie does not consider requires renewal.[81]

Samantha v. State of Andhra Pradesh[82] is another landmark case that deals with the leasing of tribal lands for mining and industrial purposes to non-tribal persons. In this case, the State of AP granted leases to several non-tribal persons to mine tribal lands. Samantha, a group representing the rights of affected tribal persons, filed a petition before the High Court of AP which was rejected. On appeal, the Supreme Court held that the Government, tribal, and forested lands in the scheduled areas cannot be leased to non-tribal persons or private companies for mining purposes. Further, the Apex Court held that mining activity in scheduled areas can only be operated by the State Mineral Development Corporation or by a coopera-

78 *Id.* at ¶ 10.
79 Ambica Quarry Works v. State of Gujarat, (1987) 1 SCC 213.
80 *Id.* at ¶ 20.
81 *Id.*
82 Samantha v. State of Andhra Pradesh, Civil Appeal 4601-02 of 1997 (Supreme Court).

tive of tribal persons with at least 20% of profits from these activities going towards infrastructure and other social services such as schools, hospitals, and sanitation. Thus, the Supreme Court cancelled all leases granted to non-tribal persons as void and in violation of the Fifth Schedule of the Indian Constitution.

The decision of the interim application in the case of *Lafarge Umiam Mining Pvt. Ltd.*[83] has streamlined the Environmental Clearance process in India to an extent. In this case, the French company Lafarge through a subsidiary had set up a two million tonne per year cement plant at Chhatak in Bangladesh. The limestone for the cement plant was proposed to be delivered from limestone mines in Nongtrai, which is in the East Khasi Hills district in Meghalaya. The limestone would be sent across the India–Bangladesh border on a conveyor belt which is 7.2 km on the Indian side of the border. Lafarge applied for the necessary Environmental Clearance in 1997 and in 2001 it commenced mining. In 2006, the Chief Conservator of Forests (CCF) noted that the mining site was surrounded by thick natural vegetation, and, since the land where the mine was located was forest land, Lafarge could not carry out operations without the necessary Forest Clearance. Thus, in addition to other clearances, it had to obtain Forest Clearance. It was objected by Lafarge that since no Forest land had been diverted for mining purposes, Forest Clearance was not required. However, the MoEF still directed Lafarge to obtain Forest Clearance under the Forest Conservation Act, 1980. The main contention was whether Lafarge had obtained initial Environmental Clearance by misrepresenting the nature of the forest land as non-forest land. The court rejected this contention and held that there was no misrepresentation as both KHADC and the DFO had certified that the land for the mine did not involve diversification of forest land and therefore there was no obligation on them to obtain Forest Clearance.

Recently, in the case of *Nature Lovers Movement v. State of Kerala*,[84] an issue pertaining to the retrospective application of the Act was raised. In the present case, the Petitioner's Society filed a writ petition before the Kerala High Court challenging an attempt of the Kerala State Government to regularise unauthorised encroachments and occupation via assignment of title deeds and invariably seeking to devise a policy with respect to the same. As the Forest Conservation Act, 1980, had tied the hands of the Government in its pursuit, after six years of the enforcement of the Act, the State Government conveyed its problem with respect to the unauthorised occupation/encroachment to the Central Government and hence requested the Central Government for permission for the regularisation of such occupation/encroachment by the issue of title deeds under State land assignment rules, to which the Central Government gave its approval. This move of the State Government was challenged on the ground of being violative of the Forest Conservation Act, 1980. In this regard, the Supreme Court clarified that

83 Lafarge Umiam Mining Private Limited (Lafarge) (T.N. Godavarman Thirumulpad v. Union of India, in W.P. No. 202 of 1995).

84 Nature Lovers Movement v. State of Kerala, (2009) 5 SCC 373.

although the Act is not retrospective in nature, the State Government is deterred from permitting any non-forest activity or the renewal of lease for any activity even prior to 1980 irrespective of its time length without the approval of the Central Government.[85]

Further, the case of *Prasad Paswan v. State of Jharkhand*[86] is also a very interesting development with respect to the implementation of FCA. In this case, the Petitioners and other co-accused individuals were discovered cultivating protected forest land without any proof of ownership. Subsequently, they resisted the forest guards' attempts to take their ploughing equipment. According to Section 33 of the Indian Forest Act of 1927, the accused was found guilty and was given a simple imprisonment sentence of six months. Although he was also found guilty under Section 2 of the 1980 Forest (Conservation) Act, no separate sentence was imposed. The High Court cleared the revision Petitioner of the charge of violating Section 2 of the Forest (Conservation) Act, 1980, holding that Section 2 of the FCA is not a penal provision and hence their conviction is not sustainable in law. However, the conviction under Section 33 of the Indian Forest Act, 1927, was confirmed by the High Court but modified to reflect the time he had already spent in detention.

2.3.3 Forest Conservation (Amendment) Act, 1988

Prior to the Amendment made to the Act in 1988, many questions arose pertaining to the application of the Act, with regard to the restrictions imposed under Section 2. The lack of clarity with respect to the term 'non-forest purpose' under Section 2(ii) of the Act had given way for the diversion of forest land for developmental activities. In many instances, the loophole in the law prompted parties to draw reference to the Indian Forest Act, 1927, to justify the diversion of forest land for various activities. Therefore, the Parliament amended the Act in 1988 to bridge the gap in the law and make it more stringent.[87]

The major amendment introduced by the 1988 Act was the introduction of the term 'non-forest purpose' in Section 2.[88] The term specifically referred to the breaking up or clearing of the land for the cultivation of crops/plants specified or for any purpose other than re-afforestation measures. Interestingly, though the amendment infused some clarity on the meaning and scope of the term 'non-forest purposes', ambiguity still persisted. For instance, many controversies arose surrounding the meaning of the term 'reforestation' or 'afforestation'. In this regard, the Supreme Court shed some light in the case of *A. Chowgule and Co. Ltd. v. Goa Foundation*.[89] The Court noted that,

85 *Id.* at ¶ 27.
86 Prasad Paswan v. State of Jharkhand, 2019 SCC OnLine Jhar 772.
87 The Forest Conservation (Amendment) Act, 1988.
88 The Forest (Conservation) Act, 1980, § 2.
89 A. Chowgule and Co. Ltd. v. Goa Foundation, 2008 (11) SCALE 482.

> Reforestation is the restocking of existing forests and woodlands which have been depleted, with native tree stock, whereas afforestation is the process of restoring and recreating areas of woodlands or forest that once existed but were deforested or otherwise removed or destroyed at some point in the past.

Stating this, the Court clarified that reforestation or afforestation cannot simply be planting new trees in numbers equal to those destroyed; this is too simplistic and archaic. Instead, both reforestation and afforestation envisage a resurrection and re-plantation of trees and other flora similar to those which have been removed and which are suitable to the area in question.[90] Therefore, the mere replanting of non-indigenous plants which does not meet the requirements of the given eco-system cannot amount to measures of afforestation.

A more specific direction on non-forest purposes was given by the Supreme Court in *T.N. Godavarman Thirumulpad v. Union of India.*[91] while analysing what measures are required to be taken to compensate for the loss of forest land and its effect on ecology when forest land is used for non-forest purposes. Recognising the importance of the forest and the need for development, the Supreme Court stressed that there is an 'absolute need to take all precautionary measures when forest lands are sought to be directed for non-forest uses as economic development at the cost of degradation of environments and depletion of forest cover would not be long lasting', a direction to pay net present value (NPV) was given. This NPV amount is to be utilized only for the protection of the environment. A committee of experts was appointed to determine NPV on economic principles.

Another salient feature of the Amendment Act is that it created statutory accountability for Government officials to comply with the law and take active measures for forest conservation. Under the mandate of Section 3A, any person – including Government departments – who contravenes or abets the contravention of Section 2 of the Act will be subject to imprisonment for a maximum of 15 days.[92] Furthermore, as per the provision of Section 3B, where an offence has been committed by any Government department or any authority, the head of the impugned department or the person in charge of the impugned authority shall be liable to punishment under the Act.[93] An exemption in this regard is available provided it is proved the offence was committed without his knowledge or that he exercised all due diligence to prevent the commission of such offence.[94]

90 *Id.* at ¶ 6.

91 T.N. Godavarman Thirumulpad v. Union of India, WP (Civil) No. 202 of 1995, Order dated 26/09/2005.

92 The Forest (Conservation) Act 1980, § 3A.

93 *Id.* § 3B.

94 *Id.* § 3B Proviso.

2.3.4 The Forest Conservation (Amendment) Act, 2023

The Forest (Conservation) Amendment Act, 2023, introduced significant legislative revisions to the Forest (Conservation) Act, 1980. Over the course of 43 years of the implementation of the FCA, several issues, challenges, and ambiguities had emerged which had to be addressed. It makes significant amendments to the FCA, including the insertion of a preamble, providing clarity regarding the application of the Act, providing statutory support to certain practised exemptions, broadening the delegated legislation power of the Central Government, etc. Key highlights of the Amendment Act are summarised as follows.

2.3.4.1 Insertion of Preamble

The Amendment Act inserts a preamble in the FCA. The preamble gives statutory recognition to India's commitment to achieving net zero emissions by 2070, its Nationally Determined Contribution (NDC) targets by 2030, and increasing India's forest and tree cover to one-third of its land area. Further, the preamble lays emphasis on India's rich tradition of preserving forests and biodiversity and envisages the enhancement of forest-based economic, social, and environmental benefits, including improvement of livelihoods for communities that are dependent on forests.

2.3.4.2 Modifying Application of the Act

The newly inserted Section 1A demarcates the land which will be covered by the FCA and also exempts certain land from the applicability of FCA. Section 1A(1) provides that the FCA will be applicable to (a) forest lands, i.e., either declared or notified as a forest under the Indian Forest Act, 1927,[95] or any other Act in force; and (b) those lands which have been recorded as forests in Government records on or after 25 October 1980. However, the Act will now not apply to those recorded forest lands that have been duly diverted for non-forest use before 12 December 1996. For clarity, the explanation appended to Section 1A(1) provides that Government records means the records 'held by' the Revenue or Forest Departments of the State Government or Union Territories, or any other authorities, local bodies, communities, or councils that are recognised by the State Government or the Union Territories.

2.3.4.3 Exemptions

Further, Section 1A(2) lists certain categories of land that are exempted from the purview of the FCA. As per this subsection, the following categories are exempted:

95 The Indian Forest Act, 1927.

- Forest land situated along rail lines or public roads maintained by the Government providing access to a habitation, rail, or roadside amenity of a maximum size of 0.10 hectare. This will assist forest-dwelling and rural communities in gaining access to civic amenities and mainstream the indigenous population with the rest of the country.
- Trees, tree plantations, or reafforestation raised on lands which are neither declared/notified as forests nor are recorded as forests in any Government records. This exemption clarifies that private plantations will not be deemed forests. This is to encourage private plantations in contributing to greater tree cover, therefore helping India achieve the goal of converting one-third of our land areas as ecological areas for our commitments in the NDC under the Paris Agreement.
- The forest land that is (i) situated within 100 km (aerial distance) of international borders/Line of Control/Line of Actual Control, to be used for the construction of strategic linear projects of national importance and concerning national security, (ii) forest land of area up to 10 hectares (10 ha) that is to be used for building security infrastructure, and (iii) forest land of area up to five hectares (5 ha) that is proposed to be used for defence-related or public utility projects or for building paramilitary camps in a Left Wing Extremism (LWE)-affected area, as notified by the Central Government.

However, it is pertinent to state that these exemptions are not blanket exemptions. They will be subject to terms and conditions laid down by the guidelines of the Central Government, which will be issued from time to time. These terms and conditions can include requirements such as compensatory afforestation activity to compensate for the felling of trees in such forest areas.[96]

2.3.4.4 Narrowing down the Ambit of Non-Forest Purpose

As stated earlier, the primary objective of the FCA is to regulate the diversion of forest land for 'non-forest purposes'. Hence, it was imperative to specify the meaning and scope of non-forest purposes. Towards this end, the Explanation appended to Section 2 of the unamended FCA stated that non-forest purpose means the 'breaking up or clearing of any forest land or portion thereof' for either cultivation of certain specified type of crops and plants,[97] or any other purpose other than reafforestation. However, the explanation also specified that certain activities that are related or ancillary to the conservation, development, and management of forests and wildlife are not to be counted as non-forest purposes. These activities included the establishment of check-posts, fire lines, wireless communications, and the construction of fencing, bridges, culverts, dams, waterholes, trench

96 The Forest (Conservation) Amendment Act, 2023, § 4 (The Forest (Conservation) Act, 1980, § 1A(3)).
97 The Forest (Conservation) Act, 1980, § 2.

marks, boundary marks, pipelines, or other like purposes.[98] The Amendment Act has further narrowed down the scope of non-forest purposes by expanding the list of activities which cannot be counted as 'non-forest purposes'. According to the Amendment Act, the following list of works are not to be considered as non-forest purposes:[99]

1. Silvicultural operations including regeneration operations;
2. Establishment of check-posts and infrastructure for the front line forest staff;
3. Establishment and maintenance of fire lines;
4. Wireless communications;
5. Construction of fencing, boundary marks or pillars, bridges and culverts, check dams, waterholes, trenches, and pipelines;
6. Establishment of zoos and safaris, that are owned by the Government or any authority, in forest areas other than protected areas;
7. Eco-tourism facilities that are included in the Forest Working Plan or Wildlife Management Plan or Tiger Conservation Plan or Working Scheme of that area; and
8. Any other like purposes, which the Central Government may, by order, specify.

Thus, apart from expanding the list of activities that cannot be considered 'non-forest purposes', the Amendment Act also empowers the Central Government to expand this list through orders.[100] Further, the newly inserted Section 2(2) also empowers the Central Government to lay down terms and conditions subject to which surveys, such as reconnaissance, prospecting, investigation, or exploration including seismic surveys, will also not be regarded as 'non-forest purposes'.[101] This was done considering the fact that such surveys and explorations in forest areas do not involve a perceptible change in the forest land use. The exception for surveys and exploration is significant considering the need to plan and strategise mines and mineral explorations, and map and keep data on activities organised in forest areas.

2.3.4.5 Creating a Level Playing Field with Respect to Grant of Forest Land

Prior to the amendment, the FCA regulated the assignment or lease of forest land by State Governments to private entities by mandating the prior approval of the Central Government before such assignment or lease. However, it did not restrict

98 *Id.*

99 The Forest (Conservation) Amendment Act, 2023, § 5(a) (The Forest (Conservation) Act, 1980, § 2(1) explanation).

100 *Id.*

101 The Forest (Conservation) Amendment Act, 2023, § 5(b) (The Forest (Conservation) Act, 1980, § 2(2)).

or mandate prior approval of the Central Government for the assignment or lease of forest land to Government agencies. This was considered unfair. Hence, the Amendment Act now creates a level playing field between state agencies and private entities. According to the amendment, now the State Government will also require prior approval of the Central Government before it assigns or leases out forest State-owned/controlled/managed agencies. The words 'not owned, managed or controlled by government'[102] that created this exemption have been removed. Further, the amended Section 2(1)(iii) also empowers the Central Government to lay down terms and conditions to regulate such grants of forest land.

2.3.4.6 Expansion of the Central Government's Power of Delegated Legislation

Prior to the amendment, the power of the Central Government to make delegated legislation was limited to making rules only. In order to ensure proper implementation of the provisions of the Act, the delegated legislation-making power of the Central Government has been expanded and it has now been bestowed with the power to issue 'directions' to any Central Government authority, State Governments, Union Territories, or to any organisation, entity, or body recognized by them.

2.3.4.7 Implication of the Amendment Act

The Forest (Conservation) Amendment Act, 2023, has brought about a paradigm shift in the regulation of forests in India and has made several significant and noteworthy changes in the Forest (Conservation) Act, 1980. The amendment is grounded on various challenges and ambiguities that were hindering the effective implementation of the Act.

First and foremost, through the amendment, the scope of the word 'forest' has been attempted to be defined and demarcated. This is a crucial legislative clarification in furtherance of the landmark decision of the Hon'ble Supreme Court in *T N Godavarman Thirumulpad v. Union of India*,[103] wherein the Apex Court has, inter alia, adopted the dictionary definition of the word forest, apart from notified and recorded forests. The adoption of the dictionary meaning of forests led to the creation of the concept of 'deemed forests', i.e., those areas which are neither notified nor recorded as forests in any Government record, but fit within the dictionary definition of forests. This made the concept of forests dynamic and subject to diverse interpretation. Gradually the concept of deemed forests evolved and it was not only interpreted differently but was also used differently, creating an ambiguity as to where the FCA is to apply. Due to this, the development of forest areas and lands fit for vegetation and habitation was severely constrained. The amendment

102 *See* the unamended Forest Conservation Act, 1980, § 2(iii).
103 T.N. Godavarman Thirumulpad v. Union of India, (1997) 2 SCC 267.

addresses and clears this ambiguity, restricting the application of the FCA to only the notified and recorded forests.

Moreover, the absence of clarity with regard to the application of the Act due to the wide definition of the term forest and the concept of deemed forests created issues and challenges for public utilities and national security and strategy-related infrastructure development. It also discouraged people from undertaking plantation, afforestation, etc., because they might come under the purview of the FCA. To address such issues and concerns, exemptions through guidelines were already in practice; however, it was necessary to give these exemptions statutory backing and to give much-needed clarity to citizens' interest in the forest and also contribute to the nation's climate ambitions. Thus, through the amendments, public utilities and national security infrastructure of specified areas are now statutorily exempted from the ambit of the FCA. The exemption related to public utilities will assist forest-dwelling and rural communities, where the poverty rate remains significantly high, to have suitable and last-mile infrastructure such as communication, electricity, and law enforcement. It is imperative that these provisions should be rigorously adhered to and enforced to fulfil the objective of the Amendment in spirit.

In addition to that, there was an ongoing debate regarding the meaning of 'recorded forests'. Should it include only the forest record or also the revenue record (as per the *T N Godavarman* judgment), or should records of any other authority also count? It is important to note that land is a State subject and revenue records of the Government also specify whether land is a forest or not. Further, there was also ambiguity regarding whether, if a land has been diverted to non-forest use for, e.g., school, Government offices or agriculture but has not been recorded as non-forest in the records, the FCA would be applicable. Both these ambiguities have now been addressed through the Amendment Act which categorically defines the meaning of the Government record to include not only forest records but also revenue records and any other record of any authority. Also, land which has been duly diverted, by Government order, towards non-forest purposes on or before 12 December 1996 (date of the *T N Godavarman* judgment) will be exempted from the purview of the FCA.

Additionally, it is equally important to highlight that the newly added preamble recognises the issues at the global level for which international and national efforts are being made. The need to achieve the targets set by India has also been acknowledged. It underscores the need to accept the fact that we can't go with the 'business as usual' mindset, as otherwise we will be lagging behind our targets. In a rapidly evolving global environmental and social landscape there is a need to go beyond conservation and management. It is also equally important to focus on the restoration of forests, the maintenance of ecological security, and the sustenance of cultural and traditional values of forests while balancing economic needs with carbon neutrality.

Lastly, with regard to the grant of Environmental clearance (EC), it is significant to note that there are no alterations and the process of obtaining EC remains unchanged. Further, on close perusal, it is evident that the authorities had been granting Environmental Clearance expeditiously. According to statistics, 3,857 Environmental Clearances were granted out of 3,957 applications in the year 2023 as of now.[104] In 2022, 12,496 applications were granted Environmental Clearance which is the highest ever.[105] It is observed that with the power to broaden the power of delegated legislation, the Central Government will issue directions and guidelines that will bring in more clarity regarding the process of obtaining EC and Forest Clearances.

2.3.5 *Scheduled Tribes and other Traditional Forest Dwellers (Recognition of Forest Rights) Act, 2006*

The Scheduled Tribes and other Traditional Forest Dwellers (Recognition of Forest Rights) Act, 2006 (FRA), or as it is popularly known, the Forest Rights Act, 2006, was enacted with the objective of addressing the difficult living conditions of the tribal groups and the primitive families living and residing in and around forests. FRA was an outcome of generations of struggle by the local inhabitants, forest dwellers, and marginalized communities, whose lives and survival were dependent on forest resources.[106] To make good the wrong that was historically perpetrated on forest dwellers, in the context of their rights to land and forest resources, the Act sought to legally recognise the entitlements and, to an extent, meet the claims of forest dwellers and Scheduled Tribes.[107] The primary aim of FRA was to give impetus to the enforcement of the rights of forest dwellers who had lived in the forests for generations but whose rights could not be recorded.[108] Thus, to provide a framework whereby the forest dwellers would be vested with such rights, the said legislation was enacted.

2.3.5.1 Forest Rights and Forest Conservation

Although FRA is primarily aimed at undoing the historical injustices done to forest dwellers and Scheduled Tribes by vesting in them certain rights *vis-à-vis* forests, the Act moots for forest conservation through the interconnectedness of forests and forest dwellers. In doing so, FRA provides an exhaustive list of expressed rights to

104 *Online Submission & Monitoring of Environmental & CRZ Clearances*, Environmental Clearance Portal, https://environmentclearance.nic.in/ (last visited June 12, 2024).

105 Simrin Suroor, *Over 12,000 Environment Clearances Granted to Projects in 2022, a 20 Times Increase Since 2018*, The Print (Mar 28, 2023), https://theprint.in/environment/over-12000-environment-clearances-granted-to-projects-in-2022-a-20-times-increase-since-2018/1477952/.

106 Savyasaachi, *Forest Rights Act 2006: Undermining the Foundational Position of the Forest*, 46(15) Economic & Political Weekly 55 (2011).

107 S. Singh, *The Forest Rights Act 2007: Implications for Forest Dwellers and Protected Areas*, 10(2) International Forestry Review (Special issue) 325–330 (2008).

108 The Scheduled Tribes and Other Traditional Forest Dwellers (Recognition of Forest Rights) Act, 2006 [hereinafter The Forest Rights Act, 2006].

which beneficiaries such as 'forest dwelling Scheduled Tribes'[109] and 'other forest dwellers'[110] are entitled.[111] FRA not only recognises the right to hold and live on forest land, but also grants primitive tribal groups and pre-agricultural communities rights to habitation, and rights to practice occupations and self-cultivation for their livelihood which include the right to collect, use, and dispose of minor forest produce and community rights. Further, it also recognises their right to protect, regenerate, or conserve or manage community forest resources which they have been traditionally protecting and conserving for sustainable use.[112]

Section 3(2) of the FRA provides a non-obstante clause which overrides the Forest Conservation Act of 1980. It states that the Central Government shall provide for the diversion of forest land for certain facilities managed by the Government, which involves the felling of trees, not exceeding 75 trees per hectare for the construction of schools, dispensaries/hospitals, *Anganwadis*, fair price shops, electric and communication lines, tanks and other drinking water supply pipelines, minor irrigation canals, etc. Further, such clearances of forest shall only be carried out if the same is recommended by the Gram Sabha. The overriding effect of the Act has been woven into the structure of the legislation to promote the overall welfare of the local communities by allowing for the provision and development of civic amenities and public utility services. To this effect, several schemes have been implemented by the Ministry of Tribal Affairs for the benefit of tribal people, including those in the forest areas such as the 'Mechanism for marketing of Minor Forest Produce (MFP) through Minimum Support Price (MSP) and development of Value Chain for MFP'.[113] Furthermore, from time to time, the Ministry of Tribal Affairs releases funds out of the Special Central Assistance to Tribal Sub Plan for infrastructure work relating to basic services and facilities viz. approach roads, healthcare, primary education, minor irrigation, rainwater harvesting, drinking water, sanitation, community halls, etc., for the development of forest villages.[114]

Section 4 of FRA provides that the Central Government shall have the power to recognise and vest forest rights in forest dwelling Scheduled Tribes and other traditional forest dwellers in respect of all forest rights mentioned in Section 3. Further, the forest dwellers recognised under FRA, such as those in wildlife habitats of national parks and/or sanctuaries, shall not be resettled or their rights shall not be affected in any manner for the purposes of creating inviolate areas for wildlife conservation, unless established that the activities as being carried out or the impact of

109 *Id.* § 2(c).
110 *Id.* § 2(o).
111 *Id.* chapter II.
112 *Id.* § 3(1).
113 Ministry of Tribal Affairs, Government of India, Guidelines for Mechanism for Marketing of Minor Forest Produce (MFP) Through Minimum Support Price (MSP) & Development of Value Chain of MFP, Notification F.No. 19/17/2018 - Livelihood dated 26.02.2019.
114 Ministry of Tribal Affairs, Government of India, Press Information Bureau, Aug 07, 2014, https://pib.gov.in/newsite/PrintRelease.aspx?relid=90114 (last visited Oct 09, 2023).

the presence of the forest dwellers is causing irreversible damage and is the cause of a threat to the existence of the species and their habitat; a resettlement package has been communicated to the forest dwellers which provides a secure livelihood and the requirements of affected individuals in the relevant laws; the free consent of the Gram Sabha has been obtained in writing; and so on and so forth, as per the relevant sub-clauses of Section 4.

Chapter IV of FRA provides for the authorities and the procedure for the vesting of forest rights. The Gram Sabha has been declared a competent authority to initiate the process of determining the nature and extent of rights, within the local limits of its jurisdiction under this Act. Any person so aggrieved by the decisions of the Gram Sabha may approach via petition the Sub-Divisional Level Committee within 60 days of the passing of the resolution by the Gram Sabha.[115] From the Sub-Divisional Level Committee, the appeal goes to the District Level Committee which has been approved by the State to keep record of forest rights. The District Level Committee's decisions shall be final and binding, and the State shall also constitute a State Level Monitoring Committee to monitor the process of recognition and vesting of forest rights and to submit to the nodal agency such returns and reports as may be called for by that agency.

Chapter V of FRA provides for offences and penalties under Sections 7 and 8. Offences under this Act are punishable by a fine which may extend up to 1,000 rupees. No court shall take cognisance of any offence under Section 7 unless any forest dwelling Scheduled Tribe in case of a dispute relating to the resolution of a Gram Sabha or a higher authority gives notice of not less than 60 days to the State-level monitoring committee and the same has not proceeded against such authority.

In 2008 the constitutional validity of FRA was challenged in *Wildlife First v. Ministry of Forest and Environment and Ors.*[116] Other issues raised in this case were whether States have implemented due process while denying forest residents' claims and regarding the validity of the procedure for filing claims under FRA. The final judgment in this case is pending; however, in 2019, the Supreme Court directed the States to file affidavits as to why eviction orders under the Act were not implemented and directed the eviction of all persons from the forest lands whose claims were rejected. Following a major public outcry, the Supreme Court stayed its order. Further in 2008, in *V. Sambasivam v. GOI, Ministry of Tribal Affairs*,[117] a writ petition was filed before the Madras High Court challenging the constitutionality of the Act. In an interim order, the High Court directed the implementation of the Act but no titles to be given without the High Court's permission. However, this order was set aside by the Supreme Court in 2016.

115 The Forest Rights Act, 2006, § 6.

116 Wildlife First v. Ministry of Forest and Environment, Writ Petition (Civil) No. 109 of 2008.

117 V. Sambasivam v. GoI, Ministry of Tribal Affairs, W.P. Np. 4533/2008.

A Joint Committee was constituted by the Ministry of Environment and Forests and the Ministry of Tribal Affairs in April 2010 to comprehensively review the implementation of FRA. This report by the National Committee on Forest Rights Act, submitted by N C Saxena to Shri Kantilal Bhuria, then Union Minister of Tribal Affairs, mentioned that the implementation of FRA has been poor and includes recommendations for implementing it effectively. According to the report, the implementation has been uneven in different States of India. In those States that are lagging, either the institutions still need to be established or they are hardly functional. There are also doubts about the FRA's applicability and relevance in some States such as the North Eastern States, whereas in States like Chhattisgarh, Naxalism and State-sponsored conflict have limited its implementation to a great extent. Additionally, in some States, the application of the Act has been limited to certain or specific regions, and in some other States, the implementation has been stayed due to High Court orders or State actions.[118]

The issue of the violation of tribal rights came to light recently in the case of *Orissa Mining Corporation Ltd. v. Ministry of Environment and Forest*. The court held that FRA is a social welfare or remedial statute, the legislative intent of which is to protect customs, usage, forms, practices, and ceremonies that are appropriate to the traditions of forest dwellers. FRA protects various rights of the forest dwellers and STs including customary rights to use forest land as a community resource and is not restricted only to property rights or areas of inhabitation.

2.3.6 Compensatory Afforestation Act, 2016

The Compensatory Afforestation Act, 2016 (the Act), was enacted for the purpose of establishing a fund solely dedicated to compensatory afforestation, additional compensatory afforestation, and penal compensatory afforestation.[119] Prior to the enactment of the Act, the Supreme Court, in the case of *T.N. Godavarman Thirumulpad v. Union of India and Ors.*, mandated that a Compensatory Afforestation Fund be created in which all the monies received from the user agencies for compensatory afforestation, additional compensatory afforestation, penal compensatory afforestation, net present value of the diverted forest land, or catchment area treatment plan shall be deposited.[120] In the said case, the Supreme Court noted that the amount collected by various States from the user agencies to whom permissions were granted for using forest land for non-forest purposes under the Forest Conservation Act, 1980, was not being utilised for such compensatory afforestation and the overall estimate indicated that the funds were being used only to the extent of 63% of the funds received by the State Governments.[121] Therefore, there was a need for

118 Ministry of Environment and Forests & Ministry of Tribal Affairs, Government of India, Report of the National Committee on Forest Rights Act (2010).

119 The Compensatory Afforestation Act, 2016, pmbl.

120 T.N. Godavarman Thirumulpad v. Union of India, AIR 2014 SC 3614.

121 *Id.* at ¶ 8.

structural changes in the way in which funds were being released for compensatory afforestation measures. To this effect, the Compensatory Afforestation Act, 2016, was enacted.

2.3.6.1 Compensatory Afforestation Fund

The Act provides for the establishment of a National Compensatory Afforestation Fund at the Central Level under the public accounts of India, which is managed by the National Authority established under the Act and controlled by the Central Government.[122] The Fund encompasses all monies collected by the State Governments and Union Territory Administrations which have been placed under the ad hoc Authority and deposited in the nationalised banks prior to the enactment of the Act.[123] Furthermore, the fund shall include all credits comprising 10% of the funds released from the user agencies in respect of the forest land diverted in their favour, which have been credited directly into the State Fund,[124] grants-in-aid received, if any, by the National Authority, any loan taken or any borrowings made by the National Authority, and any other sums received by the National Authority by way of benefaction, gift, or donations.[125] All the money so credited to the Fund shall be subject to interest, the rates of which are declared by the Central Government from time to time.[126]

Parallel to the National Fund established at the Central level, a State Compensatory Afforestation Fund shall also be established by the State Governments at the State level under the public account of the State.[127] The composition of the State fund shall be on similar lines as that of the National Fund and the State fund shall be controlled by the State Government and managed by the State Authority.[128]

For the disbursal or utilisation of funds, the Act envisages a detailed procedure providing the various heads and percentage of funds that may be disbursed. Section 5 categorically enumerates the procedure for the disbursal and utilisation of the National Fund and Section 6 deals with the procedure for the disbursal and utilisation of the State Funds.

For the collection of money for the funds, 'Net Present Value (NPV)' was a significant recommendation of the Central Empowered Committee (CEC) which was set up by the Supreme Court's Godavarman bench in 2002.[129] The concept of the Net Present Palue of Forests (NPV) was elaborated by the Supreme Court under the Forest (Conservation) Act, 1980, in *T.N. Godavarman Thirumulpad v. Union of*

122 The Compensatory Afforestation Act, 2016, § 3.
123 *Id.* § 3(3).
124 *Id.* § 3(4).
125 *Id.* § 3(5).
126 *Id.* §§ 3(6) & 3(7).
127 *Id.* § 4.
128 Id., 2016, § 4(2).
129 T.N. Godavarman Thirumulpad v. Union of India, Writ Petition (Civil) 202 of 1995.

India[130] The Supreme Court defined NPV as 'the present value of net cash flow from a project, discounted by the cost of capital'. In simple terms, it refers to the value of monetary compensation for the loss of tangible and intangible benefits from forest lands due to the diversion of forest land for non-forest purposes. Payment of NPV ensures that the new user bears the cost of these losses. The Supreme Court clarified that the payment of NPV 'is for the protection of the environment and not in relation to any "proprietary right"'. Even before the Supreme Court decision on NPV, the practice of collecting NPV was followed in several States including Bihar, Madhya Pradesh, etc. In relation to NPV, the Supreme Court in its 2005 judgement[131] considered the following issues:

(a) Whether before diversion of forest land for non- forest purposes and consequential loss of benefits accruing from the forests should not the user agency of such land be required to compensate for the diversion.

(b) If so, should not the user Agency be required to make payment of Net Present Value (NPV) of such diverted land so as to utilize the amounts so received for getting back in long run the benefits which are lost by such diversion?

(c) What guidelines should be issued for determination of NPV? Should guidelines apply uniformly to all?

(d) How to calculate NPV? Should some projects be exempted from payment of NPV?

The Supreme Court concluded by observing that payment to CAMPA including NPV is constitutional and valid. These amounts are required for achieving ecological plans and for protecting the environment and for the regeneration of forests and the maintenance of ecological balance and eco-systems. The Supreme Court further exempted Government projects like hospitals, dispensaries, and schools from paying NPV; however, all other projects are required to pay NPV subject to the final decision on this matter. It directed that the NPV, which is based on intergenerational justice, be worked out on economic principles, for which it directed the constitution of an expert committee.

2.3.6.2 Authorities Established under the Act

2.3.6.2.1 NATIONAL COMPENSATORY AFFORESTATION FUND MANAGEMENT AND PLANNING AUTHORITY

As the Act envisages a double-tiered system of compensatory afforestation funds, consequently, it also provides for a two-tiered administrative system responsible for the management of these funds. At the Central Level, the National Compensatory

130 T.N. Godavarman Thirumulpad v. Union of India, WP (Civil) No. 202 of 1995, Order dated 26/09/2005.

131 *Id.*

Afforestation Fund Management and Planning Authority (National Authority) is the designated authority responsible for managing the National Fund.[132] The National Authority is constituted by the Central Government and consists of a governing body which is headed by the Minister for Environment, Forest and Climate Change for the Government of India, who is the *ex-officio* chairman.[133] The Chairman is accompanied by the Member Secretary who shall be an officer of the rank of an Additional Director General of Forests, as the Chief Executive Officer, and other designated officials and expert members.[134] The Governing Body also is assisted by an executive committee, monitoring group, and administrative support mechanism in the performance of its functions.[135]

The primary function of the National Authority is to formulate the broad policy framework for its functioning and that of the State Authorities.[136] Apart from this, the National Authority is responsible for approving its annual audited reports, reviewing the reports of the executive committees and monitoring groups that assist it, resolving issues between State Authorities in cases involving issues of inter-State or Centre-State character, etc.

2.3.6.2.2 STATE COMPENSATORY AFFORESTATION FUND MANAGEMENT AND PLANNING AUTHORITY

At the State Level, the State Compensatory Afforestation Fund Management and Planning Authority (State Authority) is the authority in charge of managing the State Compensatory Afforestation Fund. The State Authority is constituted in each State by a notification issued by the Central Government.[137] The State Authority is headed by a governing body which is assisted by a steering committee and an executive committee.[138] In accordance with the mandate of the Act, the Governing Body consists of an *ex-officio* chairman who is necessarily Chief Minister of the State and, in the case of a Union Territory having no legislature, the Lieutenant Governor or the Administrator, *ex-officio* members, being the Minister of Forests for the State and the Chief Secretary, and other official members.[139] On similar lines as the composition of the National Authority, the State Authority shall also consist of a Member Secretary who is necessarily the Principal Secretary in charge of the Forest Department.[140]

Unlike the National Authority, the State Authority has limited functions. Some of the functions of the governing body of the State Authority include laying down

132 The Compensatory Afforestation Act, 2016, § 8.
133 *Id.* § 8(4).
134 *Id.* § 8(5).
135 *Id.* § 9.
136 *Id.* § 14.
137 *Id.* 2016, § 10(1).
138 *Id.* § 10(4).
139 *Id.* § 10(5).
140 *Id.* § 10(7).

the broad policy framework for the functioning of such State Authority within the overall framework notified by the Central Government on the recommendations of the National Authority and reviewing the working of the State Authority from time to time.[141]

The Compensatory Afforestation Act, 2016, can be lauded for streamlining the procedure of managing and distributing funds for afforestation and for creating transparency in the utilisation of funds. As the Act identifies the specific authorities responsible for managing compensatory afforestation funds, it creates accountability on the part of the State agencies and authorities in ensuring that funds are being effectively utilised for purposes of afforestation. This being said, the Act is yet to bear positive outcomes, especially considering that it is a comparatively new legislation.

2.3.7 The Indian Forest (Amendment) Act, 2017

The Indian Forest Act, 1927, was amended in the year 2017. The major change brought about by the Amendment Act was the omission of 'bamboo' from the definition of 'tree' under Section 2(7). This will waive the requirement of permission for felling bamboo grown in non-forest areas or its transportation for economic use.

141 *Id.* § 17.

Table 2.1 Best Practices Adopted by Different States as a Remedial Measure

State	*Challenge Faced/Purpose*	*Remedial Measures*
Chhattisgarh	Large-scale exploitation of natural resources, exotic flora, and fauna.	1 Granting recognition to forest rights' claims acquired by local forest dwellers and Scheduled Tribes. 2 Granting recognition to forest lands. 3 Enacted the Chhattisgarh State Forest Policy in 2001. 4 Establishment of Forest Crime Bureaus under the Policy.
Himachal Pradesh	1 Depletion of rich biodiversity, forest cover. 2 Lack of adequate protection for the rights of indigenous persons.	1 Enacting several laws such as the Himachal Pradesh Preservation of Forests and Maintenance of Supplies of Forest Based Essential Commodities Act, 1984, for conserving forests. 2 Revised the Himachal Pradesh Forest Policy, 2006, which focused on sustainable forest management. 3 The policy emphasised the active participation of the local community in forest conservation. 4 Undertook several projects such as the '*Van Samridhi*'.

(*Continued*)

Table 2.1 (Continued)

State	*Challenge Faced/Purpose*	*Remedial Measures*
Karnataka	1 Large-scale deforestation and environmental degradation of western ghats. 2 Water and energy shortage.	1 Adopting Joint Forest Planning and Management Policy to promote forest conservation. 2 Establishment of Village Forest Committees under the policy to facilitate community participation. 3 Enacting the Karnataka Forest Act of 1963 to prevent illegal exploitation of forests and promote sustainable development. 4 Notified Karnataka Forest Policy in 2013 to provide for the utilisation of silvicultural systems and rehabilitative measures for forest preservation.
Kerala	1 Extensive loss of forest cover.	1 Implementing 'Project Tiger' in 1973 to conserve tigers and other wildlife. 2 Launched 'India Eco-Development Project' in 1998 to facilitate the participation ofTribal communities in forest conservation and wildlife protection from illegal activities. 3 Adoption of Kerala State Forest Policy in 2007 to manage the State's forests through sustainable conservation.
North-Eastern States	1 Large-scale deforestation and environmental degradation.	1 Government of Mizoram launched 'New Land Use Policy' to facilitate transition from shifting agriculture to alternative sources of income. 2 The Government of Meghalaya enacted the Meghalaya Forest Regulation Act, 1973, to regulate forests and forest produce. 3 Government of Nagaland enacted the Nagaland Forest Act, 1968, to regulate forest produce. 4 The Government of Manipur enacted the Indian Forest (Manipur Amendment) Act, 2018, to provide for stricter punitive measures against illegal forest activities. 5 Government of Arunachal Pradesh enacted the Arunachal Pradesh Forest (Removal of Timber) Regulation Act in 1983 to regulate and control the removal of timber from the State.

(*Continued*)

Table 2.1 (Continued)

State	*Challenge Faced/Purpose*	*Remedial Measures*
Uttarakhand	1 Large-scale deforestation. 2 Prevalent soil degradation. 3 Diminishing biodiversity.	1 Establishment of 'Van Panchayats' to promote active involvement of rural population. 2 Implementing Joint Forest Management to conserve forest and prevent soil degradation. 3 Establishment of wildlife sanctuaries, national parks, biosphere reserves, and conservation reserves for the protection of biodiversity.

This was done with the hope that it will improve the earnings of tribal communities living around forests. The main reason for bringing this amendment was to benefit the North-Eastern States of India. These States are some of the largest producers of bamboo and it forms a large part of their traditional handicrafts, diet, and exports. Due to the earlier classification as a tree, it was very difficult to cut bamboo growing in forests, and it implied excessive paperwork and permissions for harvest and transport. The same has now been revoked. The reduced imports from South Asian countries shall prove beneficial for the rural economy and the central exchequer. It is hoped that the farmers and small entrepreneurs in North-Eastern States shall now be able to benefit from this declassification. However, bamboo growing in forest land shall continue to be classified as a tree and be guided by restrictions as per the law.

2.4 Forest Conservation at the State Level – Best Practices

Forest conservation is best understood and practised at the grassroots level. Over many decades, since pre-colonial times, local communities, forest dwellers, and indigenous people have adopted traditional practices for preserving the forests. Slowly, with advancing times and needs, these practices dwindled, while other practices evolved. Some States, with hills and mountains, have their own ways to ensure forest conservation and today, with decentralised governance and the prevalence of *Panchayats*, it was only wise to make this a localised and communal effort.

Table 2.1 illustrates the best practices adopted by the different States discussed above.

2.5 International Developments in Forest Conservation

The international legal regime on forests has witnessed a gradual development, with an array of treaties and non-binding instruments that deal with the protection and conservation of forests directly or indirectly. The increasing importance of forests as a resource pool has influenced critical interventions by the international community in addressing issues such as deforestation, protection of endangered species, loss of biodiversity, climate change, desertification, and regulation of the use of and trade in timber. While there are several legal instruments dealing with the conservation of forests, a few notable international agreements and initiatives are discussed as follows.

2.5.1 International Tropical Timber Agreement (1983)

Owing to decades of rampant exploitation and destruction of tropical forests, countries across the globe felt the need to establish an environmental body for establishing a concrete treaty regime.[142] Surprisingly, the need first materialised at the United Nations Conference on Trade and Development (UNCTAD), a body established with the purpose of facilitating greater participation from the Least Developed Countries (LDCs).[143]

Commencing in 1976, there occurred a slew of preparatory meetings up till 1982. Eventually, the International Tropical Timber Agreement (ITTA) opened for signature on 18 November 1983 and subsequently for ratification and enforcement on 1 April 1985.[144] As the consequence of a lack of State leadership, the negotiations were driven primarily by European NGOs such as the UK Friends of the Earth (FoE), World Wildlife Fund (WWF), etc., and international organisations like the International Union for the Conservation of Nature (IUCN).[145] In a step towards conserving tropical forests, the ITTA acknowledged the importance and the need for the conservation and development of timber and emphasised the establishment of a framework of international co-operation between producing and consuming members to find solutions to the problems faced by the tropical timber economy.

2.5.1.1 Legal Significance of the ITTA

The ITTA also led to the constitution of the International Tropical Timber Organization (ITTO),[146] which, since the time of its inception in 1986, has assumed the position of the supreme authority supervising and regulating tropical timber

142 Geery Nagtzaam, *Into the Woods: Analyzing Normative Evolution and the International Tropical Timber Organization*, 5(3) Arts and Social Sciences Journal 5 (2014).

143 For more information on LDCs, refer to the: United Nations Conference on Trade and Development (UNCTAD), The Least Developed Countries Report 2020: Productive Capacities for the New Decade 9, 10 (2020).

144 Michele M. Betsill and Elisabeth Corell, NGO Diplomacy: The Influence of Nongovernmental Organisations, in International Environmental Negotiations 149–206 (MIT Press 2007).

145 Fred P. Gale, The Tropical Timber Trade Regime, International Political Economy Series 87 (New York: St. Martin's Press 1998).

146 *Id.* at Ch. III, art. 3: Establishment, Headquarters and Structure of the International Tropical Timber Organization.

1. The International Tropical Timber Organization is hereby established to administer the provisions and supervise the operation of this Agreement.

trade.[147] Unfortunately, the ITTO, by virtue of its structure, facilitates environmental misappropriation, instead of precluding it.[148] The ITTO Council consists of 63 members which account for about 75% of the world's tropical forests and 90% of the international trade in tropical timber. The official member States consist of the producers and the consumers, with each having 1,000 votes.[149]

Up until 1994, various re-negotiations occurred in order to effectuate an invigorated commitment to the preservation of tropical forests. During the renegotiations, the positions of producer and consumer States were sometimes opposed: producers favoured extending the scope to cover timber from all sources, in order to bring all forests under the same stringent guidelines as agreed for tropical forests, while consumer countries held the view that broadening the convention to a global scope was beyond its mandate.

Finally, on 1 April 1994, a revised version of the ITTA was released and was subsequently enforced in 1997. The ITTA 1994 was, for the most part, a mirror image of its 1983 predecessor; however, it included some objectives including encouraging members to contribute to the process of sustainable development and information sharing on the international timber market, the transfer of technologies, and technical co-operation.[150]

As the ITTA 1994 concluded after a decade of multiple extensions and large-scale failures in attaining its objectives, another rehashed version[151] of the same was released on 27 January 2006 and enforced nearly six years later on 7 December 2011.[152] Some of the newly added objectives of the 2006 Agreement were to strengthen the capacity of members to improve forest law governance, dissemination of statistics on their trade in timber, developing strategies in the context of sustainable forest management, enhancing the capacity of local communities to

2. The Organization shall function through the International Tropical Timber Council established under Article 6, the committees and other subsidiary bodies referred to in Article 24, and the Executive Director and staff.

3. The Council shall, at its first session, decide on the location of the headquarters of the Organization.

4. The headquarters of the Organization shall at all times be located in the territory of a member.

147 Marie Claude Smouts, Tropical Forests, International Jungle: The Underside of Global Ecopolitics 144 (Palgrave Macmillan US 2003).

148 Nagtzaam, *supra* note 142, at 8.

149 The International Tropical Timber Agreement (ITTA), 1983, Ch. IV, art. 10, cl. 1. *See also* Beatrice Chaytor, *The Development of Global Forest Policy: Overview of Legal and Institutional Frameworks* 17 (MMSD Working Paper No. 3, Oct. 2001), https://www.iied.org/sites/default/files/pdfs/migrate/G00926.pdf.

150 Pamela S. Chasek, Earth Negotiations: Analyzing Thirty Years of Environmental Diplomacy 85 (Hampshire: Macmillan 1998).

151 Working Document Resulting from the First Session: Conference for the Negotiation of a Successor Agreement to the International Tropical Timber Agreement 4 (UNCTAD, Geneva, Switzerland, 2004), https://unctad.org/press-material/negotiations-begin-new-tropical-timber-agreement.

152 *International Tropical Timber Agreement (ITTA)*, University of Oslo, Faculty of Law (May 21, 2016), https://www.jus.uio.no/english/services/library/treaties/06/6-02/itta-2006.xml.

sustainably manage tropical timber producing forests, and identifying and addressing emerging issues.[153]

2.5.1.2 India and the ITTA: Obligations and the Extent of Compliance

In India, public forest resources are subject to the authority and supervision of forest departments at the State level.[154] The production of timber is moving away from natural forests to approaches grounded primarily in communities.[155] An apt example of the same is that of 'Joint Forest Management (JFM)', which essentially envisages a partnership between local communities, NGOs, and the State forest departments for the purpose of forest conservation.[156] The approach was first adduced in the country via the National Forest Policy of 1988[157] and subsequently the Joint Forest Management Guidelines in 1990.[158]

India was a signatory to the original ITTA in 1983[159] and thereafter, the country also ratified the Agreement in 1994, when the seemingly revised version of the ITTA was released.[160] However, India has not seen large-scale success under the ITTA and has consequently turned to a net importer of timber from being a net exporter.[161] This has happened as a result of the country's ever-rising demand for industrial round-wood.[162]

2.5.2 *Reducing Emissions from Deforestation and Forest Degradation Programme*

2.5.2.1 Key Attributes and Significance

Large-scale deforestation across the globe has resulted in disastrous consequences for the livelihoods of the local forest dwellers and fragile biodiversity in forest areas.[163] Being a prominent driver of climate change, it accounts for nearly 20% of global greenhouse gas emissions.[164] Seven tropical countries, such as Indonesia

153 The International Tropical Timber Agreement (ITTA), 2006, Ch. I, art. 1.

154 *The Status of Tropical Forest Management: India*, International Tropical Timber Organization, https://www.itto.int/sfm/2005/details/id=12390000 (last visited June 12, 2024).

155 *Id.*

156 Ministry of Environment & Forests, *supra* note 24, at 1.

157 The National Forest Policy, 1988, para 4.6.

158 Ram Prasad, *Joint Forest Management in India and the Impact of State Control Over Non-wood Forest Products*, 50 Unasylva (No. 198 - Non-wood Forest Products and Income Generation, 1999), https://www.fao.org/4/x2450e/x2450e0c.htm.

159 The International Tropical Timber Agreement (ITTA), 1983, Annexure A.

160 The International Tropical Timber Agreement (ITTA), 1994, Annexure A.

161 Clifford Polycarp, *India Must Rethink Timber Strategy*, Down to Earth (June 31, 2003), https://www.downtoearth.org.in/news/india-must-rethink-timber-strategy-13902.

162 *Id.*

163 *REDD: Protecting Climate, Forests and Livelihoods*, International Institute for Environment and Development (May 14, 2009), https://www.iied.org/redd-protecting-climate-forests-livelihoods.

164 *Id.*

and Brazil, contribute to deforestation, which eventually leads to carbon dioxide (CO_2) emissions.[165]

In light of the same, three prominent agencies of the United Nations (UN) – the United Nations Development Programme (UNDP), the United Nations Environment Programme (UNEP), and the Food and Agriculture Organisation (FAO) – joined hands to establish the 'UN – REDD Programme'.[166] The Programme essentially comprises a multi-donor trust fund, which facilitates the pooling of resources and financial aid to ensure the mitigation of global greenhouse gas emissions via the prevention of deforestation and environmental degradation in developing countries.[167]

From a legal standpoint, REDD was designed as a global framework within the ambit of the United Nations Framework Convention on Climate Change (UNFCCC).[168] As a concept, REDD encourages the curtailment of CO_2 emissions via financing activities that won't culminate in the indiscriminate felling of trees and soil degeneration, such as paying for forest management or carbon trading[169] in major developing countries.

Carbon or 'emissions' trading, as postulated under the Kyoto Protocol to the UNFCCC (1998),[170] permits industrialised or developed countries with spare emission units to sell this excess capacity to developing countries that have exceeded their targets.[171] Carbon trading adopts two major forms – 'cap and trade' and the process of 'offsetting'.[172] Under the 'cap and trade' scheme, governmental or intergovernmental authorities provide 'carbon permits' to prominent industries, which in turn trade these licences to pollute with entities that can make attempts to mitigate pollution at a lower cost.[173] Unfortunately, by virtue of large-scale industrial lobbying and adversities in accurate ascertainment of the prevailing emission levels, carbon trading has failed to see much success in practice.[174]

Offsetting, on the other hand, is the financing of 'emissions-saving projects' outside the domain of the aforementioned capped area at the hands of corporates,

165 *Id.*

166 *United Nations Environment Programme (UNEP)*, Sustainable Development, https://sdgs.un.org/un-system-sdg-implementation/united-nations-environment-programme-unep-44155 (last visited June 12, 2024).

167 *UN-REDD Programme*, Climate Funds Update, https://climatefundsupdate.org/the-funds/un-redd-programme/ (last visited June 12, 2024).

168 Charlotte Streck, *Who Owns REDD+? Carbon Markets, Carbon Rights and Entitlements to REDD+ Finance*, 11 Forests: Mdpi 1 (2020).

169 Arild Angelsen et al., REDD Credits in a Global Carbon Market: Options and Impacts 19 (Nordic Council of Ministers 2014).

170 The Kyoto Protocol to the United Nations Framework Convention on Climate Change, 1998, art. 17.

171 *Emissions Trading: Greenhouse Gas Emissions a New Commodity*, United Nations Climate Change, https://unfccc.int/process/the-kyoto-protocol/mechanisms/emissions-trading (last visited June 12, 2024).

172 Oscar Reyes & Tamra Gilbertson, *Carbon Trading: How It Works and Why It Fails*, 7 Critical Currents: Dag Hammarskjold Foundation 9 (2009).

173 *Id.* at 10.

174 *Id.*

governments, and even individuals.[175] This form of carbon trading hasn't yielded significant returns as far as the mitigation of greenhouse gas emissions is concerned.[176] Nevertheless, an apt example of such carbon trading is the 'Clean Development Mechanism (CDM)',[177] helmed by the United Nations.[178] A CDM project might comprise an electrification project in rural areas via the installation of solar panels or the incorporation of boilers more efficacious in terms of the units of energy consumed.[179]

2.5.2.2 Reducing Emissions from Deforestation and Forest Degradation (REDD): Mode of Implementation

The Programme was proposed in June 2008, while it became operational from September 2008.[180] Additionally, its initial phase commenced from 2011 and extended to 2015.[181] Currently, its lifespan began in 2016 and uncertainty regarding its exact duration *in toto* still looms large. The primary objectives fixed for the phase commencing from 2016 are as follows:

> Contributions of REDD+ to the mitigation of climate change as well as to the provision of additional benefits have been designed …
>
> Country contributions to the mitigation of climate change through REDD+ are measured, reported and verified and necessary institutional arrangements are in place … REDD+ contributions to the mitigation of climate change are implemented and safeguarded with policies and measures that constitute results-based actions, including the development of appropriate and effective institutional arrangements.[182]

Furthermore, at the national levels, affiliated activities are to be led by the host Government, with full support from the UN country team. The role of the Governments in the National Programme Cycle comprises of:

(a) Supervising the preparation of the National Programme.

175 *Id.* at 11.

176 *Id.* at 11, 12.

177 The Kyoto Protocol to the United Nations Framework Convention on Climate Change, 1998, art. 12.

178 Sandbag, *What is the Clean Development Mechanism (CDM)?*, THE GUARDIAN (July 26, 2011), https://www.theguardian.com/environment/2011/jul/26/clean-development-mechanism.

179 *The Clean Development Mechanism*, UNITED NATIONS CLIMATE CHANGE, https://unfccc.int/process-and-meetings/the-kyoto-protocol/mechanisms-under-the-kyoto-protocol/the-clean-development-mechanism (last visited June 12, 2024).

180 Michael Kohl et al., *Reduced Emissions from Deforestation and Forest Degradation (REDD): A Climate Change Mitigation Strategy on a Critical Track*, 4(10) CARBON BALANCE AND MANAGEMENT 1 (2009).

181 The UN-REDD Programme Strategy 2010-2015 (UN-REDD Programme 5th policy Board Meeting, Nov. 4-5, 2010), UNREDD/PB5/2010/6, at 1.

182 Draft Strategic Framework, 2016-2020 (UN-REDD Programme Thirteenth Policy Board Meeting, Nov. 3-7, 2014), UNREDD/PB13/2014/IV/4, at 4,5.

(b) Signing the final draft of the National Programme document, prior to its submission to the Secretariat for the purpose of consideration.
(c) Appointing a 'National Focal Point' to facilitate the coordination and effectuation of activities within the ambit of the Programme.[183]

2.5.2.3 Reducing Emissions from Deforestation and Forest Degradation (REDD): In the Indian Context

The aim of India's National REDD+ Strategy (NRPS) is to ensure the enforcement of the REDD+ programme within its territorial confines, specifically, in consonance with the Paris Agreement (2015), pertinent verdicts of the UNFCCC, and especially the Warsaw Framework for REDD+.[184] To facilitate the enforcement of REDD+ in the country, some of the measures that have been proposed by the Centre include:[185]

(a) Constitution of a National Governing Council for REDD+, to coordinate and guide REDD+ related activities at the national level and aid the revamping of NDE-REDD+.
(b) Establishment of a REDD+ Cell in every State Forest Department (SFD), along with the appointment of a Nodal Officer to supervise the Cell's functioning.
(c) Capacity building of all the SFD cadres to empower them to enforce and accurately ascertain the performance of REDD+ and other related activities.
(d) Capacity building of Forest Working Plan Officers post-analysis of forest carbon stocks and MRV in addition to other REDD+ associated issues to include REDD+ in the Forest Working Plans of all the Forest Divisions.
(e) Skill development of community youths for the purpose of several forestry activities, such as assisted natural regeneration, soil and moisture conservation, tree nurseries, fire protection, management of forest insects and pests, weed management, agroforestry, NTFP management, tree fodder production, bioenergy production, eco-tourism, and biodiversity management activities.
(f) Creation of supplementary infrastructure for SFDs, consisting of technical expertise, trained manpower, and the latest equipment and facilities for forest carbon measurement.
(g) Expansion of both the technical and technological capabilities of ICFRE, FSI, and the SFDs by upgradation of their current ones, and by creating supplementary technical infrastructure to empower FSI to deal with the additional responsibility of completing REDD+ measurements.

183 *UN-REDD Programme*, Climate Funds Update, https://climatefundsupdate.org/the-funds/un-redd-programme/ (last visited June 12, 2024); *See also UN-REDD Programme Focal Points (as of 31 May 2024)*, UN-REDD Programme, https://www.un-redd.org/document-library/un-redd-programme-focal-points-31-may-2024 (last visited June 12, 2024).
184 Ministry of Environment, Forest and Climate Change, National REDD+ Strategy, 2018, at 29.
185 *Id.* at 36–37.

(h) Creation of modern measuring capabilities with enhanced equipment in every State.

2.5.3 The United Nations Forest Principles, 1992

In the year 1992, during the deliberations of the United Nations Conference on Environment and Development (UNCED), the relationship between forests and international law gained great recognition. Although there were a few earlier attempts made towards gaining international consensus on the protection and conservation of forests, they were not adequate to deal with the fundamental changes taking place in the forest sector. The commercialisation of forest resources raised many issues in relation to the dimensions and scope of the existing international legal framework, thereby demanding a new and redefined law that promoted sustainable forest management. Therefore, after much deliberation, it was decided that the ideal path forward was to conclude an internationally binding treaty specially dedicated to the conservation of forests.[186] However, owing to the controversy surrounding the subject matter of forests and its allied complexities,[187] delegates at the Conference failed to conclude a legally binding instrument. Instead, recognising the need to take some initiatives, the Forest Principles titled 'Non-Legally Binding Authoritative Statement of Principles for a Global Consensus on the Management, Conservation and Sustainable Development of All Types of Forests' were adopted.[188]

2.5.3.1 Key Features of the Forest Principles

Some of the key features of the Forest Principles are as follows:

Sovereignty of States – Principle 2(a) recognises the sovereign and inalienable rights of State parties to 'utilise, manage and develop' forest resources to meet their socio-economic needs based on national laws and policies.[189] Furthermore, bearing in mind the objective of adopting a balanced approach, the Principles also take into consideration the ecological, spiritual, and cultural needs of society in utilising forest resources.[190] Having stated this, the Principles envisage caution in sustainably managing forest resources by requiring State parties to

186 C.P. Mackenzie, *Future Prospects For International Forest Law,* 14 The International Forestry Review 249–257 (2012).

187 David Humphreys, Forest Politics: The Evolution of International Cooperation 299 (Earthscan, London, 1996).

188 Report of the United Nations Conference on Environment and Development Annex III, Forest Principles, 13 June 1992, 31 I.L.M [1992]. 881 (hereinafter referred as 'Forest Principles, 1992').

189 Forest Principles, 1992, Principle 2(a).

190 *Id.* Principle 2(b).

take appropriate measures in protecting forests from the harmful effects of pollution, fires, pests, diseases, etc.[191]

Recognition of Community Interests – Principle 2(d) specifically recognises the importance of promoting and providing opportunities for the participation of local communities and indigenous people, industries, labour, non-governmental organisations, and individuals, forest dwellers, and women, in the development, implementation, and planning of national forest policies.[192] Furthermore, the Principles also advocate for adducing respect and recognition for the 'identity, culture and rights of indigenous people, their communities and other communities, and forest dwellers'.[193] In doing so, the Principles call upon State parties to take appropriate measures to promote the welfare of these communities by providing an adequate standard of livelihood, an economic stake in forests, and land tenure arrangements. Special recognition has also been rendered to the role of women in forest management as the Principles push for the active participation of women in the conservation and sustainable management of forests.[194]

Sustainable Forest Management – although the theme of sustainability is evident in the entire framework of the Forest Principles, there are specific references to the manner in which State parties can sustainably undertake the protection of forests. For instance, Principle 6 advocates for the planting of indigenous and introduced species of plants and trees to ensure the sustainable management of forests in meeting fuel and industrial needs. The Principle also States that national policies should take into account the relationship, where it exists, between the conservation, management, and sustainable development of forests and all aspects related to the production, consumption, recycling, and/or final disposal of forest products.[195] Furthermore, recognising the importance of forests to the economic development of each nation, Principle 7 calls upon States to promote a supportive international economic climate conducive to the sustained and environmentally sound development of forests in all countries.[196]

Afforestation and Reforestation – to encourage measures towards the 'greening' of the world,[197] the Principles prompt State parties to take positive and transparent actions towards reforestation, afforestation, and forest conservation. To maintain and increase forest cover and forest productivity, the Principles encourage the rehabilitation, reforestation, and re-establishment of trees and forests on unproductive, degraded, and deforested lands, as well as through

191 *Id.*
192 *Id.* Principle 2(d).
193 *Id.* Principle 5(a).
194 *Id.* Principle 5(b).
195 *Id.* Principle 6(b).
196 *Id.* Principle 7.
197 *Id.* Principle 8(a).

the management of existing forest resources.[198] Scientific and technological research and developments are also encouraged to undertake scientifically efficient methods of forest management.[199] Furthermore, in line with the holistic approach envisioned by the Principles, forest management is required to be integrated with the management of adjacent areas so as to maintain ecological balance and sustainable productivity.[200]

International Co-operation – the Forest Principles recognise that the success of forest conservation lies in the unified efforts of all nations contributing to a global outcome. Therefore, these Principles strive for achieving international co-operation in attempts to conserve forests. Principle 1(b) expressly provides for the same by stating that 'The agreed full incremental cost of achieving benefits associated with forest conservation and sustainable development requires increased international cooperation and should be equitably shared by the international community'. In addition to this, the Principles recognise the need for strengthening international institutional arrangements,[201] creating a supportive international economic climate,[202] providing financial support to developing countries to achieve their targets,[203] and exchanging information and technology to achieve best forest practices in each member nation.[204]

The Forest Principles are said to reflect the first steps towards a global consensus on forests.[205] They were celebrated as a landmark initiative by the UNCED for they included within their scope not only the conservation of tropical forests, but all kinds of forests including temperate and boreal forests. However, to a certain extent, they remain a toothless tiger. The main reason underlying their possible ineffectiveness is the fact that the Principles constitute merely a guiding instrument with no binding force on the member countries. In the absence of any legally binding obligations, it ultimately rests on the will of the individual States to take measures. Furthermore, the Forest Principles place great emphasis on the sovereignty of States to frame policies and take national measures. This strikes at the very root of international consensus as it does not truly reflect the co-operative tone required for protecting and conserving forests.

198 Forest Principles, 1992, Principle 8(b).
199 *Id.* Principle 12.
200 *Id.* Principle 8(e).
201 *Id.* Principle 3(b).
202 *Id.* Principle 7(a)
203 *Id.* Principle 7(b).
204 *Id.* Principle 12(c).
205 *Id.* pmbl.

2.5.3.2 International Conventions and Forestry

The most important global conventions related to forests are UNFCCC,[206] the Convention on Biological Diversity (CBD), the Convention on International Trade in Endangered Species of Wild Fauna and Flora (CITES),[207] and the United Nations Convention to Combat Desertification in those Countries Experiencing Serious Drought and/or Desertification, particularly in Africa (UNCCD).[208]

2.5.3.2.1 UNITED NATIONS FRAMEWORK CONVENTION ON CLIMATE CHANGE (UNFCCC)

Forests and climate concerns are closely related to one another. When their area or productivity increases, forests function as carbon sinks, acting as reservoirs for the carbon stored in biomass and soils. The most significant greenhouse gas, atmospheric carbon dioxide (CO_2), is absorbed more readily as a result. Numerous forestry techniques significantly contribute to slowing down the atmospheric build-up of CO_2. In contrast, when biomass burns or decomposes, trees become a source of greenhouse gases. Certain techniques used in agroforestry, forest management, and plantation expansion, like tilling and applying natural fertilisers, have the potential to emit greenhouse gases. While the Framework Convention mentions forests only briefly, the Kyoto Protocol is more explicit. Article 2 states that industrialised parties shall 'implement and/or further elaborate policies and measures … such as … promotion of sustainable forest management practices, afforestation and reforestation'. According to the protocol, industrialised nations may utilise specific human-induced land-use, land-use change, and forestry sector activities (referred to as LULUCF) that mitigate greenhouse gas emissions in the atmosphere, such as afforestation, reforestation, and combating deforestation, to offset their emission targets. On the other hand, adjustments to these practices – like deforestation – that reduce carbon sinks will be deducted from the total amount of emissions that are allowed. Many uncertainties and complexities surround this subject, and there is a need for further clarifications.

206 The United Nations Framework Convention on Climate Change entered into force on 21 March 1994. The aim of the Convention is to prevent dangerous human interference with the climate system.

207 Convention on International Trade in Endangered Species of Wild Fauna and Flora, March 3, 1973, 993 U.N.T.S. 243.

208 The Convention to Combat Desertification (UNCCD) is a multilateral environmental agreement effective from 1996 in Paris, France.

2.5.3.2.2 UNITED NATIONS CONVENTION TO COMBAT DESERTIFICATION IN THOSE COUNTRIES EXPERIENCING SERIOUS DROUGHT AND/OR DESERTIFICATION, PARTICULARLY IN AFRICA

This Convention aims at combating desertification and mitigating the effects of drought and contributing to sustainable development.[209] This calls for long-term plans that prioritise increasing land productivity as well as the preservation, sustainable management, and restoration of the land and its water resources, thereby creating better living conditions for people. The Convention also lays down certain prescriptions for the member nations to implement, including the preparation of National Action Programmes and implementation and evaluation indicators.[210] Due to their crucial ecological role in reducing the effects of drought and preventing desertification, the protection and expansion of forests are key components of the UNCCD. Mitigation strategies for the same are likely to also diminish losses to forests, and vice versa. Deforestation causes desertification and land degradation because intact forest ecosystems stabilise the soil. Deforestation has detrimental effects on soil erosion, water runoff, and soil fertility. The Convention focusses on measures to conserve natural resources, especially agricultural land and pastoral land, vegetation cover and wildlife, forests, water resources, and biological diversity.[211]

Furthermore, due to this ecological relationship, the underlying socioeconomic factors that contribute to desertification and forest loss are remarkably similar. In many developing nations, deforestation and other unsustainable forestry practices, carried out by impoverished rural populations for survival, economic, or commercial reasons, have led to soil fertility loss and land degradation. A key component of the corrective measures envisioned by the UNCCD to address land degradation, advance sustainable agricultural and rural development, and lessen rural poverty is sustainable forest management.

2.5.3.1.3 CONVENTION CONCERNING INDIGENOUS AND TRIBAL PEOPLES IN INDEPENDENT COUNTRIES (ILO CONVENTION NO. 169)

The lives of indigenous people are intimately linked with forests. Forests are vital for social, cultural, and economic reasons in addition to providing habitats. Concerns regarding the survival and integrity of indigenous peoples' customs and knowledge are frequently linked with concerns regarding the conservation and management of forests. The International Labour Organization (ILO) Convention, which may also be cited as the Indigenous and Tribal Peoples Convention,[212] strives to defend indigenous peoples' social, economic, and cultural rights. Parties agree to take the

209 The United Nations Convention to Combat Desertification in Those Countries Experiencing Serious Draught and/or Desertification, Particularly in Africa (UNCCD), adopted on 17 June 1994.

210 *Id.* art. 9 (Preparation of national action programmes and implementation and evaluation indicators).

211 *Id.* art. 1(f) (definition of land degradation).

212 The Indigenous and Tribal Peoples Convention, 1989 (ILO Convention 169).

necessary steps to ensure that their integrity is respected and to defend their rights using Articles – 13 to 19 of the ILO Convention.

Moreover, Article 2 gives Governments the 'responsibility for developing, with the participation of the people concerned, co-ordinated and systematic action to protect the rights of these peoples and to guarantee respect for their integrity'; and Article 7 declares that parties shall 'take measures, in cooperation with the peoples concerned, to protect and preserve the environment of territories they inhabit'.

The ILO Convention framework does not have any particular emphasis on forests. Nevertheless, its implementation programme covers things like managing natural resources, the environment, and ancestral domains. Although only 17 States have ratified the Convention, it has a significant impact on national policies and is regarded as a crucial piece of international legislation for indigenous people.

2.6 Conclusion

Even with the existence of numerous laws, conservation efforts in India will fail unless local communities' needs are carefully considered and incorporated into conservation plans. The rights of these people who live in forests are not protected enough by any legislation. Certain laws, which genuinely benefit the indigenous people, are not easily accessible. Despite the fact that women are directly dependent on the forests, the majority of forestry initiatives are instituted without taking into account their needs or the potential effects they may have on their lives. Furthermore, laws pertaining to tribal women are insufficient, and it is necessary to enact legislation that expressly addresses these issues and safeguards their rights.

Many women are now actively engaged in afforestation and forest conservation projects managed by NGOs and State organisations. Therefore, it is necessary to alter the current forest management system and implement new ones that are focused on improving the lives of tribals, specifically indigenous women. Gradually, on an international level, such practices have slowly permeated into the knowledge and awareness at the grassroots level in India. Consequently, forest conservation strategies have started taking the participative role of women more seriously. Since the REDD+ strategy has been accepted at the national level and its inclusion in the climate change mitigation strategy, a number of research and monitoring institutions have reported an increase in the forest cover in India. Judicial activism has also set a positive agenda for the conservation of forest cover and protecting the interests of people in response to the indiscriminate cutting down of forests.

However, there are instances where the stance of the judiciary has been excessively harsh, for example, in the eviction of those 'forest dwellers' who cannot prove their rights of livelihood in the forest. It constitutes a stringent step that may be said to be good in cases of actual forest encroachment issues, but is very unreasonable for those forest dwellers who don't have sufficient means to prove their identity and claim. Therefore, with the changing times and climate patterns, the role of the forest has been understood and reiterated as most important.

Review Questions

- Trace the evolution of forest conservation in pre- and post-independence India.
- What is a 'Forest'? Explain the various classifications of forest under the Indian Forest Act, 1927.
- List the various best practices adopted by States in conserving forests. Which according to you is the most effective in protecting and conserving the forests?
- How does the international timber trade affect Forest conservation? Explain the international developments in forest conservation.

3 Laws on Wildlife Protection and Prevention of Cruelty to Animals in India

3.1 Introduction

The Constitution of India emphasises the importance of wildlife and its protection. Article 48A of the Indian Constitution, covered within the ambit of Directive Principles of State Policy, lays stress on the protection and improvement of the environment. Further, it lays down provisions for safeguarding forests and wildlife. On the other hand, Article 51A(g) of the Constitution enjoins every citizen to protect and improve the natural environment including forests, lakes, rivers, and wildlife, and to have compassion for living creatures. Additionally, the Concurrent List (List III) of the Seventh Schedule prevents cruelty to animals and forests and provides the basis for the protection of wild animals and birds. In pursuance of these constitutional mandates, several laws and policies have been framed to uphold the interests of animals and to safeguard their rights. The two cardinal legal instruments that have shaped the country's efforts in the conservation of wildlife and protecting animals from unnecessary pain and suffering are the Wildlife (Protection) Act, 1972, and the Prevention of Cruelty to Animals Act, 1960. These Acts in conjunction with the Rules framed under them make provisions for all safeguards that may be necessary for the protection of animals. In addition to this, several policies and schemes have been launched by the Government from time to time and the Indian judiciary has filled the lacuna when legislative or executive efforts have failed to address the needs of wild, domesticated, and stray animals in the country.

3.2 Laws and Policies in Relation to Wildlife in India

3.2.1 The Wildlife (Protection) Act, 1972

The Wildlife (Protection) Act of 1972 is not the first legislation to have been passed in India with the aim of protecting wild fauna and flora. Prior to the enactment of this law, piecemeal efforts had been made by different States and the Central Government to protect wildlife, but such efforts were mostly limited to some specific animal species. The Tamil Nadu Wild Elephant Preservation Act, 1873, the Bengal Rhinoceros Preservation Act, 1932, and the Assam Rhinoceros Preservation Act, 1954, were some of these legislations. These legislations, besides being applicable to distinct States, were restricted to prohibiting activities harmful to individual species with little or no emphasis on the protection of their natural

DOI: 10.4324/9781032703909-3

habitats.[1] Even legislations that were not restricted to specific States were limited in their jurisdictional extent in pre-independence India such as the Elephants' Preservation Act, 1879.[2]

The first codified law, making provisions for the protection and preservation of certain wild birds and animals, was passed by the Central Government in 1912. The Wild Birds and Animal Protection Act empowered State Governments to declare the whole or part of the year as 'close time' for the whole or part of its territories during which killing, capturing, buying, selling, or possessing wild birds and animals specified in the Schedule appended to the Act was unlawful.[3] With the objective of protecting specific species, the State Government was empowered to make such declarations even with regard to female or immature wild birds or animals or any kind of wild bird or animal, other than those specified in the Schedule. Contravention of the provisions of this Act entailed punishment which could either take the form of a fine or imprisonment coupled with confiscation of the bird or animal or its parts.[4] The Act of 1912 was amended in 1935 to allow the provincial Government to set aside areas to be declared as sanctuaries for the protection and growth of wild animals and birds.[5]

Hunting was a popular sport amongst the rulers and heads of the princely states and the officials of the British Raj in the pre-independence era. The indiscriminate killing of animals prompted the enactment of laws that would preserve animals for hunting within the game reserves. The Indian Forest Act, 1927, prohibited hunting in reserve and protected forests.[6] Most of these legislations were disjointed efforts, with no Central law that comprehensively dealt with the protection of wildlife. After independence, the Indian Board for Wildlife (IBWL) was constituted by the Government in 1952, as an apex advisory body in this field to advise the Central as well as the State Governments on measures that could be adopted for the conservation of wildlife and setting up of national parks and sanctuaries.[7] On the recommendation of IBWL and the intervention of the Central Government, various State Governments established Wildlife Advisory Boards. An Expert Committee set up by the IBWL came out with a report in 1970 that advocated for policies on wildlife conservation and establishment of national parks and wildlife sanctuaries.[8] At around the same time, the international discussion on the need for the regulation of wildlife trade for conservation purposes was gaining ground in light of the

1 Nandan Nelivigi, *Biodiversity, Wildlife and Protected Area Management: A People-Centered Approach*, 37 Journal of India Law Institute 147 (1995).

2 The Elephants' Preservation Act, 1879.

3 The Wild Birds and Animal Protection Act, 1912, § 3.

4 *Id.* § 4 and § 5.

5 Sanjay Upadhyay & Videh Upadhyay, Handbook on Environmental Law: Forest Laws, Wildlife and the Environment 231 (LexisNexis Butterworths 2002).

6 Shyam Divan & Armin Rosencranz, Environmental Law and Policy in India: Cases, Materials and Statutes 328 (Oxford University Press 2002).

7 S. Raghavan, *Wildlife Conservation in India*, 95 Indian Forester 735, 738 (1969).

8 Nelivigi, *supra* note 1, at 148.

deliberations surrounding the Convention on International Trade in Endangered Species of Wild Fauna and Flora (CITES). This coupled with the report of the Expert Committee acted as a big push for India to enact a comprehensive Central legislation for the protection of wildlife in the country.[9]

Prior to the Forty Second Constitutional (Amendment) Act, 1976, 'wildlife' as a subject-matter was under the State List of the Seventh Schedule, with the exclusive power of legislating on the subject vested in the States. Thus, to enact a law on wildlife, the Indian Parliament relied on Article 252 of the Constitution which requires the legislatures of two or more States to pass a resolution, empowering the Parliament to pass a law on a subject enlisted in the State List. In 1972, the first law providing a statutory framework for protecting wild animals, plants, and their habitats was passed in the form of the Wildlife (Protection) Act after legislatures of 11 States passed the resolution empowering the Parliament.[10] The Forty Second Constitutional (Amendment) Act, 1976, moved the subject of 'wildlife' from the State List and inserted 'protection of wild animals and birds' under the Concurrent List.[11] This enabled the Parliament to bring in further amendments to the Wildlife (Protection) Act, 1972, and to legislate on the subject of wildlife, without placing reliance on Article 252 that requires the passage of resolutions by State Legislatures.

3.2.1.1 Scheme of the Act

The Wildlife (Protection) Act is spread over 14 chapters and includes 4 schedules, and was enacted in 1972. The Act was initially promulgated with the three-fold objective of providing a uniform legislation for the protection of wildlife throughout the country, to prevent hunting of wild animals and the trading of products derived from wild animals, and to set standards for the establishment and maintenance of protected areas.[12] Over time, a lot of amendments have been made to this legislation, in keeping with the needs of the changing times. The Act provides for the appointment of officers such as Directors, Wildlife Wardens, and other officers[13] and authorities such as the National Board for Wildlife, the Central Zoo Authority, the National Tiger Conservation Authority, and the Wildlife Crime Control Bureau for the implementation of the objectives of the Act. Hunting of wild animals enlisted in Schedules I and II is prohibited in general, barring certain exceptional circumstances mentioned under Sections 11 and 12.[14] The Act envisages the establishment of protected areas which may be notified as a national park,

9 *Id.* at 148–49.
10 *Id.* at 147–49.
11 India Const. sch. VII, List III, entry 17B.
12 Nalin Ranjan Jena, *People, Wildlife and Wildlife Protection Act*, 29(42) ECONOMIC & POLITICAL WEEKLY 2767 (1994).
13 The Wild life (Protection) Act, 1972, ch. II.
14 *Id.* ch. III.

a sanctuary, a conservation reserve,[15] or a community reserve.[16] It also allows for the declaration of tiger reserves.[17] Another category of 'protected area', namely 'game reserves', was recognised under the Act, till the Amendment Act of 1991 removed all references to game reserves.[18] The Act regulates trade and commerce in wild animals, animal articles, and trophies[19] and prohibits trade or commerce in trophies and animal articles derived from certain animals.[20] Stringent penalties have been prescribed for the violation of the provisions of the Act and the power of entry, search, arrest, and detention has been granted to the Director or any other officer authorised by him or the Chief Wildlife Warden or any forest officer or any police officer not below the rank of a sub-inspector.[21] Chapter VI-A has been added to the Act vide the Wildlife (Protection) Amendment Act, 2003, which provides for the forfeiture of property derived from illegal hunting or trade.

The Wildlife (Protection) Act as enacted in 1972 did not have any mention of plants. It was only after the amendment in the year 1991 that provisions on plants were incorporated under Chapter III-A of the Act, for the protection of specified plants. In the same amendment, the long title of the Act and the definition of 'wildlife' were amended to include plants within their ambit. As per Section 2(37), 'Wildlife' has been defined under the Act to include any animal, aquatic, or land vegetation which forms part of any habitat. This has been done to protect the natural habitat of wild animals and to ensure that the environmental and ecological security of the country, which is rich in biodiversity, is protected and maintained.

The Act is appended with four schedules. Schedules I to II enlist animals with varying degrees of protection afforded under the Act. Animals under Schedule I can be hunted only if they pose a threat to human life or are disabled or diseased. Trade in such animals is prohibited. Animals under Schedule II can only be hunted if they pose a threat to human life or property. Schedule III (previously Schedule VI; amended in 2022) lays down certain specified plant species in relation to which certain restrictions have been imposed with regard to their picking, damaging, acquiring, collecting, selling, possessing, or transferring, without requisite permissions from the concerned authorities.[22] Schedule IV was added in 2022 which deals with the implementation of the CITES convention by laying down scheduled specimens whose international trade is regulated by a management authority. It has three appendices appended to it. Wild animals listed under Schedule I, also referred to as 'scheduled animals' under the Act,[23] receive the maximum level of protection with strict prohibitions prescribed. Offences committed against these animals attract the

15 *Id.* § 36A.
16 *Id.* § 36C.
17 *Id.* § 38V.
18 The Wild Life (Protection) Amendment Act, 1991, § 24.
19 The Wild Life (Protection) Act, 1972, ch. V.
20 *Id.* ch. VA.
21 *Id.* § 50.
22 *Id.* ch. IIIA.
23 *Id.* § 49A(a).

maximum penalties. Species mentioned in Schedule II are also protected, but the penalties prescribed for crimes committed against such animals are less harsh.

3.2.1.2 Authorities Established and Officers Appointed under the Act

A few officers and authorities have been established under the Act to facilitate the implementation of its broad objectives.

3.2.1.2.1 OFFICERS APPOINTED BY THE CENTRAL GOVERNMENT AND THE STATE GOVERNMENTS

Under the Central Government, the highest officer for wildlife preservation is the Director of Wildlife Preservation. The Central Government may also appoint such other officers and employees as may be necessary who are required to assist the Director in the discharge of his duties and powers. The Director works under the general or special directions of the Central Government in the discharge of his duties and the exercise of powers.[24] If the Director so wants, he may delegate all or any of his powers and duties to any other officer subordinate to him. But such delegation of duties has to be with the previous approval of the Central Government and subject to such conditions as may be specified in the order in writing.[25]

The Chief Wildlife Warden appointed by the State Government is at the helm of affairs in the State in so far as the protection of wildlife is concerned. The Chief Wildlife Warden performs his duties and exercises his powers subject to the general and special directions of the State Government. The State Government may also appoint Wildlife Wardens and Honorary Wildlife Wardens and such other officers and employees who are subordinate to the Chief Wildlife Warden.[26] The Chief Wildlife Warden also has the power to delegate all or any of his powers and duties to any of his subordinate officers with the previous approval of the State Government, barring his power to permit the hunting of animals specified under Schedule I which have become dangerous to human life or are so disabled or diseased as to be beyond recovery.[27]

3.2.1.2.2 NATIONAL BOARD FOR WILDLIFE

The 2002 amendment to the Wildlife (Protection) Act, 1972, added Sections 5A, 5B, and 5C to the principal Act and gave statutory status to the National Board for Wildlife (NBWL), constituted on similar lines as that of IBWL, set up in 1952. Prior to 2002, the NBWL was referred to as the Indian Board for Wildlife. In 2002, the composition and powers of the IBWL underwent a change when the National Board was introduced. The NBWL came into existence with Gazette Notification

24 The Wild Life (Protection) Act, 1972, § 3.
25 *Id.* § 5(1).
26 *Id.* § 4.
27 *Id.* § 11(1)(a).

dated 22 September 2003, which also notified the National Board for Wildlife Rules, 2003.[28] It is an advisory body to the Central Government and the State Governments comprising 47 members headed by the Prime Minister. Nineteen members of the NBWL are ex-officio members. Other members include three Members of Parliament (two from Lok Sabha and one from Rajya Sabha), five persons to represent non-governmental organisations to be nominated by the Central Government, and ten eminent ecologists, conservationists, and environmentalists, nominated by the Central Government, and one representative each from ten States and Union Territories by rotation, to be nominated by the Central Government.[29] The minister in charge of the Ministry of Environment and Forests in the Central Government is the Vice-Chairperson. The Director-General of Forests (Wildlife) and Director, Wildlife Preservation is the Member-Secretary to the Board. The responsibility of ensuring the promotion of the conservation and development of wildlife and forests is vested with the Board. In order to fulfil its primary objective, the Board is empowered to frame policies and can also advise the Central and State Governments on promoting wildlife conservation and curbing poaching and illegal trade of wildlife and its products. Directions may be given by the Board for the setting up and management of sanctuaries, national parks, and other protected areas in furtherance of recommendations on matters relating to the restriction of activities in these areas. The Board can also conduct an impact assessment of various projects and activities on wildlife or its habitat. The Board has the power to review the progress in the field of wildlife conservation in the country and can also suggest measures for improvement. A status report on wildlife needs to be prepared and published by the Board at least once every two years.[30]

Besides advisory functions, the Wildlife (Protection) Act, 1972, has granted some special powers of granting sanctions, approvals, and recommendations to the National Board, which are of great consequence in so far as the fulfilment of the objectives of the Act is concerned. For instance, no alteration of the boundaries of a sanctuary or national park[31] can be made by the State Government except on the recommendation of the National Board.[32] The prior approval of the National Board is mandatory before the construction of any commercial tourist lodges, hotels, zoos, and safari parks is undertaken inside a sanctuary.[33] Destruction or removal of wildlife or forest produce either from a national park or a sanctuary or diversion or destruction of the habitat of any wild animal or the flow of water into or out of the national park or sanctuary is not permitted unless the State Government, in

28 Ministry of Environment, Forest and Climate Change, Gazette of India, Extraordinary Vide No. S.O. 1093 (E), Notification (Sept. 22, 2003).

29 The Wild Life (Protection) Act, 1972, § 5A(1). The membership of the National Board for Wildlife has been amended a number of times since it was first constituted in 2003, with the last reconstitution made in September 2014.

30 *Id.* § 5C(2).

31 *Id.* § 35(5).

32 *Id.* § 26(A)(3).

33 *Id.* Proviso to § 33(a).

consultation with the National Board, is satisfied that such removal of wildlife or change in the flow of water into or out of the national park or sanctuary is important for the improvement and better management of wildlife and thus issues a permit to that effect.[34] The diversion of tiger reserves and areas linking two protected areas for ecologically unsustainable uses is not permissible under the Act. However, such diversion may be made in the public interest, if the National Board gives approval for the same.[35] Even the de-notification or alteration of tiger reserves requires the recommendation of the Tiger Conservation Authority and the approval of the National Board for Wildlife.[36]

Section 5B of the Act authorises the National Board to constitute a Standing Committee if it deems fit. The Board has also been empowered to delegate powers and duties to the Standing Committee and constitute such other sub-committees or study groups from time to time as may be necessary to discharge functions as may be assigned to them.[37] In pursuance of the powers conferred by Section 5B(2) of the Wildlife (Preservation) Act, 1972, the National Board constituted its Standing Committee via a notification dated 4 November 2003. The Standing Committee was then constituted, comprising the Minister in charge of Environment and Forests, Government of India, as the Chairman of the Committee, the Director of Wildlife Preservation, and ten other members nominated by the National Board.[38] The latest amendment to the composition of the Standing Committee was made via a notification dated 22 July 2014.[39] The notification that constituted the Standing Committee also identifies the powers, duties, and functions of the Standing Committee and lays down that the Standing Committee may exercise all the powers exercisable by the National Board for Wildlife under the Wildlife (Protection) Act, 1972. It may also constitute committees, sub-committees, study groups, task forces, or advisory bodies as may be necessary. Thus, in essence, the functions of the National Board are carried out by the Standing Committee.

The Standing Committee is required to meet once every three months. The website of the Ministry of Environment, Forest and Climate Change reflects that quarterly meetings of the Standing Committee have been routinely held every two to three months since its re-constitution in July 2014. From August 2014 to February 2019 a number of proposals have been considered by the Standing Committee both within and outside protected areas and from various sectors like road construction, dams, irrigation, and mining. Questions involving policy matters have also been deliberated upon. Several proposals seeking statutory approvals for projects have come before the Standing Committee, requesting permissions for the diversion and

34 The Wild Life (Protection) Act, 1972, §§ 29 & 35(6).

35 *Id.* § 38O(g).

36 *Id.* §§ 38W(1), 38W(2).

37 *Id.* § 5B(3).

38 National Board for Wildlife, Ministry of Environment and Forests, Government of India, F. No. 6-112003 WL-I, Notification (Nov. 4, 2003).

39 National Board for Wildlife, Ministry of Environment and Forests, Government of India No. F. No. 6-46/2013 (pt-2) WL-I, Notification (July 24, 2014).

alteration of the boundaries of national parks and sanctuaries. The proposals for grant of approval of the Standing Committee are submitted by the respective State Governments in the approved format with complete details (maps, field assessments, alternatives explored, etc.) and must be accompanied by the opinion of the officer in charge of a protected area, the Chief Wildlife Warden, and the State Government, in consultation with the State Board for Wildlife.[40] Vide a letter dated 22 November, 2018, the Ministry of Environment, Forest and Climate Change has mandated that starting from 1 December 2018, all proposals seeking wildlife clearance from the Standing Committee of the National Board for Wildlife and the State Governments for non-forestry activities inside protected areas or within 10 kilometres of their boundaries have to be submitted through the online portal of the ministry – PARIVESH – a single window integrated system for environment forest and CRZ clearances.[41] This has been done to streamline the process of submission of proposals and to enhance efficiency and transparency.

In *Centre for Environment Law, WWF-I v. Union of India (UOI) and Ors.*[42] the Court contemplated the necessity of a second home for Asiatic lions (*Panthera leo persica*), an endangered species, in order to ensure their long-term survival and the protection of the species from extinction. In the research conducted by the Wildlife Institute of India, the need for a second home for Asiatic lions was pointed out. Asiatic lions were held to be prime candidates for reintroduction to ensure their survival. After the completion of a survey for alternative sites, the Kuno Wildlife Sanctuary was discovered to be most suitable for the reintroduction of Asiatic lions. In the pursuit of reintroducing Asiatic lions to the Kuno Wildlife Sanctuary, the State of Madhya Pradesh took a massive step by relocating the villagers settled in and near the sanctuary. On the directions of the State of Madhya Pradesh, the Wildlife Institute of India conducted a thorough assessment of the prey population to obtain lions from Gujarat as soon as possible. However, the Government of Gujarat did not comply with the request to translocate two lions to the Kuno Wildlife Sanctuary, as laid down in the letter by the Minister of Environment and Forests addressed to the Chief Minister of Gujarat. It was contended by the State of Gujarat that the coexistence of an almost equal number of lions as tigers already present in Kuno Palpur was unlikely. The climate and the prey base of the Kuno Wildlife Sanctuary were not adequate for the lions. Furthermore, a detailed affidavit was filed by the State of Gujarat which stated that the State had objected to the translocation of the lions and that the decision of the Standing Committee was not unanimous.

40 Praveen Bhargav, *Mandate of the Standing Committee of the NBWL*, CONSERVATION INDIA (July 20, 2010), http://www.conservationindia.org/resources/mandate-of-the-standing-committee-of-the-nbwl.

41 Ministry of Environment, Forests and Climate Change (Wildlife Division), Government of India, No. F. No. 6-137/2017 (pt-1), Notification (Nov. 22, 2018).

42 Centre for Environment Law, WWF-I v. Union of India, Writ Petition (Civil) No. 337 of 1995 decided on 15 April 2003.

The Court, after scrutinising the contentions made by the two States, directed the National Board for Wildlife to consider this matter again and file a report. The Court emphasised an ecocentric approach, instead of an anthropocentric one, while assessing the need for a second home for Asiatic lions. That the reintroduction of Asiatic lions should be in conformity with the guidelines of the International Union for Conservation of Nature (IUCN) and with active participation of experts in the arena of species reintroduction was one of the observations made by the Court.

3.2.1.2.3 STATE BOARD FOR WILDLIFE

The Wildlife (Protection) Amendment Act, 2002, also substituted newer provisions for the constitution of State Boards for Wildlife. Comprising 31 members, headed by the Chief Minister of the State as the Chairperson, the Minister in charge of Forests and Wildlife as Vice-Chairperson, and the Chief Wildlife Warden as the Member-Secretary, the State Board for Wildlife[43] primarily discharges advisory functions for the State Governments on matters related to the conservation and protection of wildlife. Regarding the choice and administration of regions to be designated as protected areas, the creation of policies for the preservation and protection of certain species of animals and plants, or any issue pertaining to the amendment of any schedule, the Act makes it obligatory for the State Government to take advice from the State Board. The State Government needs to ensure that the needs of the tribal and other dwellers of the forests are in harmony with the efforts made towards the protection and conservation of wildlife and, if the State Government requires, it may seek advice from the State Board in this regard or in any matter related to the protection of wildlife.[44]

Further, after the 2022 amendment to the Act, Section 6A of the Act authorises the State Board to constitute a standing committee if it deems fit. The board has also been empowered to delegate powers and duties to the standing committee and constitute such other sub-committees or study groups from time to time as may be necessary to discharge functions as may be assigned to them.[45]

3.2.1.3 Clearance for Projects within Protected Areas and the Role of the National Board for Wildlife

While considering project proposals for recommendation or approval, the Standing Committee may require the project proponents to comply with directions issued by the Chief Wildlife Warden of the State concerned or may also issue specific directions by itself over and above the ones stipulated by the Chief Wildlife Warden, the compliance with which would be mandatory for the grant of approval. A mention of the same can be evidenced from the 53rd Meeting of the Standing Committee

43 The Wild Life (Protection) Act, 1972, § 6.
44 *Id.* § 8.
45 *Id.* § 6A(3).

held in February 2019, where one of the proposals made pertained to the diversion of 12.218 hectares of forestland from Sardarpur Kharmor wildlife sanctuary in Madhya Pradesh for the construction of an intake well, overhead tank, and planting underground water distribution pipeline for drinking water supply in 33 villages, of which 14 villages were inside the sanctuary. At the end of discussions and deliberations, the Standing Committee pronounced that the project should be recommended, provided that the conditions imposed by the State Chief Wildlife Warden are complied with and an annual compliance certificate on the realisation of the stipulated conditions would be submitted to the State Chief Wildlife Warden by the project proponent, which then would be submitted to the Government of India.[46]

There have even been cases where the Standing Committee has prescribed additional conditions over and above the ones recommended by the Chief Wildlife Warden before approving or recommending a project or proposal. For instance, while considering a proposal for the diversion of 0.90 hectares of revenue land for the upgradation of an existing gravel road to a cement concrete road of 1.5 km length from Bamnai to Nasipur falling in Ratapani Wildlife Sanctuary in Madhya Pradesh, the Standing Committee laid down additional conditions before recommending the project. The Committee proposed that the upgradation of gravel road to concrete road should be carried out in a muddy portion only and widening of the road should be avoided. It was also stated that the State Government should permit starting the work on the project only when the road design is modified as per the animal passage plan initiated by the project proponent in consultation with the State Chief Wildlife Warden on the basis of the WII Guidelines on Eco-friendly Measures to Mitigate Impacts on Linear Infrastructure on Wildlife and if the State Forest Department prepares and implements a human-wildlife conflict mitigation plan providing for regular manual patrolling of the stretch at the project cost.[47]

While the recommendations for diversions of sanctuaries are granted subject to the fulfilment of certain conditions, to ensure that no harm is suffered by the wildlife in such protected areas, it is difficult to claim with certainty that such diversions are approved by the Standing Committee since they are considered necessary for the improvement and better management of wildlife as required under Section 29[48] and Section 35(6)[49] of the Act. It is interesting to note that these two provisions only prohibit the removal of wildlife and forest produce or diversion of a protected area without the grant of the permit by the NBWL and the State Government if the conditions laid down in the Act are not met. No activity that requires such removal or diversion has been specifically banned or forbidden under the Act. Screening of proposals received by the NBWL usually involves a subjective assessment of the

46 Ministry of Environment, Forest and Climate Change (Wildlife Division), Government of India, F. No. 6-30/2019 WL, Minutes of 53rd Meeting of the Standing Committee of National Board for Wild Life (Feb. 25, 2019), Agenda 53.3.4.

47 *Id.* Agenda 53.3.5

48 The Wild Life (Protection) Act, 1972, § 29.

49 *Id.* at § 35(6).

impact of the project on the wildlife or protected area and the presumed level of damage or degradation. Moreover, a plain reading of the provisions reveals that the process followed for the grant of approval or recommendations seems to be the same for both national parks and sanctuaries, irrespective of the difference in the degree of protection that the area enjoys.

An order rendered by the Supreme Court in *T. N. Godavarman Thirumulpad v. Union of India*[50] has added some newer procedural requirements if a project involves non-forest use of a protected area as understood in the Forest (Conservation) Act, 1980. This order banned the removal of dead, diseased, or wind-fallen trees, drift-wood, and grasses, etc., from any national park, game sanctuary, or forest, without the permission of the Supreme Court.[51]

Another procedural compliance for project proponents seeking the diversion of protected areas has been added by the Scheduled Tribes and Other Traditional Forest Dwellers (Recognition of Forest Rights) Act, 2006. As per Section 4 of the Act, traditional forest dwellers would not be resettled or relocated from a protected area for the purposes of creating inviolate areas for wildlife conservation, unless the circumstances enumerated under the Act are satisfied. Some of these factors contribute to the delay or slower clearance or approval rate for projects in land under protected areas. However, despite the large number of projects that have been on hold for the final decision by the NBWL, the rate at which projects proposing the diversion of land in protected areas under the strictest protection have been approved is far greater than the rate of rejection.[52] Between August 2014 and February 2019, the NBWL approved 682 of the 687 projects that allowed forest land in protected areas to be diverted for industry, which has earned the NBWL the moniker of 'clearance house', by a wildlife expert formerly associated with the NBWL as a member.[53] The majority of the proposals that come before the Standing Committee pertain to dams, highways, mining, quarrying, building of concrete roads, laying of power lines, and other projects that have required the diversion of wildlife habitats. In light of the large number of projects that have been passed, questions have been raised about the probity of the procedure followed by the NBWL, the Standing Committee, and the Government in granting approvals and recommendations in compliance with the provisions of the Act.

3.2.1.4 Hunting of Wild Animals

The term 'hunting' has been defined very broadly to include all its grammatical variations and cognate expressions. Since the Act prohibits the hunting of wild animals and captive animals, it is pertinent to identify the animals which have been

50 T. N. Godavarman Thirumulpad v. Union of India, Writ Petition 202/1995.

51 Kanchi Kohli et al., *Diversion of Protected Areas: Role of the Wildlife Board*, 45(26-27) Economic & Political Weekly 18, 19 (2010).

52 *Id.*

53 Jacob Koshy, *99.82% Projects in Forests Got Nod*, The Hindu (Feb. 13, 2019), https://www.thehindu.com/news/national/9982-projects-in-forests-got-nod/article26261368.ece.

included within the purview of the terms 'wild animal' and 'captive animal', since liability under the Act would only be attracted if these animals are hunted. As per Section 2(36), 'wild animal' means any animal specified in Schedule I or Schedule II and found wild in nature. The Act has defined 'captive animal' to mean any animal specified in Schedule I or Schedule II which is captured or kept or bred in captivity.[54]

Besides actual killing or poisoning of any wild or captive animal, 'every attempt' to kill or poison any wild or captive animal has also been included in the definition of hunting. Hunting also includes capturing, coursing, snaring, trapping, driving, or baiting any wild or captive animal and every attempt to do so. Injuring, destroying, or taking any part of the body of any wild animal is also considered hunting. In the case of wild birds and reptiles, not only damaging their eggs but also disturbing their eggs or nests would amount to hunting.[55] The Act provides an inclusive definition of hunting, thus making the definition enumerative and not exhaustive.[56] Thus, in addition to the general understanding of the term 'hunting', it includes a number of actions committed on wild animals, birds, and reptiles, such as capturing, baiting, injuring, disturbing nests, etc., which one would not normally bring within the import of the term 'hunting'.

Although there is a general ban on hunting animals specified in Schedules I and II, such animals may be hunted with the permit of the Chief Wildlife Warden if the conditions laid down under Sections 11 and 12 of the Act are fulfilled.[57] Under Section 11, a distinction has been made between the animals enumerated under Schedule I and the animals under Schedule II. It is interesting to note that the Act not only includes mammals, amphibians, birds, and reptiles within its ambit but also offers protection to crustaceans and insects such as different varieties of butterflies and moths, coelenterates such as corals and sea fans, and molluscs which include different varieties of snails and Echinodermata which are primarily marine animals such as sea cucumbers.[58] As far as the animals under Schedule I are concerned, the Chief Wildlife Warden may permit or cause any person to hunt such animals by an order in writing if he is satisfied that the wild animal is posing any danger to human life or has become so diseased or disabled to be beyond recovery. Since the primary objective of the Act is the protection and conservation of wildlife, orders for hunting such animals would be given only if the Chief Wildlife Warden is assured that such animals cannot be captured, translocated, or tranquilised. Unless the Chief Wildlife Warden determines that the animal cannot be rehabilitated in the wild, no such seized animal may be retained in custody, and the reasons for this determination must be documented in writing. Additionally, efforts would be made to ensure that minimum trauma is caused to the animal during their capture

54 The Wild Life (Protection) Act, 1972, § 2(5).

55 *Id.* § 2(16).

56 Bharat Cooperative Bank (Mumbai) Ltd. v. Employees Union, (2007) 4 SCC 685.

57 The Wild Life (Protection) Act, 1972, § 9.

58 *Id.* Sch. I.

or translocation.[59] Since 'hunting' has been widely defined under the Act, capturing a Schedule I wild animal would also come within its purview.

Animals enlisted under Schedule II can be hunted with the permit of the Chief Wildlife Warden or any *other authorised officer* not only if the animal has become dangerous to human life or has become disabled or diseased, but also when it poses any threat to property including standing crops on any land.[60] Hunting of animals specified under Schedule I and II for purposes other than those mentioned above would be deemed to be an offence under the Act. However, any person killing or wounding any wild animal in good faith in self-defence or to save any other person would be exonerated. Moreover, such a person would not be excused if acting in self-defence became necessary while the person was committing any act in contravention of the provisions of the Act or any other rule or order.[61] An illustration of this would be a poacher killing a lion in a national park in self-defence. If any animal is killed or wounded in self-defence or defence of any other person, such animal would be the property of the Government.

Thus, a plain reading of this provision makes it evident that the animals enlisted under Schedule I are afforded the maximum protection and cannot be hunted if they pose any threat to property such as crops. Thus, a black buck or an Indian elephant which features in Schedule I cannot be hunted if they damage property, but a common langur or a wild dog that is listed in Schedule II may be hunted for harming property including crops, with the permit of the Chief Wildlife Warden or any other authorised officer. However, most local communities located in and around protected areas have often had conflicts with animals destroying crops and posing a threat to human life. This has led to several notifications being issued by State Governments to allow the killing of Schedule II animals. Several requests have also been received by the Ministry from State Governments for permits to periodically cull Schedule I animals like elephants, wild boars, and peacocks and animals under Schedule II such as nilgais and barking deer or to declare them as vermin under Section 62[62] of the Act, to enable farmers and the local community to kill these animals without the direction of the Chief Wildlife Warden. This has often been criticised by wildlife activists who have pointed towards the lacunae in the Indian law that lays greater emphasis on the conservation of wildlife than its management. Better protection of wildlife and habitats has led to an increase in their population and consequent overflow to adjoining areas. Questions have even been raised on the impact that indiscriminate killing of a particular species declared

59 The Wild Life (Protection) Act, 1972, § 11(1)(a).

60 *Id.* § 11(1)(b).

61 *Id.* § 11(2).

62 As per Section 62 of the Wildlife (Protection) Act, 1972, the Central Government may, by notification, declare any wild animal other than those specified in Schedule II to be vermin for any area and for such period as may be specified therein.

as vermin has on the ecological balance.[63] Mitigation of human-wildlife conflict has seldom been given the attention it deserves.

In addition to the circumstances laid down under Section 11, the Chief Wildlife Warden may permit the hunting of wild animals for some special purposes specified under Section 12 such as education, scientific research, and scientific management, which has been determined as the translocation of any wild animal for an alternative suitable habitat; or for the purpose of population management of wildlife, without killing or destroying or poisoning any wild animals, derivation, collection, or preparation of snake venom for making life-saving drugs, or collecting specimens for recognised zoos or museums and other similar institutions with required permissions. The Chief Wildlife Warden shall grant permission to hunt in writing and specify the conditions that should be complied with along with the fees that the person hunting the wild animal for the aforesaid purposes would be required to pay.[64] Before the Chief Wildlife Warden grants any permit in respect of any animal in Schedule I, the previous permission of the Central Government has to be given. Likewise, for any animal in Schedule II, the previous permission of the State Government must be sought.[65]

A much-criticised exception regarding the transfer and transport of captive elephants for 'religious and any other purpose' under Section 43(2) of the Act has been added by the 2022 amendment. The new proviso creates an additional exception for the exploitation of elephants beyond the scope of activities mentioned in Section 12, for which hunting is allowed. The 2010 Report of the MoEFCC's Elephant Task Force categorically stated that most captive elephants were born in the wild but were utilised for entertainment in circus and tourism, or engaged for private/religious festivals and other purposes in religious trusts/institutions, leading to large-scale abuse and poor treatment despite being a Schedule I animal.[66]

Punishments have been prescribed for persons hunting animals in contravention of the provisions of the Act. As per Section 51, a first-time offender, if convicted, would be punished with imprisonment for a term which may extend to three years, or with a fine which may extend to one lakh rupees or both. If any animal specified in Schedule I is hunted or if any wild animal or captive animal is hunted in a sanctuary or national park or where the offence relates to a specimen of a species listed on Appendix I of Schedule IV, the offender would be punishable with imprisonment for a term which shall not be less than three years but may extend to seven years, and the person would also be liable to pay a fine which shall not be less than 25,000 rupees. For repeat offenders, the term of imprisonment would be a minimum of three years extendable up to seven years. Any person convicted more

63 Anupam Chakravartty et al., *Enemies of the State*?, DOWN TO EARTH (July 15, 2016), https://www.downtoearth.org.in/news/wildlife-biodiversity/enemies-of-the-state--54628.

64 A Viswanathan v. State of Tamil Nadu, (2022) 6 Mad LJ 517.

65 The Wild Life (Protection) Act, 1972, Proviso to § 12.

66 The Elephant Task Force, Gajah, MOEF, August 31, 2010.

than once for hunting would also be liable to pay a fine of a minimum amount of one lakh rupees.[67]

3.2.1.5 Protected Areas

The Act, when initially passed, empowered the national and the State Governments to notify only two kinds of protected areas, namely sanctuaries and national parks. The Amendment Act of 2003 widened the definition of protected area to include National Parks, sanctuaries, conservation reserves, or community reserves notified under Sections 18, 35, 36A, and 36C of the Act.[68] There are 998 notified protected areas (as of 2022) in the country, spread over an area of 173,629.52 square kilometres, covering 5.28% of the country. The primary distinction between the different classes of protected areas is about the level of protection afforded to the animals and human activities that are permitted or prohibited within their boundaries.

3.2.1.5.1 SANCTUARIES

The Act grants power to the State Governments and the Central Government to declare an area of 'adequate ecological, faunal, floral, geomorphological, natural or zoological significance', as a sanctuary for the purpose of protecting, propagating, or developing wildlife or its environment. Such powers have been granted under Section 26A, Section 38, and Section 66 of the Act. However, the area must not be within any reserve forest or territorial waters. It is important to reiterate here that the State Board for Wildlife plays an advisory role for the State Government in the selection and management of areas to be declared as protected areas.[69] The process of declaration of a sanctuary involves a number of procedures to be followed by the officers recognised under the Act. Such procedures have to be compulsorily complied with to determine the existence and extent of the rights of people on such lands and to settle those rights before the final declaration of converting such land into a sanctuary is made.

Besides this, the Wildlife (Protection) Act also empowers the State Government to declare any area comprising any reserve forest or any part of the territorial waters to be included in a sanctuary.[70] But before any part of the territorial waters is included within the confines of a sanctuary, the State Government has to seek prior permission from the Central Government, and the limits of the territorial waters to be included have to be determined in consultation with the Chief Naval Hydrographer of the Central Government.[71] While declaring territorial waters as a part of the sanctuary, adequate measures have to be taken to protect the occupational interests of fishermen, and the right of innocent passage of any vessel through

67 The Wild Life (Protection) Act, 1972, § 51(1).
68 *Id.* § 2(24A).
69 *Id.* § 8.
70 *Id.* § 26A(1)(b).
71 *Id.* Proviso 1 and 2 to § 26(1)(b).

the territorial waters shall not be affected. Once a sanctuary has been declared, its boundaries will not be altered except on the recommendation of the National Board for Wildlife.[72]

The power of notifying an area as a sanctuary normally vests with the State Governments. But an area of adequate geological, geomorphological, faunal, or floral significance may also be declared as a sanctuary by the Central Government under Section 38 of the Act. For the Central Government to exercise this power, one condition must be fulfilled – the State Government must have either leased or transferred any area under its control to the Central Government which has not been already declared as a sanctuary. Moreover, any area that was declared as a sanctuary prior to the commencement of the Wildlife (Protection) Act, 1972, shall be deemed to be a sanctuary under this Act, as per the provisions of Section 66 of the Act. There are 551 existing wildlife sanctuaries (as of May 2019) in India covering an area of 119,775.80 square kilometres.[73] Of these 551 sanctuaries, 96 are housed in Andaman and Nicobar Islands.

Restrictions and prohibitions inside sanctuaries – protected areas including sanctuaries, national parks, and community reserves are declared and notified with the primary objective of protecting, propagating, or developing wildlife or its environment and protecting the biodiversity of the region, and hence some restrictions are imposed with regard to the activities that are permissible within the protected areas and those that are not. Right of entry and residence in a sanctuary is restricted and no person is permitted to exercise such right until and unless he is a public servant on duty or has the permission of the Chief Wildlife Warden or the authorised officer to live within the boundaries of the sanctuary or a person who possesses any rights over immovable property within the boundaries of the sanctuary or is a person passing through the sanctuary along a public highway.[74] Wildlife tourism in India generates a lot of revenue for the country. National parks and sanctuaries attract many tourists yearly who want to experience the essence of eco-tourism. While the ill impacts of wildlife tourism on conservation may be debated, tourism inside a wildlife sanctuary can be permitted only after a permit has been sought from the Chief Wildlife Warden. Similarly, permission to enter or reside in a sanctuary can be sought from the Chief Wildlife Warden for investigation or study of wildlife, photography, filmmaking, scientific research, or transaction of lawful business with any person residing in the sanctuary.[75]

The overall control of the sanctuary vests with the Chief Wildlife Warden. It is his responsibility to ensure the security of the animals and the preservation of the sanctuary. The Act empowers the Chief Wildlife Warden to erect buildings, roads, bridges, walls, barrier gates, or any other work he deems appropriate for

72 The Wild Life (Protection) Act, 1972, § 26A(3).

73 *National Park v. Wildlife Sanctuary v. Tiger Reserve*, Big Cats India, https://bigcatsindia.com/national-park-vs-wildlife-sanctuary-vs-tiger-reserve/ (last visited June 12, 2024).

74 The Wild Life (Protection) Act, 1972, § 27(1).

75 *Id.* § 28.

the sanctuary. However, unless the National Board has given its prior approval, no work related to the establishment of commercial tourist lodges, hotels, zoos, or safari parks may be done inside a sanctuary. The Chief Wildlife Warden may also control, regulate, or prohibit the grazing or movement of livestock within the sanctuary in keeping with the interests of wildlife.[76] For sanctuaries falling under Scheduled Areas (where FRA 2006 is applicable and comes under the 5th Schedule), the management plan must be prepared after due consultation with the Gram Sabha concerned. Besides restrictions on entry and residence inside a sanctuary, persons are restricted from doing any of the following acts within the limits of a sanctuary:

(a) Destroying, exploiting, or removing any wildlife or forest produce from a sanctuary or destroying, damaging, or diverting the habitat of any wild animal except in accordance with the permit granted by the Chief Wildlife Warden.[77]
(b) Setting fire to a sanctuary, or kindling any fire, or leaving any fire burning, in a sanctuary, to endanger such sanctuary.[78]
(c) Entering a sanctuary with any weapon except with the permission of the Chief Wildlife Warden or the authorised officer.[79]
(d) Using chemicals, explosives, or any other substances which may cause injury or endanger any wildlife.[80]

The restrictions on the removal of forest produce from within a sanctuary are slightly diluted by the Act, where it provides that the forest produce removed from a sanctuary may be used by the people living in and around the sanctuary to meet their personal bona fide needs but not for any commercial purpose.[81] In *Consumer Education and Research Society v. Union of India*,[82] the Supreme Court considered the recommendation of the expert body and held that mining operations would not be allowed within 2.5 km of the boundaries of Narayan Sarovar Wildlife Sanctuary in Gujarat. The State Government was directed to treat this as a guideline in the matter of the renewal of mining leases.

An important case in which the Court applied the WLPA to ensure the conservation of forests is that of *Essar Oil Ltd. v. Halar Utkarsh Samiti*.[83] In this case, Essar Oil Ltd. sought to lay pipelines to pump crude oil across a portion of a Marine National Park and Marine Sanctuary to their oil refineries in Jamnagar District. On the basis of PIL petitions, the High Court held that the pipelines carrying crude oil could not be permitted to go through the park and sanctuary. The Supreme Court,

76 The Wild Life (Protection) Act, 1972,
77 *Id.* § 29.
78 *Id.* § 30.
79 *Id.* § 31.
80 *Id.* § 32.
81 *Id.* Proviso to § 29.
82 Consumer Education and Research Society v. Union of India, (2005) 10 SCC 185.
83 Essar Oil Ltd. v. Halar Utkarsh Samiti, (2004) 2 SCC 392.

while deciding the case, emphasised the significance of striking a balance between economic development on the one hand and environment protection on the other. The Court held that the State had to, while directing the grant of a permit in any case, ensure that the habitat of the wildlife was sustained and that the damage to the habitat did not result in the destruction of the wildlife. That was the implicit major premise contained in the definition of the word 'sanctuary' in the Wildlife Protection Act.

3.2.1.5.2 NATIONAL PARKS

A 'National Park' is an area declared under Section 35 or Section 38 or deemed to be declared as a national park under Section 66 of the Act.[84] National parks too may be declared by the State Government and the Central Government. Section 35 of the Act clothes the State Governments with the power of declaring an area of ecological, faunal, floral, geomorphological, or zoological association or importance as a national park for protecting, propagating, or developing wildlife in the area or its environment, by the issue of a notification. The area notified to be declared as a national park may also be within an existing sanctuary.[85] There are 106 national parks in India covering an area of 44,402.95 square kilometres of the geographical area of the country,[86] with most of them situated in the State of Madhya Pradesh.[87]

Before a national park is notified, the same procedure laid down for the notification and declaration of a sanctuary about the investigation and determination of claims, and the extinguishment of the rights of persons apply. After the period of preferring claims has elapsed, and all rights claimed are disposed of, the land proposed to be included in the national park vests in the State Government. After the settlement of rights, a notification is published by the State Government specifying the limits of the area comprising the national park.[88] Other restrictions and prohibitions with respect to entry and residence, removal of wildlife and forest produce, setting of fire, use of chemicals, etc., that apply to any area declared as a sanctuary also apply to a national park. The overall control of a national park also vests in the Chief Wildlife Warden.[89]

The Central Government may also declare an area to be a national park, irrespective of whether the area has already been declared as a sanctuary by the State

84 The Wild Life (Protection) Act, 1972, § 2(21).

85 *Id.*, 1972, § 35(1).

86 Wildlife Institute of India, Wildlife Sanctuaries, National Informatics Centre (Feb. 7, 2023) http://wiienvis.nic.in/Database/wls_8230.aspx.

87 There are nine national parks in Andaman and Nicobar Island, three each in Andhra Pradesh, Telangana, and Chhattisgarh, two each in Arunachal Pradesh, Meghalaya, Mizoram, Odisha, and Haryana, five each in Assam, Himachal Pradesh, Rajasthan, Tamil Nadu, and Karnataka, six each in Kerala and Maharashtra, one each in Bihar, Goa, Jharkhand, Nagaland, Sikkim, Manipur, and Uttar Pradesh, four each in Gujarat and Jammu and Kashmir, and six each in Uttarakhand and West Bengal.

88 The Wild Life (Protection) Act, 1972, § 35(4).

89 *Id.* § 35(8).

Government or the Central Government.[90] Provisions and restrictions that apply to a national park declared by the State Government also apply to a national park declared by the Central Government, the only distinction being that for a sanctuary or national park declared by the Central Government, the powers and duties of the Chief Wildlife Warden are exercised and discharged by the Director of Wildlife Preservation or any other officer authorised by the Director in this behalf.[91] Any national park declared by a State Government prior to the commencement of the Act, under an Act that was repealed after the coming into force of the Wildlife (Protection) Act, 1972, shall be deemed to have been declared under the latter. If rights and claims over land were not settled under the repealed enactment, they would be settled under the Wildlife (Protection) Act, 1972.[92]

In the important case of *Nagarhole Budakath Hakky Sthapna Samithi v. State of Karnataka*,[93] the Petitioner was an organisation striving to maintain the ecological spark in Nagarhole National Park and working for the wellbeing of the tribal people. It contested the Karnataka Government's leasehold rights on a few properties in the middle of Nagarhole National Park in favour of M/s Gateway Hotels Resorts Ltd., a private enterprise operating a restaurant, boarding house, and lodging facility for 18 years. The Petitioners contended that the grant of leasehold rights violated the statutory restrictions of the Wildlife Protection Act, 1972, and the Forest Conservation Act, 1980. They claimed that the Respondent company was building new buildings and expanding its operations to undeveloped forest regions by removing trees and building metalled roads under the pretense of rehabilitation. The Court held that after the declaration by the State Government of its intention under Section 35(1) to designate a region as a national park, no one may obtain any rights in or over the territory that comprises it. The Respondent corporation was directed by the court to cease all operations on the disputed forest land right away and turn over possession to the State Government.

A study of the different provisions of the Act on sanctuaries and national parks reflects that there are only two distinctions between the two classes of protected areas. The first distinction relates to the entry and grazing of livestock. In a sanctuary, the Chief Wildlife Warden may regulate, control, or prohibit the grazing and movement of livestock.[94] But in a national park, the grazing and entry of livestock is not permitted, except in cases where persons authorised to enter a national park use such livestock as a vehicle to enter the park.[95] Persons permitted to enter a national park include public servants on duty, any person who has the permission of Chief Wildlife Warden or the authorised officer to live within the boundaries of the park, or a person who possess any rights over immovable property within the boundaries of the national park, or is a person passing through the national park

90 The Wild Life (Protection) Act, 1972, § 38(2).
91 *Id.* § 38 (3).
92 *Id.*
93 Nagarhole Budakath Hakky Sthapna Samithi v. State of Karnataka, AIR 1997 Kar. 288.
94 The Wild Life (Protection) Act, 1972, §33(d).
95 *Id.* §35(7).

along a public highway. The second distinction is about the settlement of rights over land. While settling the rights of claimants over land notified to be declared as a sanctuary, if the collector admits the claim of any person over such land in part or in full, he may after consultation with the Chief Wildlife Warden allow the continuance of any right over such land within the confines of the sanctuary.[96] This right is not available to any person within the limits of a national park. No person can exercise any right over land that has been notified to be included within a national park.

With the power vested in the Governments to separately notify national parks and wildlife sanctuaries, the intent of the legislators was clearly to create two separate classes of protected areas, with the former being afforded greater protection than the latter. However, when one closely peruses the provisions of the Act, it is difficult to identify any major differences between their biological features, socio-economic objectives, and conservation functions as envisaged by the Wildlife Act. Prior to the introduction of Section 24(2)(c) by the Amendment Act of 1991, the provisions reflected no difference in the importance afforded by the legislation to the ecosystems of the two categories of protected areas or the extent to which human activities were permitted or restricted within them. Grazing and entry of livestock, prohibited within a national park but allowed within a sanctuary, was the only point of difference between the two classes. Section 24(2)(c), by allowing people to exercise rights over land within a sanctuary that is not permitted within a national park, has in a way watered down the level of protection afforded to sanctuaries by permitting human activity. This in a way seems inevitable in the present times when boundaries between animal habitats and human settlements are becoming blurry. However, the provision merely states that the continuation of rights over such land within a sanctuary shall be permitted, without giving any further clarification as to the way such rights may be exercised, or the impact that this can have on the ecology of the protected area or its conservation, activities that must be strictly avoided in the exercise of the rights.

Thus, an overview of the provisions categorising sanctuaries and national parks highlights the lack of a clear-cut demarcation between the two categories of protected areas. This gap and possible grey area have many repercussions for the different approaches and measures that may be adopted in the management of forests and sanctuaries. The current management practices as evolved by the Government for different habitats have, however, maintained the main distinction between national parks and sanctuaries is that the latter are of much lesser importance than the former. But such a crude understanding seems to have led to the blurring of the distinction between sanctuaries and protected areas under the Forest Act.[97] However, the Wildlife Amendment Act, 2002, seems to distinguish national parks and sanctuaries collectively as a class distinct from that of the protected

96 The Wild Life (Protection) Act, 1972, §25 (2)(c).

97 Indian Board for Wildlife Conservation in India, Expert Committee Report (1990).

habitats envisaged under the Forest Act.[98] This is clear from the notion that the Wildlife Amendment Act, 2002, will have Community Reserve Management and Conservation Reserve Management, along with the Biodiversity Act, 2002, which also talks in terms of maintaining a biodiversity register by the local Gram Sabha. This shows a clear conflict of jurisdiction, ideas, views, opinions, and perspectives.

3.2.1.5.3 ECO-SENSITIVE ZONES

Eco-sensitive zones are ecologically fragile corridors that fall within 10 kilometres of the boundaries of national parks and sanctuaries notified under Section 3(v) of the Environment (Protection) Act and Rule 5 Sub-Rule 5(viii) and (x) of the Environment (Protection) Rules. First envisaged under the 'Wildlife Conservation Strategy of 2002' by the erstwhile Indian Board for Wildlife, the idea of having 'All identified areas around Protected Areas and wildlife corridors' as eco-sensitive zones was also enunciated in the National Wildlife Action Plan (2002–2016). In response to this call, several States expressed their concerns since in several States human habitation and cities were located within this 10 kilometre range, and hence declaring this region as an eco-sensitive zone could adversely affect development. To resolve these concerns, the National Board for Wildlife clarified that the delineation of eco-sensitive zones would relate to the regulation of specific activities around protected areas rather than their prohibition and would have to be site-specific.[99]

Eco-sensitive zones seek to serve the role of 'shock absorbers' for protected areas that are areas of high protection, while in areas of lesser protection activities are regulated and not necessarily prohibited. These areas aim to reduce the negative impact of activities that may hamper the fragile ecosystem of protected areas. Since eco-sensitive zones are meant to be specific to the sites or protected areas that they surround, their width could vary based on the sensitivity of the corridor and its ecological importance. In principle, the width of the eco-sensitive zone could go up to 10 kilometres but, for sensitive zones or where it is important to link landscapes, its extent could go beyond 10 kilometres.

The Chief Wildlife Wardens of all States and Union Territories were directed by the Ministry of Environment and Forest in May 2005 to identify suitable areas for eco-sensitive zones and to submit proposals. A writ petition was filed in 2004 by Goa Foundation in *Goa Foundation v. Union of India*[100] before the Supreme Court regarding the delay in the declaration of eco-sensitive zones. The Supreme Court directed all States and Union Territories to forward proposals for the declaration of eco-sensitive zones around protected areas since most States had failed to forward proposals probably owing to the lack of guidelines issued by the Government in

98 The Wild Life (Protection) Amendment Act, 2002.

99 Ministry of Environment and Forests, Guidelines for Declaration of Eco-Sensitive Zones around National Parks and Wildlife Sanctuaries, F.No. 1-9/2007 WL-I (pt) (Issued on Feb. 09, 2011).

100 Goa Foundation v. Union of India, W.P. No. 460 of 2004 decided on 4 December 2006.

this regard. In pursuance of this, guidelines for the declaration of eco-sensitive zones were issued by the Ministry of Environment and Forests in February 2011 which were later revised and reissued in September 2014.[101] Some of the criteria proposed by the Ministry of Environment and Forest for the declaration of eco-sensitive zones around national parks and sanctuaries which were agreed upon by the National Board for Wildlife were the complete protection of endemic species in their full range, protection of biological corridors and complex and diversified ecosystems such as coral reefs, mangroves, etc., that are susceptible to irreversible damage, sites that act as the breeding ground of threatened and rare species: the existence of pristine forests and steep slopes and developmental activities that do not damage or destroy the habitat of critically endangered or threatened species.[102] Proposals are required to be submitted by the State Governments which are scrutinised in consultation with the Wildlife Institute of India. Once the draft notification is finalised it is legally vetted after the competent authority approves it and then it is published in the official Gazette and also released for receipt of comments from the public for 60 days, in accordance with Rule 5 of the Environment (Protection) Rules. The views, comments, and opinions received are considered by an Expert Committee before the final notification is finalised and sent for approval of the competent authority.[103]

In *Re T. N. Godavarman Thirumulpad v. Union of India & Others*,[104] the Supreme Court noted that no proposals on eco-sensitive zones had been received in respect of 21 national parks and wildlife sanctuaries across 9 States even in 2018, although 12 years had elapsed since the last direction was issued by the Apex Court in *Goa Foundation v. Union of India*.[105] In light of the casual approach taken by the States, and to expedite the declaration of eco-sensitive zones which has been long pending, the Supreme Court independently directed the Ministry of Environment, Forest and Climate Change to declare an area of 10 kilometres around these 21 national parks and wildlife sanctuaries as eco-sensitive zones.

In another move to safeguard eco-sensitive zones, the Supreme Court in *Tata Housing Development Company Ltd. v. Aalok Jagga*.[106] came down heavily on the State of Punjab since, in allowing a housing cum retail project 'Camelot' located at a distance of 123 metres on the northern side and 183 metres on the eastern side from the Sukhna Wildlife Sanctuary, the State had failed to act on the basis of the

101 Ministry of Environment, Forests and Climate Change, Guidelines for Declaration of Eco-Sensitive Zones around National Parks and Sanctuaries - Further Clarifications, F.No. 1-27/2014-WL (Issued on Sept. 25, 2014).

102 *Id.*

103 *Eco-Sensitive Zone (ESZ)*, Ministry of Environment, Forest and Climate Change, https://moef.gov.in/moef/division/forest-divisions-2/eco-sensitive-zone-esz/introduction-2/index.html (last visited June 12, 2024).

104 Godavarman Thirumulpad v. Union of India, (1997) 2 SCC 267.

105 Goa Foundation v. Union of India, (2014) 6 SCC 590.

106 Tata Housing Development Company v. Aalok Jagga, 2019 SCC OnLine SC 1419.

doctrine of public trust. The Court condemned the act of the State Government, especially since 95 MLAs of the State were recipients of flats in the project, and stepped in to protect the eco-sensitive zone around the wildlife sanctuary by quashing all clearances granted for the project.

3.2.1.5.4 CONSERVATION AND COMMUNITY RESERVES

Two new categories of protected areas that have been included under the Wildlife (Protection) Act, vide the Amendment Act of 2002, are community reserves and conservation reserves. These protected areas provide more opportunities for local communities and civil society organisations to get involved in the protection and conservation of wildlife and make room for the declaration of a special class of protected areas that cannot be strictly categorised as national parks or wildlife sanctuaries. Provisions of the Act with regard to notification, restrictions other than the right of entry and residence, prohibition on kindling fire or use of chemicals, explosives, and other injurious substances, ensuring the security of wildlife, and taking measures necessary for the improvement of the habitat of wildlife that apply in relation to a sanctuary also apply to a conservation reserve and a community reserve.[107] Considering the growing proximity between man and the wild, notifying community reserves seems to be a great initiative towards a decentralised and participatory model of conservation and protection of wild animals outside conventional protected areas. There are 99 conservation reserves and 218 community reserves in India.[108] One of the major reasons for the incorporation of these categories of protected areas in the Wildlife (Protection) Act was the reduced protection in and around existing or proposed protected areas. In addition to conservation, these protected areas help in the avoidance of resettlement programmes for communities living around protected areas and help in mitigating the impact of protected areas on local communities and vice-versa. If the full potential of these reserves in the conservation of wildlife and biodiversity of the wild habitat is to be realised, the problems plaguing them must be addressed at the earliest, and specific impetus must be given towards making them financially sound and increasing the accountability of the reserve management committees to the community and the Government.

However, apprehensions have been raised about whether community reserves would be able to fulfil the objectives with which they have been set up, considering that the provisions of the Act on the subject are not very clear and leave much room for interpretation. Some crucial questions have been raised with regard to the management of the community reserve by the Community Reserve Management Committee – a body comprising members from the rural local bodies – and the

107 The Wild Life (Protection) Act, 1972, § 6A (2) and 36C(2).

108 *Wildlife (WL)*, Ministry of Environment, Forest and Climate Change, https://moef.gov.in/moef/division/forest-divisions-2/wildlife-2/introduction/index.html (last visited June 12, 2024).

financial management of the Committee to carry out its functions. Moreover, some of the restrictions that apply to an area notified as a sanctuary also apply to a community reserve. Who would be responsible for ensuring compliance with these restrictions when most members of the Community Reserve Management Committee entrusted with the responsibility of preparing, managing, and implementing plans for the reserve and ensuring the protection of wildlife and its habitat are people from within the community? Would the community reserve allow locals to collect forest produce, as the Act has made the community responsible for managing, governing, and creating its own Rules?

A study was conducted in the months of January and February 2012 in two conservation reserves in Karnataka[109] and Tamil Nadu,[110] and a community reserve in Kerala,[111] to examine the functioning of these reserves and to identify some of their issues and challenges.[112] Interviews with local communities, conservation researchers, and Forest Department officials in the three reserves reflected that while the reserves in Tamil Nadu and Kerala were set up to protect the area from localised threats and to conserve bird diversity, the one in Karnataka was set up to conserve a threatened species of primate and specialised ecosystems with efforts to prevent the possible construction of a dam. Apart from the conservation reserve for the protection of macaques in Karnataka, where initial resistance was faced from the local community and politicians, setting up of the community reserve in Kerala also ran into trouble with the local community that resisted the declaration fearing that their resource use would be curtailed. In these reserves, interactions with stakeholders were found to be non-existent and the local community participated in the conservation efforts by abstaining from resource use.

In the community reserve of Kerala, which was set up to protect the estuarine biodiversity, there were differences of opinion among the stakeholders on the ownership of the reserve. There was clear discord between the community reserve management committee and the people of the community, whose views were not considered by the Committee and were largely nominated by the Government and not by them. Problems that were commonly encountered in all three reserves were a lack of proper communication channels between the local communities and the forest department, the dearth of proper plans for the management of these reserves and the absence of follow-up plans, a lack of cooperation amongst stakeholders, political interference, and inadequate and unstable revenue. Of all the issues identified, the most pressing issue appeared to be the lack of financial sustainability of

109 Aghanashini Lion-Tailed Macaque Conservation Reserve, Karnataka.

110 Thirupaddaimaradur Conservation Reserve, Tamil Nadu.

111 Kadalundi-Vallikunnu Community Reserve, Kerala.

112 The study was conducted with financial support from the Critical Ecosystem Partnership Fund (CEPF)-Western Ghats Small Grants Program through the Ashoka Trust for Research in Ecology and Environment (ATREE), Bangalore.

these reserves, particularly the community reserves, which could hit at the very functionality of this class of protected areas.[113]

3.2.1.5.5 TIGER RESERVES

The introduction of tiger reserves in India was through the initiatives of the Indian Government with the launch of Project Tiger in April 1973. The project was introduced to conserve India's national animal and 'to ensure maintenance of a viable tiger population in India'.[114] A country-wide assessment of the tiger population in 1970 revealed the dwindling numbers of tigers that were nearly on the brink of extinction. This led to the launch of the Project Tiger scheme which was inaugurated in Corbett National Park and initiated in nine areas.[115] From 9 tiger reserves at the inception of the Scheme, as of August 2023, Project Tiger had coverage of 54 reserves, spread out in 18 of the tiger range States, covering around 71,027.10 square kilometres or 2.21% of the geographical area of the country.[116]

While the subject 'protection of wild animals and birds' was introduced to the Concurrent List by the Forty Second Constitutional (Amendment) Act, 1976,[117] most efforts for the conservation of wild animals and birds have been State-centric. Therefore, it was deemed necessary to introduce a scheme with Central leadership and assistance as conservation efforts have ramifications that transcend State boundaries. Project Tiger was introduced as a centrally sponsored scheme of the Ministry of Environment and Forests to aid the tiger range States, in the in-situ conservation of tigers in designated tiger reserves. The field implementation of the project in the designated reserves was carried out by the respective States. A Project Tiger Directorate was established in the Ministry of Environment and Forests that was mandated to provide technical guidance, funding, and overall support to the project States.[118]

Nearly three decades after the initiation of Project Tiger, a review of its implementation highlighted the need for a statutory authority with legislative sanction to ensure tiger conservation. Recommendations were sought from the National Board for Wildlife, which suggested the setting up of a Task Force to look into the

113 Arun Kanagavel et al., *Community and Conservation Reserves in Southern India: Status, Challenges and Opportunities*, 5(17) Journal of Threatened Taxa 52756 (2013).

114 National Tiger Conservation Authority, Revised Guidelines for the Ongoing Centrally Sponsored Scheme of Project Tiger, F. No. 3-1/2003-PT (Issued Feb. 2008), at 2.

115 Valmik Thapar, *Earth Day 2019: Understanding Project Tiger, A Homegrown Conservation Success Story*, First Post (Oct. 7, 2019), https://www.firstpost.com/tech/science/earth-day-2019-understanding-project-tiger-a-homegrown-conservation-success-story-6492851.html.

116 Wildlife Institute of India, Tiger Reserves, National Informatics Centre (Feb. 7, 2023) http://wiienvis.nic.in/Database/trd_8222.aspx#tiger_reserve_india .

117 India Const. sch. VII, list II, entry 17B.

118 National Tiger Conservation Authority, *supra* note 114, at 2.

problems of tiger conservation in the country. The Task Force recommended *inter alia* to provide statutory backing to strengthen Project Tiger. A need was also felt to further strengthen the Project Tiger Directorate. This prompted the legislature to amend the Wildlife (Protection) Act, 1972, in 2006. Via the 2006 amendments, chapter IV-B was introduced into the Act to enable the conversion of the Project Tiger Directorate into the National Tiger Conservation Authority.[119] Prior to this amendment, tiger reserves were merely administrative designations to facilitate funding under Project Tiger but were not defined under the law.

'Tiger reserves' have been defined under Section 38V of the Wildlife (Protection) Act.[120] In the country, a core/buffer strategy has been adopted for tiger reserves. The core areas possess the legal status of a sanctuary or a national park, which generally exists before a tiger reserve has been notified. The peripheral or buffer areas are a combination of non-forest and forest land, managed as a multiple-use area. Agendas exclusively aimed at tiger conservation are implemented in the core areas of tiger reserves, and an inclusive people-orientated approach is sought to be implemented in the buffer zones. Under the amended Act, the State Governments can set up tiger reserves on the recommendation of the National Tiger Conservation Authority.[121] The same provisions and restrictions that apply to a sanctuary with regard to entry and residence and prohibited activities also apply to a tiger reserve.[122] Any alteration of the boundaries of the tiger reserves can be carried out only with the recommendation of the Tiger Conservation Authority with the approval of the National Board for Wildlife.[123] Similarly, the de-notification of a tiger reserve by a State Government shall be done only in the public interest with the approval of the Tiger Conservation Authority and the National Board for Wildlife.[124]

As per the Act, the tiger reserves consist of core or critical tiger habitat areas in national parks and sanctuaries and buffer or peripheral areas consisting of the area peripheral to critical tiger habitats or core areas. The core areas are identified by the State Governments in consultation with an Expert Committee constituted for the purpose, who select areas that should be kept inviolate or unharmed for the purposes of tiger conservation based on certain scientific and objective criteria. The core areas are selected bearing in mind that they should not affect the rights of the Scheduled Tribes or other forest dwellers. The buffer areas are also selected based on scientific and objective criteria in consultation with the concerned Gram Sabha and the Expert Committee. These areas require a lower degree of habitat protection to guarantee the integrity of critical tiger habitats with sufficient room for the dispersal of tiger species. The object of a buffer zone is to promote coexistence

119 *Id.*
120 The Wild Life (Protection) Act, 1972, Explanation to § 38V(4).
121 *Id.* § 38V(1).
122 *Id.* § 38V(2).
123 *Id.* § 38W(1).
124 *Id.* § 38W(2).

between wildlife and human activity with due recognition of the development, social, livelihood, and cultural rights of the local people.[125]

National Tiger Conservation Authority – the National Tiger Conservation Authority (NTCA) dispenses an overarching supervisory function in the field of tiger conservation. The NTCA has been established with a four-pronged objective. It provides a statutory authority to Project Tiger, by giving legal backing to its directives and orders; it fosters accountability of the Centre and the States in the management of tiger reserves, by providing an avenue for States to collaborate with the Centre in their efforts of tiger conservation by institutionalising an authority within our federal structure. It also seeks to address the livelihood interests of local people in the areas that surround the tiger reserves and enables the Parliament to exercise oversight.[126]

Section 38O of the Wildlife (Protection) Act enlists the powers and functions of the NTCA. Some of the powers and functions of the NTCA as enlisted under the Act are approval of the Tiger Conservation Plan which is prepared by the State Government, evaluation and assessment of various aspects of sustainable ecology and proscribing any ecologically unsustainable land, such as industry, mining, and other projects within the tiger reserves, providing information on protection measures including future conservation plans, estimating the population of tigers and natural prey species, status of habitat, disease observation, mortality survey, patrolling, reports on untoward happenings, and such other management aspects as it may adjudge fit, etc.

The Wildlife (Protection) Act authorises the NTCA to issue directions to any person, authority, or officer in writing for the protection of tiger reserves or tigers, and the person, authority, or officer so directed is bound to comply with the written directions. The issued directions must pertain to the powers and functions of the authority acknowledged under the Act. The NTCA must also ensure that the issued directions do not hinder or affect the rights of local people, particularly the Scheduled Tribes.[127]

The Act also provides for the constitution of a Tiger Conservation Authority Fund. The Central Government in pursuance of the powers granted under this Act has formulated the Tiger Conservation Authority Fund (Regulation) Guidelines, 2007.[128] The Tiger Conservation Authority Fund (Regulation) Guidelines, 2007, also allow the NTCA to provide funding support to a tiger reserve for the conservation of the tiger, its habitat, co-predators, prey animals, and for addressing eco-development and livelihood concerns of people living in and around such areas.[129] The State Governments are required to prepare a Tiger Conservation Plan that

125 *Id*. Explanation to § 38(V)(4).

126 *Objective of the NTCA*, National Tiger Conservation Authority, https://ntca.gov.in/about-us/#ntca (last visited June 12, 2024).

127 The Wild Life (Protection) Act, 1972, §38O(2).

128 Tiger Conservation Authority Fund (Regulation) Guidelines, 2007, Notification S.O. 1009 (E), June 22, 2007, Gazette of India, Extraordinary.

129 Tiger Conservation Authority Fund (Regulation) Guidelines, 2007, Guideline 6.

charts out the initiatives to be adopted by them for the proper management of the areas notified as tiger reserves within their territories. Some general directives have been provided under the Act to aid the States in devising the Tiger Conservation Plan. The Plan prepared must ensure that the natural prey-predator ecological cycle in the habitat is not disturbed or distorted while providing site-specific inputs for a viable population of tigers, prey animals, and co-predators.

Besides the broad directions provided under the Act, the National Tiger Conservation Authority released a guiding document for the States in 2007 that contains guidelines for the preparation of a Tiger Conservation Plan.[130] A perusal of the guiding document reflects that the States are advised to formulate a two-tiered approach for tiger conservation planning. The States need to submit separate Tiger Conservation Plans for the different tiger reserves within their jurisdiction, and the approved plans are valid for a period of ten years after which conservation plans must be prepared afresh and new approvals have to be sought.

The Act under Section 38X also requires the States to establish Tiger Conservation Foundations for tiger reserves within their jurisdiction. In pursuance of the powers conferred under Section 38O of the Wildlife (Protection) Act, 1972, the National Tiger Conservation Authority framed the National Tiger Conservation Authority (Normative Standards for Tourism Activities and Project Tiger) Guidelines, 2012, in consonance with the Guidelines of the centrally sponsored scheme of Project Tiger.[131] The Guidelines also elaborate on the role of the Tiger Conservation Foundations that are meant to serve as autonomous 'profit centres' for the tiger reserves. Similarly, the Guidelines additionally allow the State Government to charge a conservation fee from the tourism industry for local community upliftment works and eco-development since the major impact of the conservation efforts is faced by the local communities.[132]

Steering Committee – the State Governments within tiger range States have been given the discretionary power to constitute a Steering Committee, as evidenced by the use of the term 'may' in Section 38U of the Act. The Steering Committee shall consist of the Chief Minister, who shall serve as the Chairperson of the Committee, the Minister in charge of Wildlife, who shall act as the Vice-Chairperson of the Committee, and a maximum of five official members, amongst whom a minimum of two members shall be Field Directors of tiger reserve or Director of a national park and one member should be from the SState Government Department dealing with tribal affairs. The other members of the Committee shall be three professionals or experts with experience and qualifications in the conservation of wildlife, of which at least one shall be from the area of tribal development;

130 National Tiger Conservation Authority Ministry of Environment and Forests Government of India, Technical Document: NTCA/01/07, Guidelines for Preparation of Tiger Conservation Plan (2007).

131 National Tiger Conservation Authority, Ministry of Environment and Forests, No. 15-31/2012-NTCA.-W, Comprehensive Guidelines for Tiger Conservation and Tourism as Provided u/s 380(1)(c) of the Wildlife (Protection) Act, 1972 (Oct. 15, 2012).

132 National Tiger Conservation Authority (Normative Standards for Tourism Activities and Project Tiger) Guidelines, 2012, Part B, Guidelines 2.1.5, 2.1.6, and 2.1.7

two members from the State's Tribal Advisory Council; one representative from the State Government's Department dealing with social justice and Panchayati Raj and empowerment. The post of ex-officio Member-Secretary is to be taken up by the Chief Wildlife Warden, which is to be notified by the State Government, in the Official Gazette.[133] The Committee, formed, shall ensure the conservation, monitoring, and protection of tigers, prey animals, and co-predators within the respective States.[134]

3.2.1.6 Settlement of Rights of People vis-à-vis Protected Areas

A lot of debate has centred around the rights of forest dwellers and the settlement of their rights within protected areas, including cases of forced displacements by officials. Many of these issues have arisen owing to rights over land that have remained unrecorded for generations.[135] However, with the coming into force of the Scheduled Tribes and other Traditional Forest Dwellers (Recognition of Forest Rights) Act, 2006, efforts have been made to resolve these conflicting rights of traditional forest dwellers and wild animals. The Forest Rights Act, 2006, recognises and vests forest rights in forest dwelling Scheduled Tribes and other traditional forest dwellers over all forest lands, including protected areas such as national parks and sanctuaries. The forest rights of forest dwellers in critical wildlife habitats of national parks and sanctuaries are recognised under the Act and no forest rights holders shall be resettled or their rights affected in any manner to create inviolate areas for wildlife conservation, unless the conditions stipulated under Section 4(2) of the Act are met. As per the provisions of Section 4(5), no forest-dwelling Scheduled Tribe or other traditional forest dwellers shall be evicted or removed from forest land in the national parks and sanctuaries under his occupation, till the recognition and verification of their claims over such land is complete. Therefore, before undertaking any exercise of modification of rights or resettlement of traditional forest dwellers and forest dwelling Scheduled Tribes, notifying any protected area and publishing the final notification regarding the vesting of the land, the State Governments and Union Territories must first ensure that their rights are recognised.

3.2.1.7 Project Elephant

Project Elephant was launched in 1992 as a 100% centrally sponsored scheme of the Ministry of Environment and Forests under its wildlife division. The primary aim of the project is to assist elephant range States in the country financially and technically to ensure the protection of elephants, their habitats, and elephant

133 The Wild Life (Protection) Act, 1972, § 38U(2).

134 *Id.* § 38U(1).

135 Sarbani Sarkar, *Settling Rights* (Seminar Paper, Protecting Nature: A Symposium on Some Legal Issues Concerning the Environment, August 2000), https://www.india-seminar.com/2000/492/492%20s.%20sarkar.htm (last visited June 12, 2024).

corridors[136] that provide elephants room for securely moving between habitats without human intervention and disturbance. The other objectives of the project are to mitigate human-animal conflict and promote the welfare of captive elephants.[137]

Assistance is provided to 22 States in the country where the project is implemented to ensure that a few broad objectives are met. In addition to the elephants in reserves and in captivity, Project Elephant also prescribes measures for the management of small populations of wild elephants that may pose a threat to human life and property.[138] Further, with a view to reducing human-elephant conflict, the Ministry of Environment, Forest and Climate Change issued and circulated to all States *Guidelines for Management of Human-Elephant Conflict* in October 2017.[139]

In the recent past, the Supreme Court has intervened to ensure the protection of elephant corridors. In *A. Rangaraj v. Union of India, Ministry of Environment and Forest*,[140] in response to a public interest litigation, letters were sent to 22 States requesting details on the status of implementation of the Project Elephant scheme. Large-scale construction in the 'elephant corridor' in Tamil Nadu was questioned by the Court and the Collector of Nilgiris was directed to formulate a plan of action as to the method of identifying the construction that had been done, the purpose for which the construction was utilised, and when the construction had been carried out. Furthermore, a list of 39 resort complexes with restaurants was considered by the Court. Twenty-seven of these resorts were declared to be running commercial enterprises without having appropriate approval and were directed to be closed down or sealed.

In *Shakti Prasad Naik v. Union of India*,[141] a writ petition was filed to draw the attention of the Court to railway accidents by which the life of elephants was endangered. Although the case pertained to the north-eastern part of the country, the Court directed the railways to reduce the speed limit of moving trains that pass through dense forests all across the country. If the speed limit is not followed, action will be taken against the erring drivers and concerned officials. Certain specific directions were given to the North-Eastern Frontier Railway with regard to the construction of passes in Chapramari Wildlife Sanctuary, Jaldapara Wildlife Sanctuary, and Mahananda Wildlife Sanctuary, which fall within the State of West Bengal.

136 *Right of Passage: National Elephant Corridors Project*, Wildlife Trust of India, https://www.wti.org.in/projects/right-of-passage/ (last visited June 12, 2024).

137 *Project Elephant (PE)*, Ministry of Environment, Forest and Climate Change, https://moef.gov.in/moef/division/forest-divisions-2/project-elephant-pe/introduction/index.html (last visited June 12, 2024).

138 *Id.*

139 Ministry of Environment, Forests and Climate Change, Guidelines for Management of Human Elephant Conflicts (Issued on Oct. 6, 2017).

140 A. Rangaraj v. Union of India, WP 897 of 1996.

141 Shakti Prasad Naik v. Union of India, (2014) SCC 15 514; *see also*, Hospitality Association of Mudumalai v. In Defence of Environment and Animals, 2020 SCC OnLine SC 838.

In the year 2023, the Project Tiger division was merged with Project Elephant and a new division with the name 'Project Tiger and Elephant Division' was created under the MoEF&CC. After the merger, the staff and divisional heads of Project Elephant (PE) now report to the additional director-general of forests (ADGF), Project Tiger (PT), who has now been designated as ADGF (PT&E).[142]

3.2.1.8 Central Zoo Authority and Recognition of Zoos

The Wildlife (Protection) Amendment Act, 1991, added Chapter IV-A comprising Sections 38A to 38J for the establishment of the Central Zoo Authority of India. The body, comprising a Chairman, Member-Secretary, and not more than ten members appointed by the Central Government,[143] has a term of three years[144] and is headed by the Minister, Ministry of Environment, Forests and Climate Change.[145]

The country adopted a National Zoo Policy in 1998, but the importance of making conservation one of the primary objectives of the management of zoos was realised by the Indian Government soon after independence and the Indian Board for Wildlife made important recommendations in this regard. Acknowledging the severe pressure faced by the wildlife habitats and the growing number of wild fauna becoming endangered, it was realised that zoos had to augment the depleting populations of animals in the wild besides sustaining their own populations. Guided by the mandate of the National Zoo Policy of 1998, the Central Zoo Authority works towards complementing and strengthening the national efforts in the conservation of the rich faunal biodiversity of the country.[146]

3.2.1.8.1 FUNCTIONS OF THE CENTRAL ZOO AUTHORITY

The mission of the Central Zoo Authority is to provide better upkeep and veterinary care for the wild animals housed in zoos, ensure their conservation through the adoption of best practices of management, and inspire a feeling of empathy amongst visitors for wild animals and an understanding and awareness amongst people for the need for conservation of our wild flora and fauna.[147] One of the primary functions of the Central Zoo Authority is to grant recognition to zoos. Every zoo in the country requires the recognition of the Central Zoo Authority to operate as stipulated under Section 38H of the Wildlife (Protection) Act, 1972. In addition,

142 Aksheev Thakur, *Centre Merges Project Tiger and Project Elephant 'Without any Discussion'; Experts Demand PM Intervention*, The Indian Express (July 22, 2023), https://indianexpress.com/article/cities/bangalore/centre-merges-project-tiger-and-project-elephant-without-any-discussion-8852928/.

143 The Wild Life (Protection) Act, 1972, §38A(2).

144 *Id.* §38B(1).

145 Notification S.O. 1685(E), Ministry of Environment, Forests and Climate Change (May, 18, 2017).

146 WWF India, *National Zoo Policy, 1998, objectives*.

147 *About CZA*, Central Zoo Authority, https://cza.nic.in/page/en/introduction (last visited June 12, 2024).

the minimum standards for housing, upkeep, and veterinary care of the animals kept in the zoo are specified and evaluated by the Central Zoo Authority.[148] The overall management of animals housed in zoos and the standards and norms that have to be maintained with respect to animal housing, animal enclosures and display of animals, upkeep and healthcare of animals, veterinary and infrastructure facilities, acquisition and breeding of animals, research activities, education and outreach activities, and visitor facilities have been laid down under the Recognition of Zoo Rules, 2009.[149] The Central Zoo Authority has to evaluate and assess the functioning of zoos with respect to the standards or the norms laid down under these Rules. Section 38C contains several other functions the Central Zoo Authority is supposed to perform.

Before any wild animal or captive animal specified in Schedules I of the Act is acquired, sold, or transferred, the permission of the Central Zoo Authority has to be obtained. Moreover, such transfers and acquisitions can only be done from or to a recognised zoo.[150] Guidelines have been issued by the Central Zoo Authority for the exchange or transfer of animals between zoos, which stipulate the conditions to be fulfilled before such exchange or transfer can take place. Exchange proposals are submitted by the zoos to the Central Zoo Authority and are fundamentally decided based on the maintenance and housing resources offered by the receiving zoo and the survival of the species population group at the dominant zoo. Past track records of the zoo with regard to successful infant healthcare and breeding and upkeep are given due weight, and preference is given to unpaired animals, single animals, and animals in non-viable groups for transfer or exchange; zoos located in the normal habitat range of the species concerned are preferred while approving the exchange programmes. Randomly removing animals from a breeding group or herd is not permitted, and all animal species that are marked endangered must be marked or implanted with a microchip and detailed stud book. The Central Zoo Authority also approves the exchange of animals between foreign and Indian zoos before necessary clearances are issued under Export-Import (EXIM) Policy, and the permits are issued by the competent authority under Conservation on International Trade in Endangered Species of Wild Fauna and Flora (CITES). An exchange programme between foreign and Indian zoos generally involves seeking approvals from the Chief Wildlife Warden, the Central Zoo Authority, the zoos en route, and the Environment and Forest Ministry.[151]

148 The Wild Life (Protection) Act, 1972, § 38C.

149 Recognition of Zoo Rules, 2009, conferred by the Wild Life (Protection) Act, 1972, § 63(1)(f) and (g).

150 The Wild Life (Protection) Act, 1972, § 38I.

151 Aswin J Kumar, *Dispute over Animal Exchange Programme*, TIMES OF INDIA (July 22, 2015), https://timesofindia.indiatimes.com/city/thiruvananthapuram/Dispute-over-animal-exchange-programme/articleshow/48171802.cms.

3.2.1.8.2 COORDINATED CONSERVATION BREEDING PROGRAMME

India has also adopted the Coordinated Conservation Breeding Programme which is an effort towards ex-situ conservation breeding of endangered species in India with the involvement of both in-situ and ex-situ wildlife managers. The idea underlying the Conservation Breeding Programme is to support the conservation of endangered species by giving species which have no chance of survival in the wild a last chance of survival in ex-situ conditions through coordinated breeding. The animals bred in captivity act as insurance cover to meet exigencies and for experimental release in the wild as and when found appropriate and act as stock for the display of animals in the zoos. A total of 73 endangered animal species including the Asiatic lion, Bengal tiger, snow leopard, Tibetan wolf, red panda, and king cobra have been identified under the Conservation Breeding Programme with a few hundred or thousand left in the wild for ex-situ conservation breeding in the zoos.[152] The duty of conservation breeding of identified critically endangered species shall be assigned by the Central Zoo Authority to recognised zoos having housing facilities and technical capabilities, preferably close to the distribution range of the species. Every zoo shall help the recognised zoos in the implementation of breeding programmes.

3.2.1.9 Marine Protected Areas

Marine ecosystems around the world are protected by a network of Marine Protected Areas (MPA) or Marine and Coastal Protected Areas (MCPA). Marine Protected Area is used as a blanket term to describe a wide range of safeguarded areas for marine conservation around the world. A global definition specifically for Marine Protected Areas – different from the general definition of a protected area – was first adopted by the IUCN in 1999. The definition was amended in 2012 and the difference between terrestrial and marine protected areas was removed, placing the definition of MPAs within the definition of 'protected area' – 'a clearly defined geographical space, recognised, dedicated and managed, through legal or other effective means, to achieve the long-term conservation of nature with associated ecosystem services and cultural values'. It includes nature reserves, marine parks, and locally managed marine areas that safeguard seagrass beds, shipwrecks, reefs, tidal lagoons, archaeological sites, salt marshes, mangroves, mudflats, underwater areas on the coast, rock platforms, and the seabed in deep water.

In India, there is no standalone law that talks about the protection of marine areas. Marine and coastal protected areas are not recognised as a specific category of protected area either under the Wildlife (Protection) Act, 1972, or any other legislation. However, there are several national parks and sanctuaries that have terrestrial or freshwater components with the presence of a marine component. Such

152 *List of the Endangered Animal Species Identified Under Conservation Breeding Programme, Central Zoo Authority*, https://cza.nic.in/uploads/documents/CBP/List%20of%20CBP%20for%20website.pdf (last visited June 12, 2024).

spaces in coastal and/or marine areas are designated as national parks, sanctuaries, or community reserves under the Wildlife (Protection) Act, 1972, and are considered MPAs.[153] There are 25 marine protected areas in peninsular India, excluding the small island MPAs of the Andaman and Nicobar Islands of which 4 are located within the confines of national parks, 1 within a community reserve, and the remaining 20 within sanctuaries.[154] Of the 25 MPAs in peninsular India, the Sundarbans National Park, the Gulf of Mannar Marine National Park, the Gahirmatha Marine Sanctuary, the Gulf of Kachchh National Park, the Chilika Wildlife Sanctuary, and the Coringa Wildlife Sanctuary provide a range of ecological services to local communities and have unique marine biodiversity. In the Andaman and Nicobar Islands, there are close to 105 protected areas of which around 100 include marine areas.[155] There are 106 MPAs in the islands of India, of which 9 are in national parks and the remainder are located within sanctuaries.[156] The MPAs recognised under the Wildlife (Protection) Act, 1972, are governed by the provisions of the Act. However, MPAs were recognised in India even before the Wildlife (Protection) Act was enacted, with the oldest in India being the Point Calimere Wildlife Sanctuary in Tamil Nadu – an intertidal mud flatbed to protect migratory bird species which was declared in 1967.[157] Although the Wildlife (Protection) Act, 1972, does not make any specific mention of MPAs, it does mention that if any part of the territorial waters is to be included within a sanctuary, prior approval of the Central Government has to be sought, provided that the boundaries of the territorial water are determined in consultation with the Central Government's Chief Naval Hydrographer and requisite measures are taken to protect the occupational interests of local fishermen.

MPAs have also been recognised within biosphere reserves in India designated under the United Nations Educational, Scientific and Cultural Organization (UNESCO)'s Man and Biosphere (MAB) Programme that was launched in 1971. The MAB programme is an intergovernmental programme that allows countries to identify biosphere reserves to promote sustainable development based on local community efforts and sound science. These areas work as conservation zones of the ecosystems and in situ genetic diversity. Traditional knowledge is used in the management of the ecosystem to foster sustainable development through the involvement of the local communities and enterprises. The sites under the programme are internationally recognised under the World Network of Biosphere Reserves with a network of 686 biosphere reserves in 122 countries, including 20 transboundary

153 Ramya Rajagopalan, Marine Protected Areas in India (ICSF 2008).

154 K Sivakumar, *Editor Note*, in K. Sivakumar (ed.), Coastal and Marine Protected Areas in India: Challenges and Way Forwards (15 ENVIS Bulletin: Wildlife & Protected Areas, Wildlife Institute of India 2013).

155 Ministry of Environment and Forests, India's Fifth National Report to the Convention on Biological Diversity (2014), https://www.cbd.int/doc/world/in/in-nr-05-en.pdf.

156 *Marine Protected Areas*, WII-ENVIS Centre on Wildlife & Protected Areas, https://wiienvis.nic.in//Database/MPA_8098.aspx (last visited June 12, 2024).

157 Ramya Rajagopalan, *supra* note 153.

reserves.[158] In India, there are 18 biosphere reserves, and amongst them, the Gulf of Mannar, the Sundarbans, and the Great Nicobar have been designated as marine protected areas.[159] Thus, although biosphere reserves do not fall under a category of any of the protected areas recognised under the Wildlife (Protection) Act, they nevertheless form an important category since they are declared and notified by the Central Government under the UNESCO-MAB programme and are included in the list of MPAs in the National Report submitted by India to the Convention on Biological Diversity.[160]

3.2.1.10 Trade in Wild Animals, Animal Articles, and Trophies

The Wildlife (Protection) Act, 1972, regulates trade in wildlife and does not prohibit it completely. Chapter V of the Act is a dedicated chapter on trade and commerce in wild animals, animal articles, and animal trophies. Any article made from any captive animal or wild animal, other than vermin, has been defined as an animal article under the Act. It includes an article or object in which the whole or any part of such an animal has been used. Ivory imported into India and articles made from ivory have also been brought within the purview of the animal article.[161] A trophy of any animal, as the name suggests, means the whole of any captive animal or wild animal or its part which has been preserved by natural or artificial means and includes rugs, skins, and specimens of such animals mounted in whole or in part through a process of taxidermy, and antler, bone, carapace, shell, horn, rhinoceros horn, hair, feather, nail, tooth, tusk, musk, eggs, nests, and honeycomb.[162]

3.2.1.10.1 ANIMALS, ANIMAL ARTICLES, AND TROPHIES PROCURED IN CONTRAVENTION OF THE PROVISION OF THE ACT TO BE GOVERNMENT PROPERTY

As per Section 39, wild animals other than vermin, which are kept or bred in captivity, hunted, found dead, or killed by mistake, and animal articles, uncured trophies, trophies or meat derived from such animals, articles made from ivory, and ivory imported into India shall be the State Government's property, provided they have been procured in contravention of any of the provisions of the statute or are the subject of any offence under the statute. If the animal is hunted in a national park or sanctuary declared by the Central Government, such animal or trophy,

158 *Man and Biosphere Programme*, UN Educational, Scientific and Cultural Organization, http://www.unesco.org/new/en/natural-sciences/environment/ecological-sciences/man-and-biosphere-programme/about-mab/ (last visited June 12, 2024).

159 Jessica S. Sanders et al., *Marine Protected Areas: Country Case Studies on Policy, Governance and Institutional Issues* (FAO Fisheries and Aquaculture Technical Paper No. 556/1 Rome, 2011).

160 Ministry of Environment and Forests, supra note 155, at 25.

161 The Wild Life (Protection) Act, 1972, § 2(2); *see also* Balram Kumawat v. Union of India, 2003 SCC OnLine SC 922.

162 The Wild Life (Protection) Act, 1972, § 2(31).

uncured trophy, animal article, or meat derived from such animal shall be the Central Government's property. Any vehicle, vessel, weapon, trap, or tool that has been used for procuring these wild animals, animal articles, trophies, meat, or ivory in contravention of the provisions of the Act shall also be seized and deemed to be the property of the State Government or the Central Government as the case may be.[163] However, the seizing of tools and vehicles would be applicable only after a court of competent jurisdiction finds that the allegations made against the alleged perpetrator were true and the finding was recorded that the seized article was, in fact, used in the commission of the offence.[164]

In *Wildlife Warden v. Komarrikal Elias*,[165] the Respondent was alleged to have retrieved and stored elephant tusks, unlicensed guns, and other accessories without authorisation. The Respondent was tried under the Kerala Forest Act of 1961. The District Court Judge held elephant tusks to not be forest produce, and accordingly remanded the authority to the matter of the first instance. Following the same line of argument, the appellate authority arrived at the decision that there was no significant evidence on record to conclude that it was Government property and, hence, the presumption as anticipated under Section 69 of the 1961 Act cannot be made applicable. Learned counsel appearing on behalf of the Respondent contended that the action was taken not by treating the elephant tusk as property of the Government but by treating it as forest produce. It was held that upon a perusal of Section 39(1) of the Wildlife (Protection) Act, 1972, it is fairly certain that ivory, which is imported into India, and an article made from such ivory, in respect of which any offence against this Act or any rule or order passed has been committed, will be deemed to be the property of the State Government. If such an animal is hunted in a national park or a sanctuary declared by the Central Government, such animal or its meat, articles, etc., will be deemed to be the property of the Central Government. Hence, it attracts the presumption under Section 9 of the 1972 Act, which renders the ivory the property of the Government.

In *Cottage Industries Exposition Ltd. v. Union of India*,[166] the Petitioners made arrangements for the export of consignment containing scarves, kimonos, and shawls. On inspection of the export material, the Custom Authorities objected to the export of some shawls, suspecting them to be Shahtoosh shawls, and detained the shawls. The Petitioner contended that the shawls were made from the hair of the animal 'Chiru' which did not form a part of the animal article. The question raised before the Court was whether the phrase 'animal article' included 'animal hair'. The learned counsel for the Petitioners had contended that the definition of 'trophy' extends to include hair. However, it would not be an inclusive part of 'animal article' unless a similar provision that is inclusive is incorporated into

163 The Wild Life (Protection) Act, 1972, § 39(1).

164 Wildlife Crime Control Bureau, Ministry of Environment and Forests Government of India, Wildlife Crime Investigation – A Handbook for Wildlife Crime Investigation Officers, 39 (1st ed. 2013).

165 Wildlife Warden v. Komarrikal Elias, (2018) 8 SCC 114.

166 Cottage Industries Exposition Ltd. v. Union of India, 2007 (122) ECC 7.

the definition of 'animal article.' The Court held that as per the provisions of the Wildlife (Protection) Act of 1972, 'hair' forms a part of the animal 'Chiru'. Any person found dealing or carrying on trade in Shahtoosh was liable to proceed under the Wildlife (Protection) Act, 1972, as Shahtoosh is made from 'hair' which is a derivative of the animal 'Chiru' which comes under the category of 'scheduled animal article'. It was observed by the Court that the definitions of trophy, uncured trophy, and animal article are complementary and cannot be held to be exclusive of one another. Whether naturally shed or otherwise obtained, the hair of Chiru will form a part of an uncured trophy and the raw wool made after treating the hair will fall within the definition of a trophy. Furthermore, when this wool is processed to make a thread for the shawl, it is transformed into an 'animal article'.

Any person who obtains any property which has been declared as Government property must report the same to the nearest police station or authorised officer within 48 hours of obtaining such possession and hand over the property to such officer.[167] The Act further mandates that before acquiring or keeping in possession, custody, or control any such Government property, or transferring by gift, sale, or otherwise or destroying or damaging any Government property, it is necessary to seek prior permission from the Chief Wildlife Warden or authorised officer.[168]

In *Samir Thapar v. Union of India*,[169] the High Court of Delhi, while dealing with a petition related to the import of a leopard (*Panthera pardus*) trophy which had been hunted in Africa, established a conjoint reading of the Foreign Trade Policy, the Foreign Trade (Development and Regulation) Act of 1992, and the Act of 1972, which left no room for doubt that there was an express bar on importing *Panthera pardus* and that it was a case dealing with the import of a leopard trophy. In this case, the Petitioner sought to import a leopard trophy among other articles which he had gathered on a hunting spree in the Republic of Tanzania. On the Petitioner's return to India, in order to import the said articles and trophies, he applied for a grant of a 'no objection certificate' and furnished all necessary documents along with it. He received the clearance for the import of skin and trophies. However, the Petitioner was notified that the import of the skull and skin of *Panthera pardus*, a lookalike species, would not be allowed.

It was contended by the counsel for the Petitioner that no provision of the Wildlife (Protection) Act of 1972 and the Rules framed thereunder had been violated as the objective was only to import the said articles into the country upon the grant of a 'no objection certificate'. It was further contended by the counsel that there is no provision whatsoever banning the import of *Panthera pardus*, and hence, the request of the Petitioner was dismissed on an arbitrary basis. It was submitted that the decision was not made on any rational basis or classification. In the counter argument, the counsel for the Respondent submitted that the import of wild animals including their parts and products is prohibited, as defined in the

167 The Wild Life (Protection) Act, 1972, § 39(2).
168 *Id.* § 39(3).
169 Samir Thapar v. Union of India, 2010(171) DLT 33.

Act of 1972. According to Section 2(36) of the Wildlife (Protection) Act, 1972, 'wild animal' refers to any animal stipulated in Schedules I to IV and found wild in nature. *Panthera pardus* is listed under Schedule I, entry No. 16B, rendering the import of its skin prohibited. The Court held that upon a cursory reading, it can be established that *Panthera pardus* is an animal listed under Schedule I of the Wildlife (Protection) Act of 1972; thus there is no doubt that there is an explicit bar on importing *Panthera pardus*.

3.2.1.10.2 DECLARATION OF POSSESSION AND CERTIFICATE OF OWNERSHIP

Keeping animal trophies and animal articles was common in ancient India, especially amongst the members of royal families and those engaged by the British Government before independence, since hunting was enjoyed as a sport. However, an embargo was placed on such dealings after the commencement of the Wildlife (Protection) Act, 1972. Thus, persons who were in possession, custody, or control of any captive animal specified in Schedule I, or trophy, animal article, or uncured trophy obtained from such animals or dried or salted skins of animals or the horn of a rhinoceros or the musk of a musk deer were required to give a declaration to the Chief Wildlife Warden or the authorised officer within 30 days of the commencement of the Act together with details about the number and description of the animal, or article and the place where such animal or article is kept.[170]

After the commencement of the Act, any person seeking to receive, acquire, keep in his control, possession, or custody, offer for sale, sell, or otherwise transport or transfer any animal mentioned in Schedule I or any uncured trophy or meat obtained from such animal, or dried or salted skins of such animals or the horn of a rhinoceros or the musk of a musk deer, has to secure prior permission from the Chief Wildlife Warden or authorised officer in written form. Rules were made a little more stringent after the Wildlife (Protection) Amendment Act of 2002 and any person acquiring, receiving, or keeping in his control, custody, or possession any captive animal, animal article, trophy, or uncured trophy specified in Schedule I would have to present a certificate of ownership to prove his claim over such animal or animal article. A certificate of ownership may be issued by the Chief Wildlife Warden to a person who, as per his opinion, is in lawful possession of any wild animal or any animal article, uncured trophy, or trophy. The Chief Wildlife Warden may also mark such animal articles, trophies, or uncured trophies for purposes of identification, where possible. If the animals in question are captive animals, the Chief Wildlife Warden shall ensure that there are adequate facilities for the housing, maintenance, and upkeep of the animal before issuing a certificate of ownership.[171] The only exception allowed would be in case the person in question acquires these by way of inheritance, in which case the person would have to make a declaration of such inheritance to the Chief Wildlife Warden or the authorised

170 The Wild Life (Protection) Act, 1972, § 40(1).
171 *Id.* § 42.

officer within 90 days.[172] In addition to this, another exception made is that no certificate of ownership or declaration of inheritance would apply in the case of a live elephant.

3.2.1.10.3 REGULATION OF TRANSFER OF ANIMALS AND LICENSE FOR DEALINGS IN TROPHY AND ANIMAL ARTICLES

Persons with a certificate of ownership are only eligible to transfer captive animals, animal articles, trophies, or uncured trophies. However, transfer by way of sale or any other commercial transaction in lieu of consideration is prohibited under the Act.[173] For persons with a certificate of ownership, other transfers or transport of captive animals, animal articles, trophies, or uncured trophies are permitted. But for such transfer or transport within or outside the State, a report has to be submitted to the concerned Chief Wildlife Wardens or other authorised officer within 30 days of the transfer or transport. But these stipulations shall not apply to the tail feathers of peacocks or animal articles or trophies made from them or to captive animals transferred amongst recognised zoos and public museums.

Further, the Act requires persons dealing in trophies and animal articles to procure a licence from the Chief Wildlife Warden or the authorised officer before commencing or carrying on business as a manufacturer or a dealer in any animal article, or as a taxidermist or as a dealer in trophy or uncured trophy or captive animals or meat. As per the Act, a licence must be procured even if a person cooks or serves meat in any eating-house, or derives, collects, or prepares or deals in snake venom.[174] Eating-house as per the provisions of the Act includes any hotel, restaurant, or any place where eatables are served on the payment of food. While the Act requires persons dealing in meat and working in eating-houses to procure licences before they serve or cook meat, it can be asserted with a fair bit of certainty that this provision of the Act is not complied with in the country, bearing in mind the number of eateries, several of which function informally, and the lack of awareness about the provisions of the Act. Every manufacturer, dealer in animal articles or captive animals, trophies or uncured trophies, and every taxidermist who is desirous of acquiring a licence must make a declaration to the Chief Wildlife Warden or authorised officer about his stocks of animal articles, captive animals, trophies, and uncured trophies and the Chief Wildlife Warden and authorised officer shall make an identification mark on such animal.[175]

The application for the licence must be made before the Chief Wildlife Warden or such other authorised officer, on the payment of prescribed fees. Before the grant of any licence fee, the Chief Wildlife Warden and the authorised officer shall inquire into the antecedents and previous experience of the Applicant, the

172 The Wild Life (Protection) Act, 1972, §§ 40(2A) & (2B).
173 *Id.* § 43(1).
174 *Id.* § 44(1).
175 *Id.* § 44(2).

implications that the grant of licence would have for the status of wildlife, and other prescribed matters. The licence granted shall be subject to certain conditions. It would specify the premises and the conditions under which the licensee would carry on business, would be valid for one year from the date on which it is granted, would be renewable only once, for a period not exceeding one year at a time, and would not be transferable.[176] The licence granted for dealings in animals and animal articles and trophies can also be suspended or cancelled by the Chief Wildlife Warden or other authorised officer, subject to any special or general order of the State Government for reasons recorded in writing and after giving the holder of the licence an opportunity of being heard.[177] The Act also places restrictions on the purchase of captive animals, wild animals (other than vermin), or any animal article, trophy, uncured trophy, or meat derived from such animals. Such purchase or acquisition can only be made from a dealer or person authorised to make such transfer under this Act.[178]

Every person who is granted licences for dealing in animals, animal articles, trophies, and the like is subject to certain conditions imposed by the licence and other provisions of the Act. Thus, all acts have to be done in accordance with the rules made under this Act. Thus, no licensee can keep in his control, possession, or custody any animal, trophy, or animal article in respect of which no declaration has been made, or which has not been acquired under the provisions of this Act.[179] The licensee is further forbidden from capturing any wild animal or receiving, acquiring, or keeping in his control, possession, or custody, transporting, or selling any captive animal specified in Schedule I or animal article, uncured trophy, trophy, or meat obtained from such animals except in accordance with such rules as may be made under this Act.[180]

In *Chief Forest Conservator v. Nisar Khan*,[181] an appeal was filed against the decision of the Allahabad High Court which directed the Appellant to grant a licence for carrying out business as a dealer in birds which are bred when captive. The High Court held that the Respondent was entitled to carry on the business of birds categorised under Schedule IV of the Wildlife (Protection) Act, 1972, and hence, the issue associated with the grant of licence ought to be considered. It was argued by the learned counsel appearing on behalf of the Appellants that a bare perusal of the petition filed by the Respondent would denote that in the process of dealing with the birds, he has himself acknowledged that birds are required to be trapped, which Section 9 of the Act deems tantamount to hunting, and hence is not entitled to carry on the business. Moreover, the *Amicus Curiae* submitted that no licence can be granted under Section 44 of the Act, if as a consequence the licensee

176 The Wild Life (Protection) Act, 1972 § 44(4)–(6).

177 *Id.* § 45.

178 *Id.* § 49.

179 While the requirement of giving a declaration of inventories does not apply to dealers in meat, the need for acquiring the meat lawfully is applicable to them.

180 The Wild Life (Protection) Act, 1972, § 48(a)–(b).

181 Chief Forest Conservator v. Nisar Khan, AIR 2003 SCW 1333.

would violate any of the provisions thereof. The Supreme Court, paying regard to Section 9 of the Act which stated that 'hunting' includes 'trapping' of the birds, as specified in Schedule IV, held that before granting the licence, even with respect to the captivity of the birds, the licencing authority is placed under a statutory obligation to certify that the provisions of Section 9 of the Act are not violated. As hunting of the birds stipulated under Section 9 of the Act is prohibited, no person, dealing in birds that are in captivity, procured by hunting, which also includes trapping, can be granted a licence. Breeding birds in captivity in order to raise their population is acceptable. On the other hand, enabling the licensee to deal with the birds that are trapped before they are made captive is not acceptable.

In addition to persons dealing in animal articles and trophies, the Act also imposes obligations on persons engaged in the transportation of wild animals and animal articles. The Act requires any person, before accepting any wild animal (other than vermin) or any animal article or plant or derivative for transportation, to ascertain that requisite permissions have been granted by the Chief Wildlife Warden or other authorised officer for such transportation.[182]

3.2.1.10.4 PROHIBITION OF TRADE IN TROPHIES, ANIMAL ARTICLES DERIVED FROM SCHEDULED ANIMALS

Wild animals listed under Schedule I, also referred to as 'scheduled animals' under the Act,[183] receive the maximum protection. The Act strictly prohibits dealings in trophies, animal articles, and other substances derived from scheduled animals. Thus, no person is allowed to carry on or commence business as a manufacturer of or dealer in ivory imported into India, or dealer in scheduled animal articles, or articles made from such ivory, or a manufacturer of such articles; or a dealer in a trophy or uncured trophy obtained from any scheduled animal; or as a taxidermist with respect to any scheduled animal; or in any scheduled captive animal; or meat obtained from any scheduled animal; or cook or serve meat obtained from any scheduled animal in any eating-house. No licence granted to any dealer, manufacturer, or taxidermist shall entitle such a person to continue business in scheduled animals. However, if the Central Government deems it to be in the public interest, it may, in the public interest, allow certain institutions to deal in scheduled animals for purposes of export. Such an exemption for dealing in scheduled animals may be granted to any corporation owned or controlled by the Central Government, including a Government company,[184] or any society registered under the Societies Registration Act of 1860, or any other law for the time being in force, substantially or wholly financed by the Central Government. In a similar way, a licenced taxidermist under the Act may put a scheduled animal under the procedure of taxidermy for or on behalf of any society or corporation exempted under the Act or

182 The Wild Life (Protection) Act, 1972, § 48(A).
183 *Id.* § 49A(a).
184 *Id.* § 49B(3).

Government or on behalf of any person for scientific or educational purposes with prior written authorisation from the Chief Wildlife Warden.[185]

In *Wildlife v. Ashok Kumar*,[186] the Delhi District Court convicted three persons for committing offences under Sections 49 and 49B of the Wildlife Protection Act, 1972, since they were found in possession of and were dealing with baby leopard skin for the purpose of trade. Since the leopard is specified under Schedule I of the Act, the accused persons had contravened the provisions of Sections 49 and 49B of the Act which is punishable under Section 51. The Court directed that if in any case property is retrieved, the same should be confiscated to the State under Section 39 of the Wildlife (Protection) Act, 1972.

3.2.1.10.5 DISPOSAL OF WILD ANIMAL ARTICLE

The Wild Life Disposal of Wild Animal Article Rules, 2023, provides for the disposal of animal articles, trophies, or uncured trophies or meat derived from any wild animal. It provides for the formation of a committee by the Chief Wildlife Warden for the purpose of incineration.

3.2.2 Legislative and Regulatory Mechanism to Counter Wildlife Crimes in India

India has been a hotbed for illegal trade in wildlife, contributing to the increasing number of wildlife crimes in the country and in the world. Considered as a subset of environmental crimes, wildlife crimes prosecuted under the Wildlife (Protection) Act, 1972, rank second only to crimes committed under the Forest Act, 1927, and the Forest (Conservation) Act, 1980, in their incidence and crime rate under environment-related offences as reported by the National Crime Records Bureau in 2017.[187] Even though the ones directly affected by wildlife crimes are hapless wild animals and plants, the effect that these crimes have on the ecosystem is often far-reaching. Illegal wildlife trade is also treated as a serious economic offence since it involves huge sums of money that change hands. While the immensity of wildlife crimes is a cause for concern, the country has put in place a regulatory mechanism to impede such crimes. A series of events led to the setting up of a dedicated multi-disciplinary forum for combating organised wildlife crime in the country. The first step in this direction was taken in the year 1994 when the Ministry of Environment and Forest constituted a committee – 'Prevention of Illegal Trade in Wildlife and Wildlife Products' – which was mandated to look into the issues related to illegal trade in wildlife and wildlife products and to make recommendations for its effective control.

In 2000, seizures of wildlife articles in several parts of the country attracted international attention and the representatives of the country vowed to open a

185 The Wild Life (Protection) Act, 1972, § 49B(4).
186 Wildlife v. Ashok Kumar, CC No. 301845/2016.
187 National Crime Records Bureau, Crime in India (NCRB Ministry of Home Affairs 2017).

Wildlife Crime Cell in the 11th Conference of Parties of CITES which it had ratified in 1976 to counter the poaching of tigers and illegal trade in tiger parts and derivatives, which was made effective from July 2001. The complete disappearance of tigers from the Sariska Tiger Reserve, Rajasthan, occurred in 2005, and the report of the Tiger Task Force set up by the Ministry stated that to effectively deal with wildlife crime a multi-pronged approach that involved strengthening enforcement at the State level, investigating international trade links, and breaking the nexus of large poachers was of the utmost necessity, ultimately leading to the establishment of a wildlife crime bureau at the Central level armed with the ability to both investigate wildlife crimes and take follow-up action. Enabling provisions for the establishment of the Wildlife Crime Control Bureau were introduced into the Act by the Wildlife (Protection) Amendment Act, 2006,[188] and the Tiger and Other Endangered Species Crime Control Bureau, known as the Wildlife Crime Control Bureau, became operational in the year 2008.

Notwithstanding the fact that the Wildlife (Protection) Act, 1972, is the umbrella legislation that governs wildlife crime enforcement, there are a plethora of laws, Government institutions, and departments that closely function with the institutional machinery under the Act of 1972 in tackling wildlife crimes, primarily owing to the nature and magnitude of such crimes which involve multiple actors that often function across transnational borders. The primary enforcement agency is the State Forest and Police Department. Often the Central Bureau of Investigation steps in to investigate cases with the permission of the concerned State Government. As already pointed out, wildlife offences often have trans-border ramifications and the import and export of wildlife articles/derivatives are either restricted or prohibited under the Export-Import Policy of the country. Therefore, often a significant role is played by the Customs Department and the Directorate of Revenue Intelligence in detecting and thwarting such crimes at points of entry and exit. The authorities guarding the border, such as the Central Industrial Security Force (CISF), Border Security Force (BSF), and Indo-Tibetan Border Police, deployed at airports and border roads, aid with the prevention of the smuggling and trafficking of prohibited animals and items under the Act. Similarly, the Government Railway Police, the Railway Police Force, and the Postal Authorities also assist in combating smuggling through railways and post. Other bodies responsible for the enforcement of wildlife crimes include the State Forest Departments, the State Police Departments, the Central Bureau of Investigation, and the State and Central Forensic Laboratories.

188 The government notified the constitution of the Tiger and Other Endangered Species Crime Control Bureau to be known as the Wildlife Crime Control Bureau *vide* Order No. S.O. 918 (E) dated 6 June 2007.

3.2.2.1 Wildlife Crimes

Although the Wildlife (Protection) Act, 1972, does prohibit wildlife crimes and establishes mechanisms for countering such crimes, there is no explicit definition of 'wildlife crime' under the Act. Several activities have been prohibited under the Act, which by implication come within the fold of wildlife crimes. The Wildlife Crime Investigation Manual released by the Wildlife Crime Control Bureau of India in 2013 defines 'wildlife crime' as 'taking, possession, trade or movement, processing, consumption of wild animals and plants or their derivatives in contravention of any international, regional, or national legislation(s)'. Persecution of both animals living freely in the wild and those living in captivity is also included in the definition of wildlife crime.[189]

One of the primary challenges associated with countering wildlife crimes is that such crimes are mostly 'victim-less' as they are committed on animals and plants that are voice-less. Thus, recording wildlife crimes, like other mainstream crimes such as drug trafficking, human trafficking, murder, rape, etc., becomes a challenge. These crimes function with the involvement of organised networks of criminals who play a role in the processing, smuggling, and trading of wildlife and wildlife products through sophisticated techniques and channels across national and international boundaries. Wildlife crimes are often found in combination with corruption, fraud, counterfeiting, money laundering, and violence. The illegal theft, trade, and dealings with such natural resources of a country, besides generating losses to assets and revenues, also pose significant threats to the ecosystem and are often accompanied by the risk of life-threatening diseases that can result from the introduction of alien species to habitats unsuited for them.[190]

It is important to clarify at the outset that wildlife trade is not *per se* prohibited and the national and international bodies merely regulate trade in wildlife, so as to ensure that the ecological balance is not hampered and flora and fauna that are endangered or are on the brink of extinction are protected. The wildlife trade involves millions of different floral and faunal species that could be used for food, fuel, fodder, building materials such as timber, gums, and resins, clothing and ornaments, curios, and medicinal products made from plant and animal extracts. Wildlife trade plays a significant role in the regional, national, and international economy, and several benefits emerge from legal wildlife trade that is both sustainable and economically viable in the long run. Intergovernmental policy interventions and regulations in favour of legal wildlife trade are often implemented owing to the pressure generated by the international community and conventions to help support responsible and legal wildlife sourcing and trade practices by local businesses. This in turn persuades manufacturers and retailers to use and offer wildlife products that have legal approval and inspire consumers to choose legal and

189 Wildlife Crime Control Bureau, Wildlife Crime Investigation: A Handbook for Wildlife Crime Investigation Officers 9 (2013).

190 *Id.*

sustainable wildlife goods.[191] Illegal wildlife trade on the other hand completely undermines the advantages of legal wildlife trade. Illegal trade in wildlife commodities such as elephant ivory, rhino horn, pangolin scales, tiger bones, bear bile, and rosewood has resulted in the decline of their numbers and has pushed several plant and animal species to the brink of extinction. As per the estimates made by the United Nations in 2016, the annual value of illegal wildlife trade ranges between USD 7 and 23 billion.[192] Many actors are involved in the wildlife trade, linking the procurers or collectors of wildlife products to the ultimate users, such as specialists skilled in storage, handling, transport, manufacturing, industrial production, taxidermists, retailers, etc. The vast number of actors and middlemen involved makes it even more difficult to nab the perpetrators of illegal wildlife trade.

The major wildlife offences in India are hunting and illegal trade. Other ancillary offences include preparation, possession, transportation, and processing. Offenders committing wildlife crimes can be categorised under two heads. The first group is the poachers or hunters who kill and capture wild animals specified in Schedules I and II and the second group of persons are those purchasing killed, trapped, or harvested animals, their body parts, or their derivatives, as well as plants, for their own use or commerce, or those dealing in these items without the requisite permission and licence. Poaching often involves varying levels of violence depending upon the nature and size of the animal targeted. When large animals like elephants and rhinoceros are targeted for their ivory or horns, poaching involves the use of heavy weaponry and may even involve bloodshed. On the other hand, the poaching of smaller animals and plants such as snakes, orchids, turtles, etc., involves the use of technical skills to enable the poacher to target and identify the high-value species.[193]

A variety of tools and methods are used in India by wildlife criminals to poach, which is primarily dependent on the kind of species targeted and the environment in which the poaching is to take place and the end use for which the animal or animal parts or articles would be traded. For instance, firearms, which continue to be one of the popular modes of poaching, are used when the species poached is of sufficiently high value and the poacher is confident of getting away without attracting much attention. On the other hand, guns are not preferred if the skin of the animal commands a high price in the market, since gunshot marks may reduce the value of the product. Other methods used include leg traps, wire traps and snares, poisoning, poisoned arrows, electrocution, bird traps, nets, harpoons, and pits dug in the ground.[194]

The Wildlife (Protection) Act, 1972, which covers over 1,800 species, makes the majority of the trade in animals, plants, animal articles, trophies, etc., illegal in

191 *Legal Wildlife Trade*, TRAFFIC, https://www.traffic.org/about-us/legal-wildlife-trade/ (last visited June 12, 2024).

192 *Id.*

193 A HANDBOOK FOR WILDLIFE CRIME INVESTIGATION OFFICERS, *supra* note 189, at 10.

194 SAMIR SINHA, HANDBOOK ON WILDLIFE LAW ENFORCEMENT IN INDIA 56–60 (TRAFFIC India, New Delhi, Natraj Publishers 2010).

India.[195] Trade in species specified in Schedules I and II of the Act is illegal in India as the Act provides protection to these wild animals, plants, and their derivatives against hunting, trading, and any other form of exploitation.

Further in India, some diverse plant and animal products are illegally traded, including mongoose hair, snake skin and venom, rhino horn, claws of tigers and leopards, bones, skins, whiskers of tigers, tusks of elephants, deer antlers, Shahtoosh shawls woven from the hair of Tibetan antelopes, turtle shells, musk pods, turtles and tortoises, sea horses, tokay gecko, sea cucumber, medicinal plants, timber, red sanders, and caged birds such as parakeets, mynas, munias, etc.[196] In the recent past, animals that have been trafficked the most from India include pangolins, Patagonian seahorse, Indian star tortoise, and tokay gecko, and the demand for these animals is fuelled by their supposed use in medicine and their popularity as pets, especially the Indian star tortoise. Moreover, body parts of animals and plants are used in several traditional medicines and keeping trophies of animals, their skin, horns, and antlers, is seen as a status symbol. Superstitious and cultural beliefs also often drive illegal trade in wild animals and plants. The *Wild for Life* campaign launched in May 2019 by the Wildlife Crime Control Bureau and the UN Environment's India office identified tiger, pangolin, star tortoise, and tokay gecko as flagship species under the first phase of the campaign as they are highly endangered. China and South-East Asia are the main consumer markets for illegally traded wildlife products from India; however, live animals and body parts of animals are also smuggled to the Gulf, Europe, and North America. Besides these destinations, countries in transit such as Nepal, Bangladesh, Bhutan, Sri Lanka, and Myanmar also fall within the illegal wildlife trade ring.[197]

Red sanders is reported to be one of India's most exploited tree species and is under severe pressure from illegal logging and harvesting. Its heartwood is in demand in both domestic and international markets and is used to make furniture and handicrafts, while the red dye obtained from the wood is used as a colouring agent in textiles and medicines. Rampant illegal logging has been reported across its range State. As a native species to Andhra Pradesh, red sanders (also known as red sandalwood) use and trade are regulated by the State. Following the amendment to the Wildlife (Protection) Act, 1972, in December 2022, red sanders is now listed in Schedule IV. Under the foreign trade policy of India, the import of red sanders is prohibited, while export is restricted. Despite the regulation and legal protection, illegal logging and timber extraction remains a major conservation concern for the species.

195 World Wildlife Fund, https://www.wwfindia.org/about_wwf/enablers/traffic/resources/.

196 *Illegal Wildlife Trade in India*, World Wildlife Fund, https://www.wwfindia.org/about_wwf/enablers/traffic/illegal_wildlife_trade_in_india/ (last visited June 12, 2024).

197 Spotlight on India's Soaring Wildlife Crime, UN Environment Programme, https://www.unenvironment.org/news-and-stories/story/spotlight-indias-soaring-wildlife-crime (last visited June 12, 2024).

3.2.2.2 Wildlife Crime Control Bureau

The Wildlife Crime Control Bureau constituted under Section 38Y of the Wildlife (Protection) Act, 1972, with its headquarters in New Delhi is a multi-disciplinary body. The Director of Wildlife Preservation is the *ex-officio* Director of the Bureau. Since countering and preventing organised wildlife crime is one of its mandates, the WCCB has as its members the Inspector-General of Police as the Additional Director, the Deputy Inspector General of Police, the Deputy Inspector General of Forest, and the Additional Commissioner (Customs and Central Excise) as Joint Directors. The Chief Wildlife Warden, Wildlife Wardens, and other officers appointed by the Central Government and the State Governments may also be appointed to be members of the Wildlife Crime Control Bureau.[198] The Bureau has five regional offices at Delhi, Kolkata, Mumbai, Chennai, and Jabalpur; three sub-regional offices at Guwahati, Amritsar, and Cochin; and five border units at Ramanathapuram, Gorakhpur, Motihari, Nathula, and Moreh.[199] The increase in cases of wildlife crimes in the Western Ghats prompted the Wildlife Crime Control Bureau, in September 2019, to direct the forest department together with the CID Forest Cell to establish an intelligence cell and a crime control bureau for Karnataka with headquarters in Bengaluru.[200]

The primary aim behind the establishment of the Wildlife Crime Control Bureau has been to kerb organised wildlife crime and facilitate the investigation of cases, by assisting the State machinery in nabbing the perpetrators. In pursuance of this responsibility, the Wildlife (Protection) Act, 1972, has armed the Bureau with the power to collect and collate information on wildlife crimes, maintain a centralised data bank on wildlife crimes, and disseminate the same to enforcement agencies for immediate action. The Bureau with the assistance of its regional and border units has to coordinate the actions of different officers, State Governments, and other authorities responsible for the enforcement of the Act. It is also responsible for developing the infrastructure and capacity of officers and personnel responsible for the scientific and professional investigation into wildlife crimes and in advising the Government of India on matters relating to wildlife crimes, especially those that have national and international ramifications. The Bureau also has the duty to suggest policy and legal changes to the regulatory regime, keeping with the needs of the changing times.[201] The Wildlife Crime Control Bureau is responsible for implementing the obligations of the country under international conventions that relate to wildlife crime and wildlife trade, especially the CITES – Convention on International Trade in Endangered Species.

198 The Wild Life (Protection) Act, 1972, § 38Y.

199 *About Us*, Wildlife Crime Control Bureau, http://wccb.gov.in/index.aspx (last visited June 12, 2024)..

200 Bosky Khanna, *Karnataka to Have Its Own Wildlife Crime Control Bureau*, Indian Express (Sept. 19, 2019), https://www.newindianexpress.com/cities/bengaluru/2019/sep/19/karnataka-to-have-its-own-wildlife-crime-control-bureau-2035709.html.

201 The Wild Life (Protection) Act, 1972, § 38Z.

3.2.2.3 Enforcement Mechanism under the Act: Penalties and Their Enforcement

Section 51 lays down punishments for contraventions of the Act. Any person who breaches the provisions of the Act or any licence or permit granted under the Act, when convicted, would be punished with imprisonment for a term which may extend to three years, or with a fine which may extend to one lakh rupees, or with both. Stricter punishments have been prescribed for offences committed against scheduled animals, dealing with trophies and animal articles derived from scheduled animals and hunting of animals within a sanctuary or a national park. These offences would attract a minimum term of imprisonment of three years which could extend up to seven years, in addition to a minimum fine of 25,000 rupees.[202]

Teasing, molesting, injuring, or feeding any animal or causing disturbance to the animals by noise or in any other way, or littering the grounds in a zoo, are prohibited under Section 38J of the Act, and any person convicted of this offence can be punished with imprisonment for a term which may extend to six months, or with fine which may extend to 2,000 rupees, or with both. Subsequent offenders would attract an enhanced penalty of imprisonment for a term extending up to one year or a fine which may extend to 5,000 rupees.[203]

Once a person has been proven guilty under the Act, the Court trying the offence may order that the subjects of the perpetrator's crime such as any captive animal, wild animals, ivory imported into India, or an article made from it, any plant, or its part or derivative be forfeited to the State Government. The order of forfeiture may extend to any trap, tool, vehicle, vessel, or weapon used in the commission of the offence. The Court may also order that any permit or licence granted to the person be cancelled, which shall be in addition to any punishment that may have already been awarded for that offence.[204] The Act has been strict even against those who attempt to commit any offence in contravention of the Act or abet the commission of any offence. Such a person, if found guilty of attempting or abetting any offence under the Act, shall be deemed to have contravened the provision in question and shall be liable to be punished.[205]

In September 2008, two Czech Republic scientists were charged under Sections 27 and 29 of the Wildlife Protection Act, 1972,[206] by the West Bengal Forest Department, which dealt with illegal entry into Singalila National Park, a protected area, for collecting and being in possession of species of endangered butterflies, insects, and moths, which is punishable under Section 51 of the Act. The Court also found them guilty of violating Section 3 of the Biological Diversity Act, 2002, which prohibits non-citizens from collecting biological resources in India without approval from the National Biodiversity Authority. One of them was punished

202 The Wild Life (Protection) Act, 1972, § 51(1) & § 51(1A).
203 *Id.* § 51(1B).
204 *Id.* § 51(2) & § 51(3).
205 *Id.* § 52.
206 Shalini Bhutani & Kanchi Kohli, *Litigating India's Biodiversity Act: A Study of Legal Cases* (Foundation of Ecological Security, Nov. 2016).

with a jail term of three years and a fine of Rs. 50,000 and the other was fined Rs. 20,000.

3.2.2.3.1 FORFEITURE OF ILLEGALLY DERIVED PROPERTY

To counter and prohibit illegal trade in wild animals, animal articles, trophies, etc., and to prohibit illegal hunting, the Act has made provisions for forfeiting such ill-gotten property and a new chapter has been incorporated into the Act by the Wildlife (Protection) Amendment Act, 2002, which specifically deals with the procedures and bodies involved in such forfeiture. The chapter applies to persons convicted of an offence punishable with imprisonment for a term of three years or more under this Act, every associate of such person, and any holder of property (unless he has acquired the property in good faith in lieu of consideration) derived from illegal hunting or trading. The prohibition on holding any illegally acquired property has been made applicable from the date of commencement of the Wildlife (Protection) Amendment Act, 2002, that is 1 April 2003, and if any person holds such property it shall be forfeited to the State Government.[207]

The chapter dealing with the forfeiture of illegally derived property envisages the role of some officers in fulfilling several functions. The State Government shall authorise an officer not below the rank of the Chief Conservator of Forests to act as the competent authority, who shall be responsible for lodging complaints about persons having illegally acquired property. This information or complaint shall be given to an officer, not below the rank of Deputy Inspector General of Police, who shall have the responsibility of identifying and tracing the illegally acquired property by conducting any investigation, survey, or inquiry in respect of any person, property, place, documents, assets, books of accounting of any financial institution or bank, or any other requisite step as may be necessary. If the officer conducting the investigation or inquiry has reason to believe that the property acquired illegally could be concealed or transferred, he may make an order for the seizure of the property or make an order that the property shall not be transferred. To manage the properties forfeited to the State Government, officers not below the rank of Conservator of Forests shall be appointed to perform the function of administrators who shall be responsible for disposing of the property forfeited to the State Government. On the basis of the report of the investigating officer, the competent authority shall give an opportunity to be heard to the person who has illegally acquired property and to disclose the sources of his money, assets, or earnings, the means by which he obtained the property, the supporting documentation, and any other pertinent details. On the basis of the explanation provided, the competent authority shall record a finding on whether all or some of the property of the person in question is illegally acquired and issue a notice that such property shall stand forfeited to the State Government free from all encumbrances. If the person

207 The Wild Life (Protection) Act, 1972, § 58C.

affected can prove that the property in question was not illegally acquired, the notice in respect of such property shall be withdrawn.[208]

The Act has also made provisions for the establishment of the Appellate Tribunal for Forfeited Property consisting of a Chairman, and other members of the State Government not below the rank of a Principal Secretary to the Government to hear appeals from the decision of the competent authority, which may be filed within a period of 45 days from the date on which order of the competent authority is served on the person concerned.[209] The competent authority and the Appellate Tribunal have the powers of a civil court in so far as conducting an inquiry, receiving evidence, issuing commissions, etc., are concerned,[210] and are to be assisted by officers of the Police of the State Forest Departments, the Central Economic Intelligence Bureau, the Directorate of Revenue Intelligence, and other officers as specified by the State Government.

3.2.2.3.2 INVESTIGATION OF OFFENCES AND WILDLIFE CRIMES

Unlike offences under other legislation, offences under the Wildlife (Protection) Act, 1972, are different primarily owing to three reasons: first, these crimes are location-specific and are committed in places where the animals are housed; second, the public at large is not greatly affected by these crimes as these crimes do not instil a sense of fear or alarm in them and hence they do little for the prevention of these crimes, being mostly unaware of the adverse effects that illegal hunting and trade can cause; and third, since the general public is not as concerned, the reporting of these crimes takes longer since people do not voluntarily come forward to report them.[211] In light of these, the reporting of wildlife offences and their investigations take greater effort from the side of law enforcement agencies, and the sequence of events in the investigation may be different from other conventional crimes. For instance, in conventional crimes, the investigation of the case is initiated after the First Information Report (FIR) or complaint is filed, which is followed by the recovery and collection of evidence. However, in wildlife crimes, the seizure of the animal, animal trophy, or animal article or the apprehension of the accused may precede the registration of the case. In wildlife offences, the investigation may start after the seizure or apprehension report is filed by the officer making the seizure or arrest in a court of appropriate jurisdiction.[212]

The Act neither lays down any specific procedure for the search, arrest, and detention of alleged offenders nor does it prescribe any detailed guidelines for the investigation of wildlife offences. It merely lays down under Section 50 that the Director or officer authorised by him or the Chief Wildlife Warden or the authorised

208 The Wild Life (Protection) Act, 1972, §§ 58C, 58D, 58F, 58G, 58H & 58I.

209 *Id.* § 58N & §58O.

210 *Id.* §§ 58R & 58T.

211 A Handbook for Wildlife Crime Investigation Officers, *supra* note 189, at 10.

212 *Id.*

officer or any forest or police officer not below the rank of a sub-inspector has the power to inspect, stop any vehicle or vessel, or enter and search any premises, land, vehicle, or vessel to conduct search or inquiry, seize any captive animal, wild animal, animal article, meat, trophy or uncured trophy, or any specified plant or part or derivative and arrest without warrant and detain offenders.[213] These aforementioned officers also have the power to stop and detain any person acting without a licence, if the presence of the licence is a prerequisite for the act he is engaging in under the Act. Any authorised officer[214] who has seized any captive or wild animal may give the custody of the animal to the person from whom it was seized upon the execution of a bond which requires the person to produce the animal if and when required before the Magistrate having jurisdiction to try the offence.[215]

The Act further provides that any person detained or thing seized shall, after intimation to the Chief Wildlife Warden or officer authorised by him, be produced before the Magistrate to be dealt with according to 'law'.[216] This primarily implies that any procedure in the investigation and trial of a wildlife offence that is not specifically prescribed under the Act would be governed by the criminal law of the land, that is, the Criminal Procedure Code, 1973. However, the Act has clothed some of its officers, specifically officers holding ranks of Assistant Directors of Wildlife Preservation or Assistant Conservators of Forests authorised by the State Government or those senior in rank to such officers, with the power to investigate offences committed under any provision of this Act. This includes the power to issue a warrant, to enforce the attendance of witnesses, to compel the discovery and production of documents and material objects, and to receive evidence and record it.[217] The evidence recorded by any of the officers authorised under the Act in the presence of the accused person shall be admissible in evidence in any subsequent trials before the Magistrate.[218] This power given to the officers under the Act does not bar other officers responsible for the maintenance of law and order from investigating offences under the Act. The Act gives additional powers to the officers under the Act to investigate offences in addition to the police.

In *Moti Lal v. Central Bureau of Investigation and Anr*,[219] the question before the Supreme Court was whether the Central Bureau of Investigation was authorised to investigate an offence punishable under the Wildlife (Protection) Act of 1972. The Supreme Court ruled that under sub-section (1) of Section 50, the Act does not specifically exclude police officers from investigating offences that have been committed. Even though special powers have been conferred on other officers, such powers are in consonance with Section 4(2) of the Code of Criminal Procedure

213 The Wild Life (Protection) Act, 1972, § 50(1).

214 Any officer not inferior to the rank of an Assistant Director of Wildlife Preservation or an Assistant Conservator of Forests or their subordinate working under their authorisation.

215 The Wild Life (Protection) Act, 1972, § 50(3A).

216 *Id.* § 50(4).

217 *Id.* 1972, § 50(8).

218 *Id.* § 50(9).

219 Moti Lal v. Central Bureau of Investigation, 2002 (4) SCC 713.

which provides that all offences under any law other than the Indian Penal Code shall be investigated, inquired into, tried, and otherwise dealt with according to the Code of Criminal Procedure subject to any enactment that regulates the manner or place of investigation, inquiry, trial, or any other dealing with such offences. Accordingly, the Court ruled that there was no substance in the contention of the Appellant that the CBI could not investigate cases under the Act.

Filing a complaint is a *sine qua non* for all wildlife offences to ultimately land in Court. This is laid down under Section 55 of the Act, which provides that a Court shall not take cognisance of any offence committed against this Act except when a complaint is filed by the officers listed in the section. Thus, as per Section 55, the following persons can file a complaint under the Act for reporting a wildlife offence: the Director of Wildlife Preservation or any other officer authorised by the Central Government; the Member-Secretary of the Central Zoo Authority; the Member-Secretary of the Tiger Conservation Authority, or the Chief Wildlife Warden; or the Director of the concerned tiger reserve or any other officer authorised in this behalf by the State Government subject to such conditions as may be mentioned by that State Government; or the officer-in-charge of the zoo; or any person who has given notice of a minimum of 60 days, in the manner prescribed, of the alleged offence and of his intention to make a complaint, to the Central Government or State Government or an officer permitted under the Act.

If the officer filing the complaint is a Government servant, it is important to ensure that they are authorised to file the complaint either under the Act or by the Central Government or the concerned State Government. In several States, forest officers in the rank of range officers and above and police officers not below the rank of an Assistant Sub-Inspector of Police in charge of a police station have the authorisation to file complaints under the Act. As clarified by Section 55, Courts can take cognisance of the offence only on the basis of a complaint. A police charge sheet is not equivalent to a complaint, and the police cannot do away with the requirement of filing a complaint by directly filing a charge sheet.[220] The complaint should be filed within 60 days if the accused is in judicial custody. If there is more than one accused, the 60-day period will commence from the date of arrest of the first accused. When a complaint is filed by any of the officers authorised under the Act, it is treated as a complaint filed by a public servant acting in pursuance of the discharge of his official duties as provided under Section 200(a) of the Code of Criminal Procedure.[221]

The Act under Section 54 empowers the Director of Wildlife Preservation or any officer not below the rank of Assistant Director of Wildlife Preservation and, in the case of State Governments, the Chief Wildlife Warden or any officer not below the rank of Deputy Conservator of Forests to compound offences under the Act. Any person against whom a reasonable suspicion of having committed an offence

220 Samir Sinha, Handbook on Wildlife Law Enforcement in India 121 (TRAFFIC India, New Delhi, Natraj Publishers 2010).

221 A Handbook for Wildlife Crime Investigation Officers, *supra* note 189, at 35.

under this Act exists may approach one of the officers to compound the offence by payment of a sum of money. The sum of money paid to compound the offence shall not be more than five lakh rupees. Once the money has been paid, if the suspected offender is in custody, he shall be discharged, and no further proceedings shall be taken against him. The officer compounding the offence may on his own, or request any officer authorised to, cancel any licence or permit that may have been granted to the offender under the Act.[222] However, not all offences under the Act can be compounded. Any offence under the Act that has a minimum period of imprisonment prescribed under Section 51 of the Act cannot be compounded. Therefore, any offence involving wild animals listed in Schedule I is not compoundable.

Compounding an offence is not the same as conviction of the offender and hence when any offence has been compounded, the property seized from the offender has to be produced in court and the Chief Wildlife Warden of the concerned State has to be intimated. This issue came up for consideration before the Supreme Court in *Principal Chief Conservator of Forests v. J.K. Johnson.*[223] The question before the Supreme Court was whether the officers empowered under Section 54(1) of the Wildlife (Protection) Act, 1972, to compound offences also have the additional power to order the forfeiture of seized items. The Court held that any officer compounding any offence has no power, competence, or authority to order forfeiture of the property that has been seized in connection with the offence since compounding of any offence is not the same as conviction or admission of guilt. The officer compounding the offence is duty-bound to present the seized property before a Magistrate so that it is dealt with in accordance with the law. The Court ruled that the order passed by the Conservator of Forests of Nizamabad for forfeiting the vehicle of the accused persons and two rifles of foreign make fitted with telescopes to the State Government *dehors* the provisions of the Wildlife (Protection) Act, 1972, and hence, unsustainable.

Any case filed based on a complaint under Section 55 of the Act is tried as per the provisions of Sections 244 to 248 of the Code of Criminal Procedure. Thus, the provisions of the Code of Criminal Procedure apply to the investigation and trial of wildlife offences, unless something contrary has been specifically provided under the Wildlife (Protection) Act, 1972.

However, to uphold the interest of animals, Courts have taken an expansive view of the provisions and have even convicted offenders based on extra-judicial confessions. In *Sansar Chand v. State of Rajasthan,*[224] an appeal was filed before the apex court against the conviction order of the Appellant. The Appellant had a past record of such criminal activities, beginning with an arrest in 1974 for being in possession of 680 skins including leopards, tigers, and others. In the following years, the Appellant along with his gang established a complex, interlinking smuggling network to satisfy the demand for leopard and tiger skins and parts

222 The Wild Life (Protection) Act, 1972, §§ 54(2), 54(3) & 54(4).

223 Principal Chief Conservator of Forests v. J.K. Johnson, 2011 (10) SCC 794.

224 Sansar Chand v. State of Rajasthan, (2010) 10 SCC 604.

outside the Indian border. An appeal against the conviction of the Appellant was filed before the Court. Being a gang leader, the Appellant was infamously known for his criminal activities and had been found guilty in previous cases as well. In this case, upon an extra-judicial confession of one Balwan, who was caught with a carton containing a leopard's skin, the Appellant was tried and convicted. The counsel appearing on behalf of the Appellant submitted that the conviction was exclusively based on the extra-judicial confession of the co-accused and there was no corroborative material asserting the Appellant's guilt. The Court, differing from the Appellant's contention, stated that there was various evidence corroborating the Appellant's guilt. As the Appellant was a gang leader, although he always functioned from behind the scenes, he himself did not engage in poaching or hunting. Thus, finding direct evidence against him was, to some extent, unlikely. The Court, taking the history of his criminal activities into consideration, upheld the Appellant's conviction.

One of the long-standing cases of wildlife crimes that are yet to be resolved is the infamous case of actor Salman Khan, who was charged with poaching black bucks – a protected animal under the Wildlife (Protection) Act, also considered sacred by the Bishnoi community in Rajasthan – while shooting for one of his films in 1998. He was also charged under the Arms Act, 1959, for allegedly using illegal firearms. The case was instituted since a complaint lodged by the Bishnoi community before the Wildlife Conservator of Jodhpur. A case was registered under Sections 147, 148, 149, and 201 of the Indian Penal Code and Sections 9, 39, 51, and 52 of the Wildlife (Protection) Act, 1972.[225] Salman Khan along with other actors who were charged in this case applied for anticipatory bail which was granted. Two FIRs were lodged against the actor for killing two black bucks, one on 26 September 1998 and the other on 28 September 1998. For the alleged hunting that took place on 26 September 1998 pertaining to Criminal Case No. 207/1999, Salman Khan was convicted in February 2006 by the Chief Judicial Magistrate of Jodhpur under Section 51 of the Wildlife Protection Act and was punished with one year's simple imprisonment along with a fine of Rs. 5,000. The actor preferred to appeal against his conviction before the Sessions Judge which was later transferred to the High Court of Rajasthan as *State v. Salman Khan*.[226] In this case, the Court acquitted the actor of the charges under Section 51 of the Wildlife (Protection) Act, 1972, since the evidence adduced was found inadequate. The Court *inter alia* held that the place of incident was never recognised; no remains of the black buck were found to establish that it was killed on 26 September 1998, the Investigating Officer and the prosecution admitted that they were unable to conclude as to which weapon or knife was used for hunting, and there was no post mortem or medical report to prove whether a weapon or knife was used. Salman Khan was also acquitted under the Arms Act since the pellets recovered from the gypsy used by Salman Khan are

225 Satish Ravilal Shah v. State of Rajasthan, 1999 CriLJ 727.
226 State v. Salman Khan, S.B. C.A. No.53/2012.

used in air guns and not in firearms and it is impossible to hunt a big animal using the pellets recovered.

For the second criminal case[227] registered against the actor, he was convicted for five years for killing the second black buck on 28 September 1998 along with a fine of Rs. 25,000. An appeal was filed before the Sessions Court which was dismissed and another revision application against the conviction was filed before the High Court. The actor was ultimately acquitted in this case as well. In October 2016, a Special Leave Petition was filed by the Rajasthan Government on the ground that the Rajasthan High Court had erroneously exercised its revisional powers to set aside concurrent findings of the Chief Judicial Magistrate who had convicted him in both cases and the judgment suffered from legal infirmities since the High Court had turned down material evidence on hyper technical issues which were unsustainable. In November 2016, the Supreme Court admitted the appeal and issued notice to the actor. The actor was again convicted by the Chief Judicial Magistrate in April 2018 sentencing him to a term of five years. The actor again filed an appeal against this conviction before the District and Sessions Judge's Court and was also released on bail. The case is still pending, and there has been no definitive verdict so far.

3.2.3.1 Invasive Species

For the first time in the year 2022, a regulatory mechanism to deal with 'invasive alien species' has been inserted in the Act which defines 'any species of animal or plant which is not native to India and whose introduction or spread may threaten or adversely impact wildlife or its habitat'.[228] Several species of plants and animals found in a particular ecosystem have the potential to become invasive in another ecosystem within the nation. For instance, the hog deer, barking deer, and Asian elephant are all native to India and protected under the Act but are also designated as invasive alien species for island ecosystems in India by the National Biodiversity Authority. However, only non-native species are considered invasive as per the amended law; it fails to acknowledge ecosystem-based native species that can also be invasive.

3.3 Convention on International Trade in Endangered Species of Wild Fauna and Flora (CITES)

CITES is an international inter-governmental agreement that aims to ensure that international trade in specimens of wild animals and plants does not threaten their survival. It has its origin in the adoption of a resolution at a meeting of the members of the International Union for Conservation of Nature (IUCN) in the year 1963. The final draft of the Convention was agreed on 3 March 1973 and came into effect

227 Criminal Case No.206/1999.
228 The Wild Life (Protection) Act, 1972, § 62A.

on 1 July 1975. CITES is legally binding, and parties are required to implement the Convention; however, it does not replace the national or domestic laws. The parties are required to adopt the legal framework and procedural mechanism of the Convention to its domestic laws to ensure implementation. CITES is one of the few multilateral conventions on conservation that boasts of the highest number of members.[229]

The Convention works by imposing certain controls on the international trade of specific species of plants and animals. All species of fauna and flora listed under CITES are grouped under one of the three appendices of the Convention, depending on the degree of protection they require. The species are listed in decreasing order of threat. Approximately 5,600 animal species and 30,000 species of plants are protected under the three CITES appendices. International trade of CITES species is regulated by parties through a system of certificates and permits that are required before specimens listed in its appendices are exported, imported, or introduced from the sea[230] (or transportation into a State, specimens of any species which were taken in the marine environment not under the jurisdiction of any State) by the introduction of a system of licencing. To facilitate this process, the Convention needs State parties to designate one or more management authorities to administer the licencing system and one or more scientific authorities that advise the management authorities of the effects of trade on the status of the species.[231]

3.3.1 Structure of CITES

The two main bodies of the Convention are the CITES Secretariat[232] for administration and the Conference of the Parties[233] to make decisions. The management authorities and the scientific authorities also assist with CITES enforcement through cooperation with police, customs, and other appropriate agencies. Trade records are maintained by the parties that are forwarded annually to the CITES Secretariat, thus enabling the compilation of statistical information on the global volume of international trade in a species listed in the appendix. The functional body (SC) and two scientific committees, the Animals Committee (AC) and the Plant Committee (PC), also monitor the implementation of the Convention norms.

In *Union of India v. Zavaray S. Poonawala*,[234] the Respondent had hunted certain animals in Zambia with the permission of the Government of Zambia and

229 As of January 2022, CITES has 184 parties. *See*, Convention on International Trade in Endangered Species of Wild Fauna and Flora, *List of Parties to the Convention*, https://www.cites.org/eng/disc/parties/index.php.

230 Alice Miller et al., *Summary of the Twenty-Eighth Meeting of the CITES Animals Committee: 30 August - 3 September 2015*, 21(85) Earth Negotiations Bulletin 1 (2015).

231 Convention on International Trade in Endangered Species of Wild Fauna and Flora, Article IX, March 3, 1973, 993 UNTS 243. [hereinafter CITES].

232 CITES, art. XII.

233 CITES, art. IX.

234 Union of India v. Zavaray S. Poonawala, (2015) 7 SCC 347.

thereafter exported them to Zimbabwe for processing into items of taxidermy/hunting trophies. He wanted to bring one of the items, a trophy of a stuffed leopard, into India, which is a species in the protected and prohibited area under the Wildlife (Protection) Act, 1972, and CITES. In this case, Article IX of CITES, which deals with the functions of the management and scientific authorities was highlighted.

Article IX states that a permit of the scientific authority and management authority is necessary prior to the import of any specimen of species. However, the Court observed that the High Court erred in its judgment, by taking into regard only the management authority and overlooking the functions of the scientific authority. It is the scientific authority which determines whether the import will be unfavourable to the survival of the species involved. The Court, therefore, held that before the import of any specimen of species in Appendix I of CITES, a prior import permit of the scientific authority and management authority is required.

3.3.1.1 CITES Secretariat

The CITES Secretariat is in Geneva, Switzerland, and is administered by the United Nations Environment Programme. The coordinating and advisory function in the working of the Convention is carried out by the Secretariat. The Secretariat assists in communication and monitors the implementation of the Convention, arranges meetings of the Conference of Parties and the permanent Committees at regular intervals, assists the parties in the field of legislation, enforcement, science, and training, acts as the repository of all reports and other information submitted by the parties, issues new editions of the appendices and other information shared by the parties, and also makes recommendations regarding the implementation of the Convention.[235]

3.3.1.2 Conference of the Parties (CoP)

The first CoP was held in Bern, Switzerland, in November 1976, and the following CoPs have been held every two to three years. The latest CoP was held in Geneva, Switzerland, from 17 to 28 August 2019. The CoP meets to discuss and adopt proposals to amend the lists of species in Appendices I and II, and to review progress in the conservation of species included in the appendices. The CoP also considers proposals and recommendations from the Secretariat, State Parties, the Standing Committee, and the scientific committees. The CoP also recommends steps to improve the effectiveness of the functioning of the Secretariat and of the Convention. The list of resolutions and decisions, and the species listed in its appendices are also periodically reviewed by the CoP.[236]

235 CITES, art. XII.

236 *A Brief Introduction to the Convention on International Trade in Endangered Species of Wild Fauna and Flora*, International Institute of Sustainable Development, https://enb.iisd.org/process/biodiv_wildlife-citesintro.htm (last visited June 12, 2024).

3.3.1.3 Standing Committee

The primary task of the Standing Committee is to provide policy guidance to the Secretariat concerning the implementation of the Convention and to oversee the management of the Secretariat's budget. The work of other committees and working groups is also coordinated and overseen by the Standing Committee if a need arises for the same. To assist the CoP, the Standing Committee also carries out other tasks given to it by the CoP and also drafts resolutions for consideration by the CoP.[237]

3.3.1.4 Animals Committee and Plants Committee

The Animals and Plants Committees were formally introduced in the sixth Conference of the Parties meeting in Ottawa, Canada, in 1987. The Committees meet twice between the CoP meetings. Their main task is to provide biological and other specialised knowledge regarding trade controls in species of animals and plants. They provide scientific advice on the issue of the nomenclature of species and periodically review species to ensure a systematic categorisation of listed species in the appendices. Advising on unsustainable trade and suggesting remedial action through a mechanism called the 'Review of Significant Trade' is also one of the functions of the Animals Committee and Plants Committee.[238]

The Convention contains fundamental principles for strict regulation of all species. Species threatened with extinction whose trade is permitted only in exceptional circumstances are listed in Appendix I, all species not necessarily threatened with extinction but which may become extinct are contained in Appendix II, and all species which any State party identifies as being 'protected' and subject to regulation are contained in Appendix III.[239] In order to list a species in Appendix I or II, a party needs to submit a proposal for approval by the CoP, supported with scientifically and biologically backed data on trade trends and population. A two-thirds majority of parties present and voting must adopt the proposal. The CoP decides whether the species should be transferred or removed from the appendices relying upon the impact of trade on a species. Species may be added or removed under Appendices I and II only by the Conference of the Parties whereas species under Appendix III may be added or removed at any time, as each party is entitled to make unilateral amendments to it.[240]

For the export of listed species under Appendix I, it is mandatory to present the prior grant and presentation of an export permit, whereas a prior grant and presentation of an import permit and either an export permit or a re-export certificate are required for the import of such listed species. The re-export of such species requires prior presentation and grant of a re-export certificate. The introduction

237 *Id.*
238 *Id.*
239 CITES, art. II.
240 CITES, art. XV.

from the sea of such species requires the prior grant of a certificate from the management authority of the State of introduction.[241] Regulation of trade in listed species contained in Appendix II[242] is substantially like the regulation given under Article III. Permits or certificates for any trade of listed species shall be granted as per the provisions of Article VI. There are several exemptions and special provisions relating to trade in any listed species.[243] The Secretariat has the power to undertake international measures if it is satisfied that any listed species included in Appendix I is adversely affected or the provisions of the Convention are not being implemented.[244]

3.3.2 India's Role in the Implementation of CITES

CITES was ratified by India in 1976. India had the honour of hosting the third meeting of the Conference of the Parties held in New Delhi, in 1981, where the CITES logo was designed and unanimously adopted by the parties. After this meeting, endangered species like the great Indian rhinoceros and the Asiatic lion were added to Schedule I of the Wildlife (Protection) Act, 1972, by the Wildlife (Protection) Amendment Act, 1982, to provide effective control and protection in trade. General control and regulation on the export of animal and plant products were introduced as a result of the amendment.[245]

3.4 Legal Framework for International Trade in Fauna and Flora in India

International trade in animal and plant species is regulated through the joint operation of the provisions of the Foreign Trade (Development Regulation) Act, 1992, the Foreign Trade Policy of Government of India and Customs Act, 1962, and the Wildlife (Protection) Act, 1972.

Under Section 9 of the Wildlife (Protection) Act, 1972, the hunting of wild animals specified in Schedules I and II is prohibited except as provided under Sections 11 and 12 of the Act. Trade in every kind of imported ivory such as that of the African elephant is prohibited; however, the export or import of animal species for purposes of scientific research is allowed. The exchange of animals between zoos is allowed subject to the licence granted by the Director-General of Foreign Trade (DGFT), Government of India.

The Imports and Exports (Control) Act, 1947, was repealed by the Foreign Trade (Development and Regulation) Act, 1992, by the Central Government. The main objective of the current Act was to develop and regulate foreign trade by

241 CITES, art. III.
242 CITES, art. IV.
243 CITES, art. VII.
244 CITES, art. XIII.
245 Pushp Jain, *CITES & India,* Traffic (Apr. 2001), https://www.traffic.org/site/assets/files/10042/cites-india.pdf.

facilitating imports and augmenting exports, whereas the repealed Act was to prohibit and control imports and exports.[246] Section 3(1) of the Act empowers the Central Government to make provisions for the development and regulation of foreign trade. Subsection (2) of Section 3 makes provision for prohibiting, restricting, or regulating the export or import of goods by an order published in the official gazette by the Central Government. The Ministry of Commerce periodically announces the Foreign Trade Policy regarding the import or export of wildlife and its products. It also includes the conditions for compliance with CITES. The management authority for CITES in India is consulted on matters relating to animal and plant species for the final decision on policy. All the animal and plant species covered in the import and export policy (EXIM Policy) will be deemed to be covered under Section 11 of the Customs Act, 1962.[247]

The 2022 amendment has added Chapter VB dealing with the regulation of international trade of endangered species of wild fauna and flora as per CITES, along with Schedule IV (containing Appendix I, II, and III of CITES). The Additional Director-General of Forests has been designated as the management authority for CITES under Section 49E. This chapter also establishes a scientific authority (one or more institutions engaged in research on species) under Section 49F. The former is concerned with the issuance of permits and certificates for the trade of scheduled specimens in accordance with the Convention and with the submission of reports, and shall perform such other functions as may be necessary to implement the provisions of the Convention. The latter, on the other hand, is an advisory body charged with advising the management authority in such matters as may be referred to it. It advises the management authority to limit the grant of export permit for a species, which, in the authority's opinion, is necessary for maintaining its level corresponding to its role in the ecosystem and above the level under which it will fall into Appendix I of CITES (containing the most endangered animals and plants).

As per Section 49-I(1), the export of any specimen of species included in Appendices I or II of Schedule IV shall require the prior grant and presentation of an export permit. The export of any specimen of species included in Appendix III of Schedule IV shall require the prior grant and presentation of an export permit if the species has been listed in Appendix III of the Convention by India or a certificate of origin in other cases.[248] Grant for such an export permit shall be given by the management authority only if it is satisfied that such specimens were not obtained through the violation of any laws in place for their protection and shipping will be done minimising the risk of injury, damage to health, or cruel treatment.[249] In the case of specimens falling under Appendices I or II of Schedule IV, the scientific

246 Indian Institute of Chartered Accountants of India, Handbook on Foreign Trade Policy and Guide to Export & Import 13 (2008).

247 The Foreign Trade (Development and Regulation) Act, 1992, §3(3).

248 The Wild Life (Protection) Act, 1972, §49-I(2).

249 *Id.* §49I(3).

authority must have advised the management authority that the export will not adversely affect the survival of that species.

The import of any specimen of a species included in Appendix I of Schedule IV shall require the prior grant and presentation of an import permit and either an export permit or a re-export certificate from the country of export.[250] Conditions are attached to the grant of this import permit as well. It is subject to the satisfaction of the management authority regarding the purpose for which it is primarily used and the capability of the importer of a living specimen to provide it housing and care among other considerations.[251]

The import of any specimen of a species included in Appendix II of Schedule IV shall require the prior presentation of either an export permit or a re-export certificate issued by the country of export. The import of any specimen of a species included in Appendix III of Schedule IV shall require the prior presentation of: (a) a certificate of origin; or (b) in cases where the import is from a country which has included the species in Appendix III of the Convention, an export permit; or (c) a re-export certificate granted by the country of re-export.[252]

Section 49R clarifies that where the same species is listed in Schedules I or II and Schedule IV, then the provisions of this Act applicable to such species listed in Schedules I or II and the rules made thereunder shall apply. Further, the provisions of this chapter shall be subject to the provisions of Chapters III, IIIA, IVA, V, VA, and VIA and without prejudice to anything contained therein.

The Breeders of Species Licence Rules, 2023, issued under Sections 49N(2) and 49(O) provides for the process of licence for specimens under Appendix 1.[253] It provides for a fee of 25,000 rupees to be paid for obtaining the licence.[254] It also grants power to the Chief Wildlife Warden to cancel the licence,[255] appeals to which lie with the State Government.[256]

For CITES-related enforcement in the country, the Wildlife Crime Control Bureau is designated as the nodal agency.[257] The objective is to conserve wildlife wealth by proper and effective intervention in matters related to the capacity building of enforcement agencies in the field of wildlife crime enforcement and deter organised wildlife crime nexus.[258] Section 38(Z) of the Wildlife (Protection) Act makes it obligatory for the WCCB to assist foreign authorities and international organisations to facilitate coordination and universal action for the control of wildlife crime, to assist State Governments in prosecutions of wildlife crimes

250 The Wild Life (Protection) Act, §49J(1).

251 *Id.* at §49J(2).

252 *Id.* at §49J.

253 Breeders of Species Licence Rules, 2023.

254 *Id.* at Rule 4.

255 *Id.* at, Rule 8.

256 *Id.* at Rule 10.

257 Wildlife Crime Control Bureau, http://wccb.gov.in/WriteReadData/userfiles/file/Trade%20Facilitation/Legal%20framework%20ITC%20HS(1).pdf.

258 Wildlife Crime Control Bureau, http://wccb.gov.in/Content/VisionMission.aspx.

and advise the Government of India in matters relating to national and international wildlife crimes, to suggest relevant policy and law, and to assist the custom authorities in the inspection of animal and plant consignments, etc.[259]

The import or export of derivatives of animal and plant species in India is subject to the pre-/post-shipment inspection of export/import consignment by the CITES assistant management authority. This includes the inspection and examination of plant and animal species by the regional offices of the WCCB, designated as CITES assistant management authorities. The customs authorities are assisted and advised by these offices in the inspection of consignment, either by going to the port of entry and exit or by examining sealed samples forwarded by the customs authorities to their offices. The consignment may be imported or exported after the assistant management authorities issue a no objection certificate in favour of the importer or exporter if it is found that the species are not included within the Wildlife (Protection) Act and/or in the CITES Appendices after the inspection.[260]

3.5 Prevention of Cruelty to Animals Act, 1960

The discussion around animals would be incomplete if no reference is made to the Prevention of Cruelty to Animals Act, 1960 (PCA, 1960). This PCA, 1960, pre-dates the Wildlife (Protection) Act of 1972 and repeals those provisions of the erstwhile Prevention of Cruelty to Animals Act, 1890, that correspond to the provisions of the 1960 Act.[261] The Prevention of Cruelty to Animals Act, 1960, aims at balancing human needs with cruelty towards animals. One of the underlying purposes that the legislation seeks to serve is to give a charter of rights to animals and a charter of duties to human beings. The PCA, 1960, also applies to both domestic and captive animals. The idea of ownership of animals continues to pervade this Act and persons in charge or having the care of animals are required to ensure their well-being and prevent unnecessary pain or suffering. It is, however, worth noting that the duty of care towards animals is not restricted to their 'owners'. Owner has been defined to include not only the owners of the animals but any person having the possession or custody of the animal whether with or without the consent of the owner.[262]

259 Ministry of Environment, Forest and Climate Change, *'Not All Animals Migrate by Choice' Campaign Launched to Raise Awareness on Illegal Wildlife Trade*, Press Information Bureau (May 20, 2019), https://pib.gov.in/newsite/PrintRelease.aspx?relid=190050.

260 *Legal Framework for International Trade in Fauna & Flora*, Wildlife Crime Control Bureau, http://wccb.gov.in/WriteReadData/userfiles/file/Trade%20Facilitation/Legal%20framework%20ITC%20HS(1).pdf.

261 The Prevention of Cruelty to Animals Act, 1960, §41.

262 *Id.* §2(f).

3.5.1 Animal Welfare Board of India

The Prevention of Cruelty to Animals Act for the very first time provided for the establishment of a statutory body to promote the welfare of animals in the country. The Animal Welfare Board of India established in 1962 under Section 4 of the PCA, 1960, functions under the aegis of the Department of Animal Husbandry, Dairying and Fisheries under the Ministry of Fisheries, Animal Husbandry and Dairying and comprises 28 members. The Inspector General of Forests, Government of India, and the Animal Husbandry Commissioner to the Government of India are its ex-officio members, while the other members are either nominated or appointed in the manner prescribed under the PCA, 1960.[263]

The Board is authorised to keep a close watch on animal-related laws in the country and to advise the Government on making rules and amendments, in conformity with the objectives of the PCA, 1960. It can advise the Government to frame rules to ensure that unnecessary pain and suffering is not inflicted on animals in general especially when they are being moved, when they are kept in captivity or confinement, or when they are being utilised as performance animals. The Board can provide advice to the Government, local authorities, and other parties regarding ways to enhance vehicle designs to reduce the strain on draught animals employed for tasks like ploughing, hauling loads, and other tasks with the least amount of injury possible. The Board can encourage or provide for the construction of sheds, water troughs, rescue homes, animal shelters, sanctuaries, and veterinary assistance for animals, and give financial and other assistance to animal hospitals. The PCA, 1960, does not prohibit the killing of animals. However, it prescribes measures to be adopted for the maintenance and design of slaughterhouses and animals in such slaughterhouses to ensure that the animals are killed in a humane manner and their pain and suffering are alleviated in the pre-slaughter stages. The Board may also take steps to ensure that unwanted animals are destroyed by local authorities, when necessary, either instantly or after rendering them senseless to pain and suffering.[264]

One of the primary functions of the Board is to grant recognition to animal welfare organisations and to give financial and other assistance to such organisations. As per the Guidelines framed by the Board, to get recognition, animal welfare organisations are required to submit a registration certificate under the Societies Registration Act or the Trust Act, along with an audited statement of accounts in addition to annual reports of the previous three years, an animal welfare activities report, and copies of Memorandum of Association/Bye Laws.[265] In addition to these documents, a representative of the Animal Welfare Board has to be nominated on the managing or executive committee of the welfare association seeking recognition, so as to facilitate regular inspection of its functioning. Organisations are considered for the grant of recognition only if the inspection reports are found

263 The Prevention of Cruelty to Animals Act, 1960, §5.

264 *Id.* §9.

265 Animal Welfare Board of India, https://awbi.gov.in/view/index/recognition.

to be satisfactory. Organisations seeking financial assistance from the Board must file applications in the prescribed format to the Animal Welfare Board for the sanction of grants which may be provided under different schemes such as regular grants, cattle rescue grants, financial assistance for setting up shelter homes for animals, animal birth control programmes, ambulance for animals in distress, and natural calamity grants.[266]

3.5.2 Cruelty against Animals

Chapter III, taking a general view, elaborates on various penalties associated with treating animals with cruelty. This chapter lists several acts under Section 11 that are tantamount to cruelty against animals. According to the PCA, 1960, cruelty includes beating, kicking, over-riding, over-driving, torturing, or treating any animal in any other form which inflicts upon the animal unnecessary pain or suffering; employing any animal in a laborious task which by reason of its age, disease, or infirmity is unfit to be so employed; wilfully and unreasonably administering any injurious drug or substance; conveying or carrying an animal in any vehicle so as to subject it to unnecessary pain or suffering; keeping or confining any animal in a cage that does not afford it ample room for movement; keeping any animal chained or tethered for an unreasonable time through an unreasonably short or heavy chain or cord; abandoning any animal without reasonable cause under circumstances when it would be likely to suffer starvation or thirst; offering for sale any animal that is suffering from starvation, thirst, mutilation, overcrowding, or other ill treatment; killing or mutilating any animal by using strychnine injections in the heart or in any other unnecessarily cruel manner; or keeping or using any place for conducting animal fights or baiting any animal for money for the admission of any person to any place used for such purposes; or promoting or being a part of any shooting match or competition wherein animals are released from captivity for fulfilling the purpose of such shooting.

Section 11 lists certain acts that amount to cruelty when specifically committed by the owner of an animal. If any person being the owner neglects to reasonably exercise any dog that is habitually chained or kept in confinement; or fails to provide any animal with sufficient food, drink, or shelter; or permits any animal to be beaten, kicked, overridden, overdriven, or tortured; or permits any diseased, infirm, or aged animal that is unfit to be engaged in any laborious task, such acts would amount to cruelty. However, the owner would be held guilty of committing an offence only if he has failed to exercise reasonable care and supervision with a view to prevent offence. But, if the owner is convicted for failure of exercising care and supervision, he would not be liable for imprisonment without the option of a fine.[267] Cruelty also covers acts committed against animals for the sole purpose of providing entertainment, such as confining any animal to make it bait for

266 Animal Welfare Board of India, https://awbi.gov.in/view/index/Mandate-and-Functions.
267 The Prevention of Cruelty to Animals Act, 1960, §11(2).

other animals or tying an animal as bait in a tiger or other sanctuary; or inciting any animal to fight or bait any other animal.[268] However, Section 11(3) lays down certain exceptions to cruelty. The dehorning of cattle, castration, etc., of animals in the prescribed manner, destruction of stray dogs in lethal chambers, or extermination of any animal, etc., would not amount to cruelty, when done in the prescribed manner or under the authority of any law for the time being in force.

Persons including owners guilty of committing any of the offences listed under Section 11 of the PCA, 1960, would in case of the first offence be liable to pay a fine which shall not be less than 10 rupees and may extend to 50 rupees. If a subsequent offence is committed within three years of the previous offence, then the person would be liable to pay a fine of not less than 25 rupees which may extend to 100 rupees or may be imprisoned for a term which may extend to three months or with both. Section 12 of the PCA, 1960, penalises the administration of any drugs or performance of any operation on any milch animal to improve lactation which is injurious to the health of the animal. Any person who permits these actions to be committed on animals under his control or in his possession shall be penalised with a fine which may also extend to 1,000 rupees or with imprisonment for a term which may extend to two years, or both when convicted. Further, the Government shall take possession of the animals on which the operations have been conducted. This is a cognisable offence and the person charged with the offence may be arrested by the police without a warrant.[269]

3.5.3 Experimentation on Animals

Taking into consideration the frequency of experimentation on animals, Section 14 of the PCA, 1960, leaves experimentation on animals out of the purview of cruelty, only for the purpose of advancement by new discovery of physiological knowledge or of knowledge which shall be useful for prolonging or saving life or alleviating or combating suffering and diseases of human beings, animals, or plants. In pursuance of this, the Central Government on the advice of the Animal Welfare Board of India constituted a Committee for the Purpose of Control and Supervision of Experiments on Animals (CPCSEA) with 15 members and one Member-Secretary for the first time in 1995.[270] Since then, the Committee has been reconstituted several times and the latest reconstitution was in the year 2018.[271] Presently, the Committee, which has a term of 3 years, comprises 20 members with the Special Secretary/Additional Secretary in charge of Animal Welfare of the Ministry of Environment, Forest and Climate Change serving as its Chairman.[272]

268 The Prevention of Cruelty to Animals Act, 1960, §11(1)(m).

269 *Id.* §31.

270 *Id.* §15.

271 Ministry of Environment, Forest and Climate Change, Government of India, S.O. 2412(E), Notification (June 12, 2018).

272 *Id.*

The duties and powers of the Committee as enunciated under Section 17 of the PCA, 1960, are to ensure that no unnecessary pain or suffering is inflicted upon the animals before, during, or after the experiment in the conduct of such experiments. For that purpose, the Committee has the authority to make such rules as it deems fit and has the power of entry and inspection of any place or institution where experiments on animals are being conducted to ensure that the rules devised by it are complied with, as laid down under Section 18. Some of the basic functions of the Committee include selection and assignment of nominees for the Institutional Animal Ethics Committees of the registered establishments; registration of establishments that are eligible to conduct animal experimentation or breeding of animals for the purpose of experimentation; approval of animal house facilities based on reports of inspection; granting permissions for conducting experiments involving animals; providing recommendations to the Government for the import of animals for use in experiments; initiating action against establishments if any legal norm or stipulation is violated or breached; training the nominees of the Committee; and conducting or supporting conferences or workshops on animal ethics.[273] In pursuance of the powers conferred by the PCA, 1960, the Committee formulated the Breeding of and Experiments on Animals (Control and Supervision) Rules, 1998, to regulate the experimentation on animals. The Rules, last amended in 2006, define 'experiment' to mean any programme or project involving the use of animal(s) for the acquisition of knowledge of a biological, physiological, ethological, physical, or chemical nature, including the use of animal(s) in the production of reagents and products such as antigens and antibodies, routine diagnostics, testing activity, and establishment of transgenic stocks, for the purpose of saving or prolonging life or alleviating suffering or significant gains in well-being for people of the country or for combating any disease whether of human beings or animals.[274]

The Breeding of and Experiments on Animals (Control and Supervision) Rules, 1998, also allow breeding or trade of animals for the purpose of experiments, provided the establishments are registered with the Committee.[275] As per the Rules, every establishment engaged in experiments with animals must have an Institutional Animals Ethics Committee[276] to control and supervise experiments on animals performed in the establishment which is constituted and operated in accordance with the directions issued by the Committee. The Rules also prescribe conditions under which experiments on animals shall be conducted. As per the Rules, experiments must be performed by or under the supervision of a duly qualified person with a degree or diploma in veterinary science or medicine or laboratory animal science from a university or an institution recognised by the Government; animals intended for the performance of experiments are properly looked after both before and after

273 *Functions of CPCSEA*, Committee for the Purpose of Control and Supervision on Experimentation of Animals, https://ccsea.gov.in/WriteReadData/userfiles/file/ROLE%20AND%20RESPONSIBILITIES%20OF%20NOMINEES%20OF%20CPCSEA%20-1-.pdf.

274 Breeding of and Experiments on Animals (Control and Supervision) Rules, 1998, Rule 2(e).

275 *Id.* Rule 3.

276 *Id.* Rule 13.

experiments; if animals suffer during the course of the experiments and their recovery could be painful or if any animal suffers during the course of the experiment and they suffer abnormal or severe pain, they shall be painlessly and humanely destroyed; experiments shall not be performed by way of illustrations and public demonstrations and never performed for obtaining or retaining manual skill except in schools, colleges, and recognised training institutions.[277]

The Rules do not prescribe any penalty, but the Committee has the power to suspend the registration of any establishment or breeder or Institutional Animals Ethics Committee for a specified period or indefinitely, if on inspection it is found that the Rules are not being complied with. This would be done after giving the concerned party a reasonable opportunity of being heard.[278] In addition to these Rules, Section 19 of the PCA, 1960, empowers the Committee to prohibit experiments on animals, if it is satisfied upon inspection that the Rules laid down under Section 17 are not followed, and also to impose penalties if the order made under Section 19 is contravened. According to Section 20, the person shall be punished with a fine which may even extend to 200 rupees, and when any contravention and breach of conditions takes place within an institution, the person in charge of such an institution shall be held guilty of the offence and shall also be punished accordingly.

Irrespective of the worldwide campaigns, protests, and efforts taken by animal rights activists, associations, and organisations to kerb the use of animals in research, an estimated 192.1 million animals were used in scientific research globally, as reflected by a study conducted in 2015.[279] The absence of non-animal models or technologies that effectively convert pharmacology and toxicology data to humans can be attributed as one of the primary reasons for the lack of decline in animal experiments. While experiments on animals to check the efficacy of drugs especially before the same are administered to humans in clinical trials have been in practice for a long time, India has become the latest nation to explore more viable alternatives to animal testing. In addition to ethical concerns, another reason for this shift has been the failure of animal models to translate into successful clinical outcomes for human diseases with a failure rate of over 90% between nomination for phase I of clinical trials and the final approval of new drugs. Even after two decades of drug-discovery research using animals, not even a single new drug has been discovered in India that has made it to the market, partly because drugs that have proved to be efficacious for animals were later found to be toxic or ineffective in humans. This has led the scientific community to explore non-animal-based technologies for drug testing and trials. In 2017, the Indian Council of Medical Research set up a committee to explore alternatives to animal testing.[280]

277 Breeding of and Experiments on Animals (Control and Supervision) Rules, 1998, Rule 9 (India).

278 *Id.* Rule 14(a).

279 Katy Taylor & Laura Rego Alvarez, *An Estimate of the Number of Animals Used for Scientific Purposes Worldwide, 2015*, 47 Atla Altern Lab Anim 196–213 (2019).

280 S. Swaminathan et al., *Need for Alternatives to Animals in Experimentation: An Indian Perspective*, 149 Indian J Med Res 584 (2019).

3.5.4 Performing Animals

Chapter V of the PCA, 1960, lays down rules concerning performing animals and the training of animals for exhibitions. Section 22 states that unless a person is registered in accordance with the provisions of the PCA, 1960, and the Rules framed thereunder, any performing animal cannot be trained or exhibited by him. Also, an animal, which according to a notification in the Official Gazette should not be trained or exhibited as a performing animal, cannot be trained or exhibited as such. In a notification issued by the Ministry of Social Justice and Empowerment in October 1998, in exercise of the powers under Section 22 of the PCA, 1960, the exhibition or training as performing animals of bears, monkeys, tigers, panthers, and lions was prohibited.[281] Subsequently, a notification issued by the Ministry of Environment and Forest in July 2011 included 'bulls' in the category of animals that cannot be exhibited or trained as performing animals.[282] Section 24 of the PCA, 1960, authorises the court to prohibit or curtail the exhibition and training of any performing animals if it is established before the Magistrate that the training and exhibition of the performing animal includes inflicting unnecessary pain or suffering to the animals and should be prohibited or restricted or should be allowed only subject to certain conditions. Section 25 empowers police officers and other authorised persons to enter and inspect the premises, at all reasonable times, in which any performing animals are being trained or kept for training and exhibition.

Section 26 of the PCA, 1960, lays down the offences associated with performing animals. Training or exhibiting any performing animal, without being registered; training any performing animal or a manner of training it, in respect of which he is not registered; wilfully delaying or obstructing a police officer in the discharge of his duties with respect to inspection; and concealing any animal with a view to avoid such inspection, etc., result in offences. The person charged with such an offence and found guilty would be punished following conviction, with a fine of up to 500 rupees, a maximum sentence of three months in jail, or both . However, training any animal for military or for police purposes and exhibiting the animal trained, and keeping animals in zoological gardens or by any society for scientific and educational purposes are exceptions to offences under Chapter V of the PCA, 1960.

The Central Government has enacted the Performing Animals Rules, 1973, and the Performing Animals (Registration) Rules 2001. These Rules define 'performing animals' as animals used at, or for the purpose of any entertainment to which people are admitted through the sale of tickets.[283] The 2001 Rules extend the definition of performing animals to include those animals used for entertainment including a film or an equine event, which is an event related to horses.[284] These Rules lay down the requirements that must be fulfilled before any animal can be used

281 Ministry of Social Justice and Empowerment, GSR 619 (E), Notification (Oct. 14, 1998).

282 Ministry of Environment & Forests, GSR 528E, Notification (July 11, 2011).

283 Performing Animals Rules, 1973, Rule 2(b).

284 Performing Animals (Registration) Rules, 2001, Rule 2(h).

as a performing animal. An application for registration has to be made before the Animal Welfare Board of India or an officer authorised by the Board as stipulated under Rule 3. The general conditions for registration that the prescribed authority may impose while granting registration have been laid down under Rule 8, which include, *inter alia*, conditions such as the requirements of having a veterinarian as a regular employee for any person with ten or more performing animals; not transporting any animal by road continuously for more than eight hours except in cages of dimensions stipulated by the Rules; ensuring that no unnecessary pain or suffering is inflicted on any animal before, after, or during transportation; not depriving the animal of food or water in order to compel the animal to train or perform any trick; not keeping any animal, including horses, near shooting scenes involving explosives or loud noises, or props such as spears, nails splinters, barbed wires that may cause injury to the animal during performance, etc. Before any animal is used for any performance in a film, prior information has to be given by the owner of such animal to the Board or an authorised officer giving details about the kind of animal, its age and physical health, the nature of performance, the duration of performance, the duration and method of training for such performance, and the justification for the use of such animal in addition to any other information that the authority may seek. Every such intimation or application by the owner must be accompanied by a fitness certificate certifying the health and fitness of the animal issued by a veterinary doctor along with an ownership certificate if the animal is covered under the Wildlife (Protection) Act, 1972.[285]

The treatment and care of animals has been given a special place in the Act of 1960. Section 35, specifically dealing with this, allows the State Government to arrange infirmaries for the treatment and care of animals against which offences under this Act have been committed. Even during the pendency of a case, the Magistrate can direct that the animal concerned be taken to the infirmary for treatment and care. Except on orders of the Magistrate for the destruction of the animal or transfer to *pinjrapole*, the animal in the infirmary can only be released after attaining a certificate of its fitness for discharge issued by the veterinary officer.

3.5.5 Rules under the Prevention of Cruelty Act, 1960

The Act under Section 38 has empowered the Central Government to frame rules to fulfil the objectives of the Act and in pursuance of this, a plethora of rules have been framed that address several issues that concern the welfare of animals.

3.5.5.1 The Prevention of Cruelty to Draught and Pack Animals Rules, 1965

These Rules prescribe the maximum weight that is allowed for animals or animal-drawn vehicles to carry, the maximum load permitted on pack animals, and the maximum number of passengers for animal-drawn vehicles. The Rules also

285 Prevention of Cruelty to Draught and Pack Animals Rules, 1965, Rule 7.

suggest some general conditions for the use of pack and draught animals. They lay down that draught animals cannot be used for drawing any vehicle or carrying any kind of load for more than nine hours a day in the aggregate; in any area where the temperature exceeds 37 degrees Celsius during the period between 12.00 noon and 3.00 PM; or for more than five hours continuously without a break.[286] Animals must be disengaged from their harnesses after work and the use of spikes or any sharp object that is likely to cause severe pain to the animal is prohibited. The Rules also prescribe the manner in which animals are to be saddled.

3.5.5.2 The Prevention of Cruelty to Animals (Slaughter House) Amendment Rules, 2010

These Rules seek to monitor and regulate slaughterhouses, to ensure that animals are killed for meat in ways that cause them the least pain and discomfort. A slaughterhouse can operate, provided it is licenced or recognised under a Central, State, or Provincial Act or any rules or regulations and has ten or more than ten animals slaughtered in it per day.[287] The Rules prohibit the slaughtering of pregnant animals, animals with offspring that are less than three months old, any animal that is less than three months old, or any animal that has not been certified fit by a veterinary doctor.[288] The Rules also stipulate the other requirements of a slaughterhouse, which include a reception, the dimensions of the lair where the animals rest before the slaughter, the conditions under which the slaughtering would be done, and other requirements that have to be met such as slaughtering areas, washing facilities, etc.

These rules are supplemented and supported by the Food Safety and Standards Act of 2006 and rules framed by the Food Safety and Standards Authority of India, as well as the applicable municipal rules. Slaughterhouses often require licences from FSSAI and no objection certificates from local authorities to function and are often inspected by officers of the FSSAI, in addition to inspections carried out by the Animal Welfare Board of India or any person or any animal welfare organisation.

3.5.5.3 The Prevention of Cruelty to Animals (Dog Breeding and Marketing) Rules, 2017

This Rule prohibits the breeding of dogs without registration. Rule 8 elaborates on the conditions which must be met for sale. It states that pups less than eight weeks in age must not be sold, and dogs over six months shall not be sold without being sterilised first. It further states that dogs and pups cannot be sold for experimentation and only those dogs that are in good health and provided with medical

286 Prevention of Cruelty to Draught and Pack Animals Rules, 1965, Rule 6.
287 Prevention of Cruelty to Animals (Slaughter House) Amendment Rules, 2001, Rule 2(c).
288 *Id.* Rule 3(2).

inoculations should be sold. According to Rule 11 of the Act, reports must be furnished by the breeders to the State Animal Welfare Board, set up by the State Government. Furthermore, Part I of the Second Schedule of the Rule lays down the care and upkeep dogs should be provided with.

3.5.5.4 Prevention of Cruelty to Animals (Pet Shop) Rules of 2018

The enactment of the Prevention of Cruelty to Animals (Pet Shop) Rules of 2018 is an attempt to ensure that pet animals are being looked after in shops. It defines 'pet animals' to include dogs, rabbits, cats, guinea pigs, hamsters, rodents of the rat or mice category, pet birds, and such other types of animals, the ownership of and trade in which is not prohibited by any other law, rules, or regulations.[289] Rule 6 deals with accommodation, infrastructure, and housing. It states that a pet shop must be situated within a permanent structure, with adequate arrangements for basic amenities. Other than laying down rules for infrastructure and accommodation, the Rules prescribe that the animals for sale must be displayed or housed at all instances in an environment suitable to their species in terms of situation, temperature, ventilation, lighting, and cleanliness.[290] Sufficient food according to dietary requirements and the age of the pets must be provided to them, along with clean drinking water. Maintenance of records of breeders and suppliers of pet animals intended for sale and other details, as per Rule 8, is an essential that must be fulfilled.

3.5.5.5 Animal Birth Control Rules, 2023

The Animal Birth Control Rules, 2023,[291] were issued to find a more humane way of handling the growing issue of street dog menace in the country. As per the State of Pet Homelessness Index of 2021, India is home to 62 million stray dogs.[292] The stray dog population in India comprises dogs that were born in the streets and also dogs that were previously kept as pet dogs but eventually abandoned by owners in the streets. Huge stray populations caused by a lack of or improper birth control methods have been a source of concern as stray dog attacks have consistently grown over the years.[293] As per the World Health Organization, India accounts for nearly 60% of the rabies deaths mediated through dogs in Asia[294] and 36% of

289 Prevention of Cruelty to Animals (Pet Shop) Rules, 2018, Rule 2(j).

290 *Id.* Rule 7.

291 Animal Birth Control Rules, 2023.

292 *Index Results – India*, State of Pet Homelessness Index, https://cms.stateofpethomelessness.com/s3media/2023-07/State%20of%20Pet%20Homelessness%20Index%20-%20Market%20factsheet%20India.pdf?VersionId=Z4tejwm4NZB29orB2UGgSdDZDX3a45wF.

293 Rhea Mogul & Sania FarooquI, *The Fatal Mauling of 4-Year-Old Forces India to Grapple with Stray Dog Problem*, CNN World (Apr. 1, 2023), https://edition.cnn.com/2023/04/01/india/india-stray-dog-attack-debate-intl-hnk/index.html.

294 *Control of Neglected Tropical Diseases*, World Health Organization, https://www.who.int/teams/control-of-neglected-tropical-diseases/rabies/epidemiology-and-burden (last visited June 12, 2024).

global rabies deaths happen in India.[295] Rabies is a deadly virus that is transmitted to humans mostly through stray dog bites. The mortality rate of rabies is close to 100%; however, it can be prevented by vaccinations. Methods adopted to address the population explosion have been far from preferable in many cases including mass culling of stray dogs. Conflicts have also arisen between individuals or groups that feed street dogs in residential areas and other members of the resident's associations or communities. In certain cases, some associations have banned the feeding of strays.[296]

In *Animal Welfare Board of India v. People for Elimination of Stray Troubles*,[297] it was brought to the notice of the Supreme Court that grave cruelties were being meted out to stray dogs with committees, organisations, and clubs being formed to kill stray dogs and training imparted to children to eliminate stray dogs since stray dogs had attacked women and children. The Court condemned such acts and called upon the organisations to stop imparting such training to the children, distributing subsidised air-guns for people to kill stray dogs, publicly propagating hatred towards stray dogs, and urging people to strangulate them or offering prizes or incentives to exterminate the stray dogs. In light of this, the Court directed that stray dogs can only be culled as per the provisions of the relevant Act and Rules.

The 2023 Rules are issued in suppression of the 2001 Rules which gave directions for the capturing, sterilisation, immunisation, and release of street dogs. The 2023 Rules mandate that an 'Animal Birth Control Program' (ABC Program) has to be put in place by local authorities.[298] In the case of pet dogs, the owners are responsible for ensuring deworming, immunisation, and sterilization of them and in the case of street dogs, the responsibility falls on the local authority.[299] A Monitoring Committee shall be constituted for the effective implementation of the ABC Program, rabies eradication, and reduction of human-animal conflicts.[300] The Rules also chart out the procedure for capturing, sterilising, and releasing street dogs.[301] The team set out to capture dogs shall have two or more employees of the local authority or animal welfare organisation who are trained in the humane capturing of street dogs. Sufficient announcements shall be given to the residents nearby prior to the capturing including that they will be released into the same area after the procedure is done.[302]

295 World Health Organization, *Rabies in India*, https://www.who.int/india/health-topics/rabies (last visited June 12, 2024).

296 Bharat A. Patel, *Jalahalli Residents' Society in Soup over Ban on Feeding Strays*, Bangalore Mirror (Jul. 19, 2016), https://bangaloremirror.indiatimes.com/bangalore/others/jalahalli-residents-society-in-soup-over-ban-on-feeding-strays/articleshow/53273083.cms.

297 Animal Welfare Board of India v. People forfor the Elimination of Stray Troubles, Special Leave to Appeal (C) 691/2009 clubbed with other SLPs and petitions decided on 17.11.2016.

298 Animal Birth Control Rules, 2023, rule 3(1).

299 *Id.* rule 8.

300 *Id.* rule 9.

301 *Id.* rule 11.

302 *Id.* rule 11(3).

The Rules direct resident welfare associations or apartment owner associations to work with the individuals who intend to or are feeding stray animals in such areas to make necessary arrangements for safe and proper feeding.[303] Special areas for feeding have to be designated keeping in mind the size of the dog population and the territorial nature of the animal. Such areas shall not be close to play areas for children, entrances or exits to the apartments or building, or areas frequented by children and senior citizens.[304] The designated feeder shall also ensure that there is no littering in the area. In case of a conflict regarding this, an Animal Welfare Committee constituted for this purpose shall take a decision on it and such decision shall be final.

3.5.5.6 Prevention of Cruelty to Animals (Animal Husbandry Practices and Procedures) Rules, 2023

As per the Rules, various practices, namely dehorning, nose roping, branding, and castration, to which cattle are commonly subjected will be performed by a registered veterinary practitioner. It provides for the manner of conduct for the above-mentioned practices. Contravention of said procedures will attract a penalty under the act.[305]

3.6 Conclusion

The Wildlife Protection Act, 1972, has been the primary legislation responsible for the conservation of wild animals in the country. Efforts have been made to fill the gaps that have emerged in the statute from time to time through a series of amendments. Policies and schemes have also been framed to give effect to the broad objectives of the Act and the principles enunciated in the Indian Constitution aimed at the protection of wildlife. However, some contentious issues persist that require remedies that are more effective than amendments. For instance, the rights of humans, especially the traditional forest dwellers, continue to conflict with the interests of wildlife protection and conservation.

However, to ensure effective integration of conservation efforts and the rights of traditional dwellers, it must be ensured that local inhabitants directly impacted by the notification or expansion of protected areas play a participatory role in the decision-making process in letter and in spirit. This Act requires convergence between the forest officials, wildlife officials, and the Ministry of Tribal Affairs. Hence, it is necessary to merge the goals and efforts of the wildlife and the forest wing of the Ministry of Environment, Forest and Climate Change to successfully safeguard the protected area network of the country along with the human and wild inhabitants that live in and around protected areas. If considerable attention is given to the schemes and policies launched by the Ministry of Environment, Forest and Climate Change, a lot of emphasis has been laid on building the awareness of the local

303 Animal Birth Control Rules, 2023, Rule 20.
304 *Id.*
305 Prevention of Cruelty to Animals (Animal Husbandry Practices and Procedures) Rules, 2023.

people of the importance of wildlife conservation and increasing their engagement in the protection and management of wildlife.

This has also been emphasised in the National Wildlife Action Plan of 2017–2031, Project Elephant, and Project Tiger to name a few. This requires the building of elaborate norms and incentives and awareness-building efforts for the involvement of the local people and their proper implementation. Owing to the proximity that several tribal communities share with wild animals, instances of encroachment into one another's territory are a common occurrence, which accounts for a considerable number of deaths and killings of members of both communities. To mitigate such human-wildlife conflict, mere payment of *ex gratia* compensation as per the schemes devised by the Government may not always suffice. To successfully mitigate these conflicts a more holistic approach that involves greater involvement of wildlife and forest officials and conservation practitioners to engage and humanely interact with the locals and other stakeholders, pushing forward the values of empathy and mediation, is required. Other problems that locals may face, such as difficulty in protecting crops and livestock, should also be looked into and addressed.

While the Prevention of Cruelty to Animals Act, 1960, and the concomitant Rules seek to protect animals from unnecessary pain and suffering, the view that animals are property and are 'owned' by humans continues to underpin the legislation and the same is reflected in the Supreme Court's stance by denying them the benefit of fundamental rights which significantly differs from the view taken by other jurisdictions. Nevertheless, the Act has been instrumental in safeguarding the rights of animals in the country and has lent voice and support to the efforts of animal rights activists and organisations in upholding the rights of animals. Even though the concept of ownership of animals is deeply ingrained in the Act, the welfare of the animal is still given primacy over the rights of ownership and the rights of the owner may be forfeited to ultimately safeguard the rights of animals. However, it remains to be seen whether amendments are made to the Act to make stringent penal provisions for violation of the law.

Review Questions

- Explain the various provisions under the Wildlife (Protection) Act, 1972, prohibiting the hunting of 'wild and captive' animals.
- Discuss the various protected areas classified under the Wildlife (Protection) Act, 1972.
- Discuss the provisions of the Wildlife (Protection) Act, 1972, which prohibits trade in wild animals, animal articles, and trophies.
- What are '*wildlife crimes*'? Explain the various legislative and regulatory mechanisms adopted by India to counter wildlife crimes.
- Elucidate on different rules issued under the Prevention of Cruelty to Animals Act of 1960.

4 Regulatory Framework for Water Pollution in India

4.1 Introduction

Water, often referred to as the elixir of life or the 'cradle of life',[1] is the quintessential life force that sustains all living beings and ecosystems on our planet. In fact, what distinguishes Earth from other celestial bodies within our solar system is the sheer abundance of water on Earth, due to which it is also called a 'blue planet' or 'water planet'. Roughly 70% of Earth's surface is covered by vast oceans, and at any given moment, nearly half of Earth's surface is cloaked by clouds, which are themselves composed of water vapour.[2] Water also exists in rivers, lakes, ice caps, glaciers, ground, soil moisture, and aquifers. Further, every living things on the planet is composed mainly of water. Although water appears to be available in abundance, covering three-fourths of the Earth's surface, only 2.5% is freshwater and 98.8% of the total freshwater is locked up in glaciers, ice caps, and ground. Thus only 1.2% of all freshwater is surface water that is usable,[3] and it serves most of life's needs.[4]

This limited quantity of available freshwater is increasingly becoming scarce due to the increase in population, industries, and agricultural activities with the effect that the world today is facing a water crisis. The global water crisis also involves the pervasive and still growing issue of water pollution,[5] which has put freshwater bodies across the globe under severe and relentless pressure. Water pollution, in its various forms, poses a grave threat to the quality, quantity, and availability of water. For water to be useful, it should not be contaminated beyond a threshold. Any act polluting water affects adversely not only human beings but also animals, plants, aquatic organisms, and even non-living things as well. Further,

1 Aboud Jumbe & Nandini, *Legal Aspects of Water Pollution in India: A Review on Statutory Frameworks*, 6(1) Mapana Journal of Sciences 118 (2007).

2 *See* Matthew R. Fisher, *Water Availability and Use, in* Environmental Biology 203 (2017).

3 David Hunter, International Environmental Law and Policy Case Book 10 (2022); *See also* The World Bank, Rep. No. 15, World Development Report: Development and the Environment 5 (1992).

4 Water Science School, *The Distribution of Water on, in and above the Earth*, United States Geological Survey (Oct. 25, 2019), https://www.usgs.gov/media/images/distribution-water-and-above-earth.

5 Fisher, *supra* note 2, at 217.

DOI: 10.4324/9781032703909-4

contaminated water not only endangers aquatic ecosystems and compromises public health and food security, but it also puts an enormous burden on the economic system of the country.[6]

Hence, it is imperative to have effective legal and regulatory mechanisms for the prevention and control of water pollution. The evolution of the law in India concerning water pollution has been a combination of both bottom-up and top-down legislative approaches which are complemented enormously by the activism of the Indian higher judiciary. This means that the focus initially centred on enacting specific pollution control measures which gradually expanded to encompass broader environmental protection. Thus, the Water (Prevention and Control of Pollution) Act[7] was enacted first in 1974, followed by the Air (Prevention and Control of Pollution) Act, 1981,[8] and then the Environment (Protection) Act, 1986.[9] However, the trend in western countries has been a slightly top-down approach, i.e. starting with a general policy on the environment, followed by an overarching law on the environment, and then addressing the specific aspects of pollution control. For instance, in the United States, the National Environmental Policy Act[10] was enacted way back in 1969, which was then followed by a series of legislations dealing with clean air and clean water, all contributing to environment protection.

Furthermore, courtesy of the proactive stance of the Indian judiciary, the legislative measures on water pollution in India have been well complemented by a plethora of landmark pronouncements. To start with, the right to water has been declared as a fundamental right in cases such as *Narmada Bachao Andolan v. Union of India*[11] and *M.C. Mehta v. Union of India.*[12] In *F K Hussain v. Union of India*[13] and *Attakoya Thangal v. Union of India*[14] it was held that the right to sweetwater and the right to free air are attributes which sustain life itself. Recently, in *Madan Lal v. State of HP*,[15] it was held that water and electricity supply form a part of the right to life under Article 21 of the Constitution of India, and electricity connection is integral to access to water.[16] A similar stance has been adopted by the Tripura High Court in *P Roy Barman v. A Bhowmik*,[17] and by the Kerala High Court in *K N*

6 C. M. Jariwala, *Book Review, Water Pollution in India: Law and Enforcement by Bharat Desai*, 35(1) Journal of the Indian Law Institute 202 (1993).
7 The Water (Prevention and Control of Pollution) Act, 1974.
8 The Air (Prevention and Control of Pollution) Act, 1981.
9 The Environment (Protection) Act, 1986.
10 The National Environmental Policy Act, 1969 (USA).
11 Narmada Bachao Andolan v. Union of India, (2000) 10 SCC 664.
12 M.C. Mehta v. Union of India, 1988 SCR (2) 530.
13 FK Hussain v. Union of India, AIR 1990 Ker 321.
14 Attakoya Thangal v. Union of India, 1990 (1) KLT 580.
15 Madan Lal v. State of Himachal Pradesh, 2018 SCC OnLine HP 1495.
16 *See* Bhumika Indulia, *Water and Electricity Supply form a Part of Right to Life under Article 21 of the Constitution of India: Himachal Pradesh HC*, SCC Blog (Oct 25, 2018), https://www.scconline.com/blog/post/2018/10/25/water-and-electricity-supply-form-a-part-of-right-to-life-under-article-21-of-the-constitution-of-india-h-p-high-court/.
17 P Roy Barman v. A Bhowmik, WP (C) No. 482 of 2022.

Raveendranadhan v. The Kerala State Electricity Board.[18] Furthermore, the stance of the Supreme Court in the *Ganga Pollution Case*,[19] *Vellore Citizens Welfare Forum v. Union of India*,[20] and *A P Pollution Control Board v. M.V. Nayudu*[21] have contributed immensely to strengthening the water pollution control framework in India. The present chapter is a comprehensive enquiry, exploration, and evaluation of the intricate legal and regulatory framework established to combat water pollution in India. In this chapter, we will get into the specifics of the pollution control legal regime, which refers to the law, its enforcement, the obligation of compliance, and the manner of compliance.

4.2 Sources of Water Pollution in India

The sources of water pollution are multiple, and can be natural as well as anthropogenic. However, certain sources and industries can be specially implicated for causing most pollution of water. In India, water pollution comes from three main sources: domestic sewage, industrial effluents, and runoff from agriculture. The largest source of water pollution in India is untreated domestic sewage, which is discharged into water bodies owing to insufficient infrastructure to treat it before discharge. Domestic waste includes human excreta, urine and the associated sludge (collectively known as black water), and wastewater generated through bathing and kitchen work (collectively known as grey water), both of which need to be treated in different ways before discharge.[22] The Central Pollution Control Board has stated that there remains a 78.7% gap between sewage generation and installed sewage treatment capacity. Untreated sewage is most often dumped in surface water sources such as rivers; it is a major contributor to pollution in the large rivers of the Indo-Gangetic plains, especially the Ganga and Yamuna.

Another major source of water pollution in India is industrial effluents, which are again discharged into both surface water bodies and groundwater without proper cleaning or treatment. One of the distinguishing characteristics of effluents of industrial origin, as compared to municipal wastewater, is that often they may contain a mixture of different and highly toxic substances.[23] Industrial effluents tend to be chemical compounds such as sulphates, nitrates, and phosphates, as well as some inorganic compounds and toxic heavy metals. The nature of the effluents is also dependent on the industry in question – oil refineries, chemical plants, and textile and sugar mills are often implicated in causing pollution, but they all release

18 K N Raveendranadhan v. The Kerala State Electricity Board, WP (C) No. 34061 of 2014(G) decided on March 15, 2021.

19 M.C. Mehta v. Union of India, AIR 1988 SC 1037 (Ganga Pollution Case).

20 Vellore Citizens Welfare Forum v. Union of India, 1996 5 SCR 241.

21 A.P. Pollution Control Board v. Prof. M.V. Nayudu, 1999 (2) SCC 718.

22 Central Pollution Control Board, *Newsletter: Sewage Pollution* (2013), ENVIS, https://cpcbenvis.nic.in/cpcb_newsletter/sewagepollution.pdf.

23 R. Guerra, *Water Analysis: Industrial Effluents* in ENCYCLOPEDIA OF ANALYTICAL SCIENCE 289 (2nd edn., 2005).

effluents that require different kinds of treatment. Such treatment, while regulated by the Government and subject to certain standards that industries have to follow, is very often not profitable for industries to do. As a result, compliance issues may arise, owing to the covert discharge of toxic pollutants which are mainly colourless and odourless.[24] The National Green Tribunal has continued to affirm, such as in *Paryavaran Suraksha Samiti v. Union of India*,[25] that the treatment of effluents is a primary condition of industries being granted Consent to Operate as part of an environmental assessment.

A third major source of water pollution in India is agricultural runoff, which is what happens when water used for the irrigation of crops runs down the natural gradient of the land towards a surface water source, carrying with it the pesticides, fertilisers, and other chemical compounds used for the growth of crops and to protect them from diseases and infestations, along with vast amounts of sediment. These chemical compounds are most often inorganic salts like phosphates and nitrates. Surprisingly, the Food and Agriculture Organisation has found that in many developed countries, this runoff has surpassed industrial effluents to become the largest source of water pollution.[26] Such runoff impacts both surface and groundwater and can often lead to groundwater containing far beyond the permissible levels of certain chemicals — fluorides, arsenic, metals, and even uranium have been found in India's groundwater. CGWB studies indicate the occurrence of fluoride and arsenic beyond permissible limits in isolated pockets. Excess fluoride has been encountered in point sources in 370 districts in 23 States, and arsenic in point sources in 152 districts in 21 States.[27] This renders groundwater unsafe and unfit to use.

Apart from these three main sources of water pollution, there are several smaller ones. For example, activities such as animal husbandry also generate waste that gets flushed or dumped into rivers. The restaurant, hospitality, and retail industries are also major sources of point water pollution. Flooding during monsoons worsens India's water pollution problem, as it washes and moves solid waste and contaminated soils into its rivers and wetlands. There are also other kinds of pollution that arise from these. Microbiological pollution refers to the excessive presence of bacteria and other microorganisms in water sources, which may be bearers of waterborne diseases or indicate a chemical imbalance within the ecosystem of the water source that could in turn be the result of pollution. Thermal pollution refers to the discharge of hot water or heat into water sources, most often from power plants discharging into rivers the water used to cool their turbines; this practice is not only a consumptive process as held by the Supreme Court in *Delhi Electric Supply*

24 T. Rajaram and Ashutosh Das, *Water Pollution by Industrial Effluents in India: Discharge Scenarios and Case for Participatory Ecosystem Specific Local Regulation*, 40 Futures 56 (2008).

25 Paryavaran Suraksha Samiti v. Union of India, 2017 (5) SCC 326.

26 Food and Agriculture Organisation, *Water Pollution from Agriculture: A Global Review – Executive Summary* (2017), https://www.fao.org/3/i7754e/i7754e.pdf.

27 Ministry of Jal Shakti, *Contamination of Ground Water*, Press Information Bureau (Mar. 24, 2022), https://pib.gov.in/PressReleasePage.aspx?PRID=1809264.

Undertaking v. Central Board for the Prevention and Control of Water Pollution,[28] but also has an impact on the overall ecosystem.

4.3 Water (Prevention and Control of Pollution) Act, 1974

4.3.1 Historical and Legislative Background of the Water Act

In 1974, the Indian Parliament initiated a comprehensive review of environmental regulations in India. This stocktaking and assessment exercise was promoted by events of 1972, when India participated in the United Nations Conference on Human Environment (Stockholm Conference, 1972). This international summit catalysed nations, including India, to formulate specific legislations to address the crisis problem of environmental degradation and the looming threat to life on Earth.[29] At that time, India had adopted and primarily relied on general administrative principles and laws such as common law and criminal law pertaining to nuisance, negligence, and liability to tackle environmental concerns. These legal tools, however, were aged and were found somewhat inadequate. Furthermore, they encompassed a wide spectrum of issues, including pollution. The need of the hour was not a general law but a very focused attention for effective pollution control. Moreover, India had made international commitments for formulating its own dedicated environmental laws. Hence, the need to come up with a sharp, effective, and focused piece of legislation was evident. Further, a need was also felt to establish a dedicated specialised body of enforcement with all the skills and capabilities as required to deal with a wide variety of pollution issues. Hence, in the year 1974, India enacted the Water (Prevention and Control of Pollution) Act[30] (Water Act) which was India's first dedicated environmental law. And after seven years of its enactment, the Air (Prevention and Control of Pollution) Act, 1981,[31] (Air Act) was enacted. In the interim period between these two legislations, India introduced another small legislation, the Water (Prevention and Control of Pollution) Cess Act, 1977,[32] which aimed to assist the institutional machinery to become a self-sustaining body by facilitating the collection of a cess for the consumption of water that is used by industries. Although these were different legislations made at different points in time, the administration remains the same and collectively, they constitute the pollution control legal regime in India. Additionally, after the enactment of the Environment (Protection) Act, 1986,[33] (EPA) the source of authority of these two legislations and the institutions created under them has expanded. Under the EPA several delegated legislations have been made, under which additional

28 Delhi Electric Supply Undertaking v. Central Board for the Prevention and Control of Water Pollution, LAWS (SC) – 1994-3-41.

29 *See* United Nations, Report of the United Nations Conference on the Human Environment (Stockholm, 5–16 June, 1972).

30 The Water (Prevention and Control of Pollution) Act, 1974.

31 The Air (Prevention and Control of Pollution) Act, 1981.

32 The Water (Prevention and Control of Pollution) Cess Act, 1977.

33 The Environment (Protection) Act, 1986.

functions, beyond the prescription of the Water Act and the Air Act, have been assigned and entrusted to these bodies.

At this juncture, it is pertinent to highlight that water is a State subject under the Constitutional division of legislative powers covered under Entry 13 of the State List in the Seventh Schedule.[34] Thus, only the States have the constitutional authority to make a law on water.[35] However, Article 249 (national interest supported by resolution of two-thirds of the States), Article 250 (Proclamation of Emergency), Article 252 (resolution by two or more States and adoption by other States), and Article 253 (giving effect to international agreements) of the Constitution provide certain situations where the Parliament can legislate on the subjects under the State List. Consequently, in pursuance of Article 252 of the Constitution, resolutions were passed by the States of Assam, Bihar, Gujarat, Haryana, Himachal Pradesh, Jammu and Kashmir, Karnataka, Kerala, Madhya Pradesh, Rajasthan, Tripura, and West Bengal regarding the regulation of water pollution by a Central law, thereby allowing Parliament to legislate on a State subject.[36] Further, the need for a Central law was also felt by the States because, by enacting their own separate State laws concerning water pollution, some of them had stringent provisions and some of them had very few provisions, with the result that the pollution in one area may affect other areas. And since pollution, especially of the atmosphere and the water bodies, does not really know the barriers of the State, district, taluk, etc., it is necessary that there should be some kind of a uniform law all over India. Thus, although water is a State subject, a Central legislation was enacted in exercise of the Union's powers under Article 252, and the Water Act was finally passed in 1974.

4.3.2 Objectives of the Water Act

The Water Act is essentially intended to achieve three fundamental objectives, each of which holds significant implications for improving water quality in India. The primary objective is to prevent and control water pollution.[37] Thus, it signifies the critical importance of preserving the water resources. However, the Act extends beyond mere pollution control with the secondary objective, which is to maintain and restore the wholesomeness of water.[38] Thirdly, the Act establishes the Pollution Control Boards which are envisaged as pollution control regulators and entrusted to implement and carry out the various functions under the Water Act.[39] The Act envisages a proactive role on the part of the Pollution Control Boards such that they will strive for not only prevention and controlling contamination of water

34 India Const. Seventh Schedule, List II, entry 13 ('Water, that is to say water supplies, irrigation and canals, drainage and embankments, water storage and water power').

35 The Water (Prevention and Control of Pollution) Act, 1974, pmbl.

36 *Id.*

37 *Id.*

38 *Id.*

39 *Id.*

but are also entrusted to work actively to maintain the quality of water, ensuring that it remains wholesome and fit for various uses.

4.3.3 Salient Features of the Water Act

The Water (Prevention and Control of Pollution) Act, 1974, embodies several notable characteristics aimed at preventing and managing water pollution effectively. These salient features include:

- **Scope and extent**: the application of the Water Act is not confined to mere pollution, but it also extends to contamination and alteration of the properties of water and discharges into water that cause nuisance as well as harm to human health, plant varieties, animals, and ultimately to the entire environment.[40] Initially, the Act was made applicable to only those States which passed the resolution for enactment of a Central law on water pollution. Further, the Act is also applicable to all Union Territories.[41] However, today the Act is applicable to the whole of India, upon adoption by all the States, i.e. it is operative all over India.
- **Administrative architecture for pollution administration**: the administration of pollution control under the Water Act is structured around various authorities. These include the Central Government (via the Ministry of Environment, Forests and Climate Change), the Central Pollution Control Board (CPCB), Regional Offices of the CPCB, State Governments, and State Pollution Control Boards.[42] Further, in India, given the diverse nature and size of each State (big States, small States, and almost microstates – especially in the north-eastern region), many times, due to budgetary constraints, some small States will not be in a position to have an independent Pollution Control Board exclusively for themselves. In such a situation, provisions for a Joint Board have been made in the Water Act.[43]
- **Overriding effect over other laws**: one of the major features of the Water Act is that it has an overriding effect over all other laws as per Section 60.[44] However, unlike the Environment Protection Act of 1986, this status is confined to the Water Act alone, and not for the rules made thereunder. Under the EPA, the status of overriding effect is there for the rules also over other laws.[45]
- **Consent to establish and operate**: an important facet of the Water Act is the introduction of a consent mechanism. The Water Act requires that industries and other establishments obtain consent from the respective Pollution Control Boards for the discharge of pollutants into water bodies. The two main types of

40 *Id.* § 2(e).
41 *Id.* § 1(2).
42 *Id.* Ch. II–IV, §§ 3–18.
43 *Id.* Ch. IV.
44 *Id.* § 60.
45 The Environment (Protection) Act, 1986 § 24(1).

consent under the Water Act are Consent to Establish and Consent to Operate which are together known as Environmental Clearance.

- **Inspection and monitoring provisions**: the Water Act contains provisions which empower the Pollution Control Boards to conduct regular inspection and monitoring of sewage, effluents, and other pollutants in order to check compliance with the specified standards and consent conditions. To carry this out, the PCBs are empowered with the power to obtain information,[46] power to take samples of effluents,[47] power of entry and inspection,[48] etc. Further the Boards are empowered to establish or recognise laboratories to assist them in analysis of the samples.[49] The Central and State laboratories can also be used in this regard.[50]
- **Elaborate set of penal provisions**: the Water Act prohibits and regulates a host of activities that cause water pollution and has quite an elaborate set of penal provisions to deal with almost every kind of violation (Ss. 41, 42, 43, 44, 45, 45A), which includes fines as well as imprisonment. This serves as a deterrent against contraventions and non-compliance.
- **Citizen suit provisions**: the Water Act was amended in the year 1988 and a provision was inserted which empowers 'any person' to make a complaint before the magistrate for violation of the Water Act.[51] This provision is called citizen suit provision. However, the complaint directly to the magistrate can be filed only after giving 60 days' notice to the Board or its authorised officer of the alleged offence and the person's intention to make a complaint. This significant provision of the Water Act remains under-utilised in India so far.

4.4 Important Terms Defined under the Water Act

The Water Act adopts a large number of nuanced definitions in order to help with the fulfilment of these ambitions. The definitions are broad and, for the most part, inclusive. As a consequence, the legislation is forward-facing, to ensure that the goal of environmental preservation and protection does not become secondary while industrial expansion takes place. Section 2(e) of the Water Act provides a broad and comprehensive definition of 'water pollution'. 'Water pollution' denotes:

1. Contamination of water.
2. Alteration of physical, chemical, or biological properties of water.
3. Direct or indirect discharge of sewage or trade effluents or liquid, gaseous, or solid substances.
4. Provided that such contamination, alteration, or discharge *may*:

46 The Water (Prevention and Control of Pollution) Act, 1974, § 20.
47 *Id.* § 21.
48 *Id.* § 23.
49 *Id.* §§ 16, 17.
50 *Id.* §§ 52, 53.
51 *Id.* § 49.

a. Create nuisance.
b. Or render such water injurious to public health and safety.
c. Or render such water harmful for domestic, commercial, industrial, agricultural, or other legitimate uses.
d. Or render such water injurious to the life and health of aquatic flora and fauna.[52]

It is noteworthy that the definition does not require actual pollution. The usage of 'may cause' or 'may render' shows that even a *risk* or *probability* of pernicious effects (from the contamination, alteration, or discharge) is sufficient to constitute 'pollution'. This incorporates the 'precautionary principle' which imposes a higher duty of care on the polluter. In essence, this principle stresses the need for precautionary measures to prevent harm to public health, even in the absence of scientific certainty. It suggests that if an action might cause significant harm to the environment, the onus of proving the action's benign nature falls on those advocating the action.[53] Thus, this principle prevents even a potential threat of environmental damage. In *Vellore Citizens Welfare Forum v. Union of India*, the precautionary principle was recognised as a part of the Water Act and Indian environmental law in general.[54] This was reiterated by the Supreme Court in *Tirupur Dyeing Factory Owners Assn. v. Noyyal River Ayacutdars Protection Assn.*, where the Court opined that 'risk of harm to the environment or human health' is the requisite standard for pollution under the Water Act.[55] Such 'risk' has to be determined using a reasonable person's perspective, keeping in mind the public interest.

Further, recognising the different sources of pollution, the Water Act defines two types of effluents:

1. Sewage effluent is the 'effluent from any sewage or sewer disposal works, and includes sullage from open drains'. This essentially includes the two types of sewage waste recognised by the CPCB: both bathroom wastewater and kitchen runoff in the form of sullage.[56]
2. Trade effluent is also defined broadly, as 'any liquid, gaseous or solid substance which is discharged from any premises used for carrying on any industry, operation or process, or treatment and disposal system, other than domestic sewage'. Thus, any effluent that does not emanate from a domestic source is classified as trade effluent.[57]

52 *Id.* § 2(e).
53 Mathew John, *Judicial Scrutiny of Environmental Risk and the Legislative Scheme of the Water Act: A Comment*, 13 Socio-Legal Rev. 70 (2017).
54 Vellore Citizens Welfare Forum v. Union of India, (1996) 5 SCC 647.
55 Tirupur Dyeing Factory Owners Assn. v. Noyyal River Ayacutdars Protection Assn, (2009) 9 SCC 737.
56 The Water (Prevention and Control of Pollution) Act, 1974, § 2(g).
57 *Id.* § 2(k).

The definition of a 'stream', which receives special protection in Sections 24 and 32, is expanded to include both surface water and underground water – rivers, watercourses both flowing and dry, natural or artificial inland water and groundwater. The scope of the definition of 'occupier'[58] is also very broad, as it encompasses either the person with control over the factory or premises or the person in charge of the polluting substance at that time. There have not been many cases outlining the scope of these definitions, but the scheme of the legislation seems to suggest that the definitions are to be interpreted broadly so as to regulate various sources and types of water pollution, even those not specifically mentioned in the act.

4.5 Establishment of Administrative Architecture for Pollution Control

The heart and soul of governance of the pollution control laws lie in the hands of the Pollution Control Boards. The Act creates two levels of statutory bodies in which the power of regulating pollution is vested: the Central Pollution Control Boards (CPCB) and State Pollution Control Boards (SPCBs). This section of the chapter undertakes a comprehensive examination of the establishment of PCBs, their composition, role, responsibilities, and functions.

4.5.1 The Central Pollution Control Board

The CPCB was constituted on 23 September 1974, in pursuance of Section 3 of the Water Act, 1974, to exercise the powers and perform the functions assigned to it under the Act.[59] It is a statutory authority at the Central level and performs its functions under the Ministry of Environment, Forests and Climate Change (MoEFCC) of the Government of India. Additionally, it was also entrusted with authorities and responsibilities under the Air Act, 1981.[60] As per Section 3 of the Water Act, the CPCB is a body corporate having perpetual succession and a common seal with the power to acquire, hold, and dispose of property. It can also enter into contracts with any other person or party in its name. Further, it can also sue and be sued in its own name.[61] CPCB acts according to the directions of the Central Government. Its primary role encompasses overseeing air and water quality monitoring services, along with addressing various pollution-related concerns.

4.5.2 Constitution and Composition of Central Pollution Control Board

The membership of the CPCB is laid out in Section 3 sub-section 2 of the Water Act and includes the following members:

58 *Id.* § 2(d).
59 *See About Us,* CENTRAL POLLUTION CONTROL BOARD, https://cpcb.nic.in/Introduction/ (last visited Oct. 24, 2023).
60 The Air (Prevention and Control of Pollution) Act, 1981.
61 The Water (Prevention and Control of Pollution) Act, 1974.

- A full-time **Chairman**, having special knowledge and practical experience in environmental protection and administrative institution matters as specified under Section 3 (2)(a) of the Act, who is to be nominated by the Appointments Committee of the Cabinet of the Central Government. As per the Central Pollution Control Board (Qualifications and other Terms and Conditions of Service of Chairman), Rules, 2015,[62] he is required to have a master's degree in a science-related field or a bachelor's degree in engineering, as well as special knowledge and 15 years of practical experience relating to environment protection and to have rendered 25 years of service. He may also be a member of certain specified services.
- One full-time **Member-Secretary** to be appointed by the Central Government who possesses qualifications, knowledge, and experience of scientific and engineering or management aspects of pollution control.[63]
- A maximum of five **official representatives**, who are to be nominated by the Central Government for representation of their interests.[64]
- A maximum of five members nominated from amongst members of the State Pollution Control Boards by the Central Government. Not more than two members can be nominated from a particular SPCB.[65]
- A maximum of three **non-official members** to be nominated by the Central Government. They are persons who represent the interests of agriculture, fishery, or industry or trade or any other interest, which the Central Government thinks ought to be represented.[66]
- Two members nominated by the Central Government to represent the companies or corporations owned, controlled, or managed by the Central Government.[67]

4.5.3 Powers and Functions of Central Pollution Control Board

Section 16(1) of the Water Act, states that the main function of CPCB is to promote the cleanliness of streams and wells in different areas of the States.[68] Some of the significant powers and functions of the CPCB are as follows:

A. **Provide guidance to the Central Government**: CPCB offers their expert advice and recommendations or suggestions to the Central Government regarding the framing of new policies or amendments in such pre-existing policies, framing strategies, and actions aimed at preventing and effectively managing

62 The Central Pollution Control Board (Qualifications and Other Terms and Conditions of Services of Chairman) Rules, 2015.
63 The Water (Prevention and Control of Pollution) Act, 1974 § 3(f).
64 *Id.* § 3(b).
65 *Id.* § 3(c).
66 *Id.* § 3(d).
67 *Id.* § 3(e).
68 *Id.* § 16(1).

water pollution. The suggestions or recommendations which are made to the Central Government are based on scientific research, knowledge, and expertise in the field of water pollution with the primary aim to effectively prevent and manage water pollution.[69]

B. **Coordinate the activities and mediate disputes of State Boards**: CPCB acts as a governing body, facilitating cooperation and collaboration among State Boards. SPCBs work under the directions and instructions laid out by the CPCB. In the event of any disagreements or disputes between different State Boards, the CPCB intervenes to mediate and find mutually acceptable solutions, ensuring a collective approach to tackling water pollution across States.[70]
C. **Provide technical support to State Boards**: CPCB provides specialised technical support and guidance to State Boards in enforcing its guidelines and addressing water pollution challenges. It also assists and guides the SPCBs while conducting research and investigating water pollution matters. CPCB also conducts and funds research and provides preventive measures for understanding water pollution issues and developing effective strategies for the prevention, control, or reduction of water pollution.[71]
D. **Design programmes for preventing, controlling, or reducing water pollution**: CPCB takes responsibility for creating structured training programmes that educate and train such personnel who are engaged in activities related to the prevention and control of water pollution. These programmes adhere to specific guidelines and standards set by CPCB, in order to effectively reduce water pollution.[72]
E. **Collect, compile, and publish data and lay down standards regarding water pollution**: CPCB collects, organises, and publishes accurate technical and statistical data related to water pollution. This data is updated frequently and serves as a valuable resource for researchers and the general public in the development and evaluation of effective pollution prevention and control measures. This data also serves as a great tool and provides deep insights to the policymakers through which they can form effective policies to manage water pollution. It also acts as a check on Governments, such as in the case of Ganga water pollution, in which the CPCB was mandated to monitor pollution interstate boundaries by the Supreme Court in the *M.C. Mehta case*, as a way of keeping a check on how each State was monitoring river pollution. The standards that are set, updated, or modified by CPCB, as well as the measures implemented for maintaining or improving water quality, are done in collaboration and deep discussion with the State Governments, and are based on thorough scientific assessments and extensive study after taking into account factors such as water quality, flow characteristics, and intended use and other

69 The Water (Prevention and Control of Pollution) Act, 1974, § 16(1)(a).
70 *Id.* § 16(1)(b).
71 *Id.* § 16(1)(c).
72 *Id.* § 16(1)(d).

relevant factors. Thus, the standards combine policy interests with raw scientific data.[73]

F. **Implementation of a nationwide initiative**: CPCB develops a strategic plan to comprehensively address water pollution at a national level. It oversees the execution of this plan, ensuring alignment and taking all necessary actions with the aim of achieving set goals and objectives to effectively prevent, control, or reduce water pollution across the country. It collaborates with and directs all established SPCBs in pursuit of its set plans and goals and collective work in the manner necessary for achieving such goals.[74]

G. **Performing the functions of State Boards in certain circumstances**: the Act empowers CPCB to perform the functions of any State Board in pursuance of an order made under Section 18(2) of the Water Act, 1974.[75] As per this Section, the Central Government may pass an order to direct the CPCB to take over the functions of any State Board if that State Board has defaulted in complying with any direction given by the CPCB under Section 18(1), and due to such default, a grave emergency has arisen and it is necessary or expedient in the public interest to do so.[76] Further, in relation to Union Territories, since no State Board is constituted, it is CPCB which exercises the powers and performs the functions of a State Board for Union Territories.[77] However, the CPCB does not have to perform the functions of State Boards in the UTs directly, but it can delegate them to the Pollution Control Committee (PCCs) which are appointed by the Central Government. As of the present, there are six PCCs in the different UTs, namely the Delhi Pollution Control Committee (DPCC), Puducherry Pollution Control Committee, Chandigarh Pollution Control Committee, Daman and Diu and Nagar Haveli Pollution Control Committee (a Joint Committee for the UTs of Daman, Diu, and Dadra and Nagar Haveli), Andaman and Nicobar Islands Pollution Control Committee, and Lakshadweep Pollution Control Committee.[78]

H. **Any additional functions**: CPCB is open to assume any other responsibilities or functions specified by regulations, laws, or relevant authorities such as the Government of India, as long as they are in line with its mission or intention to address water pollution effectively and efficiently and prevent or improve quality of water. For example, although it was put in place for the purpose of preventing water pollution, its functions were extended to air pollution by the Air Act of 1981.[79] Further, under Section 57 of the Water Act, the CPCB is duty-bound to furnish such reports, statistics, accounts, and other information

73 The Water (Prevention and Control of Pollution) Act, 1974, § 16(1)(f).

74 *Id.* § 16(1)(h).

75 *Id.* § 16(1)(ee).

76 *Id.* 1974 § 18(2).

77 *Id.* § 4(2).

78 *SPCBs & PCCs*, Central Pollution Control Board, https://cpcb.nic.in/spcbs-pccs/ (last visited Oct. 24, 2023).

79 The Water (Prevention and Control of Pollution) Act, 1974 § 16(1)(i).

with respect to its funds or activities as the Central Government may, from time to time, require.[80]

I. **Power to direct the State Boards to furnish reports**: Section 57 of the Water Act provides that the CPCB may, from time to time, ask the State Boards to furnish such reports, statistics, accounts, and other information with respect to their funds or activities as it may require. The State Boards are duty-bound to furnish such reports.[81]

J. **Power to seek information and assistance from local authorities**: in order to discharge its responsibilities efficiently, CPCB requires assistance from local authorities and hence, it can request the same from local authorities. Section 55 of the Water Act explicitly provides that all the local authorities are duty-bound to render such help and assistance and furnish such information to the Board. Further, the Board, to discharge its functions, can also inspect and examine records, maps, plans, and other documents. The local authorities are obligated to make the same available to the Board.[82]

K. **Establishment of Central Board laboratories an Central Board analysts**: Section 16(3) of the Water Act empowers the Central Pollution Control Board to either establish or recognise a laboratory or laboratories. Such laboratories play an important role in assisting the Board to carry out its functions.[83] The most significant role of such laboratories is to conduct analysis of samples of water or trade effluents collected by State Boards in the exercise of its sampling power under Sections 21 and 22 of the Water Act.[84] Further, the CPCB is also authorised to appoint Central Board analysts with the approval of the Central Government. The Central Board analysts, so appointed, are the persons in charge of carrying out the analysis of samples of water or sewage or trade effluents sent for analysis by the Board.[85]

L. **Power to constitute committees and engage persons**: the CPCB is authorised under Section 9 of the Act to constitute as many committees and for such purpose or purposes as it deems necessary. These committees can either be fully composed of Board members or non-board members, or they can be comprised partly of members and partly of non-members. Further, the Board can also prescribe their time and place of meeting along with the rules for the procedure for the transaction of business.[86] Furthermore, the CPCB can also engage any person on a temporary basis for assistance or advice in performing its functions. Such persons associated with the Board are not regarded as Board members, and although they have the right to take part in the Board discussions, they do

80 The Water (Prevention and Control of Pollution) Act, 1974, § 57.
81 *Id.* § 57.
82 *Id.* § 57.
83 *Id.* § 16(3).
84 *Id.* § 21.
85 *Id.* § 53.
86 *Id.* § 9.

not have the right to vote in Board meetings.[87] Additionally, the Board also has the responsibility to prescribe the fees and allowance to be paid to non-Board members of committees constituted by it under Section 9 and also to the other persons it decides to associate under Section 10.

M. **Power to delegate powers to the Chairman**: the CPCB being a legal entity required a human agency to exercise its powers and carry out its functions. Hence, one of the most significant powers of the CPCB is to delegate its power and functions to the Chairman who will then exercise such powers and perform such duties as have been delegated to him by the Board.[88]

4.5.4 Disqualification of Members of Central Pollution Control Board

Disqualification of members of a Pollution Control Board typically involves criteria or circumstances that make an individual ineligible or incapable of serving as a member. The aim of these disqualifications is to uphold integrity, impartiality, and effectiveness within the board. Disqualifications can vary depending on the nature of the post, and may be as prescribed by the Government from time to time. However, certain broad potential disqualifications may be noted.

1. **Conflict of interest**: a conflict of interest arises when a member's personal or financial interests clash with their responsibilities to regulate pollution. CPCB's powers are extensive for the simple reason that regulating pollution is a complex process involving balancing a multitude of interests. It cannot be that a board member favours personal interests over the welfare of the public and the environment. Even for persons serving in scientific roles, the board makes it necessary for them to have a no objection certificate if they are already employed in Government, autonomous, or statutory bodies, PSUs, corporations, or companies.[89] This is to ensure that their scientific assessments are unbiased. Thus, any person who has directly or indirectly, by himself or any partner, any share or interest in any firm or company carrying on the business of manufacture, sale, or hire of machinery, plant, equipment apparatus, or fittings for the treatment of sewage or trade effluents cannot be a member of the Board.[90] Further, a person who is a director, or a secretary, manager, or other salaried employee of any company or firm having a contract with the Board, or with the Government constituting the Board, or with a local authority in the State, or with a company or corporation owned, controlled, or managed by the Government, for the carrying

87 The Water (Prevention and Control of Pollution) Act, 1974, § 10.

88 *Id.* § 11A.

89 Central Pollution Control Board, Declaration of Result of Online Examination Held on 18.06.2023 for the Post of Scientist 'B' in Central Pollution Control Board (CPCB) – Reg (September 26, 2023), https://cpcb.nic.in/employee/jobs/Result-Scientist-B-26092023.pdf.

90 The Water (Prevention and Control of Pollution) Act, 1974 § 6(1)(e).

out of sewage schemes or for the installation of plants for the treatment of sewage or trade effluents cannot be a member of the Board.[91]

2. **Convictions or criminal history**: disqualifying individuals with specific criminal convictions or a history of unlawful activities ensures that the integrity and reputation of the Pollution Control Board are maintained. The Water Act prescribes that a person who is or has been convicted of an offence which in the opinion of the Central Government involves moral turpitude cannot be a member of CPCB.[92] Further, criminal history may indicate a lack of trustworthiness and can undermine the credibility of the board, making it essential to prevent such individuals from serving on the board. The rules pertaining to the appointment of the Chairman and the Member-Secretary also specify that such individuals should not be guilty of the offence of bigamy. Further, if a person has been convicted of any offence under the Water Act, he/she also cannot be a member of the Board.[93]
3. **Incompetence or insufficient qualifications**: disqualification due to incompetence or lack of qualifications is crucial to uphold the high standards of expertise and knowledge required to effectively address pollution-related challenges. The rules pertaining to appointments specifically mention a very high level of scientific knowledge, because individuals lacking the necessary qualifications and expertise might make uninformed decisions that could have detrimental effects on the environment and public health. The Supreme Court has said in *Techi Tagi Tara v. Rajendra Singh Bhandari*[94] that 'Such appointments should not be made casually or without due application of mind considering the duties, functions and responsibilities of the SPCBs'. The Jharkhand High Court also prevented an unqualified person from continuing as the chairperson of the SPCB in the case of *Binay Kumar Sinha v. State of Jharkhand*.[95]
4. **Misuse of position**: misuse of position for personal gain or activities contrary to the objectives of the Pollution Control Board undermines the board's purpose and effectiveness. Thus, the Water Act prescribes that a member who has abused his position as a member so as to render his continuance on the Board detrimental to the interest of the general public can be removed from his position. Disqualification in such cases ensures that the board's members act in the best interest of the public and the environment, rather than for personal advantage.[96]
5. **Mental incapacity, bankruptcy, or insolvency**: Disqualification due to mental incapacity or being bankrupt or insolvent is necessary to ensure that board

91 The Water (Prevention and Control of Pollution) Act, 1974, § 6(1)(f).

92 *Id.* § 6(1)(c).

93 *Id.* § 6(1)(d).

94 Techi Tagi Tara v. Rajendra Singh Bhandari, Civil Appeal No. 1359 of 2017, decided on 22 September 2017 (Supreme Court of India).

95 Binay Kumar Singh v. State of Jharkhand, W.P. (S) No. 3956 of 2010, decided on 27 April 2016 (Jharkhand HC).

96 The Water (Prevention and Control of Pollution) Act, 1974 § 6(1)(g).

members can effectively carry out their duties and make informed decisions. Mental incapacity could impair judgment and hinder the ability to fulfil responsibilities effectively and responsibly. Disqualification in cases of financial issues like bankruptcy or insolvency prevents conflicts of interest and potential misuse of the position due to financial instability.[97]

However, a member of the Board cannot be removed by the Central Government without giving him a reasonable opportunity of showing cause against such removal.[98] This is to ensure compliance with the principles of natural justice in administrative adjudication. Further, the Act provides that any member who has been removed from his position shall not be eligible for renomination as a member.[99]

4.5.5 State Pollution Control Boards

The State Pollution Control Boards (SPCBs) are the real operating functional arm of the pollution control regime in India. The SPCBs are constituted by the respective State Governments under Section 4 of the Water Act, 1974.[100] At present, there are 29 SPCBs that have been constituted in India.[101] They consist of a Chairman and members representing various interests such as Government, local authorities, industry, agriculture, fisheries, etc.[102] One of the most important functions entrusted to the SPCBs is the issuance of Consent to Establish (CTE) and Consent to Operate (CTO) to industries and establishments that discharge effluents into water bodies.[103] This consent is granted only after a thorough assessment of the potential environmental impact and compliance with prescribed standards. Further, the SPCBs are also tasked with monitoring the effluent quality to ensure adherence to set parameters. This process helps in maintaining water quality at permissible levels, thus safeguarding the health of both ecosystems and communities dependent on these water sources.

The State Boards are also mandated to plan a comprehensive programme for the prevention, control, or abatement of water pollution in their States.[104] They also collect and disseminate information relating to water pollution and its prevention, and advise the State Government on any matter concerning water pollution.[105] The SPCBs also collaborate with CPCB and other agencies in matters relating to water

97 The Water (Prevention and Control of Pollution) Act, 1974 § 6(1)(a) & (b).
98 *Id.* § 6(2).
99 *Id.* § 6(3).
100 *Id.* § 4(1).
101 *See SPCBs & PCCs*, Central Pollution Control Board, https://cpcb.nic.in/spcbs-pccs/ (last visited Oct. 24, 2023).
102 The Water (Prevention and Control of Pollution) Act, 1974 § 4(2).
103 *Id.* § 27.
104 *Id.* § 17(1)(a).
105 *Id.* § 17(1)(b), (c).

pollution.[106] They also conduct investigations, and inspect sewage or trade effluents for the treatment of water.[107] The SPCBs are also mandated to lay down, modify, or annul effluent standards for the sewage and trade effluents and for the quality of receiving waters (not being water in an inter-state stream).[108]

4.5.6 Constitution and Composition of State Pollution Control Boards

In terms of its composition, the SPCB is a bureaucracy-heavy body. It consists of a total of 17 members, which include the Chairman and a Member-Secretary. A Member-Secretary is generally a representative of one of the departments of the Government and hence is part of the Government itself. In addition to these 2, there are 15 other members and they are drawn from various departments of the Government. Further, there are three non-official members which represent agriculture, trade, and industry and other expert groups. There is representation provided for local bodies also. The exact composition of the SPCBs is as follows:

- A **Chairman** nominated by the State Government.[109] However, unlike the CPCB, the Chairman of the SPCBs can either be a full-time or a part-time member as decided by the State Government.[110]
- A full-time **Member-Secretary** appointed by the State Government.[111]
- A maximum of five officials to be nominated by the State Government to represent the State Government.[112]
- A maximum of five members nominated by the State Government from amongst local authorities functioning within the State.[113]
- A maximum of three non-official members, nominated by the State Government, who represent the interests of agriculture, fishery, or industry or trade or any other interest which, in the opinion of the State Government, ought to be represented.[114]
- Two members, nominated by the State Government, to represent the companies or corporations owned, controlled, or managed by the State Government.[115]

As per Section 5 of the Act, the term of office of members, except the Member-Secretary, is three years. The provision to Section 5(1) also provides that at the end of the third year, if no provision is made for some new person to take over their

106 The Water (Prevention and Control of Pollution) Act, 1974, § 17(1)(e).
107 *Id.* § 17(1)(f).
108 *Id.* § 17(1)(g), (k).
109 *Id.* § 4(2)(a).
110 *Id.* § 4(2)(a) proviso.
111 *Id.* § 4(2)(f).
112 *Id.* § 4(2)(b).
113 *Id.* § 4(2)(c).
114 *Id.* § 4(2)(d).
115 *Id.* § 4(2)(e).

position or there is no renewal given for an extension by another three years, still the members will continue to hold office till the appointment of their successor takes place.[116] This provision provides for the contingency which unfortunately happens on a regular basis in many of the SPCBs, that even after the expiry of the three-year period, no fresh appointments are made. Then in such a situation, the existing members will continue to hold the same position and discharge the same function under the law. The idea behind this provision is that since the SPCB takes care of the entire State on all matters concerning pollution, it shall not be found wanting in the performance of its functions by way of vacancies, i.e., it should not be found wanting in taking decisions in the absence of a member.

Further, the provisions laid down for the disqualification under Section 6 of the Act also apply to the SPCBs. Thus, it is quite possible for a member to be removed from his office or to cease to hold office because of some disqualification, or the member, except the Member-Secretary, can himself resign from his office.[117] The disqualifications prescribed include insolvency, unsoundness of mind, and conviction of offences involving moral turpitude. Hence, a criminal cannot become a member. It also extends to somebody who is a partner, a holder of a share or an interest in a firm involved in carrying out a business of sale, manufacture, hiring, etc., of equipment for the treatment of sewage or trade effluent associated with an organisation or an entity owned, controlled, or managed by the Government, having a contract with the board for carrying out sewage schemes or for the installation of plants, etc., for the same purpose.[118] The idea behind this detailed provision is that a member should not become an interested party when he becomes the decision-maker. Because the pollution control board takes important decisions affecting various stakeholders, it is a quasi-judicial body, and a very important and a very peculiar kind of authority. It is not merely any governmental agency where only administrative actions are taken. Though it takes administrative action, it performs many more functions than that; it takes decisions and passes several orders which are equal to the orders of a court of law.

The position of the Member-Secretary is one of the most significant and prestigious positions at the PCBs. The Member-Secretary is a full-time member possessing qualifications, knowledge, and experience in scientific engineering or management aspects of pollution control. He is a State Government appointee and his term of office is determined by the order of appointment given by the Government.[119] There is no minimum prescribed period of three years or even two years. The State Government can transfer him at any time. Further, the Government can even stipulate that he will hold office only for a period of six months. Thus, as per the order of the Government or the order issued by the Government from time to time, the tenure of the Member-Secretary is determined. Although the qualifications stipulated

116 The Water (Prevention and Control of Pollution) Act, 1974, § 5(1) proviso.
117 *Id.* § 5(4).
118 *Id.* § 6.
119 *Id.* § 12.

for the Member-Secretary are essential to ensure proper functioning of the board, it was noted by the Supreme Court Monitoring Committee in a 2005 *communique* that 'in several States, persons from IFS or from the PWD, especially from the PHE departments, are either being appointed or deputed to the post of Member Secretary without the necessary statutory qualifications'.[120]

An important case related to the appointment of the Member-Secretary of the SPCB is that of *Karnataka State Pollution Control Board Officer's Association v. State of Karnataka*.[121] In this case, the Petitioners claimed that the person appointed as the Member-Secretary did not have the necessary educational qualifications or could not be said to have achieved any knowledge or experience of scientific, engineering, or administrative aspects of pollution control in terms of the provisions of the Water Act. However, the court observed that the person appointed as the Member-Secretary held a BA degree and was an IAS Officer. As a member of the Service, she had held various posts such as Assistant Commissioner, Chief Executive Officer, Managing Director, Joint Registrar, and Deputy Commissioner. In some of her posts, she was responsible for the collection, segregation, and transportation of solid waste and was also associated with all other aspects of health and sanitation. She had also worked with the management of effluents of co-operative sugar factories. Furthermore, as a Sub-divisional Magistrate (SDM), she exercised power under Section 133 CrPC for monitoring public nuisance, noise, water/air pollution, etc. The Court further observed that, at the time of its enactment in 1974, Section 4(2)(f) of the Water Act prescribed that the Member-Secretary should be 'qualified in public health engineering and have administrative experience in environmental protection'. However, in its wisdom the Parliament broadened the qualification requirement for the post of Member-Secretary to its present wide and general formulation. Hence, the Court held that in the current formulation of Section 4(2)(f) the Member-Secretary could not be said to have lacked the necessary knowledge or qualifications as she was managing certain aspects of pollution in her various capacities.

The most important position in the Pollution Control Board is that of the Chairman. The qualifications of a Chairman are stipulated in the Water Act. He must have special knowledge or practical experience in matters relating to environmental protection or administration of such issues. Thus, a very general qualification has been prescribed for a very important position in pollution administration and enforcement of standards. In fact, a study carried out by the Centre of Policy Research (CPR) highlights that if we look at the profile of the Chairman of the Pollution Control Boards, there is no definite qualification that has been prescribed. The Government always has the discretionary power because it is a nominated

120 Rajendra Singh Bhandari v. State of Uttarakhand, (2016) 08 NGT CK 0029.

121 Karnataka State Pollution Control Board Officer's Association v. State of Karnataka, W.P. No. 8460-8466 of 2004.

position, and so the Government can use the discretion to appoint anyone to become the Chairman of the Pollution Control Board.[122]

The landmark case of *G. Jagannath Pillai v. State of Karnataka*[123] highlights this situation. In this case Dr Bangeri, a lecturer in zoology in a pre-university college, was appointed as the Chairman of the Karnataka State Pollution Control Board by the State Government. His appointment was done in a very opaque manner. It was found that a selection committee was nominated which was called as a search committee comprised of very eminent people that shortlisted three names and submitted them to the Government. The Government returned the file of three nominations to the search committee informing them that these three names were insufficient and the State Government was including a fourth name. The search committee was directed to consider this candidate's name also for selection and then take a decision and come up with a recommendation. The search committee looked at their own list and found that the fourth name was not even among the top ten shortlisted by them. And so, they refused to change their previous set of three recommendations.

Overlooking the recommendation of the search committee, the State Government appointed Dr Bangeri as the Chairman of the State Pollution Control Board. This decision of the State Government created two issues. Firstly, despite a particular procedure that was laid down whereby the Government would pick and choose among the three recommendations made, the Government did not follow the recommendation. Secondly, the Government went beyond the list and came up with someone out of the blue and nominated him as a Chairman. Hence, the question in this case was whether the Government could do so. However, the case dragged on for a long time. Further, even the secretary to the Government dealing with the environment and forests had given a dissenting note to the decision of the Government, saying that this was not the proper procedure to follow. Defying even that, the State Government had taken the decision because it is a governmental decision, and as per the Act the Government is given the power to make any nomination. However, the court held that this was not the appropriate course of action and directed a fresh appointment. The court gave the Government a very short period of time before the term ended. Despite the court's direction, the Government had still not acted even though the three-year period elapsed and the term of the Chairman came to an end. The matter came up again before the court of law and the court directed the State Government to comply with the previous instructions immediately within three months. At the end of the third month, the Government finally came up with a new appointment. This case highlights that a person who did not have the approval of the search committee was appointed as the Chairman of SPCB. He not only completed a three-year term but also an extended three months in office because

122 Shibani Ghosh, et al., *The State of India's Pollution Control Boards: Who is at the Helm?* (Centre for Policy Research, 2022).

123 G. Jagannath Pillai v. State of Karnataka, 1998 (6) KarLJ 126.

until the next Chairman takes over he was under the law entitled to continue as the Chairman.

The Case of Jharkhand Pollution Control Board Chairman (2002) is another case which highlights the abuse of discretionary powers in the appointment of the Chairman of the Pollution Control Board.[124] The High Court had certain doubts regarding a pollution matter. Each time they had a doubt they would seek clarification from the Chairman, Shri Thakur Bal Mukund Shahdeo, who was present in the court. On several of the clarifications sought from the Chairman, the Chairman replied that he would revert back to the hon'ble court after getting the advice. This continued for a number of occasions, and each time when clarifications were sought, the Chairman would buy time. The Court then enquired about the selection of the Chairman and his qualification for appointment as the Chairman of the Pollution Control Board. It was revealed that there is no evidence to show that Shri Shahdeo, who is a matriculate, had any technical expertise to qualify for the chairmanship of the board. He was actually the follower of the minister of environment and forest in that particular State. Considering that it is a specialised position, the Jharkhand High Court quashed the appointment of Shahdeo and directed the State Government to make a proper appointment. The Government, however, showed reluctance to follow the instructions of the court. It submitted that it was a discretionary power and that the Government is very much within its powers to make this appointment. But luckily, the friction with the court ended, and the Government made a fresh appointment. This case highlighted that since there is no fixed qualification for holding a specified position, the Government has made all kinds of political appointments. A study conducted by Down to Earth stated that at one point of time, out of 32 PCBs in the country, almost 22 (about 70%) had 'part-time' Chairmen. Around 15 of them were appointed by the Government from the general services such as the IAS and the IFS (forest officers). Among the remaining 15, it could be anybody – it could be a scientist, it could be an activist, it could be a political heavyweight, it could even be a minister. It could be somebody who was denied a ministership and made into the Chairman.[125] Hence, the recruitment of the chairperson of the PCB is a bit of a weak position in the working of this law. The Water Act makes the qualifications very general. Thus, it is high time to revise this particular provision so as to limit the discretion of the Government and to limit it to those who have the knowhow, the knowledge, the skill, and the expertise in this particular area to hold this important position.

Yet another aspect of the status of Chairman comes to light with a greater degree of force in the case of *Suma Traders v. Karnataka State Pollution Control*

124 *See Unfit for Office*, Down to Earth (June 30, 2002), https://www.downtoearth.org.in/news/unfit-for-office-14774; *Realities Unmasked*, Down to Earth (Oct. 31, 2002), https://www.downtoearth.org.in/news/realities-unmasked-15346; TNN, *Jharkhand Pollution Board Chief Sacked*, Times of India (May 18, 2002), https://timesofindia.indiatimes.com/india/jharkhand-pollution-board-chief-sacked/articleshow/13217094.cms.

125 *Id.*; *see also* Shibani Ghosh, et al., *The State of India's Pollution Control Boards: Who is at the Helm?* (Centre for Policy Research, 2022).

Board.[126] In this case, an industry was releasing certain gaseous substances into the atmosphere from the chimney of that industry. This disturbed the people who were living in the neighbourhood. They felt that the dark cloud-like fumes that were coming out of this industry had contaminated the entire atmosphere, and they were finding it very difficult even to breathe. They complained to the Chairman of the Pollution Control Board over the telephone. Without any delay, the Chairman came to the spot, looked at the situation, summoned the occupier of the premises, and ordered the closure of this industry. The occupant resisted on the grounds that no notice was served upon him and no explanation was sought from him before passing the order. He was not even accorded an opportunity to give an explanation. The industry approached the court, and the question is whether the Chairman can make a decision like that. The court held that it is the Pollution Control Board that makes the decision and not an individual, including the Chairman. The power of the Chairman is to convene meetings, to chair the proceedings, and in the board the issues are deliberated and decisions are made. Among the decisions, the board can assign the task of executing the decision to any individual, and that individual will implement the orders of the PCB. However, in this case, the Chairman, instead of convening a meeting, made a decision and acted on that decision. Hence, such a decision is bad in law.

4.5.7 Powers and Functions of State Pollution Control Boards

Within the framework of this Act, the duties of a State Board extend into both civil and criminal jurisdictions. The civil functions of the SPCB include its advisory role to the State Government on matters under its purview,[127] planning comprehensive programmes for the prevention, control, or abatement of pollution of streams and wells in the State and securing their execution,[128] the laying down and enforcement of standards,[129] and evaluation of the consent to operate granted to industries and other units likely to cause water pollution. The criminal functions, laid out in Chapter VII, allow the board to take cognisance of environmental offences such as water pollution. Some of the important functions that the State Pollution Boards perform are as follows:

a) **Consent to Establish and Consent to Operate**: one of the pivotal functions of the State Pollution Control Boards is to grant Consent Orders. There are two types of Consent Orders envisaged under the Water Act: (i) Consent to Establish (CTE); and (ii) Consent to Operate (CTO). Any person establishing (or expanding) any industry, operation, or process or any treatment and disposal system, which is likely to discharge sewage or trade effluent, is required

126 Suma Traders v. Karnataka State Pollution Control Board, AIR 1998 Kar 8.
127 The Water (Prevention and Control of Pollution) Act, 1974 § 17(b).
128 *Id.* § 17(a).
129 *Id.* § 17(g) & (m).

to obtain CTE from the concerned SPCB under Section 25 of the Water Act. Once the industry is established (i.e. the equipment has been installed, and other measures have been taken, in accordance with CTE), it must apply for CTO before it can commence operations. CTE is generally a one-time activity and remains valid for three to five years. If the project proponent requires an extension of the period, it can apply for an extension on the basis of requirement. CTO, on the other hand, is a periodic activity. Once granted, it remains valid for a period of 5, 10, and 15 years according to the red, orange, and green categories of the industry respectively. The industry has to apply for renewal of the CTO before the expiry of the period of the previous CTO. The grant, extension, and renewal of both these consents are based on compliance with the environmental norms laid down by the PCB.[130]

In *Andhra Pradesh Pollution Control Board v. M.V. Nayudu*,[131] the court stressed that seeking permission from the State Pollution Control Board during the establishment of an industry is mandatory. Further, consent may also be 'deemed' under Section 25(7); the Karnataka High Court further ruled, in *Vijayanagar Educational Trust, Bangalore v. The Karnataka State Pollution Control Board*,[132] that it would be totally unjustified to deny such deemed consent when there was nothing on record either before the Board or before the Appellate Authority to show that the uncertain danger to the environment was 'non-negligible'. Any rejection of a request for the establishment of an industry, when the risk is certain but its nature is 'negligible' or 'non-negligible', could be made only after proper identification of the amount and nature of pollutants and the danger to which the environment is exposed by such pollution. However, there can be subsequent revocation if industries fail to comply or if the environmental damage turns out non-negligible, such as in *Tamil Nadu Pollution Control Board v. Sterlite Industries (I)*,[133] where the CTO was granted but the TNPCB later revoked it and ordered that the plant be shut down for major pollution concerns, including a 2013 leak of sulphur dioxide gas. The NGT ordered the plant to be reopened, but the Supreme Court struck down the NGT order.

b) **Monitoring compliance**: the SPCBs play a crucial role under the Water and Air Acts in monitoring the pollution caused by industries even after the grant of the CTO. Section 17(f) provides that the State Board may inspect sewage and trade effluents, and review plants and other systems of disposal of sewage or trade effluents which may arise in connection with the grant of consent as

130 The Water (Prevention and Control of Pollution) Act, 1974, § 25.
131 Andhra Pradesh Pollution Control Board v. M.V. Nayudu (2001) 2 SCC 62.
132 Vijayanagar Educational Trust, Banglore v. The Karnataka State Pollution Control Board, AIR 2002 Kant 123.
133 Tamil Nadu Pollution Control Board v. Sterlite Industries (I) Ltd., (2019) 19 SCC 479.

required under this Act.[134] Under Section 27(2), the board has the power to from time to time review industrial units to which it had previously granted consent, and refuse or withdraw such consent in cases of non-compliance.[135] This review includes but is not limited to reviewing plans, specifications, or other relevant data concerning water treatment facilities, purification works, and sewage or trade effluent disposal systems. In the case of *Madura Coats Private Limited Coats India v. The Appellate Authority Tamil Nadu Pollution Control Board and Ors*[136] it was held by the Madras High Court that the Board is well within its capacity to set standards of compliance with regard to such parameters, and revoke the CTO if such standards are not met. The Uttarakhand High Court also held in *Devendra Singh Adhikari v. State of Uttarakhand*[137] that industries that have previously received CTO under now-superseded standards are still required to comply with the new standards. Thus, the monitoring role of the SPCB primarily relates to compliance, and it has the right to revoke previous consent if such compliance is not found on review of the unit.

c) **Refusal to give consent or withdrawal of consent and Appellate Authority**: the State Pollution Control Boards are statutorily empowered to grant CTE and CTO to certain industries and activities, with a view to preemptively block activities that may cause considerable water pollution. It is mandatory, in fact, to obtain the consent from the SPCB.[138] However, it is not mandatory for the State Boards to grant consent to every Applicant. Under Section 27 of the Water Act, the State Boards have the power to refuse the grant of a consent order to Applicants if it is of the opinion that the person who has applied for such consent order is not in a position to comply with the conditions imposed by the Board.[139] Further, Section 27 also empowers the Board to (i) review any conditions imposed while granting a consent order, (ii) review the refusal of consent orders; and (iii) review grant of consent orders without any conditions. While doing such review, the SPCB can make any reasonable variation in the consent order or it may revoke the consent order, or may impose conditions (in the case of unconditional orders) or it may make any such orders as it deems fit. Any such variation made pursuant to Section 27 will supersede any condition imposed under Section 25 or Section 26 and will continue to remain in force unless and until it is revoked.

Orders of the SPCB granting or refusing consents are not only administrative orders but are also appealable orders. Thus, any person aggrieved by orders made by the SPCB under Section 25, 26, or 27 can, within 30 days from the date of

134 The Water (Prevention and Control of Pollution) Act, 1974, § 17(f).
135 *Id.* § 27.
136 Madura Coats Private Limited Coats India v. The Appellate Authority, Tamil Nadu Pollution Control Board, MANU/TN/0973/2009.
137 Devendra Singh Adhikari v. State of Uttarakhand. MANU/UC/0002/2023.
138 The Water (Prevention and Control of Pollution) Act, 1974, § 25.
139 *Id.* § 27.

communication of the order to him,[140] appeal to the Appellate Authority established under Section 28 of the Water Act.[141] Appellate Authority (AAs) are statutory bodies constituted by the State Governments to hear appeals against the orders made by their respective State Pollution Control Boards. Section 58 of the Water Act bars the jurisdiction of civil courts from entertaining any suit or proceeding related to matters for which the Appellate Authority has been constituted. It also prohibits any court or authority from granting injunctions against actions undertaken or to be undertaken in accordance with the powers conferred by or under the Water Act.[142] Thus, in other words, disputes falling within the purview of the Water Act must be addressed exclusively by AA, and civil courts are barred from intervening in such matters. This ensures that the disputes related to the Water Act are addressed in a streamlined manner.

In relation to the composition of the Appellate Authority, Section 28 of the Water Act provides that the AAs shall consist of either a single person or three persons (both odd numbers) as the State Government may think fit. However, generally as a matter of practice AAs are usually composed of three members. The members of the AAs are appointed by the State Governments. Thus, this creates a quasi-judicial forum, where such administrative orders passed by the SPCB may be challenged by those aggrieved or affected by them.[143] The statute does not specify the qualification and exact composition of the Appellate Authority, but the Supreme Court in *AP Pollution Control Board v. Prof. MV Nayudu*[144] reiterated the need for both judicial and technical members in forums deciding environmental cases, as both bring necessary qualifications to the adjudicatory process. It recommended that such appellate authorities should comprise 'a Judge of the High Court, sitting or retired, and a scientist or group of scientists of high ranking and experience, to help in the adjudication of disputes relating to the environment and pollution'.

The Madras High Court also said in *Puducherry Environment Protection Association v. Union of India*[145] that the existence of the NGT as a judicial body did not obviate the need for a judicial member in the Appellate Authority, which is a body of first appeal. This hierarchy of appeal against orders under Section 27 — first to the Appellate Authority and then to the NGT – must be maintained. The Supreme Court in the *Sterlite* case[146] clarified that

140 *Id.* § 28 proviso (the AAs are empowered to entertain appeals after the expiry of a 30-day period if the AA is satisfied that the Appellant was prevented by sufficient cause from filing the appeal on time).

141 *Id.*

142 *Id.* § 58.

143 Shibani Ghosh, Sharachchandra Lele & Nakul Heble, *Appellate Authorities under Pollution Control Laws in India: Powers, Potential and Problems*, 14 Lead 45 (2018), https://lead-journal.org/content/18045.pdf.

144 AP Pollution Control Board v. Prof. MV Nayudu, (1999) 2 SCC 718.

145 Puducherry Environment Protection Association v. Union of India, (2014) SCC OnLine Mad 947.

146 Tamil Nadu Pollution Control Board v. Sterlite Industries (I) Ltd., (2019) 19 SCC 479.

> an appeal against an order made under Section 27 of the Water Act is appealable to the appellate authority under Section 28 of the said Act. Under Section 33B (a) of the said Act, if a person is aggrieved by an order or decision of the appellate authority under Section 28, it is then appealable to the NGT. This is made clear also by Section 16(a) of the NGT Act.

Thus, it clarifies that even in cases where the appellate authority has not yet been constituted, 'a leapfrog appeal to the NGT cannot be countenanced'. It is also important to note that there is no strict requirement of locus for appeals to this authority; in *Gujarat Pollution Control Board v. Parmar Devusinh Shersinh*[147] it was held that not being a party to the consent order did not prevent someone from appealing to the authority if their interests would be impacted if the unit were indeed allowed to operate.

d) **Testing, sampling, and other evidentiary functions**: the SPCB also has the scientific functionality of testing and sampling the pollution capacity of various units, as well as the levels of various pollutants in the effluents of the plant. Such samples are used as evidence in cases both of previous cancellation of consents obtained, and in assessing environmental compensation, such as in the case of *Akhil Bhartiya Mengela Samaj Parishad v. Maharashtra Pollution Control Board,*[148] where it was used as grounds to justify cancellation of consent to operate a common effluent treatment plant.

However, there have been a number of questions pertaining to whether the collection of such samples violates the principles of natural justice by not giving the unit an opportunity to be heard. In *Delhi Bottling Company v. Central Pollution Control Board,*[149] the court went into the scope of Section 21 – power to take samples of effluents. The court observed that proceedings under Section 33 are legal proceedings, and so Section 21 samples must be taken in accordance with the requirements of Section 33, and samples must be taken only when the analysis is admissible under that section. At times the collection itself may be incorrect and thus incriminating, such as in the case of *Gujarat Pollution Control Board v. Nicosulf,*[150] where the effluent was collected prior to a final treating process. It was further held in *Maharashtra Pollution Control Board v. Deepak Fertilisers and Petrochemicals Corporation Ltd*[151] 'that [if] the factum of collection of sample was itself doubtful, all further steps taken in pursuant thereto like that of obtaining report does not carry prosecution case any further'. These cases shed light on the

147 Gujarat Pollution Control Board v. Parmar Devusinh Shersinh, 2000 SCC OnLine Guj 132.
148 Akhil Bhartiya Mengela Samaj Parishad v. Maharashtra Pollution Control Board, MANU/GT/0018/2022.
149 Delhi Bottling Company v. Central Pollution Control Board, AIR 1986 Del 152.
150 Gujarat Pollution Control Board v. Nicosulf, (2009) 2 SCC 171.
151 Maharashtra Pollution Control Board v. Deepak Fertilisers and Petrochemicals Corporation Ltd, Criminal Appeal No.1237 of 2002, Bombay HC.

legal intricacies surrounding the collection of samples for analysis under the Water Act. They also emphasise the importance of adhering to prescribed procedures to maintain the admissibility and reliability of evidence in legal proceedings related to environmental pollution.

Apart from its functions specifically related to the environmental consent framework of the law, the SPCB also has broader functions of regulation and the setting of standards, as well as framing policies pertaining to water pollution. These include:

- **Effluent and treatment standards for sewage and trade effluents and for the quality of local waters resulting from effluent discharge**: setting, updating, and nullifying standards for effluents discharged into local waters is vital for pollution control, as is tailoring treatment standards to specific streams. The State Board sets these standards considering the local conditions and the capacity of the stream to dilute and absorb effluents without causing pollution.[152] This ensures that levels of pollutants in the water remain within acceptable limits.
- **Developing effective and efficient methods for waste treatment and disposal**: the State Board localises treatment methods to the unique conditions of different regions, considering factors like soil type, climate, and water flow characteristics.[153] Finding sustainable ways to utilise treated sewage and trade effluents in agriculture is an important initiative. The State Board explores methods to safely and effectively use these resources in agriculture to reduce environmental impact.[154] The Board also devises efficient approaches for land-based disposal of sewage and trade effluents, which is essential due to prevailing conditions of low stream flows for a significant part of the year, making it challenging to achieve the minimum dilution degree for proper waste management.[155] At times the Board may also direct erring units to implement these methods to reduce the amount of pollution being caused.[156] For example, in the *Madura Coats* case, it directed the unit to implement a continuous TDS monitor to measure the level of pollutants being discharged. The courts may also order that certain measures be taken, as per these newer and more efficient approaches; for example, in *Vellore Citizens Welfare Forum v. Union of India*,[157] it was directed that tanneries in the State of Tamil Nadu should avail of the subsidies already being provided by the State on the SPCB's advice in order to set up common effluent treatment plants that multiple small industries could share the costs of.
- **Enacting, modifying, or revoking orders to prevent, control, or mitigate waste discharges into streams or wells**: the State Board can issue, amend, or

152 Water (Prevention and Control of Pollution) Act, 1974, § 17(1)(k).
153 *Id.* § 17(1)(j).
154 *Id.* § 17(1)(i).
155 *Id.* § 17(1)(k).
156 *Id.* § 17(1)(l)(ii).
157 Vellore Citizens Welfare Forum v. Union of India, 1996 5 SCR 241.

revoke orders to ensure waste discharges into streams or wells are controlled, reduced, or prevented to protect the water bodies effectively.[158] Such powers, if exercised in the interest of environmental protection, are not subject to scrutiny; for example, an order limiting the kinds of Ganesha idols that could be immersed in water bodies to prevent toxic paints and chemicals entering them was upheld by the Karnataka High Court in *Bengaluru Mahanagara Ganesh Utsav Samiti v. State of Karnataka*.[159]

- **Providing guidance to the State Government on matters concerning the prevention, control, or reduction of water pollution**: the State Board acts as an advisory body, offering expert advice and recommendations to the State Government on various aspects related to water pollution.[160] This could encompass suggesting policy changes, technological advancements, or specific actions required to kerb pollution effectively. The Board also advises the State Government to help prevent industrial pollution in critical water bodies.[161]
- **Gathering information related to water pollution and its prevention, control, or reduction**: the State Board actively collects data and information regarding water pollution and prevention strategies. This involves conducting research, investigations, and studies focused on understanding the dynamics of water pollution.[162] The findings from these activities can be used to formulate effective strategies and policies to combat pollution effectively.
- **Collaborating with the Central Board**: the SPCB is required to collaborate with the Central Pollution Control Board to organise training programmes for individuals engaged or planning to be engaged in initiatives related to the prevention, control, or reduction of water pollution. Collaboration is key to the implementation of the Board's orders. Working closely with the Central Board, the State Board helps in organising training programmes to educate individuals involved in pollution control efforts. This also includes educating the broader public through mass awareness campaigns.[163]
- **Power to seek information and assistance from local authorities**: similar to the CPCB, the State Boards will also require assistance from local authorities and hence, the State Boards also can request the same from local authorities. Section 55 of the Water Act explicitly provides that all the local authorities are duty-bound to render such help and assistance and furnish such information to the Board. Further, the Board, in order to discharge its functions, can also inspect and examine records, maps, plans, and other documents. The local authorities are obligated to make the same available to the Board.[164]

158 The Water (Prevention and Control of Pollution) Act, 1974, § 17(1)(l).
159 Bengaluru Mahanagara Ganesh Utsav Samiti v. State of Karnataka, (2017) Writ Petition Nos. 35047 and 35448 of 2017 (Kar HC).
160 The Water (Prevention and Control of Pollution) Act, 1974, § 17(1)(b).
161 *Id.* § 17(1)(n).
162 *Id.* § 17(1)(d).
163 *Id.* § 17(1)(e).
164 *Id.* § 57.

- **Establishment of State Board laboratories and State Board analysts**: Section 17(2) of the Water Act empowers the State Pollution Control Boards to either establish or recognise a laboratory or laboratories. Such laboratories play an important role in assisting the Board to carry out its functions.[165] The most significant role of such laboratories is to conduct analysis of samples of water or trade effluents collected by the Board in exercise of its sampling power under Sections 21 and 22 of the Water Act.[166] Further, the SPCBs are also authorised to appoint Board analysts with the approval of their respective State Governments. The Board analysts, so appointed, are the persons in charge of carrying out the analysis of samples of water or sewage or trade effluents sent for analysis by the Board.[167]
- **Power to constitute committees and engage persons**: similar to the CPCB, the SPCBs are also authorised under Section 9 of the Act to constitute as many committees and for such purpose or purposes as it deems necessary. These committees can either be fully comprised of board members or non-board members, or they can be comprised partly of members and partly of non-members. Further, the SPCBs can also prescribe their time and place of meeting along with the rules for the procedure for the transaction of business.[168] Furthermore, similar to the CPCB, the SPCBs can also engage any person on a temporary basis for assistance or advice in performing its functions. Such persons associated with the Board are not regarded as Board members, and although they have the right to take part in the Board discussions, they do not have the right to vote in Board meetings.[169] Additionally, the SPCB also has the responsibility to prescribe the fees and allowance to be paid to non-board members of committees constituted by it under Section 9 and also to the other persons it decides to associate under Section 10.
- **Power to delegate powers to the Chairman**: just like the CPCB, the SPCBs are also juridical entities and hence they require a human agency to exercise its powers and carry out its functions. Hence, similar to the CPCB, the State Board is also empowered to delegate its power and functions to the Chairman who will then exercise such powers and perform such duties as have been delegated to him by the Board.[170]

Apart from these functions, the SPCBs are required to carry out additional functions as prescribed or as entrusted by the Central Board or the State Government on a periodic basis: the State Board's functions are broad, but they also change based on the circumstances and necessity.[171] Further, In instances of violations or

165 The Water (Prevention and Control of Pollution) Act, 1974, § 17(2).
166 *Id.* § 21.
167 *Id.* § 53.
168 *Id.* § 9.
169 *Id.* § 10.
170 *Id.* § 11A.
171 *Id.* § 17(1)(o).

non-compliance with the Act, SPCBs can impose penalties and fines on industries or individuals. These penalties act as a deterrent, promoting strict adherence to pollution control norms and regulations. The fines are to be calculated as per the various formulae for environmental compensation laid down by the CPCB. Overall, these provisions grant the State Board the necessary powers to gather crucial data, monitor water usage and pollution, and obtain insights into various activities that could potentially affect water sources. This information is vital for making informed decisions and formulating strategies to prevent, control, and mitigate water pollution effectively. Further, the State Board is duty-bound under Section 57 of the Water Act to submit and furnish to the respective State Government and the Central Pollution Control Board reports, returns, statistics, accounts, and other information with respect to its funds or activities which the State Government or the CPCB may ask it to provide from time to time.[172]

4.5.8 Joint Boards

In India, given the diverse nature and size of each State (big States, small States, and almost microstates – especially in the north-eastern region), many a time, due to budgetary constraints, it might happen that some small States will not be in a position to have an independent Pollution Control Board exclusively for themselves. In such a situation, provisions for a Joint Board have been made in the Water Act.[173] Joint Boards are formed: (i) through an agreement between two or more Governments of contiguous States, or (ii) through an agreement between the Central Government (in respect of one or more UTs) and one or more Governments of States contiguous to such UT(s).[174] A Joint Board has the same status as the State Pollution Control Board, which has representation from two or more States that have come together to constitute the joint board. Its status, role, responsibilities, and functions are the same as the State Pollution Control Board.

The Joint Board has a full-time Chairperson, a full-time Member-Secretary, and other members nominated by each participating State or the Central Government, as the case may be. It is envisaged to have equal representation from each participating State.[175] A perusal of the provisions of the joint board's composition elucidates that it is intended to bring together a rich pool of knowledge, expertise, and representation, allowing for a holistic approach to combatting environmental pollution. However, currently, there is no Joint Board in operation, and each State has its own separate Pollution Control Board. Only the UTs of Daman, Diu, and Dadra and Nagar Haveli have a Joint Pollution Control Committee.

172 The Water (Prevention and Control of Pollution) Act, 1974, § 57.
173 *Id.* Ch. IV.
174 *Id.* § 13(1).
175 *Id.* § 14.

4.5.9 Role, Responsibilities, and Powers of the Central and State Government under the Water Act

The Water Act, 1974, envisages a significant role for both the Central and State Governments in implementing the provisions of the Act. Although the role, responsibilities, and powers of both these tiers of the Government enumerated under the Act are distinct and specifically demarcated, at the same time, they are also similar and interconnected. This section outlines some of the key functions entrusted to both these Governments.

a. **Power to appoint key functionaries and members of the Pollution Control Boards**: one of the most significant functions of the Central and State Governments is to appoint and nominate key functionaries to the Pollution Control Boards. The Central Government makes the appointments and nominations in relation to the Central Pollution Control Board, whereas the State Government makes appointments and nominations in relation to State Pollution Control Boards and Appellate Authorities. They are also empowered to lay down the conditions for terms and services, allowances, etc., for such functionaries. They are also empowered to remove the appointed persons from their office.

Given the wide powers of the Central Government with regard to appointment, they are also amenable to great abuse upon the change of Government. The case of *N Bhoomand Manay v. State of Karnataka*[176] highlights this concern. In this case, the Petitioner, who held a postgraduate qualification in engineering from Karnataka and from Yale University, was nominated as Chairman of the Karnataka State Pollution Control Board. The notification prescribing the period of his appointment stated that he shall be Chairman for a period of three years (from the date of his nomination) or *until further orders*. This appointment was made by the Government before the general elections of 2004. After the elections a new Government took over and it took the decision to seek resignation of all the directors and chairmen of various corporations and boards who were appointed by the previous Government, and in case the resignations were not tendered, the Government directed that they were to be relieved and the secretaries of those departments should take charge. This direction of the Government was challenged by the Petitioner in this case. The Government defended its action on the ground that the phrase '*until further orders*' in the appointment notification empowers the Government to order the removal of the Chairman even before the end of the three-year period.

The Karnataka High Court in this case observed that Section 5 of the Water Act fixes the tenure of a member (including Chairman) for a term of three years from the date of his nomination. Further, the proviso of Section 5 makes it clear that notwithstanding the expiration of his term, he continues to hold office until his

176 N. Bhoomanand Manay v. State of Karnataka, 2006 (1) Kar LJ 407.

successor enters office. Therefore, it is clear that the term of the office of a member (including the Chairman) is statutorily fixed; it would not come to an end automatically with the expiration of that period but rather will come to an end only when their successor enters office. Hence, he does not hold office at the pleasure of the Government. Although Section 5 also empowers the State Government to remove any member (including Chairman) before the expiry of the term, before doing so he has to give such a member a reasonable opportunity of showing cause against the same. Thus, though the removal of a member is also statutorily provided under the Act, such removal has to be in accordance with the law. In the instant case, however, no notice was served upon the Petitioner asking him to show cause, and in fact, his multiple letters addressed to the Chief Minister asking for clarification regarding his removal remained unanswered.

Further, it is not the case that the appointment of the Chairman was being questioned on the ground of his lack of qualification or his continuation as Chairman was being hit by any disqualification mentioned in Section 6. Thus, the Court held that the removal of the Chairman by the State Government was contrary to law, illegal, and could not be sustained. Lastly, the hon'ble court expressed its distress as to how responsible qualified persons appointed to posts of cabinet rank in terms of statutory requirements were treated after the change of Government. The court stated that

> If such appointments were purely political in nature, the only criteria being loyalty to the party in power, the government would have been justified in removing such persons from office. However, this rule cannot be applied to statutory appointments made based on qualification in public interest.

Another important question that emerges with respect to the appointments made by the Central and State Governments is whether such appointments can be challenged before the National Green Tribunal. In *Rajendra Singh Bhandari v. State of Uttarakhand*,[177] the Applicant contested the constitution of Uttarakhand SPCB on the ground that the members appointed as Chairman and Member-Secretary lacked the necessary training, expertise, and experience in environmental protection and pollution control as required by the Water Act and the Air Act. Initially the petition was filed before the High Court of Uttarakhand, which directed the Applicant to approach the NGT. The Applicant further claimed that environmental degradation and natural disasters were caused by the Uttarakhand SPCB illegally granting polluting industries no objection certificates (NOCs) without taking the area's carrying capacity and eco-sensitivity into account. The Tribunal observed that on many previous occasions various High Courts and the Supreme Court have laid down direction with respect to the appointment of the Chairman and Member-Secretary of the Pollution Control Boards. However, a large number of States and Union Territories have disregarded these directives and appointed individuals who did not

177 Rajendra Singh Bhandari v. State of Uttarakhand, OA No. 318 of 2013 (NGT).

meet the requirements as the Chairman or Member-Secretary of their respective SPCBs. The Tribunal held that these appointments were unlawful, arbitrary, and in violation of the Air Act's and the Water Act's express mandates. Within three months, the Tribunal ordered all States and Union Territories to reconstitute their SPCBs in compliance with the guidelines and the law. In addition, the Tribunal instructed the MoEF to keep an eye on and guarantee adherence to its ruling.

Later on, the issue of whether the NGT has the power to quash such appointments came before the Supreme Court in *Techi Tagi Tara v. Rajendra Singh Bhandari*.[178] In this case, the State Governments were instructed by the NGT to reevaluate the selection of the Chairperson and members of the SPCBs, and guidelines for these appointments were released. The Appellants contested the NGT's order, arguing that the tribunal went beyond its jurisdiction and that there was no significant environmental question or dispute that the NGT could resolve concerning the SPCBs' appointment. It was held by the Supreme Court that the appointment of the SPCBs as a matter could be challenged before the constitutional courts and not before the NGT. Accordingly, the Supreme Court overturned the NGT's order because of a lack of jurisdiction. But at the same time, the apex court also underlined how crucial it is to appoint competent and experienced individuals to the SPCBs to effectively protect the environment.

In the case of *T. Narasimhamurthy v. State of Karnataka*,[179] the Petitioner challenged the appointment of the Chairman of Karnataka State Pollution Control Board arguing that the person appointed lacked the qualifications to be appointed as Chairman. However, the Petitioner was not able to put any material on record to show that the person appointed lacked the necessary qualifications. This case highlights that it is the responsibility of the person challenging the appointment to provide evidence in support of his claim.

b. **Power to establish Central and State water laboratory and framing of related rules**: Section 51 of the Water Act grants the Central Government the authority to either establish a Central water laboratory or designate an existing laboratory or institute as a Central water laboratory. Similarly, the Water Act makes provisions for the establishment of a State water laboratory. Section 52 of the Water Act grants the State Government the authority to either establish a State water laboratory or designate an existing laboratory or institute as a State water laboratory. Additionally, the Central Government, in consultation with CPCB, is also empowered to frame rules that specify the functions of the Central water laboratory, the procedure for submitting water, sewage, or trade effluent samples for analysis, the format of laboratory reports, the associated fees, and any other additional aspects that are required to enable the laboratory to perform its functions effectively.[180] A similar power has been given to

178 Techi Tagi Tara v. Rajendra Singh Bhandari, Civil Appeal No. 1359 of 2017 (SC).
179 T. Narasimhamurthy v. State of Karnataka, WP No. 39682 of 2016 (Kar HC).
180 The Water (Prevention and Control of Pollution) Act, 1974 § 51.

the State Government, which formulates such rules in consultation with the respective SPCB.[181] Both the Central Government and State Governments can appoint Government analysts to their respective laboratories to analyse samples of water or of sewage or trade effluent sent to the Central water laboratory for analysis.[182] The analysis reports signed by such Government analysts may be used as evidence of the facts stated therein in any proceeding under this Act.[183]

c. **Power of the Central Government to supersede the Pollution Control Boards under certain circumstances**: Sections 61 and 62 of the Water Act provide for supersession of Pollution Control Boards by their respective Governments. Section 61 empowers the Central Government to supersede the Central Pollution Control Board or any Joint Board for specific reasons. This section provides that if the Central Government is of the opinion that (i) the CPCB or any Joint Board has persistently defaulted in performance of its functions under the Act; or (ii) circumstances are such that it is necessary in the public interest to take such action, then the Central Government by issuing a notification in the Official Gazette can supersede the Board for a maximum period of one year.[184] This period can be extended by a further period not exceeding six months.[185] However, the Central Government must give the respective Board a reasonable opportunity to show cause and it should consider any explanation or objections made by the Board before issuing the notification.[186] The effect of issuing the notification superseding the Board is that during the period of supersession all board members have to vacate their offices, and the powers and functions of the Board are taken over and exercised by the Central Government or any person appointed by it, and the property of the Board is also taken over by the Central Government.[187] The Central Government will continue to do so until the Board is reconstituted.[188] However, the Central Government cannot exercise the functions and powers of the Board forever, and hence, before or on the expiry of the initial or extended time of supersession, it has to reconstitute the Board with fresh appointments.[189] A similar power to supersede the State Pollution Control Board on the same grounds has been given to the State Governments under Section 62 of the Water Act.
d. **Rule-making power of the Central Government**: the Water Act confers wide rule-making powers to the Central Government subject to three conditions: (i) the rules should be made in respect of the matters listed in Section 63(2);[190]

181 The Water (Prevention and Control of Pollution) Act, 1974, § 52.
182 *Id.* § 53.
183 *Id.* § 54.
184 *Id.* § 61(1).
185 *Id.* 61(3)(a).
186 *Id.* § 63(1), proviso.
187 *Id.* § 61(2).
188 *Id.* § 61(2).
189 *Id.* § 61(3).
190 *Id.* § 63(1).

(ii) once the Central Board has been constituted, no rule shall be made, varied, amended, or repealed without consulting the board, i.e. the Central Government is required to mandatorily consult the CPCB while exercising its rule-making power,[191] and (iii) parliamentary supervision of delegated legislation, i.e. any rule made by the Central Government shall be laid down before the Parliament which has the power to modify them.[192] The matters listed in Section 63(2) cover a wide range of subjects such as terms and conditions of services of CPCB members, the schedule and procedure for Board meetings, the fees and allowances of non-board members of the committees constituted under Section 9(3), the engagement of individuals by the CPCB, the terms and conditions of service of the Chairman and Member-Secretary and their respective powers and duties, and the powers and functions of CPCB in relation to Union Territories. Additionally, the Central Government by rules may also specify the formats of reports, budgets, annual reports, accounts, and the manner in which the notice of intention to make a complaint shall be given to the CPCB or its authorised officer under Section 49.[193]

e. **Rule-making power of the State Governments**: Section 64 of the Water Act confers authority upon the State Government to make rules to carry out the purposes of the Water Act. However, this power of the State Governments is not unlimited. It is subject to two key constraints: (i) once the State Board for that particular State has been constituted, then the creation of any new rule or variation, amendment, or repeal of the already existing rules cannot be done by the State Government without consulting the SPCB;[194] (ii) the State Government can only make rules on matters which do not fall within the purview of Section 63, i.e. the State Governments cannot make rules on those matters for which the rule-making power is vested with the Central Government.[195]

Apart from these two limitations, the rule-making power of the State Governments is still extensive and can encompass a wide array of subjects, including the terms and conditions of service of the SPCB members (excluding the Chairman and Member-Secretary), the time, place, and conduct of SPCB meetings (including the quorum required), fees and allowances of non-board members of the committees constituted under Section 9(3), conditions for the engagement of individuals with the State Boards, the other terms and conditions of the Chairman and Member-Secretary under Section 5(9), and the powers and duties to be exercised by the Chairman and Member-Secretary. Additionally, through rules, the State Government may specify the required format for the various notices, reports, consent applications, appeals, budget preparation, annual reports, maintenance of accounts, the manner in which an inquiry under

191 The Water (Prevention and Control of Pollution) Act, 1974, § 63(1), proviso.
192 *Id.* § 63(3).
193 *Id.* § 63(2).
194 *Id.* § 64, proviso.
195 *Id.* § 64(1).

Section 25(3) may be made in respect of an application for obtaining consent, and the manner in which notice of intention to file a complaint shall be given to the Board or its authorised officer under Section 49, etc.[196] Lastly, it is very interesting to note that, unlike the rules made by the Central Government, the rules made by the State Governments are not required to be laid down before the State Legislature for approval. Thus, legislative supervision of delegated legislation is not contemplated for the State Government Rules under the Water Act.

f. **Power of the Central Government and State Government to demand reports from Pollution Control Boards**: Section 57 of the Water Act provides that the Central Government and the State Government, may, from time to time, ask the Pollution Control Boards to furnish such reports, statistics, accounts, and other information with respect to its funds or activities as it may require. The Central Government can demand such reports from the Central Pollution Control Boards whereas the State Government can demand the same from its respective SPSB. Both the Central Board and the State Board are duty-bound to furnish such reports.[197]
g. **Power to acquire land for the State Board**: Section 56 of the Water Act provides that if the State Board requires any land for the effective execution of its duties under the Water Act, such land can be acquired for the State Board under the provisions of the Land Acquisition Act, 1894 (now repealed), or under any other corresponding law for the time being in force (LARR, 2013).[198] Both the Central Government and the State Governments have the power to acquire land under the legal regime for land acquisition in India. The Water Act makes it clear that the land required by the SPCB for the effective performance of its functions is deemed to be for a public purpose.[199]
h. **Power of the State Government to restrict the application of the Water Act and notify 'pollution control areas'**: under Section 19 of the Act, the State Governments have the power to extend or restrict the application of the Water Act to any part of that particular State.[200] These parts are called 'Water pollution, prevention and control areas' which can either be declared with reference to a map or by reference to the line of any watershed or the boundary of any district or partly by one method and partly by another.[201] This provision makes it a very unique legislation because the State may adopt it in its entirety but restrict it in terms of application. To exercise the discretion under Section 19, the State is required to come up with a clear gazette notification to the effect that this law is applicable to the entire State or is confined to a particular area or it does not

196 The Water (Prevention and Control of Pollution) Act, 1974, § 64(2).
197 *Id.* § 57.
198 The Right to Fair Compensation and Transparency in Land Acquisition, Rehabilitation and Resettlement Act, 2013.
199 The Water (Prevention and Control of Pollution) Act, 1974 § 56.
200 *Id.* § 19(1).
201 *Id.* § 19(2).

operate in a particular area. Upon such a gazetted notification, the Act, rules, regulations, and notifications issued under it will be applicable only where it has been designated to be operative. Further, the States by a subsequent notification can alter, extend, and reduce any existing water pollution, prevention, and control areas. The States can also define new water pollution, prevention, and control areas by merging one or more such areas or by merging any part or parts of such areas.[202]

i. **Power to revise non-appealable consent orders of the SPCB**: the State Government is empowered under Section 29 of the Water Act to revise the orders made by the SPCBs with regard to consent (i.e. grant, refusal to grant, or withdrawal of grant of consent) under Section 25, 26, or 27 of the Water Act,[203] and there is no provision of appeal of such orders.

4.5.10 Relationship between the Administrative and Pollution Control Bodies

Firstly, it is important to highlight that generally pollution control laws are made by the Central Government and these Central laws are enforced as a general rule by the State functionaries, i.e. the State Pollution Control Boards. This means that the Central Pollution Control Board lays down the standards and prescribes the norms as to how pollution needs to be controlled and managed,[204] and the State agency, in the form of the State Pollution Control Board, is responsible for implementing and enforcing them. The CPCB is not envisaged as an enforcement body; it will not enforce the standards it creates. It is the SPCBs which are entrusted with that responsibility and have to enforce the standards. However, in the case of Union Territories, it is the Central Pollution Control Board which performs the function of a State Pollution Control Board and enforces the Central law.[205]

Secondly, along with the standards set by the Centre, the States also have the power to make their own rules with regard to standards.[206] Every State will have its own unique requirements. So, in order to give that elbow space, rules can be framed by the States also. But these laws have to be aligned and in consonance with their respective Central law and the prescriptions made thereunder and with the condition that the rules made by the State should not go beyond the Central rules, meaning that the State rule can prescribe a far stricter standard than what has been fixed by the Centre but it cannot relax or dilute this standard.[207] The State can prescribe the maximum permissible (setting a strict standard), but it cannot dilute the standard set by CPCB. Thus, the States can be stricter in laying down the standards but they cannot be more relaxed. Hence, the strictest standard of the two will be enforceable in that particular area.

202 The Water (Prevention and Control of Pollution) Act, 1974, § 19(3).
203 *Id.* § 29.
204 *Id.* § 16.
205 *Id.* § 4.
206 *Id.* § 17.
207 CPCB, Guidelines for Development of Location Specific Stringent Standards (2009).

Thirdly, in the performance of its functions, the Central Pollution Control Board is bound by the directions issued by the Central Government.[208] As stated earlier, the CPCB is primarily envisaged to have an advisory role, the role of an expert, the role of an educator, the role of a trainer. It can be described as a think tank, a brain trust, a guide, advisor, and monitor. It is supposed to train and equip all the States and State agencies in the performance of their duties at the State level.[209] The second primary function of CPCB is that it will perform the function of SPCBs in the case of Union Territories. Similarly, the State Pollution Control Board is bound by the obligations prescribed to it by the State Government.[210] However, in addition to the State Government, the SPCB is also bound by the directions given to it by the CPCB. Thus, in a way, whereas the CPCB has only one master – the Central Government – the SPCB, on the other hand, has two masters – the CPCB and the State Government. Suppose, in a hypothetical case, an action of the SPCB is based upon the directions issued by the State Government. Unfortunately, it may be that the directions of the State Government are at variance with the directions given by the CPCB, i.e. there is an inconsistency between the directions of the State Government and the CPCB. In such a situation, the Water Act mandates that the matter shall be referred to the Central Government, and its decision on the matter will be binding on all.[211]

Fourthly, a direction given by the Central Pollution Control Board is binding on the State Pollution Control Board. But in the case of a default or if the SPCB defies the direction given the CPCB, the Water Act makes it very clear that, if such defiance or a default in compliance with a direction of the CPCB, by the SPCB, leads to a grave emergency (such as the law is not put to work, or made inactive and no action is taken), and hence it is necessary or expedient in the public interest, the Central Government can direct the CPCB to take over the functions of the State Pollution Control Board and perform those functions in such areas and for such a period as stipulated in its order by the Central Government.[212] The effect of this direction is that the Water Act can become a highly centralised law. This provision is to a degree parallel and inspired by the Centre-State relation and president's rules under the Constitution. In other words, if there is a kind of breakdown of the machinery of implementation of the Act because of a conflict between CPCB and SPCB and SPCB is not complying with the directions of CPCB, in such an event law will have the grave danger of becoming redundant. And to prevent that, the Water Act has contemplated the Central rule over the State by empowering the Central Government to order the CPCB to take all such functions in that area.

Furthermore, Section 61 of the Water Act contemplates that the Central Government has the power to supersede the Central Pollution Control Board and

208 The Water (Prevention and Control of Pollution) Act, 1974 § 18.
209 *Id.* 16.
210 *Id.* § 18.
211 *Id.* § 18(1) proviso.
212 *Id.* § 18 (2).

Joint Boards.[213] Similarly, under Section 62 the State Government has the power to supersede the State Pollution Control Board.[214] Due to the State Government's power to supersede the State Board, scope for another legislative dilemma is created which has the potential to put the SPCB essentially in a devil and the deep blue sea situation. For instance, the Water Act states that the SPCB has the duty to follow every instruction of the State Government. But suppose there is a situation where the SPCB is given two different sets of instructions – one by the State Government and another by the Central Government – and they are in conflict or there is an inconsistency. In such a case which direction should the SPCB follow? It becomes very difficult to answer this question for the simple reason that if the SPCB does not follow the instructions of the CPCB, it may invite the wrath of the Central Government and it may take away its powers and functions, and hand it over to the CPCB. On the other hand, if the SPCB does not comply with the directions of the State Government, it has the power to supersede the State Board. Unfortunately, this anomaly has not been completely ironed out as yet. However, fortunately, there has been no such occasion where such a dilemma has actually occurred.

Lastly, under Section 29 of the Water Act, the State Government has the power to revise every order passed by the SPCB under Sections 25, 26, or 27 (except where the order passed by the SPCB is appealable, and there is an appellate authority constituted for hearing such appeal).[215] Thus, where provision and scope for seeking appeal before an appellate authority exist the State Government has no power to revise the orders of the State Pollution Control Board. The matter should go for resolution before the concerned appellate authority. But if there is no such appellate body, and the SPCB as a final authority has given the decision which is binding on the industry, in such a case, an application for revision can always be made to the State Government. Further, the State Government can take it up for revision, *suo moto*, and can pass appropriate orders. In *T.N. Pollution Control Board v. Sterlite Industries (I) Ltd.*, the Supreme Court held that there cannot be an appeal before any other authority (such as the National Green Tribunal) unless the appellate remedy before the State Government is exhausted.[216]

4.6 Provisions for Prevention and Control of Water Pollution under the Water Act

4.6.1 Other Civil Powers of the Pollution Control Boards

The Water Act grants substantial powers to the SPCBs necessary for the regulation of pollution, investigation of polluting incidents, and issuance of directions. There

213 The Water (Prevention and Control of Pollution) Act, 1974, § 61.
214 Under the Air Act, the state government even has the power to dissolve the board constituted under the Air Act.
215 The Water (Prevention and Control of Pollution) Act, 1974 § 29.
216 T.N. Pollution Control Board v. Sterlite Industries (I) Ltd., (2019) 19 SCC 479.

has also been a plethora of case laws which further clarify the extent and scope of these powers, many of which are auxiliary to its key civil and criminal functions.

1. **Power to obtain information**: in order to perform its responsibilities under the Act, the SPCB or its authorised officer is granted the authority to conduct surveys in any area, gather data, keep records, and monitor various aspects of water sources (streams and wells). This includes recording the flow, volume, and other characteristics of these water sources, as well as tracking rainfall patterns. The Board can also install and maintain equipment like gauges for this purpose. Additionally, the Board can take any necessary steps to collect information essential for its functions.[217] Furthermore, the SPCB has the power to issue directions to any person who is either extracting a substantial amount of water from the water sources or is discharging sewage or trade effluents into them. The Board can direct such individuals to provide specific information about their activities.[218] Lastly, in order to prevent or control water pollution, the SPCB can also require any person who is in charge of any establishment where any industrial operation or process or treatment and disposal systems are being carried out to furnish details about the construction, installation, or operation of these facilities, including any extensions or additions.[219] This information gathering activity is vital for the SPCBs to effectively regulate and control activities impacting water quality.

However, in exercising powers under this section, the Board cannot go beyond the scope of its authority and demand any sort of information that is not connected with its functions. For instance, in the case of *Shrushti Agro & Cold Storage v. State of Karnataka*,[220] the Petitioner was carrying on the activity of procuring meat and processing the same or storing it in the cold storage in his premises. The Board issued a communication to the Petitioner which, *inter alia*, required the Petitioner to submit documents regarding legal sources of procurement of meat and a copy of the KIADB allotment letter for permission to carry on the activity. The Court held that such a request is beyond the powers of the Board.

2. **Power to collect samples of effluents**: the power of the SPCBs to take samples and send them for analysis is one of the most important powers of the Boards. It is one of the major processes of collecting evidence related to water pollution. Section 21 of the Water Act outlines the authority related to taking samples of water, sewage, or trade effluents for analysis and lays down the procedure in this regard. The State Board or its authorised officer can collect samples from streams, wells, or places where sewage or trade effluents are discharged and can

217 The Water (Prevention and Control of Pollution) Act, 1974, § 20(1).
218 *Id.* § 20(2).
219 *Id.* § 20(3).
220 Shrushti Agro & Cold Storage v. State of Karnataka, W.P. No. 111502/2019 (GM-RES) (Kar HC).

send them for analysis.[221] However, the results of this analysis cannot be used as evidence in legal proceedings unless the specified conditions with regard to the procedure for obtaining samples are complied with.[222]

Section 21 prescribes that when a sample is taken, the person collecting the sample must serve a notice of his intention, then and there, to any of the following persons: (i) the person in charge of or having control over the plant or vessel; or (ii) the occupier, i.e. the person who is in occupation of the place;[223] or (iii) any agent of such occupier. After serving the notice, the procedure for collecting the sample and the laboratory to which it will be sent will depend upon the conduct and cooperation of the occupier or his agent. In normal cases where the occupier or his agent cooperates, the person taking the sample, after taking the sample, must divide it into two parts. This division has to be done in the presence of the occupier or his agent. Each part is placed in a separate container which is properly labelled and sealed. The containers should also be signed by both the person taking the sample and the occupier or his agent. One container is then sent forthwith for analysis to either the laboratory designated by the Central Board (if the sample is taken in a UT area) or the State Board laboratory (in all other cases). Further, if the occupier or his agents make a request, the second container can be sent for analysis to either the Central water laboratory (in case the sample is taken from a UT area) or the State water laboratory (in any other case).[224]

However, if, after serving the notice, the occupier wilfully absents himself from the process, then the person taking the sample should proceed as follows. Firstly, he should proceed with taking the sample. Secondly, the sample taken should be placed in one container (no division of the sample in this case). This container shall also be marked, sealed, and signed by the person taking the sample. Thirdly, the container should be sent forthwith to either the Central water laboratory (in case the sample is collected from a UT area) or the State water laboratory (in any other case). In this case, the person taking the sample cannot send it to the Board laboratory. Further, the person taking the sample must also inform the Government analyst in writing about the wilful absence of the occupier or his agent. Any expenses incurred in getting the sample analysed in this case can be recovered from the occupier as arrears of land revenue or of public demand, after giving a reasonable opportunity of being heard to the occupier or his agent.[225] Lastly, in case the occupier or his agent who was present at the time of taking the sample does not make a request for the sample to be divided into two parts, then in such a case, the duly taken sample should either be sent to the Central Board laboratory or the State Board laboratory, as the case may be.[226]

221 The Water (Prevention and Control of Pollution) Act, 1974, § 21(1).
222 *Id.* § 21(2).
223 *Id.* § 2(d) (defining the term occupier).
224 *Id.* § 21(3).
225 *Id.* § 21(4).
226 *Id.* § 21(5).

Section 22 further elaborates the procedure for reporting of results of the sample analysis. Firstly, when a sample is sent for analysis to a laboratory established or recognised by the Central or State Board, the Board analyst will conduct the analysis and prepare and submit three copies of the report (triplicate) to the concerned Board.[227] One copy is sent by the concerned board to the occupier or his agent, another copy is retained for potential legal proceedings, and the third copy is kept with the concerned board.[228] However, if a sample is sent to either the Central or State water laboratory, then it is the Government analyst at the laboratory who provides a report (in triplicate) to the concerned Board. In this case also, one copy is sent to the occupier or his agent, another is kept for potential legal proceedings, and the third copy is kept with the concerned board.[229] Interestingly, in case of an inconsistency or variation or discrepancy in the results of analysis carried out by different laboratories, the report from the Government analyst from the Central or State water laboratory prevails.[230] This provision is there to avoid any conflict of interest or misuse of the influence the Board may have over its own laboratory and its staff. It also ensures that independent and impartial expert analysis prevails. Lastly, any costs associated with analysing a sample at the request of the occupier or their agent are the responsibility of the occupier and can be recovered as arrears of land revenue or public demand in case of non-payment.[231]

The procedure for collection of samples as prescribed under Section 21 of the Water Act is a mandatory one. Not adhering to the prescribed procedure can vitiate legal proceedings commenced after analysing the sample. Section 21(2) expressly states that the result of any such analysis of a sample which has not been collected in conformity with the procedure laid down in Section 21 will not be admissible in evidence in any legal proceeding. In the case of *Delhi Bottling Co. Pvt. Ltd. v. Central Board for the Prevention and Control of Water Pollution*,[232] a sample of trade effluent was taken by the Board from the bottling company's discharge stream and after the analysis, it was found that the sample was non-conforming with the requirements of the Consent Order granted to the company. The Board filed a suit under the Water Act and accordingly, an injunction was issued by the court requiring the company to establish a treatment plant. The bottling company challenged this order. The Delhi High Court observed that the representative of the company was duly present at the time of taking the sample; however, the sample was not divided by the officials of the Board into two parts and no part thereof was given to the company's representative in spite of his request on that behalf. Hence, the hon'ble court held that the sample was not taken in strict compliance with the

227 The Water (Prevention and Control of Pollution) Act, 1974, § 22(1).
228 *Id.* § 22(2).
229 *Id.* § 22(3).
230 *Id.* § 22(4).
231 *Id.* § 22(5).
232 Delhi Bottling Co. Pvt. Ltd. v. Central Board for the Prevention and Control of Water Pollution, AIR 1986 Delhi 152.

procedure laid down under Section 21 of the Water Act and hence this evidence cannot be regarded as admissible.

3. **Powers of entry and inspection under Section 23**: Section 23 confers the power of entry and inspection to the State Pollution Control Boards.[233] This power is crucial in ensuring that the regulatory body can effectively monitor and enforce compliance with the provisions of the Act and its associated rules. The section enumerates the specific purposes for which such entry and inspection can be conducted which include execution of the functions of the board, ensuring compliance, examination of material, investigation of offences, and seizure of evidence. Thus, individuals authorised by the State Board can enter a premises to perform any function that has been entrusted to them by the Board. This could include activities related to pollution prevention, control, or abatement, as outlined in the Act.[234] The authorised individuals have the right to inspect locations to ascertain whether the prescribed functions are being carried out effectively. This involves assessing adherence to the Act and its rules, as well as any notices, orders, directions, or authorisations issued under the Act.[235] The inspection allows for the examination of various materials such as plants, records, registers, documents, or any other tangible objects relevant to pollution control. This is essential to verify compliance and gather evidence.[236] If there are reasonable grounds to suspect an offence under the Act or its rules, authorised individuals can conduct a search at a specific location. This is crucial for investigating violations and maintaining the integrity of the regulatory framework.[237] Further, in cases where there is a belief that certain materials might contain evidence related to an offence under the Act, authorised individuals have the power to seize such material. This ensures that potential evidence is preserved for further investigation and legal proceedings.[238]
4. **Power of the Board to obtain restraining orders from the Court (judicial remedy)**: Section 33 of the Water Act deals with such cases where there is an apprehension on the part of the CPCB or SPCB that the water in a stream or well might become polluted due to the disposal or likely disposal of substances in a stream, well, sewer, or land. In such cases, Section 33 grants the CPCB and the SPCBs the authority to approach a court, which is not inferior to that of a Metropolitan Magistrate or a Judicial Magistrate of First Class. The board can make an application before the court to grant restraining orders prohibiting the person, who is likely to cause pollution, from causing such pollution.[239] The court upon receiving such an application has the discretion to issue an

233 The Water (Prevention and Control of Pollution) Act, 1974, § 23(1).
234 *Id.* § 23(1)(a).
235 *Id.* § 23(1)(b).
236 *Id.* § 23(1)(c).
237 *Id.* § 23(1)(c).
238 *Id.* § 23(1)(c).
239 *Id.* § 33(1).

appropriate order. If the court makes a restraining order to stop a person from polluting the water, then in that order, the court may also instruct that person to either cease the activities causing pollution or remove the pollutants from the water source. Additionally, in the restraining order, the court can also authorise the Board to take action to remove and dispose of the pollutants if the person fails to comply with the court's order.[240] Any expenses incurred by the Board in removing and disposing of pollutants, as authorised by the court, can be covered by the funds obtained from the disposal, and any outstanding costs can be recovered from the responsible person as land revenue or a public demand in the form of arrears.[241]

5. **Power of the State Pollution Control Board to carry out certain works and take emergency measures (administrative justice – I)**: one of the significant developments in recent years has been the emphasis on obtaining speedy justice through the help of the administrative structure. Sections 30, 32, and 33A of the Water Act signify this trend. To start with Section 30 deals with situations where the State Board while granting consent orders under Section 25 or 26 has imposed certain conditions, and these conditions *inter alia* require the person to execute any necessary associated work within a given timeframe. If such work is not completed within the stipulated time, the State Board can issue a notice to the person, giving him at least 30 days to complete the work. If despite the notice, the person defaults in carrying out the work required, the State Board can step in and it can either execute the work itself or arrange for its execution. The expenses incurred by the State Board in doing so, along with interest, can be recovered from the person responsible as arrears of land revenue of public demand.[242] Next, Section 32 of the Act authorises the State Pollution Control Boards to take prompt and immediate action in cases of pollution of a stream, well, or land due to the release of poisonous or harmful substances due to any accident or unforeseen acts or events.[243] This action can involve removing the harmful substances from the stream/well/land, addressing pollution issues caused by the presence of such substances in the stream or well, and issuing immediate orders to prevent further discharges or unsanitary use of the affected stream or well. However, under this section, the authority of the SPCB is limited to temporary measures and it does not include the construction of permanent structures.[244] Further, the reasons for taking any such action by the SPCB must be recorded in writing.[245]
6. **Power to issue directions conferred under Section 33A (administrative justice – II)**: as per Section 33A of the Act, both the CPCB and the SPCBs have the power to issue directions in pursuance of powers granted under the

240 The Water (Prevention and Control of Pollution) Act, 1974, § 33(2).
241 *Id.* § 33(3).
242 *Id.* § 30.
243 *Id.* § 32(1).
244 *Id.* § 32(2).
245 *Id.* § 32(1).

Act to any person, officer, or authority, and such directions are binding.[246] This includes the power to direct the closure of any industry, operation, or process,[247] and the stopping or regulating of supply of any service like water or electricity.[248] In the case *In Re: Bhavani River – Sakthi Industry* case, the TNPCB issued some directions to Sakthi Industries, some of which were not complied with. On failure of the industry, the Board directed closure of operations. The court observed that the order of closure was justified due to the failure to carry out directions. Further, the court directed the industry to take remedial action.[249] A similar conclusion was reached in *Stella Silks v. State of Karnataka*, where it was held that the Petitioner continued the industry despite the notice of withdrawal of consent and continued to pollute the water. This went against their argument that the order was passed without an adequate opportunity for hearing. Further, it laid down that in the case of a grievance against withdrawal of consent, the procedure under Section 28 is to be followed.[250]

Although Section 33A of the Water Act is envisaged as an effective administrative enforcement mechanism in the hands of Pollution Control Boards to implement the Water Act, the case of *M/S Devi Enterprises v. The Environmental Officer, Karnataka State Pollution Control Board*[251] illustrates how the implementation of Section 33A itself could become a victim of bureaucratic impediments. In this case, an industry was operating without obtaining valid consent orders from the KSPCB. Show cause notices were issued by the Board and the industry was also called for personal hearing. But no one from the industry attended. Thus believing that industry was not interested in complying with the direction of the Board, it issued closure orders against the industry under Section 33A of the Water Act. The industry was directed to close the industrial operation or process 'forthwith' and until further orders. Simultaneously, the managing directors of the Bengaluru Electricity Supply Company (BESCOM) and Bengaluru Water Supply and Sewerage Board (BWSSB) were directed to issue necessary directions to the concerned engineers to stop/cut off the electricity and water supply to the industry 'forthwith' and until further orders. Additionally, the Commission of Bruhat Bengaluru Mahanagara Palike (BBMP) was also directed to withdraw the licence issued to the industry, under municipal laws, 'forthwith' and until further orders.

In pursuance of the said orders the concerned Managing Director of BESCOM wrote to his subordinate, who in turn wrote to his subordinate, and that subordinate further wrote to his subordinate. All this communication was done through letters sent by post. The resultant effect of this chain of communication was that the order

246 The Water (Prevention and Control of Pollution) Act, 1974, § 33A.
247 *Id.* § 33A(a).
248 *Id.* § 33A(b).
249 In Re: Bhavani River – Sakthi Industry, AIR 1998 SC 2059.
250 Stella Silks v. State of Karnataka, AIR 2001 Kant 219.
251 M/S Devi Enterprises v. The Environmental Officer, Karnataka State Pollution Control Board, WP No. 44828 of 2013 (Kar HC).

of 'forthwith' cutting of power and water supply issued by the Board on 3 July 2013 was not implemented till 22 August 2013. Furthermore, it was revealed that there is no record to show whether and when the MD of BWSSB had issued any direction for cutting the water supply. Moreover, the Commissioner of BBMP, instead of complying with the orders of the Board, attempted to press into service its own rules or procedure and only issued a show-cause notice to the industry on 28 August 2013, and there is no record to show what happened thereafter. Extremely agitated by this, the High Court of Karnataka not only dismissed the writ petition of the industry challenging the closure orders, but also reprimanded the KSPCB, the Electricity Company and Water Board, and the BBMP for delay in the enforcement of the orders. It was observed by the Court that the agencies have 'openly displayed a callous attitude in discharge of their duties', while the activity prohibited by the mandatory orders of the Boards merrily continued in flagrant violation of law through which the purpose of the stringent provisions of the Water Act has been defeated. Hence, the court, *firstly*, held that delay in the implementation of the orders 'forthwith' on the part of the Electricity Company and Water Board, *prima facie*, amounts to not only dereliction of duty, but a serious criminal offence under Section 41 of the Water Act. *Secondly*, the Court directed the KSPCB to file necessary complaints against all the officers of the electricity and water supply agencies as well as the Petitioner for non-implementation of the orders issued under Section 33A.

Thus, the *Devi Enterprises*[252] case reaffirms three main points of law in relation to Section 33A of the Water Act: (i) orders and directions issued under Section 33A are mandatory in nature; (ii) the agencies to whom such orders are issued cannot seek to enforce their own rules of procedures, including show-cause notice, while implementing the orders. The Water Act being a special law prevails over such requirements; and (iii) failure to comply with orders or unreasonable delay in implementing the orders issued under Section 33A can result in criminal prosecution of the agencies for the offence under Section 41 of the Water Act.

4.6.2 Criminal Penalties under the Water Act

The Water Act has quite an elaborate set of penal provisions to deal with almost every kind of violation (sec. 41, 42, 43, 44, 45, 45A). Chapter VII of the Water Act deals with penalties and procedure. The following acts are penalised as per the scheme of the Act:

1. **Failure to comply with orders**: failure to comply with an order under Section 20(2) or 20(3) to furnish information regarding extraction from or discharge into a water stream is criminalised under Section 40.[253] The punishment is

252 M/S Devi Enterprises v. The Environmental Officer, Karnataka State Pollution Control Board, WP No. 44828 of 2013 (Kar HC).

253 Water (Prevention and Control of Pollution) Act, 1974, § 20.

imprisonment up to three months, or a fine up to 10,000 rupees, or both. There may also be an additional fine of 5,000 rupees for each day the failure continues.[254] Further, failure to comply with orders issued under Section 32(1)(c) restraining or prohibiting a person from discharging polluting matter into a stream or well is criminalised under Section 41.[255] The punishment is imprisonment not less than one year and six months, up to six years, and with a fine. The same provision for continued failure is present.[256] If the failure continues for more than a year, the imprisonment period is not less than two years and can extend up to seven years.[257] In *Delhi Bottling Co. Pvt. Ltd. v. Central Board for the Prevention and Control of Water Pollution*,[258] the Delhi High Court has observed that if the Board gives a direction to the industry for setting up a treatment plant, then for non-erection of the treatment plant the Board has the power to launch prosecution against the defaulting company under Section 41 of the Water Act.

2. **Section 42 offences**: under Section 42, the following offences are criminalised:
   a. Destroying or defacing any matter put up by a Board, obstructing a Board from exercising its functions.
   b. Damaging of Board property.
   c. Failure to furnish information required by the Act.
   d. Failure to intimate occurrence of any unforeseen event or accident under Section 31 to the Board.
   e. Giving false information knowingly.
   f. Obtaining consent under Sections 25 or 26 by making any false statements.[259]

The punishment for these acts is imprisonment up to three months, a fine up to 10,000 rupees, or both.[260] Further, Section 42(2) also punishes altering a measuring or monitoring device used for the purposes of Section 25 or 26. The punishment may be imprisonment up to three months, a fine up to 10,000 rupees, or both.[261] As observed in *Karnataka State Pollution Control Board v. B. Heera Naik*, the terms 'any person' and 'whoever' under Section 42 are broad enough to convict functionaries of companies.[262] It was further held that the term 'body corporates' under Section 47 of the Water Act enables the prosecution and cognisance of offences against even public sector companies and statutory bodies like municipal

254 The Water (Prevention and Control of Pollution) Act, 1974, § 41(1).
255 *Id.* § 41(2), 32(1)(c).
256 *Id.* § 41(2).
257 *Id.* § 41(2).
258 Delhi Bottling Co. Pvt. Ltd. v. Central Board for the Prevention and Control of Water Pollution, AIR 1986 Delhi 152.
259 Water (Prevention and Control of Pollution) Act, 1974, § 42.
260 *Id.* § 42.
261 *Id.* § 42(2).
262 Karnataka State Pollution Control Board v. B. Heera Naik, (2020) 16 SCC 298.

corporations.[263] *Rajasthan State Board for Prevention & Control of Pollution v. Sharif Dyeing Works* ruled that the offence under Section 42 is a non-cognisable offence, because the maximum imprisonment thereunder is three years.[264]

3. **Penalty for use of a stream or well to dispose of polluting matter**: Section 24 of the Water Act prohibits the knowing emission of poisonous or polluting matter into a stream, well, sewer, or on land. It also prohibits knowingly allowing any matter which may cause a stream to stop flowing, either directly or in combination with other matter.[265] The standard here is to 'knowingly cause or permit'.[266] As observed in *Paryavaran Suraksha Samiti v. Union of India*, State Pollution Control Boards must undertake a rigid implementation of the standards under Section 24.[267] For this purpose, constant data collection and monitoring of industrial effluents must be undertaken by the Pollution Control Boards.[268] Further, Section 24(2) deals with some exceptions. It provides that any person who merely does the following acts shall not be guilty of an offence under this section:

i. Constructing, improving, or maintaining any structure in or across the bank or bed of a river or stream, that they have a right to be constructing.
ii. Depositing materials on the bank or in the bed of a stream for reclaiming land, or for protecting the bank or bed of the stream, provided such materials are not polluting.
iii. Putting into a stream any natural deposit that has been deposited by the stream.
iv. Causing deposit accumulated in a well, pond, or reservoir to enter into a stream with the consent of the State Board.[269]

Further, Section 24(2) vests power in the State Government to exempt any other persons from Section 24(1) by notification in a gazette, after consultation with the State Board.[270] The violation for Section 24 has been criminalised under Section 43. For the contravention of Section 24, Section 43 provides imposition of imprisonment for a term not less than one year and six months, and up to six years, and with a fine.[271] In the 2017 case of *Vikash Bansal v. Delhi Pollution Control Committee*,[272] better known as the *Haryana Paneer Bhandar case*, the polluter

263 *Id.*, at ¶ 17–22.
264 Rajasthan State Board for Prevention & Control of Pollution v. Sharif Dyeing Works, 1998 SCC OnLine Raj 497.
265 Water (Prevention and Control of Pollution) Act, 1974, § 24(1).
266 *Id.* § 24(1).
267 Paryavaran Suraksha Samiti v. Union of India, (2017) 5 SCC 326.
268 *Id.* ¶ 13.
269 Water (Prevention and Control of Pollution) Act, 1974, § 24(2).
270 *Id.* § 24(3).
271 *Id.* § 43.
272 Vikash Bansal v. Delhi Pollution Control Committee, (2017) Criminal Appeal No. 112/17 (Delhi).

was sentenced to two years' imprisonment for the discharge of effluents into the Yamuna; while the conviction was notably rare, this was not because of a lack of incidents but because of inadequate enforcement.

An interesting question with regard to the application of Sections 24, 25, and 43 is who can be included within the ambit of 'person', and whether a local body such as a Town Panchayat (i.e. a juridical body) or any official of the same can be held to be guilty of contravention of Sections 24 and 25. This issue came up for discussion before the Karnataka High Court in the case of *V.T. Wilson v. Karnataka State Pollution Control Board.*[273] In this case, the Karnataka Pollution Control Board filed a case against the Town Panchayat of *Tirumakudalu Narasipura*, commonly known as T. Narasipura or T.N. Pura (a town in Mysore District of Karnataka), and the chief officer of the Town Panchayat. It was observed by the Court that the Town Panchayat and its officials had failed to discharge the obligations cast on them under various provisions of the Water Act. The Town Panchayat was vested with all the drains and sewers of the area. Through these drains and sewers, polluting material was being let into the *Kabini* river. Although pollutants are let into the drains by various other agencies like other villages (not coming under the jurisdiction of T.N. Pura's Town Panchayat), on account of the failure of the Town Panchayat to prevent the flow of pollutants into the Kabini river, the Town Panchayat had knowingly permitted the pollutants to enter the river, thereby making out the contravention of Sections 24 and 25 of the Water Act. The High Court of Karnataka upheld the initiation of action under the Water Act against the Town Panchayat and its chief officer. Thus, a local body head of a local body could be held liable under Section 24 for failing to prevent the discharge of effluents.

4. **Contravention of Sections 25 and 26**: Section 44 of the Water Act penalises the contravention of Sections 25 and 26 with a punishment of imprisonment (ranging from one year and six months to a maximum of six years) in addition to fines.[274]
5. **Other penal provisions**: Section 45 of the Water Act provides for enhanced penalties after a previous conviction. The section provides that any person who is convicted of any offence under Sections 24, 25, and 26 who is found guilty of an offence contravening the same provision, shall be punishable with imprisonment from two years to seven years, and with a fine. The proviso provides that the time limit for this is two years, and any convictions before this shall not be taken into account.[275] Further, Section 45A of the Water Act provides for a penalty for contravention of provisions for which there has been no penalty elsewhere. It provides that this shall be punishable with imprisonment up to three months, a fine up to 10,000 rupees, or both. If there is a continuing failure,

273 V.T. Wilson v. Karnataka State Pollution Control Board, Criminal Petition No. 5314 of 2016, decided on 6 September 2019 (Kar HC).
274 The Water (Prevention and Control of Pollution) Act, 1974, § 44.
275 *Id.* § 45.

a fine of 5,000 rupees per day of such continuance shall be imposed.[276] Further, Section 46 provides for the publication of names of repeat offenders. It provides that, if a person commits an offence, similar to the one for which he has been convicted earlier, for the second time or more, it shall be lawful for a court to cause the name, place of residence, offence, and penalty to be published at the offender's expense in a manner directed by the court.[277]

4.6.3 Who Can Take Cognisance of Offences

Cognisance of offences is dealt with in Section 49 of the Water Act. The section lays down that no court shall take cognisance of any offence, except on a complaint. This complaint may be made by a Board (either CPCB or SPCB), or any officer authorised by the Board on this behalf. Additionally, any person who has given at least 60 days' notice to the Board or any officer of it is also eligible to make a complaint. This provision is also known as the Citizen Suit Provision. If such a complaint has been made by a person, the Board is also vested with the duty to make available any relevant reports to the person making a complaint that are in its possession, except where doing so is against the public interest.[278]

The lowest courts that can try any offences under this Act are those of a Metropolitan Magistrate or a Judicial Magistrate of the First Class. Such a court shall be competent to pass sentences greater than two years or fines greater than 2,000 rupees, notwithstanding the provisions of the CrPC.[279] As noted in *Nalin Thakor v. State of Gujarat*, an order of cognisance based on such a complaint by the Board must show an application of mind by the Magistrate, otherwise it is liable to be set aside.[280] However, at the stage of taking cognisance, it is not imperative to place all the materials before the Magistrate. As noted in *U.P. Pollution Control Board v. Dr. Bhupendra Kumar Modi*, it is sufficient if the relevant materials placed before him prima facie point towards an offence under the Act.[281]

In *Lipton India Ltd. v. the State of U.P.*,[282] the UP Pollution Control Board resolved to file a complaint and for that purpose authorised an officer of the Board to be nominated by the Assistant Secretary. The Assistant Secretary nominated Shri. Pramod Mishra, Assistant Environmental Engineer, to file the complaint. Praying for a writ of *certiorari* for quashing the complaint as non-maintainable, it was argued on behalf of the company (Petitioners) that this nomination of the Assistant Environmental Engineer to file the complaint suffers from the principle of *delegatus non potest delegare*, i.e. a delegated power cannot be further delegated, and in the instant case not only has the delegated power been further delegated

276 The Water (Prevention and Control of Pollution) Act, 1974, § 45A.
277 *Id.* § 46.
278 *Id.* § 49.
279 *Id.* § 49.
280 Nalin Thakor v. State of Gujarat, (2003) 12 SCC 461.
281 U.P. Pollution Control Board v. Dr. Bhupendra Kumar Modi, (2009) 2 SCC 147.
282 Lipton India Ltd. v. State of U.P., AIR 1996 All 1996.

but the Board has allowed the further sub-delegation of the power by allowing the Assistant Secretary to nominate the Assistant Environmental Engineer of the Board to file the complaint. The Allahabad High Court observed that, firstly, the Board is not a natural person but it is a legal person, and hence resolutions passed by it have to be acted upon by some officers of the board representing it. Secondly, in the instant case, the Board resolved to file the complaint; therefore, naturally the act of filing complaint was to be performed by some officer of the Board well conversant with the facts of the case. Thus for performing the aforesaid action of filing a complaint, the Board authorised one of its officers to be nominated by the Assistant Secretary. Accordingly, the Assistant Secretary nominated the Assistant Environmental Engineer. Therefore, the mere nomination by the Assistant Secretary does not amount to further delegation of a delegated power or further sub-delegation of sub-delegated power. Thirdly, the complaint states that the complainant is the State Board and not the Assistant Environmental Engineer. Hence, it is the Board who has filed the complaint and not the Engineer. The signature of the Engineer on the complaint is not in his personal capacity but in the capacity of a representative of the Board, duly authorised by the Board to do so. Fourthly, in the instant case, it is the Board and the Assistant Secretary who authorised the Environmental Engineer to file a complaint. It is not the case that the Board authorised the Assistant Secretary to file a complaint and in turn the Assistant Secretary authorised the Engineer to file a complaint. Based on this reasoning, the Hon'ble High Court held that the provisions of Section 49 have been complied with and the complaint is maintainable.

A similar situation arose in the case of *Nitin Majumdar v. State of Karnataka*,[283] in the context of the Air Act, 1981[284] (provisions of which are *pari materia* with the provisions of the Water Act, 1974). In this case, the State Board by resolution authorised the Chairman of the Board to initiate legal action under relevant sections against the polluting industries. The Chairman of the Board by an order authorised Regional Officer, Karwar, to initiate criminal action by filing criminal cases in competent courts against 17 occupiers of the Iron Ore Stack Yards located in and around Karwar, Ankola, and Jolda Taluks of Uttara Kannada District, which include the names of the Petitioners also. Thus, it was argued by the Petitioners that the Chairman had not lodged the complaint but the same was lodged by the Regional Officer of the SPCB and thus the complaint was not maintainable on the ground that the Chairman (the delegatee) had further delegated his powers to lodge the complaint to the Regional Officer and hence the act of lodging the complaint suffered from the principles of *delegatus non potest delegare*. The Hon'ble High Court of Karnataka rejecting this argument and applying the same reasoning adopted in *Lipton case*[285] held that the complaint had been lodged by the Board itself. However, the Board is represented by the Regional Officer in these mat-

283 Nitin Majumdar v. State of Karnataka, ILR 2007 Kar 2969, 2007 (4) Kar LJ 569.
284 The Air (Prevention and Control of Pollution) Act, 1981.
285 Lipton India Ltd. v. State of U.P., AIR 1996 All 1996.

ters. The Board has authorised the Chairman who could have signed the complaint and could have lodged the complaint. However he chose to authorise the Regional Officer of the area to lodge the complaint. This action of the Chairman of nominating the Regional Officer does not amount to sub-delegation of his power. He has merely authorised the Regional Officer to initiate criminal action. The complaints are still filed in the name of the Board who is the complainant. And hence, the mere delegation of authority of lodging and signing the complaints on behalf of the Board is not hit by the principle of *delegatus non potest delegare.* Further the court held that

> the maxim *delegatus non potest delegare* does not embody a rule of law. It merely lays down a rule of construction of a statute. However, looking at the facts and circumstances of each case, the construction that would best achieve the purpose and object of the statute should be adopted … even otherwise the defect or irregularity not affecting the merits of the matter and which do not prejudice the case of the accused is to be ignored.[286]

4.6.4 Provision for Offences Committed by Companies and Government Departments

The Water Act also lays down provisions for cases where offences under the Water Act are committed by companies and Government departments. Section 47 deals with offences by companies whereas Section 48 deals with offences by Government departments. Under Section 47, where an offence is committed by a company, several people are held guilty. Every person who was in charge of the company or the business of the company shall be deemed guilty, as long as they cannot prove the offence was committed without their knowledge, or that they exercised all due diligence to prevent the commission of the offence.[287] Further, if the offence can be attributed to the neglect of any officer of the company, or was committed with their consent or connivance, they would also be deemed guilty.[288] Section 47 was expounded by the Supreme Court in *U.P. Pollution Control Board v. Mohan Meakins Ltd.* In this case, the Court held that 'any director, manager or other officer' of the company, who has 'consented to or connived' in the commission of the said offence is covered by Section 47.[289] This followed up on *U.P. Pollution Control Board vs Messrs Modi Distillery*,[290] in which the court held that the director and members of the Board of Directors of M/s Modi Industries Limited, the company owning the industrial unit, could be proceeded against on a complaint against the said industrial unit. It should also be noted that the definition

286 Nitin Majumdar v. State of Karnatak, ILR 2007 Kar 2969, 2007 (4) Kar LJ 569 ¶ 21.
287 Water Pollution (Prevention and Control of Pollution) Act, 1974, § 47.
288 *Id.* § 47(2).
289 U.P. Pollution Control Board v. Mohan Meakins Ltd., (2000) 3 SCC 745.
290 *Id.*

of 'company' in the Act is 'any body corporate', including a firm or association of individuals.

Further, Section 48 of the Water Act lays down a similar provision with regard to offences committed by government departments. It prescribes that where an offence is committed by a Government department, the head of the department shall be deemed guilty of the offence. The same exception is available as Section 47, i.e. proving that the offence was committed without knowledge or that all due diligence was exercised. Section 48 of the Water Act has created a host of controversies in recent times where the PCBs have started to initiate criminal prosecution against Government departments. One of the issues that emerges with regard to the application of Section 48 is *whether the bar prescribed under Section 197*[291] *of the CrPC for initiating criminal action against a public servant is still applicable to cases where the public servant is being sued under Section 48 of the Water Act?* This question has been answered in the negative as per the concurrent judgments of Karnataka High Court and the Supreme Court of India in the case of *V.C. Chinnappa Goudar v. Karnataka State Pollution Control Board*.[292] In this case, criminal prosecution under Section 48 of the Water Act was initiated against persons who were holding the post of Commissioner and Chief Officer Grade II, both being public servants. The Petitioners argued that they both were public servants and, hence, criminal prosecution against them under Section 48 of the Water Act could not be initiated without obtaining sanction from the Government under Section 197 of CrPC, i.e. the Magistrate cannot straight away take cognisance of an offence *de hors* non-compliance with the requirements under Section 197.

The Court, elucidating Section 48 of the Act, explained that where any department of the Government commits an offence under Section 48 of the Act, the head of the department shall be liable to be prosecuted and punished accordingly because they shall be deemed guilty of such offence. This creates a legal fiction that obviates the need for mens rea and places the burden of proof on the head. However, this is a rebuttable presumption, and the head of the department will get an opportunity to demonstrate that the offence was committed without his knowledge or in spite of due diligence to prevent the commission of such an offence. Further, Section 5 of the Code of Criminal Procedure stipulates that

> nothing contained in this Code shall, in the absence of a specific provision to the contrary, affect any special or local law for the time being in force, or any special jurisdiction or power conferred, or any special form of procedure prescribed, by any other law for the time being in force.[293]

Moreover, Section 60 of the Water Act gives it an overriding effect over any other enactment. Since there is no specific provision providing for any sanction to be

291 The Code of Criminal Procedure, 1973 § 197.

292 V.C. Chinnappa Goudar v. Karnataka State Pollution Control Board, MANU/KA/0507/2008 & Criminal Appeal No. 755 of 2010, decided on 10 March 2015 (Supreme Court).

293 The Code of Criminal Procedure, 1973 § 5.

secured for proceeding against a public servant under the Water Act, it is not required to be obtained for the purpose of Section 48 of the Water Act. Section 48 of the Water Act being a special law will prevail over the general law of Section 197 of CrPC courtesy to Section 5 of the Criminal Procedure Code and Section 60 of the Water Act. This construction avoids the situation where sanction is sought under Section 197 but is denied. Such a situation will virtually negate the deemed fiction under Section 48 of the Water Act and render the provision inoperative despite it being a special law. This position of law was further affirmed in the later cases of *Noorulla Khan v. Karnataka State Pollution Control Board*[294] and *V.T. Wilson v. Karnataka State Pollution Control Board*.[295]

Another interesting issue with regard to the application of Sections 47 and 48 emerged in the case of *Karnataka State Pollution Control Board v. Heera Naik*.[296] In this case, the issue before the Supreme Court was *whether the Commissioner of the City Municipal Council and Chief Officer of the City Municipal Council (both local authorities) can be prosecuted under the Water Act, and if yes, then under which Section? Section 47 or 48?* The KSPCB in this case filed a complaint in 2006 against the then-Commissioner of the Municipal Council and its ex-commissioners who held the office from 2004 until the date of filing the complaint. The allegation of the Board was that it had given Consent Orders to accused persons to discharge sewage effluents after treatment. One of the conditions of the Consent Order was the establishment of a sewage treatment plant to treat the sewage in the city municipal council area. No such treatment plant had been established nor had any steps in this regard been taken by the accused persons. Moreover, the consent order given by the Board had expired, it had not been renewed, and the accused had continuously been discharging untreated sewage into the water bodies. The court held that the violation of Section 25 of the Water Act and offences under Section 44 had been made out and directed the Magistrate to proceed with the complaint.

Nextly, the Court dealt with the issue of whether a municipal council is a Government department and whether the Commission of the municipal council can come within the purview of 'Head of the Government Department'. The Court referred to the various provisions of the Water Act, 1974, the Karnataka Municipal Corporation Act, 1976, the Karnataka Municipalities Act, 1964, and the Constitution of India. It observed, *firstly*, that municipalities and municipal corporations are defined uniformly and constantly under various laws as 'a body corporate'; *secondly*, a perusal of the constitution of the State's Pollution Control Board elucidates that separate and different provisions deal with nominating Government official members (who represent the Government) and members from local authorities functioning within the State. Thus, the intention of the Water Act is to treat both of them separately and distinctively; *thirdly*, the definition of the term company

294 Noorulla Khan v. Karnataka State Pollution Control Board, MANU/SC/0454/2021.

295 V.T. Wilson v. Karnataka State Pollution Control Board, Criminal Petition No. 5314 of 2016 decided on 6 September 2019 (Kar HC).

296 Karnataka State Pollution Control Board v. Heera Naik, (2020) 16 SCC 298.

under Section 47 of the Water Act includes 'any body corporate'. Based on this reasoning, the Supreme Court held that a municipality is not a Government department as per the provisions of Section 48 of the Water Act. Rather, a municipality comes under Section 47 as a 'body corporate' and hence its Commissioner is not a 'Head of Government Department' but rather should be treated as the person in charge of a company. Further, the court can also take cognisance of such offences as per the rule in s. 49. Additionally, following the *V.C. Chinnappa Goudar v. Karnataka State Pollution Control Board*[297] case, the Supreme Court reaffirmed the position that Section 197 of CrPC is not applicable under Section 48.

The position of law established by *Heera Naik* was again followed by the Supreme Court in *Noorulla Khan v. Karnataka State Pollution Control Board*.[298] In this case, the Petitioner was a Chief Officer of Gram Panchayat, who was convicted of offences under Sections 43 and 44 of the Water Act. The conviction was challenged on the ground of non-compliance with Section 197 of CrPC. The Supreme Court rejected the petition and held that: (i) following *Heer Naik*, the Chief Officer cannot be held to be the head of the department and thus he will not come under Section 48 but will be covered under Section 47; (ii) following *V.C. Chinnappa Goudar*[299] the defence of Section 197 of CrPC is not applicable to the offences committed under the Water Act.

4.6.5 The Curious Case of Haryana Paneer Bhandar: Common Facts, Uncommon Conviction

Despite the robust and comprehensive penal provisions of the Water Act, the rate of conviction remains very low. In fact, the incidents of conviction are very rare. In this context, the conviction of the accused in the case *Vishal Bansal v. Delhi Pollution Control Committee*[300] is a very rare occurrence against the background of its very common factual matrix. In this case, a complaint was filed by the Delhi Pollution Control Committee (DPCC) against the accused Vikash Bansal and Jagdish Prasad (deceased at the time of judgment) who were partners and in the firm M/s Haryana Paneer Bhandar, a manufacturer of sweets and *namkeen*. They were also the occupiers of the same. A Vigilance Squad of the Delhi Government (comprising the SDM and engineers of DPCC) carried out an inspection of the sweet shop (the industry in this case) which found that the unit had no treatment facility and the entire trade effluent generated during the washing process of sweet/namkeen preparation moulds/containers/utensils, etc., was being discharged

297 V.C. Chinnappa Goudar v. Karnataka State Pollution Control Board, MANU/KA/0507/2008 & Criminal Appeal No. 755 of 2010, decided on 10 March 2015 (Supreme Court).

298 Noorulla Khan v. Karnataka State Pollution Control Board, MANU/SC/0454/2021.

299 V.C. Chinnappa Goudar v. Karnataka State Pollution Control Board, MANU/KA/0507/2008 & Criminal Appeal No. 755 of 2010, decided on 10 March 2015 (Supreme Court).

300 Vishal Bansal v. Delhi Pollution Control Committee, Criminal Appeal No. 112/17 in CC No. 535235/16 Delhi Pollution Control Committee v. Haryana Paneer Bhandar, decided on 21 November 2017 (Delhi District Court).

without treatment into the public sewer. It was alleged in the complaint that (i) while discharging such untreated trade effluent into the drain, the owners were causing severe pollution; (ii) they were running the sweet/namkeen manufacturing workshop without any treatment facility and without obtaining any consent under the Water Act. Conviction of the accused was sought for the offences committed under Sections 24, 25, 26, and 33A read with Sections 41, 42, 43, 44, and 49 of the Water Act. The trial court convicted the accused under Sections 24, 43, 26, 25, and 44. The conviction was appealed before the CBI Court. The CBI Court partially allowed the appeal (by setting aside the conviction under Sections 25 and 26) but upheld the conviction under Section 24. This judgment of the CBI Court discusses several interesting points related to and elucidating the application of the Water Act that emerged in this case, which are summarised as follows:

- **Whether the unit was discharging 'trade' or 'sewage' effluents which require consent**: to convict a person for not obtaining consent, it has to be established that the activity conducted by the person was of such a nature that it required consent, i.e. whether the person was discharging 'sewage' or 'trade effluent'. Section 2(k) defines trade effluent as including 'any liquid, gaseous, or solid substance which is discharged from any premises used for carrying on any industry, operation, or process, or treatment and disposal system, other than domestic sewage'. This section has to be read with Section 17(m) of the Act which obligates the Pollution Control Boards to set standards for sewage and trade effluents. In the instant case, though such standards have been prescribed, a sample of the trade effluent was required to be taken and tested in the laboratory based on which it could be concluded that the industry was discharging a trade effluent which violated the standards set and such an activity required consent.
- **Notice under Section 25(5) is mandatory**: Section 25(5) stipulates that where a person has established or taken steps to establish an industry operation or process without obtaining prior consent, in such a situation the DPCC has to serve notice on the person imposing any such conditions as it might have imposed while granting consent. In the instant case, no such notice was served. Thus, in the absence of any laboratory report establishing that the unit was discharging trade effluent that required consent and non-compliance with the notice requirement under Section 25(5), the conviction under that section was held liable to be set aside.
- **Date of establishment is required for conviction under Section 26**: Section 26 of the Act places a responsibility on the persons who were discharging trade effluents, before the commencement of the Water Act, to also obtain consent under Section 25. Contravention of Section 26 is punishable under Section 44. However, in this case, it was observed by the Court that there was no evidence on record produced by the DPCC as to when the unit was in operation. Thus, it cannot be said that the unit was functioning before the enactment of the Water Act.

- **Conviction under Section 24(1)(a) also requires sample collection and a laboratory report**: Section 24(1)(a) prescribes that no person shall discharge any 'poisonous, noxious, or polluting matter' into any water source (stream, well, sewer, or land). Whether a matter is poisonous, noxious, or polluting has to be determined in accordance with 'such standards' that have been set by the State Board. In order to make such a determination, sample collection and laboratory testing are essential. And hence, in the absence of the same, the accused cannot be convicted under Section 24.
- **Conviction under Section 24(1)(b) does not require sample collection or a laboratory report**: Section 24(1)(b) bars the discharge of 'any other matter' in any stream which may tend to impede proper flow of water of the stream in a manner that leads to or can likely lead to substantial aggravation of pollution. However, unlike Section 25 or Section 24(1)(a), this section does not obligate the Board to set standards which will necessitate sampling and laboratory testing before initiating prosecution. It is sufficient if it can be established that this 'any other matter' would either impede the proper flow of water to aggravate pollution. Hence, relying on various judgments of the Higher Courts and other reports that have stated that the food and dairy industry is a highly polluting industry, coupled with the fact that the inspection reports and testimony of witnesses established that the unit was discharging its entire effluent into the sewer, the conviction of the accused under Section 24 was upheld.
- **Application of the polluter-pays principle**: lastly, the court applied the polluter-pays principle and directed the accused to pay a compensation of Rs. 2.5 lakhs to the victims. The victims were collective members of the society at large. Since it would not be possible for the Court to pay individual compensation, the Court directed the accused to deposit the same in the PM Relief Fund.

4.7 Other Legal Mechanisms for Controlling Water Pollution

4.7.1 Environmental Impact Assessment

Environmental impact assessment (hereinafter referred to as EIA) is a study that is undertaken to predict the effect of a proposed plan, project, or other activity on the environment.[301] It is a tool used by the authorities to assess or examine the positive and adverse consequences of the said plan/project on the environment. Ideally, it is a formal process that involves community participation, thereby reducing the possibilities of conflict or resistance to the project in the said region. Currently, an ideal EIA model is expected to have a broad approach, dealing with matters such as social, economic, environmental, and biodiversity health. The concept and process of EIA was first introduced in the United States of America in the National Environmental Policy Act in the year 1969. It was the first time that environmental consideration was included as a requirement for sanctioning

301 *Understanding EIA*, Centre for Science and Environment, https://www.cseindia.org/understanding-eia-383 (last visited June 12, 2024).

large-scale development projects. This model was gradually implemented in the then-developed countries such as Canada (1973), Australia, and New Zealand (1974). The notion of environmental impact assessment in India dates back to the 1970s when one of the initial cases of environmental clearance was for river-valley projects. Until the 1990s, Environmental Clearance was subject to the approval of the Central Government, as its administrative function, with no legal backing. It was in the year 1994 that the Central Government enacted the EIA Notification, which required a mandatory Environmental Clearance for projects in Schedule I, which includes petrochemical complexes, manufacture of bulk drugs and pharmaceuticals, thermal power projects, mining, and highway projects.

EIA Notification, 1994: the 1994 notification prescribed that the expansion or modernisation of any activity, leading to a pollution load in excess of the existing one, or new project will be undertaken only upon the grant of Environmental Clearance by the Central Government. Schedule II lays out the requirements and procedure to apply for this clearance. The application is to be made as per the form in Schedule II, along with a project report containing an Environmental Impact Assessment Report or Environment Management Plan in accordance with the guidelines of the MoEFCC. Information such as the objective of the project, land requirement, climate and air quality, disaster management plans, power, and labour force requirements, a plan for the rehabilitation of displaced people, etc., is expected to be included in the form.

These documents shall be reviewed and evaluated by the Impact Assessment Agency, which is the Ministry. The IAA may consult an Expert Committee constituted under Schedule III of the Notification. Functions of the IAA include entry and inspection of premises, preparing recommendations based on the assessment of reports, inspection, and interaction with interested groups, and the preparation and publishing of a summary of reports subject to public interest. However, consultation with the local people was done in the later stages of the clearance stage. The assessment must be completed within a period of 90 days and the Environmental Clearance, if granted, shall be valid for a period of 5 years. The project authorities are expected to submit a half-yearly report. Such reports shall be made publicly available, subject to the public interest. If no comments are made by the IAA within the prescribed time limit, the project is deemed to be approved, though it can be revoked upon false data or reports. Schedule III provides for the members constituting the aforementioned Expert Committee, who are from the fields of air/water pollution control, land planning, flora/fauna conservation, management, etc.

EIA Notification, 2006: the EIA Notification, 2006,[302] creates a regulatory authority for dealing with matters falling under Category B in the Schedule known as the State Environmental Impact Assessment Authority (SEIAA). This is apart from the Central Government which deals with matters provided under Category A in the Schedule. The SEIAA is a regulatory body constituted under the

302 Ministry of Environment, Forests and Climate Change, Notification SO 1533(E) (issued on September 14, 2006).

Environment Protection Act by the Central Government. The Notification provides for the constitution of this authority with a maximum of three members including a Chairman and Member-Secretary.[303] Apart from this, the Notification classifies all projects and activities into two categories in the Schedule: Categories A and B. This classification is done based on the spatial extent of the potential impact on human health and natural as well as man-made resources.

The Notification also provided for the creation of an Expert Appraisal Committee at the national level as well as at the State level (SEACs), upon whose recommendations the respective Impact Assessment Authority shall approve or reject an application. The EAC and SEACs have the power to enter and inspect premises for the screening, scoping, and appraisal of the project. The constitution of the Committee is provided for under Appendix VI. Members include 'professionals' and 'experts' in environment quality, project management, risk assessment, and forest and wildlife experts. Further, an Environmental Clearance that is granted under the Notification for a particular project or activity can be transferred to a legal person without the intervention or permission of the Expert Appraisal Committee.

As per the notification, the procedure for Prior Environment Clearance involves four main stages:[304]

1. **Screening**: under this stage, the application form made under Form 1 is scrutinised to determine whether Category B activities require further environmental studies for an Impact Assessment Report before the grant of Environmental Clearance or not. Projects requiring environmental impact assessment are classified as Category B1, and the remaining projects not requiring the same are termed as Category B2.
2. **Scoping**: in this stage, the EACs/SEACs determine the terms of reference based on the information provided in the application form as well as environmental concerns entailed by the activity or project.
3. **Public consultation**: at this stage, the respective State Pollution Control Boards undertake the function of ascertaining the various concerns of the local people who are likely to be affected by the Applicant's project. The Notification exempts certain projects from the purview of such consultation. Such projects include the expansion of roads and highways, the modernisation of irrigation projects, and activities concerning defence and national security. The public consultation stage comprises two components: a public hearing for ascertaining the concerns of locally affected people and obtaining responses from other persons who could have a stake in the environmental concerns of the project. The hearing and other due procedures are to be conducted by the respective

303 Ministry of Environment, Forests and Climate Change, Notification SO 1533(E) (issued on September 14, 2006) cl. 3.
304 *Id.* cl. 7(i).

State Pollution Control Board or Union Territory Pollution Control Board. The procedure regarding the same is provided in Appendix IV.

4. **Appraisal**: in the final stage of the process, an appraisal involves final scrutiny of the documents including the application, EIA report, and outcome of the public hearing. For projects not requiring public consultation, the appraisal will be carried out solely based on the application form and any other valid information. The appraisal of the application must be completed by the EAC or SEAC as the case may be, within 60 days of receiving the final EIA report along with necessary documents as required by the Committee. Upon due consideration and recommendations of the EAC/SEAC, the regulatory authority must convey its decision with regard to Environmental Clearance within 45 days of the receipt of the recommendations from the Committee or within 105 days from the receipt of the final EIA report.

4.7.1.1 Types of Environmental Clearances

In 2016, the Ministry of Environment, Forest and Climate Change notified the division of industries into colour-coded categories, based on their Pollution Index (PI)[305] The PI is based on emissions (air pollution), effluents (water pollution), and utilisation of raw materials and resources along with the manufacturing process. The PI range is between 0 and 100 and the industries with PI '60 and above' fall under the 'Red category', those having a score between '41 and 59' fall under the 'Orange category', those having PI between '21 and 40' fall under the 'Green category', and those with a PI score from '0 to 20' fall under the 'White category.' Understanding the categorisation of the industries is relevant, so as to know what categories of industries are required to seek consent to establish and consent to operate. The 'consent' refers to the permission issued by the authorities of PCBs to discharge or release pollutants according to the specified limits as set by the authorities. In other words, any industry that is likely to discharge emissions or effluents through a conveyance system is compulsorily required to seek and obtain permission from the authorities specified under the Water Act. Primarily there are two types of consent, i.e.:

- Consent to establish: this is to be applied for and obtained while setting up a new establishment or in case of enlargement of operations in the existing industrial establishment or in case of alteration in product mix or changing outlet. Here, the impact of the establishment on the surrounding environment would be taken into consideration.
- Consent to Operate: here, the pollution management mechanism for the operations would be taken into consideration. Proposals with respect to the renewal

305 Ministry of Environment, Forest and Climate Change, *Environment Ministry Releases New Categorisation of Industries*, PRESS INFORMATION BUREAU (Mar. 05, 2016), https://pib.gov.in/newsite/printrelease.aspx?relid=137373.

of consent issued earlier would also fall within the category of consent to operate. Every industry that is said to be or proposed to be discharging emissions or effluents, whether they are newly established or desirous to expand or alter existing processes, must apply for this consent. Whereas in the case of the expansion of an existing establishment there is a continuation of discharge of such effluents. Consent to operate would be given for a period of 5, 10, or 15 years depending on the category of industry such as red, orange, and green respectively and also depending upon the kind of effluents discharged from the said industry. The industries that fall under the green and white categories are exempted from obtaining consent to set up and operate. They are however required to submit pollution control devices based on the processes and activities they are engaged in and are required to have a self-regulatory regime to check their impact on the environment

It was held in *Indian Oil Corporation Limited v. V.B.R. Menon*[306] that as per Section 21 of the Air (Prevention and Control of Pollution) Act, 1981, Environmental Clearances encompass two concepts – one, the consent for the purpose of establishing an industrial plant, and the other for operation of that plant. When a unit or an industrial plant is given consent to operate, the unit ought to have satisfied all the conditions stated in the order of consent to establish and would have installed the requisite technologies to prevent pollution in the operational stage. Thus, consent to establish is necessary before consent to operate can be issued. Further, once an Environmental Clearance is granted, it remains open to scrutiny by the courts, for a range of reasons. There may be procedural concerns, such as if the State Environment Impact Assessment Authority (SEIAA) did not adequately consider the information presented to it. The Bombay High Court in the case of *Gram Panchayat Navlakh Umbre v. Union of India*[307] cited this as grounds for the vitiation of the decision to grant the EC, along with the material fact of the Applicant breaching the condition which prohibits work prior to the receipt of Environmental Clearance. Thus, the Applicant's actions during the period of waiting for the EC can also be grounds for revocation of the EC.

Even if the grant of the EC is procedurally sound, there can be subsequent revocation in the event of the industry causing more pollution than at first envisioned. This was the situation in the case of T*amil Nadu Pollution Control Board v. Sterlite Industries (I) Ltd.*[308] where the EC was granted but the TNPCB later revoked it and ordered that the plant be shut down for major pollution concerns, including a 2013 leak of sulphur dioxide gas. The NGT ordered the plant to be reopened, but the Supreme Court struck down the NGT order; while this was largely on procedural grounds as to the NGT's appellate powers, it led to the EC grant being cancelled.

306 Indian Oil Corporation Limited v. V.B.R. Menon, (2023) 7 SCC 368.
307 Gram Panchayat Navlakh Umbre v. Union of India, 2012 (114) BOM LR 2695.
308 Tamil Nadu Pollution Control Board v. Sterlite Industries (I) Ltd., (2019) 19 SCC 479.

Further, certain types of projects, as notified by the MoEFCC, are also exempt from the need for such clearances, as per the schedule to EIA 2006. For example, in a May 2022 circular, the ministry clarified that schools, colleges, and hostels for such institutions would be exempt from the EC requirement but would still have to implement sustainable practices. In July of that year, it exempted highways within 100 km of international borders or the Line of Control. However, such exemptions are not absolute, even for the State; it was held in the case of *Jammula Choudariah v. Union of India*[309] that the State would have to pay compensation for environmental damage arising as a result of its irrigation scheme, which had been exempt from the original requirement of an EC.

Apart from exemptions, there is also the possibility of ex post facto clearance, or the grant of an EC after the commencement or expansion of a project. The controversial EIA Notification of 2020, which remains in draft format, also allowed for the grant of ex post facto clearance in clause 22. The provision said that a committee would appraise the situation, the lack of Environmental Clearance, and its consequences for a project that has already been started; if it is compliant with environmental norms, a clearance is granted, and if not, closure is recommended. While this provision was extremely controversial, the judiciary has already in its pronouncements envisioned the grant of such clearances in a more limited sense.

Further, various judicial precedents have said that the Environmental Clearances may also be granted *post facto*. The case of *D. Swamy v. Karnataka State Pollution Control Board*[310] is a landmark case in this regard. In this case, the validity of the CTO granted to a common bio-medical waste management facility (CBWTF) was challenged at the Supreme Court because there was no prior approval of EC. The judgment was delivered by Justice Indira Bannerjee, and held that *ex post facto* clearance should not ordinarily be granted but can be granted in 'exceptional circumstances'. The court found that the operation of the bio-medical waste management facility was in the interest of prevention of environmental pollution. The closure of the facility only on the ground of want of prior clearance would be 'against public interest'. Thus, while dismissing the appeal, the Court also laid down the conditions for the grant of *ex post facto* Environmental Clearance: *firstly*, *ex post facto* clearance should ordinarily not be granted routinely but rather, there should be exceptional circumstances wherein all relevant environmental factors have been considered; (ii) the adverse consequences of denial of *ex post facto* clearance outweigh the consequences of grant of such clearance; (iii) the concerned establishment should have complied with all other necessary pollution norms; and (iv) the *ex post facto* clearance has to be given in accordance with and in strict conformity with all the applicable statutory rules, and in an appropriate case the non-compliant industry may be penalised by an imposition of a heavy penalty on the basis of the polluter-pays principle.

309 Jammula Choudariah v. Union of India, MANU/GT/0263/2021.
310 D. Swamy v. Karnataka State Pollution Control Board, 2022 SCC OnLine SC 1278.

Further, the Supreme Court in the *D. Swamy case* also clarified its position vis-à-vis the previous case of *Alembic Pharmaceuticals*[311] in which the Supreme Court had held that the grant of an *ex post facto* EC was in derogation of fundamental principles of environmental jurisprudence. The Supreme Court read down the ratio of *Alembic Pharmaceuticals* by highlighting that even the *Alembic* judgment had not directed the closure of the units but had rather explored measures to reduce the damage to the environment, because the units had existed for a long time and employed a number of workers. In *Electrosteel Steels Limited v. Union of India*,[312] the court again used economic imperatives to decide that it was within the powers of the Government to allow a *post-facto* Environmental Clearance, as the law did not expressly prohibit it. However, this goes against the key idea highlighted in Chapter 4 of environmental rights having the elevated status of fundamental rights as per Indian courts. Thus, as courts are compelled to balance the need to protect the environment with the push towards industrialisation and protecting jobs associated with the industrial sector, the legality of *post facto* ECs has gradually become more established if there is an economic reason to grant the EC.

4.7.2 Factories Act, 1948

In order to make the legal provisions surrounding water pollution enforceable for a variety of sources of pollution, the Factories Act of 1948 was amended in 1987 to insert a number of provisions pertaining to hazardous processes. This included Section 41A, which provides for a Site Appraisal Committee to 'consider applications for grant of permission for the initial location of a factory involving a hazardous process or for the expansion of any such factory'. The Committee includes a representative of both the Central and State Pollution Control Boards for both water and air pollution, as well as a representative of the State Department of Environment. As per the section, the Committee is required to 'examine an application for the establishment of a factory involving hazardous processes and make its recommendation to the State Government within a period of ninety days of the receipt of such application in the prescribed form'.

There is, however, an overriding provision in Subsection 5, which says that where the State Government has approved the establishment or expansion of a factory involving a hazardous process, any further approval from the Central or State Government under the Water or Air Act is not required. This effectively limits the powers of these boards. However, there has been very little litigation pertaining to the admissibility of this particular subsection, and in fact Section 41A as a whole is not a very commonly used section in cases of pollution by factories.

A key case, however, was decided by the Guwahati High Court in *Moirangthem Dhaneshor Singh v. State of Manipur*, in which a tyre manufacturing company was

311 Alembic Pharmaceuticals Ltd. v. Rohit Prajapati, (2020) 17 SCC 157.

312 Electrosteel Steels Limited v Union of India, Civil Appeal No. 7576-7577 of 2021, decided on December 9, 2021 (SC).

required to mitigate the impact that its processes were having on the surrounding environment, especially the air pollution that it was causing.[313] The State was also directed to file a complaint against the factory managers for offences punishable under Section 92 of the Factories Act. Thus, the case is precedent that those in charge of a factory that causes pollution can be charged for offences both under the Water or Air Acts, and under the Factories Act. Thus, the provisions under the Factories Act create a specific responsibility for factories and other industrial establishments not to cause pollution.

The Factories Act of 1948 will be repealed by the Occupational Safety, Health and Working Conditions Code, 2020. However, the Central Government has not yet notified this Code into force so it is only a draft law at this stage. Section 2(za) of this Code defines 'hazardous process' as any industrial activity that can potentially harm workers' health or pollute the environment in general. Such industries are listed in Schedule I of the Code. Several obligations, such as maintaining updated records, are outlined for industries with hazardous processes under Section 85 of the Code. While the Code incorporates and builds on the provisions of the Factories Act, courts and tribunals have not based their decisions on it since the Code has not yet been notified into force.[314]

4.7.3 Public Nuisance Actions under the Code of Criminal Procedure

Certain provisions under Chapter X of the CrPC empower executive magistrates to pass any order as they may deem fit to prevent 'public nuisance'. Most importantly, Section 133 of the CrPC provides for a preventive and remedial measure to protect the public from any harm or inconvenience caused by 'public nuisance'. The authorities empowered by Section 133 of the CrPC include the District Magistrate, the Sub-Divisional Magistrate, or any other executive magistrate. Under this section, they are empowered to pass a conditional order ordering entities to desist from the acts causing such nuisance. Such an order may be based on a police report or any evidence collected by the magistrates themselves.

However, does the enactment of the Water Act, which confers similar powers on the Pollution Control Boards, take away this power under Section 133 of the CrPC? This issue is also pertinent because of the Act's overriding effect over other previous legislations. This was the subject matter of several High Court and Supreme Court judgments. The Andhra Pradesh High Court first decided upon this in *Nagarjuna Paper Mills Ltd. v. Sub Divisional Magistrate and RDO Sangareddy*. In this case, the magistrate had passed an order directing the stoppage of polluting factories if they failed to prevent the discharge of toxic effluents into rivers. This order was challenged on the ground that only the Pollution Control Boards had that power and the Water Act had impliedly overruled Section 133 of the CrPC. The Andhra Pradesh High Court held that the Water Act does not eclipse the provisions

313 Moirangthem Dhaneshor Singh v. State of Manipur, 2009 SCC OnLine Gau 385.
314 NTPC Ltd. v. M.P. Power Management Co. Ltd., 2022 SCC OnLine CERC 414.

under Section 133 of the CrPC.[315] Thus, the magistrate was fully empowered to pass the restraining orders, especially if the State Pollution Control Board failed to act in a timely manner. This proposition was upheld by several other High Courts as well.[316]

However, in a series of inconsistent rulings, some High Courts ruled that Section 133, insofar as it pertains to the prevention of water pollution, had been impliedly overruled by the Water Act.[317] Whereas in a few other cases, such as *Lakshmi Cement v. State*,[318] the high courts have opined that Section 133 of the CrPC does not automatically or impliedly get repealed after the commencement of the Water and Air Acts, so as to bar the proceedings under Section 133. This confusion was finally settled by the Supreme Court in *State of M.P. v. Kedia Leather & Liquor Ltd.* In this case, the Supreme Court reasoned that the provisions of the Water Act and Section 133 of the CrPC are mutually exclusive and operate in different domains.[319] This is because Section 133 of the CrPC is solely preventive in nature and deals with 'public nuisance' which is a much broader term than water pollution. In contrast, the Water Act deals with only water pollution and its provisions are not just preventive but also of a curative and penal character. Thus, there arises no question of implied repeal of Section 133. In short, the law as it stands today empowers executive magistrates to pass preventive orders against water pollution.

4.7.4 Regulation of Groundwater Pollution

One of the limitations of the Water Act is that it does not provide for the contamination and pollution of groundwater resources. However, there are other legislative frameworks for the regulation of groundwater which include the Indian Easements Act, 1882, and other allied laws. Further, the Central Ground Water Authority also regulates the use of groundwater resources. However, there have been a few judgments of various courts concerning groundwater. For instance, in *Hindustan Coca-Cola Beverages v. Perumatty Grama Panchayat*,[320] a unanimous decision was made by the village governing body to revoke the licence of Hindustan Coca-Cola Beverages Pvt. Ltd.'s bottling plant operations. The decision was based on the observation that Coca-Cola's excessive use of groundwater in Plachimada was causing a severe shortage of drinking water in Perumatty Panchayat and nearby areas. This action was taken in the interest of the public, with the intention of

315 Nagarjuna Paper Mills Ltd. v. Sub Divisional Magistrate and RDO Sangareddy, 1986 SCC OnLine AP 59.

316 Harihar Polyfibers v. Sub-Divisional Magistrate, 1996 SCC OnLine Kar 657; Ayyappa Stone Crusher v. Mandal Revenue Officer, 2000 SCC OnLine AP 918; Orient Paper Mills v. State of M.P., 1988 SCC OnLine MP 297.

317 Tata Tea Ltd. v. State of Kerala, 1983 SCC OnLine Ker 129; State of M.P. v. Kedia Leather & Liquor Ltd., (2002) 10 SCC 382; Abdul Hamid v. The Gwalior Rayon Silk Mfg., 1989 CriLJ 2013.

318 Lakshmi Cement v. State, 1994 CriLJ 3649 (Raj. HC).

319 State of M.P. v. Kedia Leather & Liquor Ltd., (2003) 7 SCC 389.

320 Hindustan Coca-Cola Beverages v. Perumatty Grama Panchayat, 2005 (2) KLT 554.

not renewing the company's licence. Coca-Cola contested this decision, prompting the State Government to temporarily halt the cancellation. The Panchayat was instructed to establish an expert committee to conduct various environmental tests to determine the accuracy of the claims. The Panchayat challenged the State Government's decision in the High Court of Kerala, where a single judge sided with the Panchayat's argument, asserting that the private overuse of a public resource was contrary to the public interest. Coca-Cola disputed allegations of excessive exploitation and pollution and filed an appeal.

In 2005, the High Court's divisional bench stated that it found no compelling grounds to rule against the multinational's right to extract water, nor did it consider the extraction of natural resources to be in violation of the law. The court further argued that Coca-Cola had legitimately exercised its property rights in extracting water from its own land. As part of its ruling, the appellate court pointed out that the Kerala High Court had imposed impractical conditions and propositions, thus treating the multinational unfairly. The appellate court granted permission for the company to extract 500,000 litres of groundwater per day in the 2005–2006 period. The Court also affirmed that the Village Council was not justified in revoking Coca-Cola's operating licence until a comprehensive scientific assessment had been conducted. In the absence of a specific legal provision, the Court held that the Panchayat lacked the authority to prohibit private individuals or companies from extracting groundwater from their land. The Court rejected the applicability of the Public Trust Doctrine as a theoretical foundation for upholding the Panchayat's authority and upheld the landowner's right to extract groundwater from their property as a fundamental right that could only be restricted by explicit statutes.

Further, in the case *Plachimada Kashara Samrakshana Samithy v. State of Kerala*[321] against a Coca-Cola factory that had depleted groundwater levels and turned it brackish, the MNC's right to extract groundwater was weighed against the public trust that local bodies held over the land, and the limits of the decision-making powers of these bodies. However, the plant was eventually closed, and the company said it had no plans to reopen it. It should be noted that the cause of action was not pollution as much as it was depletion of groundwater; however, the water in the area remains polluted and unusable. A compensation bill for the same was passed by the Kerala legislature but was struck down for legislative incompetence. The Supreme Court eventually dismissed the appeals on the subject after the company stated its plans not to reopen the plant.

Recently, in *Sunita Pandey v. Union of India*,[322] the NGT issued several directions related to groundwater contamination by arsenic in multiple districts of Uttar Pradesh and other Indian States. As a carcinogen, arsenic can harm the environment and result in serious illnesses. In order to monitor, mitigate, and prevent arsenic contamination, the NGT provided guidelines and recommendations to the SPCBs, the Central Ground Water Authority (CGWA), the Chief Secretaries of the

321 Plachimada Kashara Samrakshana Samithy v. State of Kerala, 2009 (Ker HC).
322 Sunita Pandey v. Union of India, (OA No. 384/2019) (NGT).

concerned States, the Ministry of Jal Shakti (MoJS), and other departments. The NGT also accepted the recommendations made by the former High Court judge-led Oversight Committee for the State of Uttar Pradesh on a number of issues, including water harvesting, impact assessments, health surveys, and the disassembly of hand pumps. The ruling further stated that additional consideration may be given to irrigation as well as other geogenic pollutants that are detrimental to the health of humans and animals, such as nitrate and fluoride. However, despite these guidelines, the issue of groundwater pollution continues to be a serious issue in India.

Review Questions

- Elucidate the administrative structure established under the Water Act for the prevention and control of water pollution in India.
- The State Pollution Control Boards are the real operational arm entrusted with the enforcement and implementation of the Water Act, 1974. Explain.
- Discuss the power of sampling, search, and seizure of the Pollution Control Boards.
- What are the various offences under the Water Act? Can a Government department be held responsible for committing an offence under the Water Act? Elucidate.
- What are the traditional common and criminal law remedies for the prevention and control of water pollution in India?

5 Regulatory Framework on Air and Noise Pollution in India

5.1 Introduction

Air pollution has been one of the most concerning issues, not only in India but across the globe. In common parlance, the term air pollution generally refers to the existence of any solid, liquid, or gaseous substance in the atmosphere, in a concentration harmful to humans, other beings, plants, property, or the environment. The Council on Industrial Health, American Medical Association, has also similarly defined it to mean 'the concentration of foreign matter in the air which adversely affects the wellbeing of the individual or causes damage to the property'.[1] Air pollution may be said to be the harmful pollutants present in the atmosphere that pose detrimental effects not only to human health and the quality of living but also drastically impair the quality of the environment. The release of harmful gases such as carbon monoxide, carbon dioxide, nitrogen oxides, sulphur dioxide, and fine particles has blanketed the earth, thereby trapping excess heat and contributing to global warming and climate change, rising sea levels, changes in vegetation, and aggravated weather conditions. Air pollution may not be considered to be an isolated phenomenon, since it has wide-reaching ramifications on other aspects of the environment as well, thereby making it a much more serious issue to be dealt with.

The Association of South East Asian Nations (ASEAN) published a report titled the 'Sixth State of the Environment Report', wherein the 'state of environment' has not been described in the best of situations and the Report foresees many complex environmental challenges and issues in the coming future. Although the global temperature has risen by just 1.09 degrees, the Report notes various other impacts of pollution like an increase in sea level, extreme weather conditions, and lower crop productivity. Air pollution has been described as one of the most severe categories, causing harm to around 667 million people in the ASEAN region.[2] The situation in India is no better as Indian cities, reeling under the siege of excessive pollutants in the air, are battling not only pollution of the environment but also grave medical conditions of citizens and animals together. The year 2015–16, particularly, had

1 *Air Pollution*, American Medical Association, https://www.ama-assn.org/ (last visited June 12, 2024).

2 ASEAN Secretariat, ASEAN Cooperation on Environment, Sixth ASEAN *State of the Environment Report* (SOER5) ASEAN Cooperation on Environment, https://asean.org/serial/sixth-asean-state-of-the-environment-report/ (last visited on June 12, 2024).

DOI: 10.4324/9781032703909-5

been an eye-opener for the State Capital when the Central Pollution Control Board declared an emergency situation owing to the deadly smog that engulfed the city of New Delhi and the National Capital region and had detrimental effects on the well-being of the human environment. The situation has failed to improve subsequently. As recently as in October 2023, Delhi experienced extreme levels of air pollution, with the air quality index falling into the 'very poor' and 'severe' categories, resulting in respiratory and cardiovascular problems for people. Although the winter of 2022 has been described as the 'cleanest' since 2015, the quality was still rated as 'toxic'.[3] The improvement, however marginal, resulted from the Government's Graded Response Action Plan, which is planned to be scaled up. Air pollution as an environmental problem calls for a robust legal and regulatory framework that can address this problem. In this context, this chapter delves into the existing Indian framework that addresses air and noise pollution.

5.2 Prevention and Control of Air Pollution – Legislative Developments

The leading legislation that provides a comprehensive legal framework to address and resolve the issue of air pollution in the country is the Air (Prevention and Control of Pollution) Act, 1981 (Air Act). Before the passing of the Air Act,[4] there was no comprehensive legislation that was solely dedicated towards addressing the issue of air pollution. The Air Act was passed in pursuance of the 1972 Stockholm Conference, though there was a considerable lag in the enactment of the statute. The Air Act was designed to address the problem of air pollution by empowering certain authorities known as the Pollution Control Boards to take necessary actions under the Act and the Rules made thereunder. The duties, powers, functions, and constitution of these Boards are outlined in detail in the Act. Similarly, the Air (Prevention and Control of Pollution) Rules, 1982, were made by the Central Government in pursuance of the power conferred under the Act. These rules prescribe the procedure to be followed by the Boards and their Committees. In addition to these Rules, in 1983, the Central Government notified another set of Rules which were to be exclusively applicable in the Union Territories. In 1987, an amendment was made to the provisions of the Air Act. However, the most noteworthy amendment was the insertion of Section 22A, which empowers the State Boards to request the court to issue directions to any person to prevent air pollution if there is an apprehension that such person is causing or is likely to cause air pollution. The Air Act, along with the Rules made thereunder, envisions a comprehensive system to address the problem of air pollution. Besides the aforesaid, the Environment (Protection) Act, 1986, also serves as an umbrella legislation that

3 Jacob Koshy, *2022 Winter Air in Delhi NCR `Cleanest' in Five Years but `Toxic': CSE Report*, The Hindu (Mar. 07, 2023), https://www.thehindu.com/news/national/2022-winter-air-in-delhi-ncr-cleanest-in-five-years-but-toxic-cse-report/article66587949.ece.

4 The Air (Prevention and Control of Pollution) Act, 1981, pmbl.

empowers the Government to make rules for the protection of the environment, which as a corollary includes the subject matter of air pollution.

5.3 Air Pollution and the Role of Pollution Control Boards

Along the lines of the Water Act, 1974, the Air Act envisions a two-tiered system[5] of regulatory bodies consisting of the Central Pollution Control Board (CPCB/Central Board) at the Central Level and in the Union Territories[6] and the State Pollution Control Boards (SPCBs/State Boards) at the State Level.[7] The main function of the Central Board is to improve the quality of air/water and to prevent, control, or abate pollution in the country.[8] Apart from this, the Central Board may also perform related functions such as advising the Central Government on matters relating to the prevention and control of air pollution, coordination of activities of State Boards and resolution of disputes between them, providing technical assistance to State Boards, information dissemination, and the planning and execution of nation-wide programmes for the prevention, control, and abatement of air pollution.[9] The State Boards have similar functions as the Central Board, and in addition to these have certain other specific functions, such as the inspection of air pollution control areas at such intervals as they may deem necessary, and the inspection of control equipment, industrial plant, or manufacturing process. The Boards may also issue orders directing persons as they may consider to take steps for the prevention and control of air pollution.[10] Over and above these powers, the Pollution Control Boards wield specific powers which include the following:

(a) Monitoring of pollution control areas – the State Boards play a pivotal role in assisting and consulting their respective State Governments in identifying certain areas as pollution control areas.[11] After consulting their respective State Boards, the State Governments may alter any air pollution control area whether by way of extension or reduction; or declare a new air pollution control area in which may be merged one or more existing air pollution control areas or any part or parts thereof.[12] This power with respect to pollution control areas also includes the power to prohibit the use of certain fuels or appliances which cause or are likely to cause air pollution. It is to be noted that in exercising its powers to declare an area as a pollution control area, the appropriate Board

5 Before the passing of the Air Act, 1981, the Pollution Control Boards were referred to as the 'Water Pollution Control Boards'. However, with the passing of the Air Act, the Boards constituted under the erstwhile Water Act, 1974, were granted an extension of powers under the Air Act as well.
6 The Air (Prevention and Control of Pollution) Act, 1981, § 3.
7 *Id.* § 4.
8 *Id.* § 15.
9 *Id.* § 16.
10 *Id.* § 17(1).
11 *Id.* § 19.
12 *Id.* § 19(2).

must take caution in fulfilling all the procedural and substantive formalities. Failure to fulfil all the requisite formalities in declaring an area as a pollution control area impedes the Board from taking action against any industry for not complying with the provisions of the Act.[13]

(b) Power to give instructions for ensuring emission standards – the State Boards also aid the State Governments through consultations for ensuring emission standards of automobiles.[14] After such consultations, the State Government may give instructions to the authority in charge for the registration of vehicles under the Motor Vehicles Act, 1939, and the subsequent amendments, to comply with the said instructions. Currently, the vehicular emission standards are set by the Ministry of Road Transport and Highways (MoRTH) known as the 'Bharat Stage' emission standards. They reflect the output of air pollutants permitted from compressed ignition engines and spark engines. The most recent standards set by the Ministry are the BS VI Standards[15] which apply to light- and heavy-duty vehicles, as well as two- and three-wheeled vehicles.[16]

(c) Power to impose restrictions on certain industrial plants – the State Boards are empowered to issue certificates of consent for certain categories of industrial plants to operate in the pollution control areas.[17] Any person desirous of operating an industrial plant in such areas is required to make an application for consent to operate, along with the requisite fee. Upon the receipt of such an application, the State Board shall conduct an inquiry and within a period of four months communicate its decision in writing to the applicant.[18] The State Board may issue the consent certificate subject to certain conditions.[19] Furthermore, the State Boards shall regulate the discharge of emissions by industrial plants beyond a particular limit prescribed in the pollution control areas.[20] These provisions are mandatory, and no exemption can be provided in this regard. In the event any industry emit pollutants under the Act, neither the State Boards nor the Government can exempt such industry from the purview of the Act.[21]

13 Dayabhai K Solanki v. N J Industries, (1996) 1 Guj LH 466.

14 The Air (Prevention and Control of Pollution) Act, 1981, § 20.

15 BS VI standards increased much in notoriety after the administration chose to avoid the BS V standard and legitimately jump to this standard. The Auto Fuel Policy proposed the execution of this standard by 2024. Yet, after the Supreme Court requested the legislature to uphold BS VI measures before the proposed due date of April 2021, the move from BS IV to BS VI occurred. With this, India also follows the class of standards followed in Japan, European Union, and the United States of America in terms of the Euro Stage VI standards.

16 *India Bharat Stage VI, Emission Standards*, GSR No 187(F), Ministry of Road, Transport and Highways, Government of India, http://egazette.nic.in/WriteReadData/2016/168300.pdf (last visited June 12, 2024).

17 The Air (Prevention and Control of Pollution) Act, 1981, § 21.

18 *Id.* § 21(4).

19 *Id.* § 21(5).

20 *Id.* § 22.

21 K. Muniswamy Gowda v. State of Karnataka, (1998) 3 Kar. LJ 594.

(d) Power to restrain any person from causing air pollution – even though the State Boards are conferred with ample power to conduct due diligence in the form of inquiries before permitting the establishment of industrial plants, there may be circumstances where such plants may tend to violate the conditions prescribed. As such, to kerb this menace and to ensure preventative measures, the State Boards may apply to a Judicial Magistrate or Metropolitan Magistrate seeking to restrain such class of persons, who, through the operation of an industrial plant, are likely to cause air pollution in excess of the standards prescribed by the Boards.[22]

(e) Power to require the furnishing of information – when the emission of any air pollutant into the atmosphere exceeds the State Board standards or is apprehended to exceed due to some unforeseen event, the Boards shall require the furnishing of all relevant information as to the occurrence of such event from such person in charge of the premises.[23] On receipt of such information, the State Boards may take remedial measures as deemed fit to mitigate the air pollution and prevent the exacerbation of air pollution. The Court has observed that upon the receipt of information under Section 23, the Boards are duty-bound to take remedial measures to mitigate or kerb the emissions at the earliest.[24] Apart from this, the State Boards are also conferred with the general power to obtain information – including information relating to the level of emissions and type of pollutants released – from the occupier of any industrial plant or oil industry.[25]

(f) Power of entry and inspection – the State Boards are vested with the right to enter at any reasonable time, any premises for the purposes of ensuring whether or not the orders, directions, or authorisations issued by it are complied with or for the purpose of examining and testing any control equipment, industrial plant, record, register, document, or any other material object or for conducting a search of any place in which there is reason to believe that an offence under this Act or the Rules made has been or is being or is about to be committed and for seizing any such materials.[26] Every person who is the occupier of such premises under inspection or who is in control of the equipment situated therein is required to render all assistance necessary, the failure to do so amounting to an offence under the Act.

(g) Power to take samples – similar to the Water Act, the State Boards under the Air Act are also empowered to take samples of air or emissions from any chimney, flue, or duct or any other outlet in such manner as may be prescribed for the purpose of analysis.[27]

22 The Air (Prevention and Control of Pollution) Act, 1981, § 22A.
23 *Id.* § 23.
24 Chaitanya Pulverising Industry v. Karnataka State Pollution Control Board, AIR 1987 Kar. 82.
25 The Air (Prevention and Control of Pollution) Act, 1981, § 25.
26 *Id.* § 24.
27 *Id.* § 26(1).

(h) Power to issue directions – the Pollution Control Boards are also empowered to issue directions in exercise of their powers and functions under the Act.[28] This power, as provided under Section 31 A is a residuary power to enable the Boards to perform their functions conferred under the Act and is in addition to the powers enumerated under Section 17.[29] The Boards may issue any directions in writing to any person, officer, or authority who shall be bound to comply with such directions. These powers include directions ordering the closure, prohibition, or regulation of any industry, operation, or process or the stoppage or regulation of supply of electricity, water, or any other service.

Apart from this, the Pollution Control Boards have undertaken the mammoth task of monitoring the national ambient air quality so as to assist the Government in making the required action plans to abate environmental pollution and maintain the wholesomeness of the environment. This is being carried out under the project 'National Ambient Air Quality Monitoring', popularly known as NAAQM. Under this programme, the Boards have set up hundreds of monitoring stations spread all over the country. These stations are to monitor the air quality round the clock on selected days of the week and pass on the data to the Central Pollution Control Board. The CPCB, after analysing the data, would formulate the desired action programme to maintain the air quality by advising the Government to take necessary action and if necessary, to declare an area as air pollution control area.

5.4 Contributors to Air Pollution: A Sectoral Analysis

Air pollution is an outcome of a plethora of activities and cannot be narrowed down to one or a few causal factors. From emissions arising out of day-to-day household activities to the ever-increasing vehicular pollution, there are several contributing factors that by and large aggravate the worsening quality of air in the country. Some of the major sectors are identified as follows.

5.4.1 Household/Indoor Air Pollution

As the name suggests, 'indoor air pollution' refers to the pollutants found indoor. While indoor air pollution in rural areas is largely sourced to harmful emissions from fuel/firewood used for cooking, the sources of indoor pollution are different for urban areas. Key pollutants in urban buildings include nitrogen dioxide, carbon monoxide, radon (from building materials, water, and soil), formaldehyde (from insulation), asbestos, mercury, man-made mineral fibres, volatile organic compounds, allergens, and tobacco smoke – as well as organisms like bacteria which are harmful to health. According to The State of Global Air Report 2020 by

28 The Air (Prevention and Control of Pollution) Act, 1981, § 31 A.
29 Bihar State Pollution Control Board v. Hiranand Stone Works, AIR 2005 Pat 62.

the Health Effects Institute, household air pollution is responsible for about 64% of neonatal deaths caused by air pollution.[30]

In light of these serious issues rising from household air pollution, in 2016, the Central Government launched a major scheme, i.e., 'Pradhan Mantri Ujjwala Yojana (PMUY)', to raise the utilisation of liquefied petroleum gas (LPG) for cooking purposes since it is a relatively less-polluting fuel.[31] The Scheme aims to safeguard women's health by providing them with clean cooking fuel – LPG – as an alternative to firewood and kerosene. To ensure this, the connections are issued in the name of women of the households.[32] Following the implementation of the scheme, overall household LPG coverage grew swiftly to reach 94.3% as of 1 April 2019.[33] However, as per the survey published by the National Family Health Survey (NHAS-V) in December 2020, there has only been a 20% surge in the use of alternative cleaner fuel in the past five years.[34] The Scheme was initially successful but failed to thrive afterward owing to the considerable waiting period and cost incurred in becoming a PMUY beneficiary, despite the loans and subsidies available.[35] It is of paramount importance to ensure that the implementation of the scheme is sustained over a long period of time, until actual changes are witnessed in society, and that the scheme is not just a one-time success.

In addition to the launch of PMUY, another initiative taken by the Central Government is the development of 'NEERDHUR', a novel domestic cooking stove with multi-fuel options. The Council of Scientific and Industrial Research and National Environmental and Engineering Research Institute (NEERI) undertook the conceptualisation and subsequent production of NEERDHUR.[36] This initiative presented poor households with improved stove efficiency, high overall thermal efficiency, and reduced fuel consumption and emissions through design

30 Health Effects Institute, State of Global Air 2020: A Special Report on Global Exposure to Air Pollution and Its Health Impacts (2020).

31 *Pradhan Mantri Ujjwala Yojana*, National Portal of India, https://www.india.gov.in/spotlight/pradhan-mantri-ujjwala-yojana (last visited June 12, 2024).

32 Deepak Upadhyay, *PMUY: How to Avail Full Benefits of Ujjwala Yojana,* Live Mint (Sept. 14, 2019), 2019 https://www.livemint.com/news/india/pmuy-how-to-avail-full-benefits-of-ujjwala-yojana-1568387408556.html.

33 Sumant Sen, *How Effective Has the Pradhan Mantri Ujjwala Yojana Been?,* The Hindu (Dec. 18, 2019), https://www.thehindu.com/data/data-how-effective-has-the-pradhan-mantri-ujjwala-yojana-been/article30338388.ece.

34 National Family Health Survey, Rep. No. 5, Key Indicators: 22 States/UTs from Phase-I, at 11 (2013).

35 Kundan Pandey, *Ujjwala Scheme Had a Great Start, But It Failed to Maintain Momentum*, The Federal (Jan. 27, 2021), https://thefederal.com/news/pradhan-mantri-ujjwala-yojana-has-claimed-success-with-almost-98-percent-coverage-of-lpg/.

36 Manka Behl, *NEERI's Stove Reduces Smoke, Promises Better Rural Health*, The Times of India (Oct. 04, 2016), https://timesofindia.indiatimes.com/city/nagpur/neeris-stove-reduces-smoke-promises-better-rural-health/articleshow/54665243.cms.

improvements and technological innovations, to address issues such as stove cost, maintenance, fuel affordability, and availability.[37]

Another initiative undertaken to combat indoor air pollution is the development of 'microwaves', which treat contagious waste and eradicate air emissions, which include highly poisonous 'persistent organic pollutants (POPs)'. The large-scale commercialisation of the same was carried out by the Union Ministry of Micro, Small and Medium Enterprises, the United Nations Industrial Development Organization and the Global Environment Facility.[38]

5.4.2 Vehicular Pollution and the Automobile Industry

Vehicular pollution is an issue that never ceases to perplex policymakers in the country. As India is home for around 1.3 billion people, it is inevitable that the number of vehicles required to meet the needs of this population will be tremendous. The IQ AirVisual 2018, World Air Quality Report,[39] published by IQ AirVisual, a USA-based company, indicates that India holds the third position among the list of countries having the worst air quality in the world. Moreover, in the south-eastern region, 13 of the 15 most polluted cities in terms of air quality are situated in India.

5.4.2.1 Vehicular Standards

To tackle the issue of vehicular pollution at the source, attempts were made in the late 20th century when the first mass emission standards to kerb vehicular pollution were laid down in 1991.[40] These standards required vehicle manufacturers to adopt and incorporate technology upgrades such as catalytic converters to cut exhaust emissions. While this signified an attempt to encourage cleaner technology, these standards were not widely implemented. Taking note of the ameliorating air quality, the Supreme Court thought it fit to address the situation by ensuring appropriate action is taken by the concerned State authorities. Therefore, in 1999, on the basis of the suggestions made by the Bhure Lal Committee, the Supreme Court directed the Government to lay down emission standards for various classes of vehicles.[41] The directions by the Supreme Court were the required matchstick to the trail of

37 *NEERDHUR*, National Environment Engineering Research Institute, https://www.neeri.res.in/file_abouts/99365234_NEERDHUR.pdf (last visited June 12, 2024).

38 Rene Van Berkel, *Five Indian Innovations to Beat Air Pollution*, United Nations in India, https://uninindia.sitslive.com/blogs/five-indian-innovations-to-beat-air-pollution/ (last visited June 12, 2024).

39 IQAir AirVisual, 2018 World Air Quality Report: Region & City PM2.5 Ranking (2018).

40 *Vehicular Exhaust*, Central Pollution Control Board, https://cpcb.nic.in/vehicular-exhaust/ (last visited June 12, 2024).

41 M C Mehta v. Union of India, (1999) 6 SCC 12 ¶3.

fire that followed suit, as they led to the formulation of Bharat Stage Emission Standards for fuel.

Following the mandate of the Supreme Court, the Government rolled out the first nationwide set of emission standards in 2000, known as the Bharat Stage (BS) I norms, in line with the EURO emission standards. These emission standards were primarily set in place as an attempt to control and check the amount of air pollutants released from internal combustion equipment. This was followed by an upgraded set of standards in 2001 known as the Bharat Stage II norms. However, unlike the first set of emission standards, which were applicable to the whole of India, the BS II standards were applicable only to the four metropolitan cities – NCR, Mumbai, Chennai, and Kolkata – as these cities were reeling under the pressure of air pollution the most. However, these norms failed to achieve the desired outcome thereby necessitating a need for laying down a structured plan of action that addresses vehicular pollution in India. To this effect, the Auto Fuel Policy, 2003, was formulated under the chairmanship of Shri Prahlad Joshi, which laid down a specific policy directive for the required technological changes to the automobile sector by choosing fuels that are less harmful to the atmosphere and cause less air pollution.[42] The policy made recommendations which *inter alia* included a road map for the implementation of Bharat Stage II fuel emission norms and Euro III equivalent norms.[43] Subsequent to the Auto Fuel Policy, 2003, an Expert Committee was formed under the chairmanship of Shri Saumitra Chaudhuri to formulate a road map allowing for periodic revisions in the policy framework. In this regard, this Expert Committee formulated and submitted the Auto Fuel Vision and Policy 2025.[44]

In 2005, Bharat Stage III norms were introduced which were to be implemented in 15 selected cities by the end of that year and nationwide by the end of 2010. Following these norms, in 2010, the next stage of norms – Bharat Stage IV – was introduced. As per the mandate of BS IV norms, automakers were required to make their vehicles compliant by the year 2017. Interestingly, though India gradually adopted the European standards, it appeared to lag behind their implementation. Therefore, to expedite the process, the Ministry of Road Transport and Highways announced a direct leap to the rather stringent and comparatively robust Bharat Stage VI norms to be implemented by 1 April 2020.[45] The Government's intent to leapfrog the BS V norms was based on the rapidly declining air quality in the country.

On similar lines of standards set for four-wheeler and two-wheeler vehicles, the law also categorically enumerates minimum standards for auto-rickshaws. The Motor Vehicles (Amendment) Act, 2014, for example, was introduced to define

42 Ministry of Petroleum & Natural Gas, Auto Fuel Policy, 2003.
43 *Id.* at 10.
44 Ministry of Petroleum & Natural Gas, Auto Fuel Policy, 2014.
45 Ministry of Road, Transport and Highways, Draft Central Motor Vehicles (Amendment) Rules, 2016.

the scope of e-rickshaws and e-carts in India and provided information regarding their possession and usage on the roads.[46] In addition to this, the Motor Vehicles (Amendment) Act, 2015, along with the Central Motor Vehicles (Amendment) Rules, 2015, laid down specific standards that were to be compulsory incorporated in e-rickshaws.[47] The 2015 Rules expressly provided that e-rickshaw models were to be approved by the International Centre for Automotive (ICAT) at Manesar, Vehicle Research and Development Establishment (VRDE) Ahmednagar, Automotive Research Association of India (ARAI) in Pune, or the Indian Institute of Petroleum (IIP) in Dehradun to ensure energy efficiency of the vehicles.[48]

5.4.2.2 Emission Reduction Schemes and Policies

Besides laying down emission standards, the Government has also undertaken welfare measures through the introduction of various schemes and missions. The first of such initiatives was taken in the year 2011, when the Ministry of Heavy Industries and Public Industries launched the National Electric Mobility Mission for setting up the National Board for Electric Mobility and the National Council for Electric Mobility – which were the authorities responsible to 'achieve greater synergy through common vision, roadmap and priorities amongst all stakeholders involved in promoting electric mobility'.[49] Furthermore, the Mission was accompanied by a comprehensive plan titled National Electric Mobility Mission Plan, 2020, which was formulated as a roadmap to transform India into a world leader in the electric automotive market.[50]

The Central Government also launched the National Urban Livelihood Mission (NULM) in 2013, which *inter alia* included measures to encourage the urban poor to adopt greener vehicles such as e-rickshaws.[51] Similarly, in 2015, the Ministry of Heavy Industries and Public Enterprises launched the scheme for Faster Adoption of Electric/Hybrid Vehicles to provide incentives and subsidies for manufacturing electric vehicles.[52] Along with this initiative, the Smart Cities Mission (2015) also

46 Notification SO 2590 (E), Ministry of Road Transport and Highways, Government of India (2014).

47 Motor Vehicles (Amendment) Act 2015, § 2(2) – the definition of e-rickshaws was improved and changed to 'a special 3 wheeled vehicle of powers not exceeding 4000 Watts' instead of 2,000 Watts and thereby allowed for better performance.

48 Ministry of Road Transport and Highways, Government of India, Notification dated Jan. 13, 2015.

49 National Mission for Electric Mobility, File No. 12(89)/2009 AEI, Ministry of Heavy Industries and Public Enterprise, Government of India, (2011).

50 Ministry of Heavy Industries and Public Enterprise, Government of India, *National Electric Mobility Mission Plan 2020*.

51 Ministry of Housing and Urban Affairs, Government of India, Deendayal Antyodaya Yojana – National Urban Livelihoods Mission (2020).

52 Department of Heavy Industry, *Faster Adoption and Manufacturing of (Hybrid &) Electric Vehicles India*, Ministry of Heavy Industries & Public Enterprises, Government of India (Jan. 13, 2020), https://dhi.nic.in/writereaddata/UploadFile/Gazette_Notification_FAME_India.pdf.

gave impetus to the electrification of e-rickshaws by earmarking a budget for their purchase and development in 29 out of 100 smart cities.[53]

Policies to encourage electric mobility and cleaner vehicular technology have also been adopted at the State level. In September 2017, the 'Karnataka Electric Vehicles and Energy Storage Policy 2017' was introduced by the State of Karnataka to incentivise and attract investment and jobs in the EV segment of the country.[54] In line with the initiative by the Karnataka State Government, the States of Kerala,[55] Uttar Pradesh,[56] and Andhra Pradesh[57] followed suit.

5.4.2.3 Aviation Industry

The aviation sector is said to be one of the major contributors to air pollution across the world. As an industry that has grown exponentially over the past three decades, the civil aviation sector has created significant pressure on the atmosphere owing to the large quantum of toxic emissions released by aircraft. In 1999, the Intergovernmental Panel on Climate Change ('IPCC') had highlighted the impact of the aviation industry on the global atmosphere, which accounted for 13% of carbon emissions from the transport industry to the aviation sector.[5859] Recently, a study by the International Civil Aviation Organisation ('ICAO') revealed that by the year 2050, carbon emissions in the international aviation sector may tend to increase sevenfold.[60]

India, being one of the leading civil aviation industries in the world,[61] is facing a growing concern that the burgeoning demand in the domestic aviation sector may place increasing pressure on the atmosphere. As the Indian air transport sector has seen steady growth over the past few years, the magnitude of the environmental

53 Ministry of Urban Development, Government of India, Smart Cities Mission.

54 Commerce and Industries Department, *Karnataka Electric Vehicles and Energy Storage Policy – 2017*, Government of Karnataka (Jan. 13, 2020), https://kum.karnataka.gov.in/KUM/PDFS/KEVESPPolicyInsidepagesfinal.pdf.

55 *Policy on Electric Mobility*, Government of Kerala (Jan. 13, 2020), https://www.acma.in/uploads/doc/EV-policy-Kerala.pdf.

56 *Uttar Pradesh Electric Vehicles (EVs) Manufacturing Policy 2018*, Government of Uttar Pradesh (Jan. 13, 2020), https://www.acma.in/uploads/doc/Uttar_Pradesh_Electric_Vehicles.pdf.

57 *Industries & Commerce Department, Electric Mobility Policy 2018–23*, Government of Andhra Pradesh, (Jan. 13, 2020), https://www.acma.in/uploads/doc/AP%20Policy_final.pdf.

58 IPCC Working Group, Special Report, Aviation and the Global Atmosphere (1999), https://www.ipcc.ch/site/assets/uploads/2018/03/av-en-1.pdf (last visited Apr. 29, 2019).

59 *Id* at 6.

60 International Civil Aviation Organisation, *The Next Chapter DESTINATION GREEN* (Environmental Report on Aviation and Environment (2019)), https://www.icao.int/environmental-protection/Documents/ICAO-ENV-Report2019-F1-WEB%20(1).pdf (last visited June 12, 2024).

61 Ministry of Civil Aviation, Government of India, *White Paper on National Green Aviation Policy* (2018), www.civilaviation.gov.in/sites/default/files/Whitepaper on National Green Aviation Policy.pdf (last visited June 12, 2024).

impact caused by this growth is estimated to be bleak.[62] To address this concern, sector-specific schemes and measures have been adopted.

In 2015, the Director General of Civil Aviation ('DGCA'), the affixed unit of the nodal authority, the Ministry of Civil Aviation issued a circular on Climate Change Initiatives and Local Air Quality Monitoring in Civil Aviation.[63] According to these requirements, all airport operators and airline operators are required to develop annual emission management reports including the following criteria: (i) the carbon footprint of emissions; (ii) the voluntary measures adopted to reduce carbon emissions; and (iii) the certification in accordance with ISO standards, Airport Carbon Accreditation, or such other certified standards.[64] Besides this, the Requirements also included provisions on local air quality monitoring, fuel management by airport operators, and emission management by airports.

In 2018, the DGCA introduced the Carbon Offsetting and Reduction Scheme for Civil Aviation (CORSIA).[65] The objective of the Requirements of the Scheme is to manage the adverse impact of aviation activities on the atmosphere, leading to sustainable growth of the industry by offsetting the carbon emissions generated due to international operations of their flights.

The Central Government introduced the National Green Aviation Policy in 2019 'to enable, promote and strengthen all inclusive, green and sustainable growth of air transportation in India'.[66] The Policy delved into varied nuances of sustainability in the civil aviation sector. To ensure this, it lays down broad policy areas which address environmental concerns arising from the aviation sector including waste management, environment management systems, green infrastructure programmes, airport master planning, noise management, local air quality, solar, and other renewable energy, etc.[67]

5.4.2.4 Crop Residue Burning

Typically known as the 'slash and burn' method of clearing crop residue, the burning of residual crop or stubble to prepare the land for the new crop season is said to be an issue that the country, particularly the northern plain of India, grapples with on an annual basis. While this method of farming is economically efficient for farmers, it has wreaked havoc for the environment and human health. A report

62 *National Green Aviation Policy - Presented by India* (International Civil Aviation Organization, Working Paper A40-WP/372 EX/151 15/8/19 presented at the 40th Assembly Session 2019).

63 Directorate General of Civil Aviation, Circular No F. No. 04-01/2010-AED (Vol. II), Ministry of Civil Aviation, Government of India.

64 *Id.* Cl. 4.

65 Directorate General of Civil Aviation, Carbon Offsetting and Reduction Scheme for Civil Aviation (CORSIA), (2018).

66 Ministry of Civil Aviation, National Green Aviation Policy, 2019, Vision Statement.

67 *Id.* at 9.

prepared by the Parliament's Standing Committee in 2018[68] delved into the underlying cause for the smog-filled atmosphere in Delhi, especially in the winters, which highlighted that the incessant resort to crop-burning in the adjoining areas of Haryana, Punjab, and other bordering States led to poor air quality in Delhi. This, accompanied with the vehicular pollution in the Capital and the bursting of firecrackers, causes the national capital to be engulfed with a blanket of smog every year.

To tackle this situation, the Central and State Governments have implemented certain measures against stubble burning. For instance, in 2014, under the mandate of the twelfth five-year plan, the Central Government initiated the Sub-Mission on Agricultural Mechanisation, which *inter alia* included financial assistance to farmers for adopting equipment for better land and crop residue management.[69] In the same year, the Government also introduced the National Policy for Management of Crop Residue.[70] The broad mandate of the Policy was to steer State Governments towards identifying various interventions, formulating suitable work plans, and monitoring their implementation at the State Level.[71] Following this, in 2018, the Ministry of Agriculture and Farmers Welfare rolled out a scheme on 'Promotion of Agricultural Mechanization for In-Situ Management of Crop Residue in the States of Punjab, Haryana, Uttar Pradesh and NCT of Delhi' for the period of 2018–19 to 2019–20.[72] The Scheme was devised with the main objectives of providing financial assistance to promote the use of in-situ crop residue management machinery among farmers and to create awareness of the effective utilisation and management of crop residue.[73]

At the State level, various Governments have independently taken steps to kerb air pollution caused by stubble burning. In Punjab, the Government took the incentive route as opposed to the command-and-control mechanism, to encourage greener alternatives among the farmers.[74] Similarly, the Government of Haryana issued a notification under Section 19(5) of the Air Act which prohibits crop

68 Parliamentary Standing Committee on Science & Technology, Environment & Forests, Report on Air Pollution in Delhi and National Capital Region (2018).

69 Department of Agriculture & Cooperation, Ministry of Agriculture, Government of India, *Sub-Mission on Agricultural Mechanization, 2014*, https://agri.punjab.gov.in/sites/default/files/Guidelines%20%20of%20SMAM.pdf (last visited June 12, 2024).

70 Ministry of Agriculture, National Policy for Management of Crop Residue, 2014.

71 *Id* at 7.

72 Ministry of Agriculture and Family Welfare, Government of India, *Promotion of Agricultural Mechanization for In-Situ Management of Crop Residue in the States of Punjab, Haryana, Uttar Pradesh and NCT of Delhi*, https://agrimachinery.nic.in/Files/Guidelines/CRM.pdf (last visited Apr. 21, 2019).

73 *Id.* at 2.

74 *Punjab Govt to Set up 400 Processing Plants to Convert Paddy Straw into Bio-Energy to Curb Pollution,* First Post (Nov. 16, 2017), https://www.firstpost.com/india/punjab-govt-to-set-up-400-processing-plants-to-convert-paddy-straw-into-bio-energy-to-curb-pollution-4212351.html.

residue burning (CRB). Strict monitoring of this situation has been promulgated and a jail term has been imposed, along with a fine.[75]

The Courts in India have played a rather proactive role in tackling the issue of air pollution caused by crop residue burning. The NGT, in particular, has deliberated upon this issue with serious thought. In the case of *Vikrant Kumar Tongad v. Environment Pollution (Prevention & Control) Authority*, the NGT displayed its conviction to resolve this issue by prohibiting agricultural residue burning in all parts of NCT of Delhi, the State of Rajasthan, the State of Punjab, the State of Uttar Pradesh, and the State of Haryana.[76]

The approach taken by the NGT in the *Vikrant Kumar Tongad* case did not prove to be highly effective as the growing instances of stubble burning could not be entirely regulated or kerbed by the State. The inability of farmers to clear the residue before the consecutive cropping season and the lack of resources created a financial burden on the farmers.[77] A need was felt to approach the problem through a market-based mechanism rather than a punitive system. Therefore, in the case of *Ganga Lalwani v. Union of India*,[78] the NGT opined that economic incentives and disincentives were viable options to encourage greener farming techniques among farmers.

In another instance where the NGT took *suo motu* cognisance of the burning of *parali*[79] in the Agricultural Institute, Durgapur, Jaipur, the Tribunal has shown active interest in tackling the unchecked menace of crop residue burning in the country.[80] The Tribunal observed the peculiarity of this case as it was 'a case where not our farmers but government and its instrumentalities are themselves taking the steps which had been of serious concern for the public at large and the State is duty bound to prevent/prohibit such practices'. Taken aback by the actions of the State and its instrumentalities, the NGT considered taking action under the polluter-pays principle.

Besides the NGT, the Supreme Court has also demonstrated an active stance on addressing this issue. In 2019, the Court took note of the striking and concerning statistics on pollution caused in the northern States such as Delhi, Haryana, Punjab, and UP[81] and thought it fit to remedy the dreary situation. Considering the lackadaisical approach and negligence by the State, the Court resorted to mak-

75 *Economic Survey 2019–20: Stubble Burning Incidents Come Down*, The Hindu (Jan. 31, 2020), https://www.thehindu.com/news/national/stubble-burning-incidents-come-down/article30705487.ece.

76 Vikrant Kumar Tongad v. Environment Pollution (Prevention & Control) Authority, Original Application No. 118/2013 (10.12.2015 – NGT).

77 Sucha Singh Gill, *Possible Solutions to Residual Crop Burning*, The Wire (Oct. 23, 2017), https://thewire.in/agriculture/crop-residue-burning-punjab-haryana.

78 Ganga Lalwani v. Union of India, 2018 SCC OnLine NGT 339.

79 *Parali* refers to the dry grass left behind as residue after harvesting the paddy crop.

80 Suo Moto v. Union of India, MANU/GT/0047/2019.

81 Environment Pollution (Prevention and Control Authority), Rep. No. 106, 2019, Special Report on Pollution Hot Spots in NCR with Request for Urgent Directions to Improve Enforcement and Pollution Control.

ing the appropriate authorities in these States responsible for keeping a check on stubble burning. By considering a holistic approach to kerbing this menace, the Supreme Court directed Chief Secretaries of the State Governments, District Collectors, Tehsildars, Director General, IG/SP, and other police officers of the area of the concerned police station and the entire police machinery to ensure that not even a single incident takes place of stubble burning, failing which, the concerned authorities would be held liable for violating the orders of the Court.[82] Furthermore, to infuse stringency in the monitoring process, the Court cautioned the State Governments that in the event that they failed to implement the Court's order, they would be liable to pay compensation as tortious liability and for violating the public trust doctrine.[83]

Similarly, in the case of *M. C. Mehta v. Union of India*,[84] the Supreme Court took note of the drastic effects of stubble burning on the atmosphere in the national capital and its surrounding areas. The Court directed the Central Government and the Governments of Uttar Pradesh, Punjab, and Haryana prepare a scheme for making available alternative measures such as combine harvesters, happy seeders, hydraulically reversible MB ploughs, paddy straw choppers, mulchers, rotary slashers, zero till seed drills, and rotavators and balers especially dedicated to small and marginal farmers to be made available either free of charge or on a nominal rental basis.[85]

Recently, the Delhi High Court sought the Centre's response on a plea seeking immediate steps to prevent stubble burning in the neighbouring States of Punjab and Haryana, on the ground it would aggravate COVID-19 related problems.[86] Further, the Supreme Court appointed a one-man committee composed of a retired judge, Justice Madan B Lokur, to monitor stubble burning in the States of Punjab, Haryana, and Uttar Pradesh. However, it was suspended later on, when the Central Government assured the Supreme Court of enacting a new legislation that would create a permanent body to deal with the annual air pollution problem in Delhi and its surrounding areas.[87] Towards this, the Central Government, on 29 October 2020, introduced a new law through an ordinance, titled the Commission for Air Quality Management in National Capital Region and Adjoining Areas Ordinance, 2020, to tackle the problem of air pollution in the Delhi-NCR Region and the adjoining areas of Punjab, Haryana, Uttar Pradesh, and Rajasthan where the Ordinance

82 M.C. Mehta vs. Union of India, (2020) 7 SCC 573, ¶7.

83 *Id.* at ¶9.

84 M. C. Mehta v. Union of India, (2020) 7 SCC 530.

85 *Id.* at ¶57.

86 *Delhi HC Seeks Centre's Reply on Plea to Stop Stubble Burning by Punjab and Haryana,* The Print (Sept. 28, 2020), https://theprint.in/environment/delhi-hc-seeks-centres-reply-on-plea-to-stop-stubble-burning-by-punjab-haryana/512122/.

87 Sunil Prabhu & Anindita Sanyal, *Stubble Burning: Supreme Court Agrees to Request after Centre Assures Law,* NDTV (Oct. 26, 2020), https://www.ndtv.com/india-news/stubble-burning-supreme-court-puts-on-hold-order-on-one-man-monitoring-panel-after-centre-says-it-will-bring-law-to-tackle-problem-2315840.

shall be in force.[88] The subsequent Act constituted the Commission for Air Quality Management (CAQM).[89] Further, it provides for the power to take measures, issue orders, and hear complaints for the purpose of maintaining air quality in the region.[90] It can also order investigations[91] or restrict a certain area for industries.[92]

Under the farmers' protests against the contentious Farm Bills, the Government also agreed to their demand of decriminalising stubble burning. However, the move has been balanced by a recent rule that allows the CAQM to collect fines for burning stubble.[93] Failure to pay the compensation will, in effect, make it an arrear on land revenue.[94] Even though it has been decriminalised, policy mechanisms like looking for greener alternatives (as undertaken in Punjab) may provide incentives to avoid stubble burning.

5.4.3 Industrial Air Pollution

Industries are said to be one of the major contributors to air pollution in India. In India, the legal and statutory framework addresses the problem of industrial air pollution through a multi-scalar approach. For instance, the Factories Act, 1948, which was one of the earliest legislations to raise awareness regarding the toxic work environment, made specific provision for artificial humidification and ventilation in factories.[95] It was only after the enactment of the Air Act, 1981, that specific legal provisions were introduced to categorically regulate and control industrial air pollution, which were further strengthened by the passing of the Environment (Protection) Act, 1986.

The Air Act, 1981, is the primary legislation that sets out specific legal provisions for the regulation of industrial air pollution. It sought to regulate the quantity and quality of air pollutants being emitted by industries, among other activities.[96] Therefore, it created parallel and additional responsibilities on the Pollution Control Boards already established under the Water Act, 1974, *albeit* with specific reference to preventing and controlling air pollution. With respect to regulating industrial air pollution, the Pollution Control Boards – more specifically the State

88 *Centre Introduces New Law Through Ordinance to Tackle Air Pollution in Delhi-NCR,* Economic Times (Oct. 30, 2020), https://economictimes.indiatimes.com/news/politics-and-nation/centre-introduces-new-law-through-ordinance-to-tackle-air-pollution-in-delhi-ncr/articleshow/78930582.cms.

89 The Commission for Air Quality Management in National Capital Region and Adjoining Areas Act 2021, § 3.

90 *Id.* § 12.

91 *Id.* § 12(vi).

92 *Id.* § 12(v).

93 Notification GSR 322(E) § 3, Commission for Air Quality Management in NCR and Adjoining Regions.

94 The Commission for Air Quality Management in National Capital Region and Adjoining Areas Act, 2021, § 4(4).

95 The Factories Act, 1948, § 15.

96 The Air (Prevention and Control of Pollution) Act, 1981, Statement of Objects and Reasons.

Boards – are vested with the power to prescribe standards for industrial plants,[97] prescribe prerequisites for industrial equipment, conduct inspections as and when necessary, and advise the Government on the location and spatial planning of industrial plants.[98]

Besides this, any person operating an industrial plant in any air pollution control area with the consent of the State Board shall not permit the emission of air pollutants in any quantity beyond the prescribed limit[99] and in the event of any apprehension of excess emissions such person is required to inform the appropriate Board of such measures to enable the Board to take remedial measures.[100] The State Board is empowered to seek court restraint against any person if it is apprehended that such person is emitting excess air pollution.[101]

5.4.3.1 Industrial Emission Standards

Industrial Emission Standards are one of the major constituents of the air quality strategies in India. Although the Central Pollution Control Board specifies minimum air quality standards in the form of the National Ambient Air Quality Standards (NAAQ),[102] there are specific industry-based standards that cater to the identified industries.[103] The standards are prescribed for a broad range of industries varying from major polluting industries such as aluminium smelting, copper smelting, etc., to minor polluting industries such as dairy, tanneries, and hospitality. On a broader categorisation, the Central Pollution Control Board has categorised industries into four main categories based on their pollution index,[104] which *inter alia* include the level of air pollutants being emitted. For the purpose of categorisation of the industrial sector, the four colour-coded categories are the red category,[105] the

97 Section 2(k) defines an 'industrial plant' to which the provisions of the Act and the Rules made thereunder shall apply.

98 *Id.* § 17.

99 *Id.* § 22.

100 *Id.* § 23.

101 *Id.* § 22(A).

102 Central Pollution Control Board, Rep. No. 45, National Ambient Air Quality Status & Trends, 97 (2019).

103 Central Pollution Control Board, Standards for Emission or Discharge of Environmental Pollutants from various Industries (2021).

104 Central Pollution Control Board, Modified Directions under Section 18(1)(b) of the Water (Prevention and Control of Pollution) Act, 1974, and the Air (Prevention and Control of Pollution) Act, 1981, for the Harmonisation of Classification of Industry Sectors into Red/Orange/Green/White (2016).

105 The 'red' category refers to industrial sectors having a pollution index of 60 and above. This category includes 60 industries.

orange category,[106] the green category,[107] and white category.[108] Industries that are not categorised expressly under any category are to be designated under a particular category by a Committee appointed by the concerned State Pollution Control Board in accordance with the revised criteria.[109] The demarcation of industries into different categories was done to identify the pollution load and capacity of the various industries so as to enable the State Pollution Control Boards to modify or tighten the criteria for granting consents under the Air Act, 1981, and the Water Act, 1974.

5.4.3.2 Judicial Expositions on Industrial Air Pollution

Though the law adequately deals with the regulation of industrial air pollution, the courts have intervened time and again to place certain checks on the release of toxic and harmful emissions into the atmosphere. Such intervention is often evident in matters involving an invasion into the rights of citizens or in matters concerning the general degradation of the environment. The first case which brought the issue of industrial air pollution to the limelight was the infamous *Taj Trapezium Case.*[110] The case, the facts of which have been discussed in the following section of the chapter, was a landmark ruling as it brought to the fore the growing concerns of toxic emissions generated by industries. The case not only exemplified the role of the courts in ingeniously addressing the environmental problem but also raised many concerns of the drastic consequences of unchecked industrial emissions. By striking a balance between environmental sustainability and industrial development, the Court paved the way for scrutinising the role of industries as a causal factor for the degrading atmosphere and environment. Following this case, the issue of industrial air pollution was frequently raised before the courts as a policy concern as well as a matter of violation of human rights.

A relevant example of the emergence of rights-based litigation against industrial air pollution is the case of *A. Citizen v. District Collector R.R. District.*[111] The case dealt with illegal stone crushing plundering the natural resources, its subsequent air pollution, and the inaction of law implementing authorities. Pursuant to this, a committee of experts was appointed to report on the issues and it was reported that there was significant air pollution in the adjoining areas due to stone crushing.

106 The 'orange' category refers to industrial sectors having a pollution index of 41 to 59. This category includes 83 industries.

107 The 'green' category refers to industrial sectors having a pollution index of 21 to 40. This category includes 63 industries.

108 The 'white' category refers to industrial sectors having a pollution index up to 20. This category includes 36 industries.

109 Central Pollution Control Board, Modified Directions under Section 18(1)(b) of the Water (Prevention and Control of Pollution) Act, 1974, and the Air (Prevention and Control of Pollution) Act, 1981, for the Harmonisation of Classification of Industry Sectors into Red/Orange/Green/White, No. CPCB/IPC-VI/ROGW (2021).

110 M.C Mehta v. Union of India, (1997) 2 SCC 353.

111 A Citizen v. District Collector R.R. District, 1998 (4) ALD 389.

Based on the findings of the Committee report, the High Court held that the proximity of the quarrying activities posed a significant health hazard to the residents of the adjoining residential area. Therefore, the Court ordered the closing down of all illegal stone crushers situated within the impermissible limit of 1 km and directed the State Government to re-examine the leases granted to those stone crushers situated within a distance of 2 km from the residential area and to pursue relocation of such stone crushing activities.

Similarly, in the case of *K. Muniswamy Gowda v. State of Karnataka*[112] the Petitioners filed a writ petition for directing the shutting down of the rice mills set up by the eighth respondent situated in the residential area where the petitioners lived. The petition was adduced on the grounds of health hazards posed by the rice mill which emitted husk and dust in the entire atmosphere surrounding the area, thereby resulting in a gross violation of fundamental rights. The Karnataka High Court relied on the ruling in *Subhash Kumar v. State of Bihar*,[113] wherein the Supreme Court laid down that the 'Right to live is a fundamental right under Article 21 of the Constitution of India and it includes the right of enjoyment of pollution free-water and air for full enjoyment of life'. The Court held that both the State Government and Pollution Control Board have no power to exempt industries from the purview of the pollution control laws and exemplary damages were awarded to the petitioner which is in consonance with *Common Cause v. Union Of India*,[114] 'the legal position that exemplary damages can be awarded in a case where action of a public servant is oppressive, arbitrary or unconstitutional is unexceptional'. Therefore, the Courts have viewed the problem of air pollution with great stringency that public authorities are also made equally liable for aggravating industrial air pollution.

In an interesting case, adjudicated upon by the NGT, the Tribunal has ingeniously addressed the issue of industrial pollution by not only penalising the violating industries but by holding them responsible for undertaking remedial measures to make good the environmental harm perpetuated by such violations. In the case of *Aam Janta v. State of M.P*[115] the Petitioner sought the directions of the tribunal against the respondent No. 5, Prism Cmt Ltd, to put a halt to the pollution from its plant and to improve sanitation in the open area of the Gram Panchayats where the plant was located. The Tribunal, after considering all the reports from the MPCB and the Agriculture Department and the contentions from both sides, issued the following directions:

1. The company had to maintain a good relationship with the villagers and its stakeholders and should demonstrate its commitment by way of undertaking various welfare measures.

112 K. Muniswamy Gowda v. State of Karnataka, AIR 1998 Kar 281.
113 Subhash Kumar v. State of Bihar, AIR 1991 SC 420.
114 Common Cause v. Union of India, 1996 (6) SCC 593.
115 Aam Janta v. State of M.P, 2014 SCC OnLine NGT 6897

2. The company had to set a required amount of profit to remedy the damage caused to the environment to enforce the provisions of the Environment (Protection) Act, 1986.
3. To address the environmental degradation, the factory and mining areas including the truck yards required revamping, upgrading, and modernisation.
4. The company had to undertake the planting of trees on village roads, tracks leading to mining sites, leftover factory premises, blank space of community, etc.
5. The company had to devise a detailed plan to attend to the issues raised by the villagers, particularly with regard to providing drinking water facilities, improving sanitation, and drainage.
6. Emergency medical facilities were to be provided to the villagers who had succumbed to any health issues.
7. The Tribunal also directed the District collector, Sub divisional officer to monitor the CSR activities of the company and report the same to MPCB on a six-monthly basis and shall then give it to the Tribunal.

5.4.4 Tobacco Smoke

Although smoking tobacco contributes to air pollution by a very marginal amount, it is one of the major sources of indoor air pollution. Environmental tobacco smoke is often said to constitute a negligible portion of smoke and dust particles in the air; however, the chemicals present in such smoke can be lethal as they are composed of toxic and carcinogenic components. The smoke is said to be a concern among many, as the harmful substances can affect persons inhaling the same through what can be termed as 'passive smoking'. It is estimated that in India, tobacco smoke is responsible directly or indirectly for approximately eight lakh deaths annually in the country. Thus, to kerb this menace, prohibition on the manufacture and sale of tobacco has been suggested from time to time. However, tobacco cigarette production and export contribute to the GDP of the country by a significant margin. India is said to be the third largest producer of tobacco after China and the USA and also the sixth largest exporter of tobacco and accounts for 6% of the global tobacco trade. Hence, imposing a complete ban was not seen as a viable option. On the contrary, it was possible to regulate the production and consumption of cigarettes.

5.4.4.1 Central Laws

Earlier attempts to regulate the consumption of tobacco-related products were evident in legislation that sought to restrict smoking in certain specified places. For example, under the Railways Act, 1989, the smoking of cigarettes and other tobacco products was banned in train compartments.[116]

116 The Railways Act, 1889, § 167.

So, to regulate the production, supply, and distribution of cigarettes and tobacco products, in 2003, the Cigarettes or Other Tobacco Products (Prohibition of Advertisement and Regulation of Trade and Commerce, Production, Supply and Distribution) Act, 2003 (COTPA), was enacted with the objective of prohibiting advertisements relating to the sale and purchase of cigarettes and regulating the tobacco business in India.[117] The Act put restrictions on tobacco products including cigarettes, *gutka*, *pan masala*, cigars, cheroot, *beedi*, snuff, chewing tobacco, hookah, and tooth powder containing tobacco.

As per the mandate of Section 5, any person engaged in the production, supply, or distribution of cigarettes or any other tobacco products is prohibited from advertising directly or indirectly the use or consumption of cigarettes or any other tobacco products.[118] The Act, however, makes an exception for advertising cigarettes or any other tobacco product on a package containing cigarettes or any other tobacco product or which is displayed at the entrance of or inside a warehouse or a shop where cigarettes and any other tobacco products are offered for distribution or sale.[119] With regard to the sale of cigarettes and other tobacco products, there is a strict prohibition on the sale of such products to a person below the age of 18 years or within an area located within a radius of 100 yards of any educational institution.[120] This distance is to be measured from gate to gate, as has been held by the High Court in the case of *Joy v. State of Kerala*.[121] In *Godawat Pan Masala Products IP Ltd. v. Union of India*,[122] the Court held that this provision of the COTPA overrides the provisions of Section 7(iv) of the Prevention of Food Adulteration Act, 1954, with regard to the power to prohibit the sale or manufacture of tobacco products, since the COTPA is a special law in this matter, while the other Act is only a general law. Furthermore, no person is permitted to produce, supply, distribute, or sell cigarettes or any other tobacco-related product unless the package includes a label that specifies a warning which may include pictorial depictions of the same.[123] The warnings must be legible and prominent, being conspicuous as to size and colour, in such a style or type of lettering as to be boldly and clearly presented in distinct contrast to any other type, lettering, or graphic material used on the package or its label, and shall be printed, painted, or inscribed on the package in a colour that contrasts conspicuously with the background of the package or its labels[124] and in such language as is specified under the Act.[125] The warnings specified thereunder

117 The Cigarettes or Other Tobacco Products (Prohibition of Advertisement and Regulation of Trade and Commerce, Production, Supply and Distribution) Act, 2003 [hereinafter COTPA, 2003], pmbl.

118 *Id.* § 5.

119 *Id.* § 5, proviso.

120 *Id.* § 6.

121 Joy v. State of Kerala, 2016 SCC Online Ker 31899.

122 Godawat Pan Masala Products IP Ltd. v. Union of India, (2004) 7 SCC 68.

123 COTPA, 2003 § 7.

124 *Id.* 8.

125 *Id.* § 9.

are also applicable to cigarettes and tobacco-related products that are imported.[126] Furthermore, all such products must contain the details of the quantity of nicotine and tar contents of each cigarette in a clear and specified manner, and such contents shall not exceed the permissible limits.[127]

In order to keep a check on the sale and distribution of cigarettes and tobacco products within the permissible ambit of the law, the Act also empowers certain authorities with ancillary powers to search any premises where such products are being stored or supplied, to confiscate and seize such products, and to impose fines where necessary. The Act also authorises the concerned authorities to confiscate cigarettes, tobacco products, or advertisement material pertaining to the same in the event any person who is in possession, control, or management of such property contravenes any provisions of the Act.[128] In the alternative, the Court is also authorised to order the payment of costs amounting to the value of goods confiscated in lieu of confiscation.[129]

5.4.4.2 State Laws

Apart from this Central legislation, the State Legislatures have also taken efforts to kerb public smoking. In Delhi, the Delhi Prohibition of Smoking and Non-Smokers Health Protection Act, 1996, prohibits smoking in public places, including place of work and public transport in the National Capital Territory of Delhi.[130] Similarly, in Maharashtra, while there is no specific legislation that prohibits smoking generally, there is the Maharashtra Opium Smoking Act, 1936, which prohibits the smoking of opium or the possession of any instrument or apparatus for the purpose of smoking opium.[131]

In Tamil Nadu, the State Legislature enacted the Tamil Nadu Prohibition of Smoking and Spitting Act in February 2003 with the objective of prohibiting these activities in any place of public work or use and in public service vehicles in the State of Tamil Nadu.[132] Along the same lines as that of the Delhi State Legislation, this Act prohibits smoking in public places[133] as well as public service vehicles.[134]

126 COTPA, 2003, § 7(3).

127 § 7(5) and §10. *See also,* the Rules which specify the height and manner in which each letter or figure pertaining to the contents of nicotine and tar are to be specifically provided.

128 *Id.* § 14.

129 *Id.* § 15.

130 The Delhi Prohibition of Smoking and Non-Smokers Health Protection Act, 1996, § 5 and § 6.

131 The Maharashtra Opium Smoking Act, 1936, § 6.

132 The Tamil Nadu Prohibition of Smoking and Spitting Act, 2002, pmbl.

133 *Id.* § 4.

134 *Id.* § 5, According to Section 2(*e*) 'public service vehicle' means a vehicle as defined under clause (35) of Section 2 of the Motor Vehicles Act, 1988.

5.4.4.3 Judicial Expositions

The judiciary has also played a significant role in preventing and prohibiting smoking in public places, etc., through some landmark judgments in this regard. In the case of *Murli S. Deora v. Union of India,*[135] the Supreme Court held that the fundamental right guaranteed under Article 21 of the Constitution of India provides that none shall be deprived of his life without due process of law. Smoking is injurious to health and may affect the health of smokers but there is no reason that the health of passive smokers should also be injured. There is also no reason to compel non-smokers to be helpless victims of air pollution. Recognising this, the Court directed the Government to take steps to prevent smoking in public places.

In the case of *Narinder S. Chadha v. Municipal Corporation of Greater Mumbai,*[136] the Supreme Court observed that the Cigarettes Act was enacted in furtherance of the implementation of the World Health Assembly Resolutions, to put a total ban on the advertising of tobacco products, to prevent the sale of tobacco products to minors, and to implement Article 47 of the Constitution, which imposes upon the State a duty to take steps to improve public health and prohibit the consumption or use of drugs which are harmful or injurious to health.

In the case of *J. Anbazhagan v. Union of India,*[137] a writ petition was filed before the Madras High Court under Article 226 of the Constitution, praying for the constitution of a Special Investigation Team to take steps to seize and eradicate banned items like *Gutkha* and *Pan Masala* containing tobacco and/or nicotine and investigate the involvement of Government officials and public servants in the manufacture, sale, and distribution of such items in the State of Tamil Nadu. The Court held that the underground *Gutkha* business is a crime against society which needs to be kerbed.

In the case of *Health for Millions Trust v. Union of India,*[138] the Supreme Court dealt with the issue of whether mandatory health warnings on cigarette and tobacco products as per COTPA are violative of Article 19 (1) (g). The Court held that the health of a citizen has primacy and he or she should be aware of that which can affect or deteriorate the condition of right.

5.4.5 Thermal Power Sector

Thermal power plants are one of the major contributors to air pollution in India. They are point sources for particulate emissions such as fly ash, over and above other toxic air pollutants such as carbon dioxide, sulphur, mercury, and nitrates. As coal remains the major fossil fuel for power generation in the country,[139] the

135 Murli S. Deora v. Union of India, (2001) 8 SCC 765.

136 Narinder S. Chadha v. Municipal Corporation of Greater Mumbai, (2014) 15 SCC 689.

137 J. Anbazhagan v. Union of India, 2018 (3) CTC 449.

138 Health for Millions Trust v. Union of India, (2018) 14 SCC 152.

139 In India, coal remains the dominant source of energy. *See* Anissa Suharsono et al., *Tackling Air Pollution in India,* International Institute for Sustainable Development (IISD), 9 (2019).

environmental impact of emissions generated from coal-fired plants is comparatively problematic when compared to other sectors.[140] Interestingly, despite the volume of emissions arising from thermal power plants, the regulation of the sector has been very minuscule. Critics attribute the minimal state intervention to the dichotomy of balancing conflicting interests of energy security and environmental sustainability.[141] Nevertheless, there have been some positive strides towards controlling emissions generated from the power sector.

Within the ambit of the general law, emissions from thermal power plants are regulated by the National Ambient Air Quality Standards prescribed by the Central Pollution Board.[142] Besides this, in 2014, the MOEFCC laid down certain rules prescribing the maximum limit of ash content in coal used by thermal power plants.[143] The Notification mandated that coal-based thermal power plants shall not use raw or blended or beneficiated coal ash exceeding 34%. Furthermore, the Notification specified limits on the supply and use of coal as fuel in thermal power plants.

In 2015, the Ministry of Environment, Forest and Climate Change notified power plant-specific emission standards for curbing pollutants emitted by thermal power plants.[144] Interestingly, to crack down on outdated power generators, separate sets of standards are prescribed for thermal power plants installed before 2003, after 2003 but before 2017, and after 2017.[145] Power plants which do not comply with the set standards face the risk of being shut down. They also lay down specific standards for water use and consumption by the power plants. Apart from the sector-specific standards laid down by the Ministry in 2015, another set of standards was devised in 2018.[146] While these standards were primarily aimed at regulating the water consumption level of coal and lignite power plants, they invariably prompted emission reduction.

5.5 Judicial Interventions in the Control of Air Pollution

5.5.1 Role of the Supreme Court

Besides the compact legal framework in place, the judiciary has also played a vital role in imposing pollution control mechanisms through various judgments. It is a universal truth that the right to life includes the right to a qualitative living which

140 Sarath Guttikunda, Puja Jawahar & Debi Goenka, *Regulating Air Pollution from Coal-Fired Power Plants in India*, 50(1) Economic and Political Weekly 62 (2015).

141 *Id.*

142 Central Pollution Control Board, National Ambient Air Quality Standards (2009).

143 Notification GSR(2)(E), Ministry of Environment, Forest and Climate Change, Government of India (2014).

144 Notification GSR 354 (E), Ministry of Environment, Forest and Climate Change, Government of India (2011).

145 *Id.*

146 *Emission Standards for Thermal Power Plants,* Central Pollution Control Board, https://cpcb.nic.in/displaypdf.php?id=SW5kdXN0cnktU3BlY2lmaWMtU3RhbmRhcmRzL0VmZmx1ZW50LzQyOC5wZGY= (last visited June 12, 2024).

inter alia includes the right to a clean and healthy environment. The quality of air that we breathe has an inextricable link to a healthy and clean environment. Towards ensuring the right to a clean environment along with the right of humans to live with dignity, the higher judiciary has time and again mandated certain measures that will ameliorate the quantum of air pollution in the country.

The sparse yet effective environmental litigation through the method of instituting public interest litigation has managed to bring the attention of the judiciary to the rising concern of air particulate matter and the rising deterioration of human health, property, and eventually the overall state of the environment. One of the boldest moves of the Government is the drastic measures taken when M.C. Mehta, a staunch environmental activist and litigant, in a case concerning vehicular pollution[147] brought the matter to the attention of the Supreme Court contending that the quality of air around the National Capital Region had become extremely polluted due to the excessive amounts of vehicular pollution caused largely by diesel-consuming vehicles. The Supreme Court took note of this dire situation and understood the need to phase out such vehicles which were the primary cause for the deteriorating quality of air in NCR Delhi. This intervention of the Court led to a positive shift from the use of diesel to that of compressed natural gas (CNG) in Delhi's State transport and public transport vehicles such as buses and auto-rickshaws. This decision of the Supreme Court was not easily accepted and enforced in the city. It required strict monitoring by the Supreme Court. Nevertheless, it paved the way for the momentum of litigants approaching the courts to resolve issues relating to air pollution.

Another case concerning industrial air pollution was one concerning the pollution caused by the emissions let out from oil refineries in the vicinity of the iconic Sarnath temple. A letter written by the *Chhetriya Pardushan Mukti Sangharsh Samiti*[148] alleged that the Jhunjhunwala Oil Refinery and other industries located within the green belt surrounding the famous Sarnath temple were emitting toxic pollutants which caused a blanket of thick smoke in the surrounding vicinity, thereby affecting the health of the local inhabitants. The smoke and dust emitted from the chimneys of the mills and oil refineries were turning out to be an environmental and health hazard. The Supreme Court in its judgment observed that

> Every citizen has a fundamental right to have the enjoyment of quality of life and living as contemplated by Art. 21 of the Constitution. Anything which endangers or impairs by conduct of anybody either in violation or in derogation of laws, that quality of life and living by the people is entitled to recourse of Art. 32 of the Constitution.

The Court, however, noted that since the petitioner did not approach the court with clean hands and with an ulterior motive, the matter was devoid of any merit and the same was dismissed.

147 M.C Mehta v. Union of India, AIR 1996 SC 12.
148 Chettriya Parushan Mukti Sangarsh Samiti v. State of U.P., AIR 1990 SC 2060.

Another landmark case concerning the degradation of the Taj Mahal was brought before the Supreme Court.[149] In what is famously known as the '*Taj Trapezium*' case, the petitioner M. C. Mehta filed a writ petition in 1984, alleging that the Taj was suffering corrosion and degradation due to the increasing amount of air pollution in the Taj Trapezium area. It was alleged that the foundries, refineries, and industries located within the Taj Trapezium area were releasing sulphur dioxide into the atmosphere, which when combined with rain, resulted in acid rain that severely corroded the marble of the Taj Mahal. This corrosion causes the marble of the Taj Mahal to turn a pale yellow colour, thereby ruining its lustre and charm.[150] After considering the submissions made by the petitioner, the Supreme Court took cognisance of the report on the 'Control of Urban Pollution' by the Central Pollution Control Board and concluded that the main sources of pollution are iron foundries, ferroalloy industries, rubber processing industries, lime processing industries, engineering, chemical industry, brick refractory, and vehicles. The Court, speaking through Justice Kuldip Singh, further directed the UP Pollution Control Board to conduct a survey on the number of industries and foundries which are sources of pollution in the area and to issue notices to such industries to comply with the stipulated anti-pollution measures. The UP Pollution Control Board identified 511 industries and among these identified industries, the Court ordered 292 industries to avail of gas connection and the rest of the industries were to be relocated outside the Taj Trapezium Zone. Based on the reports submitted by the *Vardharajan Committee* and the NEERI, the Supreme Court observed that such a stringent measure was imperative in order to protect this heritage landmark.

Interestingly, while the above-mentioned case was being decided by the Court, parallelly, the petitioner knocked on the doors of the court to address the concerns of air pollution, but with respect to a different cause. In this case, the petitioner, M.C. Mehta, challenged the actions of proprietors of stone-crushers whereby stone dust and smoke were allowed to pass into the air, and due to pollution, the lives of the people living in some parts of South Delhi, especially those in rural areas and workers, their families living at the site as well as people living in the villages bordering Haryana were suffering from different diseases and their lives were in danger.[151] The Court observed that while industrial development comes at the cost of some environmental degradation, the quality of the environment cannot be permitted to be damaged. The Court thus directed the Delhi Development Authority, the Haryana Development Authority, and the Central Pollution Control Board to inspect the stone crushing plants and submit a report as to whether the provisions of the Air Act and the Environmental Protection Act were being violated. Orders were passed to relocate these stone crushers and the Government was asked to take measures to abate pollution from these units.

149 MC Mehta v. Union of India, AIR 1997 SC 734.

150 Michael Martin Reddy & Bruce R. Doe, *Marble Dissolution by Acid Rain and Sulfur Dioxide* (Conference Paper, Godschmidt Conference Sept. 3-8, 2000, Oxford, UK).

151 MC Mehta v. Union of India, 1991 SCC (2) 353.

Similarly, in another case concerning the Master Plan for Delhi, 2001, the petitioner M.C. Mehta filed a case against the release of noxious gases by industries.[152] The case began as a public interest litigation against the dumping of toxic effluents in the river Yamuna in 1987. However, as the case evolved, it became embroiled with the technicalities of the operation of the industries themselves and thus, the issue of air pollution was also addressed in the same matter. The process effectively began in March 1995, where the Court expressed its agony over the levels of pollution in Delhi and stated, on the basis of an affidavit filed by the Development Commissioner and Secretary, Government of India, that it was estimated that there were 93,000 industries which were operating in Delhi and the majority of these industries were in non-conforming zones. The Supreme Court issued orders to the CPCB directing it to issue individual notices to 8,378 'non-conforming' units, indicating that 'these industries have to stop functioning in the city of Delhi and be relocated elsewhere'.

This case brings into sharp focus the issue of equity in addressing environmental concerns. It also interrogates the discourse and politics which inform 'urban planning' in a globalising economy. In order to attain the status of 'global cities, urban centres are increasingly neglecting and marginalizing their urban poor'. The approach of the Supreme Court in this case, that of relocating pollution outside Delhi's residential (and therefore necessarily middle and upper class) backyard, ignores the question of the rights of the workers who would nevertheless have to work in those units, irrespective of where they were located. The problem with the 'not in my backyard' approach is that it not only ignores the workers' relationship with pollution, it also ignores the health concerns of the population in the areas where pollution is shifted. Much like the racist dumping of toxic wastes near Indian reservations in the USA, and the trade in wastes that dumps hazardous and toxic waste in the Third World, it shows a fundamental disregard for the lives and livelihood of those who exist on the periphery.[153]

Besides vehicular and industrial pollution, the Courts have also delved into the issue of air pollution triggered by the use of firecrackers during festive seasons. In the case of *Arjun Gopal and Ors. v. Union of India and Ors.*,[154] the Court noted that the indiscriminate use of firecrackers during the season of Diwali led to the release of harmful particulate matter as PM 2.5 or PM 10 at alarming levels, thereby bringing about a situation of emergency. The petitioner prayed for the issuance of possible measures for checking pollution at the source, which included causes such as seasonal crop burning and indiscriminate dumping of dust and other pollutants, and in particular sought a ban on firecrackers, sparklers, and minor explosives in any form during festivals or otherwise. However, it was argued by the respondent that the use of firecrackers was part of the fundamental right of citizens to practice

152 AIR 1996 SC 2231.

153 Jayati Ghosh, *Pollution and the Right of Citizens*, FRONTLINE (Dec. 9, 2000), http://www.flonnet.com.

154 AIR 2018 SC 5731.

their religion and therefore, the ban on firecrackers would amount to a violation of the right guaranteed under Article 25 of the Constitution. The Union of India, however, suggested that in place of a total ban, restrictions on the use of firecrackers would be a viable option. The Supreme Court accepted the measures as suggested by the Union of India and directed it and other concerned authorities to implement the same with immediate effect. Only crackers with reduced emissions and green crackers were permitted to be manufactured and sold. Certain restrictions on e-commerce websites, including Flipkart, Amazon, etc., were imposed with respect to the acceptance of any online orders and affecting online sales. Furthermore, the Court prescribed limited time periods within which firecrackers were to be burnt.

The Supreme Court's stance on firecracker regulation has become more stringent. In the *Arjun Gopal case*, the Court rejected the plea of using reduced quantities of barium nitrate, even though it would be 30% less polluting. It grounded its reason on the fact that a large number of patients were being admitted during festivals because of pollutants from crackers.[155]

> We are aware that we are only issuing interim directions, and much is left to be heard, discussed and said about the rival claims and contentions. What is however indisputable is that the harmful effects of fireworks on the ambient air and the lungs, eyes and ears of people. What is also obvious is the extreme nuisance, noise the fireworks cause to citizens particularly the ailing and the aged. Therefore, though much can be argued as always about the significance and even joy of bursting fireworks. But at the same, prima facie, a just constitutional balance, must overwhelmingly prioritize the harmful effects of this hazardous air on present and future generations, irreversible and imperceptible as they are, over the immediate commercial constraints of the manufacturers and suppliers of fireworks. Secondly, this Court recognizes that the duty to ensure a healthy environment not only falls on the State in terms of Article 48-A of the Constitution of India but also on all citizens Under Article 51A(g) of the Constitution. This Court has previously held that fundamental duties in Part IV A of the Constitution could be a guiding factor in testing the reasonableness of restrictions under Article 19(2)–(6) of the Constitution of India [see State of Gujarat v. Mirzapur Moti Kureshi Kassab Jamat[156]]. The principle of inter-generational equity, recognized and applied by this Court in a number of decisions, beaconing us to the health and needs of the future generation, also favours the issuance of interim directions. Lastly, the precautionary principle, affirmed by this Court in Vellore Citizens Welfare Forum v. Union of India,[157] mandates that where there are threats of serious and irreversible damage, lack of scientific certainty should

155 Arjun Gopal v. Union of India, IA No. 48692 of 2022 and IA No. 104836 of 2023 in Writ Petition (C) No. 728 of 2015.
156 State of Gujarat v. Mirzapur Moti Kureshi Kassab Jamat, MANU/SC/1352/2005.
157 Vellore Citizens Welfare Forum v. Union of India, MANU/SC/0686/1996.

not be used as a reason for postponing measures to prevent environmental degradation.

Similarly, efforts have been made towards combating the environmental impact of diesel generators through their constant CO_2 emissions during service life.[158] A diesel generator used to power a BTS consumes about 18,000 litres of fuel per year. CO_2 emissions from one litre of diesel fuel are 2.68 kg, which further emits about 46.5 metric tons of CO_2 annually.[159] Overall, diesel generator sets contribute 7–18% of the ambient air pollution in non-attainment cities according to National Clean Air programme. Diesel generators as per the NCAP emit toxic air pollutants PM and NOx that pollute the air, and health experts have concluded that pollutants emitted by diesel engines adversely affect human health and contribute to acid rain, ground-level ozone, and reduced visibility.[160] Long-term exposure to such particulate matter is highly dangerous since it is associated with an increase in the long-term risk of cardiopulmonary mortality by 6–13% per µg/m.[161] The Centre for Science and Environment (CSE) released a report titled 'GOING *SOLAR:* Action Plan to Tap Gurugram's Solar Rooftop Potential 2018' on 22 June 2018. The report attested to the fact that diesel generator sets are highly polluting. A subsequent study by CSE on 'Pollution in Residential Societies from Diesel Generators Sets' concluded that diesel generator sets resulted in a huge spike in air pollution levels in the local surroundings. Owing to these developments, State Pollution Control Boards across India have issued circulars/orders calling for the 'retrofitting' of diesel generator sets. The Central Pollution Control Board ('CPCB') in collaboration with the Union Ministry of Environment and Forestry has issued certain guidelines for regulating all the diesel generator sets which are manufactured, assembled, or imported into India. However, these guidelines aren't applicable to those diesel generator sets which are manufactured for the sole purpose of exporting to foreign countries or for sample use.[162] Under the Environment (Protection) (Third Amendment) Rules, 2013, environmental standards exist in India for new generator sets with capacity up to 800 kW and specify emission limits for three different

158 See, Notification No. TNPCB/Labs/DD(L)/02151/2019 dated June 10, 2020.

159 *Environmental Impact*, Renewable Energy Systems and the Environment Group Project, https://www.esru.strath.ac.uk//EandE/Web_sites/10-11/Mobile_mast/environ.htm (last visited June 12, 2024).

160 W. L. Chameides & Ellis Brevier Cowling, The State of the Southern Oxidants Study (SOS): Policy-Relevant Findings in Ozone Pollution Research, 1988-1994 (College of Forestry, North Carolina State University 1995).

161 Lindsay Wichers Stanek et al., *Attributing Health Effects to Apportioned Components and Sources of Particulate Matter: An Evaluation of Collective Results*, 45(32) Atmospheric Environment 5655 (2011).

162 Team ProductLine, *Permissible Emission Limit and Other CPCB Regulations That Diesel Generator Manufacturers and Users Need to Aware of*, Economic Times, https://economictimes.indiatimes.com/small-biz/productline/power-generation/permissible-emission-limit-and-other-cpcb-regulations-that-diesel-generator-manufacturers-and-users-need-to-be-aware-of/articleshow/69097147.cms (last updated Apr. 29, 2019).

size classes: up to 19 kW, 19–75 kW, and 75–800 kW (MOEFCC 2013). Emission limits for NOx + HC, CO, and PM apply for type approval and conformity of production. In contrast, in-use environmental standards apply to generators with capacity above 800 kW or 0.8 MW (or 1,000 kVA), as applicable to diesel engines for application in power plants, generator set applications, and other requirements, under the Environment (Protection) Third Amendment Rules, 2002. It is observed that under the current regulatory regime for the control of in-use emissions which is applicable only to the high horsepower capacity segment, load conditions are not mentioned during the periodic emission testing of diesel generator sets.

The latest guidelines are broadly divided into three parts as per the power rating of the diesel generator sets. Further, each diesel generator set requires a Type Approval Certificate and a Conformity of Product Certificate which essentially mean that the diesel generator set meets the minimum standard of regulatory, technical, and safety requirements of the State. No diesel generator set is allowed into the market without these certificates of approval.[163] Further, there is a requirement that the term 'Genset Engines' should be engraved in the cylinder block of the diesel generator set engine and a durable and legitimate conformance label (containing details like the name and address of the manufacturer, a statement that the product is in conformance with the Environment (Protection) Rules, 1986, number of type approval, date of manufacture/import, rated speed, and gross power of the generator) should be attached to an integral part of the engine which is clearly visible and seldom replaced.[164] In some cases, the user of the diesel generator set needs to obtain environmental clearance for which an environmental impact assessment (EIA) needs to be conducted as informed by stakeholders. India's emission standard for diesel generators is comparable to Euro Stage IIIA which was prevalent in Europe till 2010 for all size categories. However, the quality of diesel (in terms of sulphur content in ppm) is an important consideration while setting emission norms for diesel engines in other countries. Sulphur content in diesel plays a role in determining the choice and effectiveness of emission control technologies. The lower the sulphur content, the wider the range of emission control options available. A study on diesel generators' emissions concludes that all models of diesel generators marginally met old PM and CO norms while satisfactorily surpassing the old NOx + HC limits (on average 20 to 25% less emissions compared to the limit). However, there was no regulation for generators in-use after commissioning (except the 800 KW and above category). Ninety-one per cent of diesel generator sets have no regulations beyond the point of manufacture. Studies show that as diesel generator sets get older, they might emit 11 times the standards set for the manufacturers.

163 *Id.*
164 *Id.*

5.5.2 Role of the National Green Tribunal

Apart from the higher judiciary, the National Green Tribunal (NGT) has also played an instrumental role in imposing control on air pollution through various orders. In the case of *Charudatt Pandurang Koli v. M/s. Sea Lord Containers Ltd.*,[165] the main issue involved was the air pollution caused due to emissions of volatile organic compounds (VOC) as a result of the loading, storage, and unloading of chemicals by the Respondent. The NGT ordered the Director ICT, Matunga-Mumbai, to submit a Report on the issue within six weeks. Later on, the Tribunal found that the operation of the unit was causing respiratory diseases in the area, and direction was issued for the preparation of an action plan to take remedial measures, particularly to check excessive polluting odour to mitigate pollution of the area having a health impact on the inhabitants in the area. Further, the Tribunal permitted the Respondent to continue to operate but subject to depositing a sum of Rs. 1 crore with the CPCB for restoration/relief to the victims for damage already caused.[166]

In *Sandplast (India) Ltd. V. Ministry of Environment and Forest*,[167] the NGT stated that the non-utilisation and improper disposal of fly ash leads to an increase in air pollution and causes severe health problems. It also affects horticulture and agricultural crops. It referred to the 'precautionary principle' and the 'polluter-pays' principle to be applied under Section 20 of the National Green Tribunal Act, 2010, and also the principle of 'extended producer's liability'. In its order, it directed that a Joint Committee of the representatives of the Ministry of Environment, Forest and Climate Change, Central Pollution Control Board, and IIT Roorkee be constituted to finalise an action plan to achieve 100% utilisation of fly ash and ensure its scientific and environmentally sound disposal. It also directed all thermal power stations who failed to dispose of 100% fly ash to deposit damages for environment restoration.

Another landmark case is that of *Saloni Ailawadi v. Union of India.*[168] In this case, the NGT dealt with the issue of pollution caused by Volkswagen India, a company that manufactures vehicles. The engines manufactured by the company were found to be in violation of norms in the USA and Europe on account of the employment of 'deceit devices', defeating the test of the actual state of affairs. The expert committee constituted by the Tribunal recommended a conservative sum of damages against Volkswagen to the tune of Rs. 100 crores due to a lack of methodologies for calculating the overall impacts of NOX on the environment and health. However, the Tribunal enhanced the fine to Rs. 500 crores to create a deterrent effect.

165 2015 SCC OnLine NGT 99.

166 Charudatt Pandurang Koli v. Maharashtra Pradesh Pollution Control Board, 2018 SCC OnLine NGT 2755.

167 2018 SCC OnLine NGT 1810.

168 2019 SCC OnLine NGT 69.

In another case,[169] the issue for consideration before the NGT was the remedial measures to be taken to improve the air quality of 102 cities identified as 'non-attainment cities', which did not meet the National Ambient Air Quality Standards, prescribed under Section 16(2)(h) of the Air (Prevention and Control of Pollution) Act, 1981. Earlier, the Tribunal had directed the States to prepare and furnish an action plan to the Central Pollution Control Board, to bring the air quality up to the prescribed norms. Thus, the Tribunal held that the States that failed to submit action plans were liable to pay environmental compensation of Rs. 1 crore each.

In another major case, the NGT took *suo moto* cognisance of the gas leak in the LG Polymers India Chemical[170] Plant which occurred in the early hours of 7 May 2020 in Visakhapatnam. As a result of this, there was a formation of vapour cloud over a radius of around 3 km, which affected the surrounding areas. This incident also led to the death of 13 people and another 1,000 people suffered injuries after exposure to leaked gas. The Tribunal ordered Rs. 50 crores to be deposited as an initial amount with the District Magistrate, Visakhapatnam, to mitigate the damages caused. Notably, the Tribunal found the company absolutely liable for the pollution caused. The said principle was formulated in the Bhopal Gas Tragedy Case.[171] Absolute liability, as opposed to strict liability, does not allow for any exceptions like negligence. The polluter will be held liable even if the safety standards were adhered to. The case therefore affirms the use of absolute liability when hazardous substances are employed. For the sake of protecting the environment, it is hoped that the Court will continue to apply the standard of absolute liability for a case on the use of hazardous substances leading to damage.

The activist stance of the NGT is visible in its *suo moto* cognisance of air pollution due to the release of gas from pipelines. The NGT took cognisance of the fact based on a news report. The pipeline was laid by GAIL without any environmental clearance. Therefore, the Court ordered the Tamil Nadu Government to take appropriate action against the company. Further, GAIL was ordered not to continue laying the pipeline without complying with the necessary clearances under different environmental laws.[172]

Even in *Gautam Sharma v. State of UP*, the NGT ordered compensation due to the pollution caused. In this case, the petitioner complained of illegal mining of sand and murram near residential areas. The terms and conditions notified under the Air Act were breached. However, no action for compensation was taken by the UP PCB. The Court took cognisance of the fact that the industry was causing air

169 NCAP with multiple timelines to clean air in 102 cities to be released around August 15, In re, 2019 SCC OnLine NGT 1358.

170 O.A. No.73/2020, In re: Gas Leak at LG Polymers Chemical Plant in RR Venkatapuram Village, Vishakhapatnam, Andhra Pradesh, dated 8 August 2020, National Green Tribunal, Principal Bench, New Delhi.

171 M.C Mehta v. Union of India, AIR 1996 SC 12.

172 Panic due to gas released out for 15 feet height from the pipeline of Natural Gas Co. v. State, 2022 SCC OnLine NGT 243.

pollution. Thereby, it ordered action to be taken with respect to compensation. The same was ordered to be used for remedying the environmental damage caused.[173]

5.6 Obligations of India under International Law to Address Air Pollution

Air pollution is an environmental and health concern that has been deliberated upon at the global level. Nations across the world have recognised the ghastly consequences of unchecked air pollution and have resolved to address the issue on a united front. Many treaties and agreements have been concluded to this effect. One of the many significant agreements that address the issue of air pollution is the Convention on Long-Range Transboundary Air Pollution, 1979.[174] The Convention has addressed some of the major environmental problems of the UNECE region through scientific collaboration and policy negotiation. The Convention has been extended by eight protocols that identify specific measures to be taken by Parties to cut their emissions of air pollutants.[175] It is said to be one of the fairly effective Conventions in terms of its enforcement. However, much to our dismay, India is not a party to this Convention. Despite this, India has shown positive strides in the international efforts to combat air pollution by being party to agreements that are dedicated to addressing allied issues such as climate change and ozone depletion.

5.6.1 Actions under the Climate Change Regime and the Paris Accord, 2015

The main instrument that represents global consensus on battling climate change is the United Nations Framework Convention on Climate Change ('UNFCCC'), a culmination of international negotiations on climate change in 1992. The construction of the UNFCCC as well as negotiations in the following years in relation to the Convention have revealed fundamental disagreements between the industrialised North and the developing South.[176] This is because not only does the UNFCCC require developed countries to take the lead in combating global climate change, but it also refers to the differing circumstances and responsibilities of developed and developing countries. Further, the Convention notes that it is the developed countries who are responsible for the largest share of historical and current emissions. It also states that the emissions of developing countries will have to grow, while those of developed countries will have to be reduced. Major developing countries such as India, Brazil, and China played a crucial role in the formation of this Convention as they were at the forefront of developing countries' demands

173 Gautam Sharma v. State of U.P., 2023 SCC OnLine NGT 222.

174 Convention on Long-Range Transboundary Air Pollution, 1979, UN Doc. ECE/GE 79-42960 (1979), reprinted in 18 ILM 1442 (1979).

175 *Air*, United Nations Economic Commission for Europe, https://unece.org/environmental-policy-1/air (last visited June 12, 2024).

176 The terms 'developing' and 'the South' are used interchangeably for those countries that are viewed from a Northern perspective as 'less developed countries'.

for 'new and additional funding' to help them implement measures to help combat climate change.

India signed the UNFCCC at the UNCED in Rio in 1992, on 10 June 1992 and was the 38th country to ratify it on 1 November 1993. Post-ratification, three major concerns of the Indian Government had arisen: (1) the implementation of convention-specific commitments by industrialised countries, in relation to their goals to stabilise national GHG emissions at the 1990 level by the year 2000, and make technological and financial transfers to developing countries; (2) to ensure that the concept of 'common but differentiated responsibilities' is followed; (3) the availability of additional sources (transfer of technology and additional funding), required for the fulfilment of India's commitment to submit its national communications.[177]

In 1997, the Kyoto Protocol[178] was adopted by the Parties to the UNFCCC. Via the Kyoto Protocol, developed countries agreed to specific targets for cutting their emissions of greenhouse gases. A general framework was defined for this, with specifics to be detailed over the following few years. India acceded to the Kyoto Protocol on 26 August 2002. Since the Protocol required the developed countries to reduce emissions of GHG by an average of 5.2% below the 1990 level by 2012, India was not required to reduce emissions under it. Besides supporting India's position that developed and developing countries have differentiated responsibilities towards stabilizing emissions of GHG, the Protocol enables India to engage in clean technology projects with external assistance to ensure it sticks to national sustainable development priorities. The Protocol was thus seen as beneficial for India by enabling the transfer of technology and additional foreign investments into renewable energy, energy generation, and efficiency promotion and afforestation projects.

The Protocol also led to the creation of three cooperative mechanisms – Emissions Trading, Joint Implementation, and the Clean Development Mechanism[179] – allowing member countries to have some flexibility in meeting their commitments in relation to reductions in emissions.[180] The Clean Development Mechanism is quite

177 Under the UNFCCC, developing countries are differently situated than the developed countries, also referred to as the Annex I countries, to the extent that the former category is not subjected to any quantified ceiling on emissions, but are, just like developed countries, obliged to submit national communications on greenhouse gas emissions as under Article 12.5 of the Convention.

178 The Kyoto Protocol committed industrialised countries and economies in transition to limit and reduce GHG emissions in accordance with agreed individual targets.

179 Kyoto Protocol to the UNFCCC, art. 12.

180 The Kyoto Protocol is an international and legally binding commitment according to which industrialised countries will reduce their combined greenhouse gas emissions by at least 5% as compared to 1990 levels by the period 2008 to 2012. The Protocol promises to produce a historical reversal of the upward trend in emissions that started in these countries about 150 years ago. The Protocol will enter into force 90 days after it has been ratified by at least 55 Parties to the Convention, including developed countries accounting for at least 55% of the total 1990 emissions from this industrialised group. Presently, 96 nations have ratified or accepted the Protocol, covering a total of 37.4% of global emissions. It was pointed out at the Johannesburg World Summit for

significant for India, since it enables developed countries to use certified emission reduction credits from project activities in developing countries, and also helps developing countries to achieve sustainable development objectives.[181]

5.6.1.1 Clean Development Mechanisms

India's first UNFCCC-compliant Clean Development Mechanism project is a Gujarat-based, publicly owned business partnership with INOX Leisure Limited, Gujarat Fluorochemicals Ltd. (GFL).[182] Driven by its belief in the principles of sustainable development and corporate social responsibility, GFL developed the Project, which earned 'carbon credits' by the thermal oxidation of a waste gas, HFC23, generated in its refrigerant gas manufacturing plant. This was the first CDM Project in the world to seek registration under the Kyoto Protocol and has been approved by the Governments of India, the United Kingdom, the Netherlands, Japan, and Italy. From its commencement to December 2012, this Project has reduced 54 million tonnes of greenhouse gas emissions, and the carbon credits so earned have been sold to leading companies across the globe for compliance purposes. GFL not only has business in air coolant manufacturing but also in a host of other sectors such as energy generation, leisure, wind power, renewable energy, etc.

With the Kyoto Protocol coming to an end in 2016, a huge change was witnessed in the international environmental law scenario, especially in the area of pollution and climate change. The Paris Agreement, formed out of the COP-21 of the Kyoto Protocol, laid down an extensive plan for the coming years and highlighted the harsh realities of the increasing pollution of natural resources, which has had severe repercussions for the overall climate. India underwent major policy changes for the implementation of strict measures to reduce emissions, after signing and ratifying the Paris Agreement. The United States of America, the world's largest air polluter with the maximum number of operating thermal plants after China, is the only country which did not sign the Paris Accord.

5.6.1.2 The International Solar Alliance

To fulfil the targets set in the Paris Agreement, and to lower the emission rate, the Government of India has laid special emphasis on the development of solar power in the country through indigenous means. To this end, India, in partnership with France, has established the International Solar Alliance (ISA), a programme which aims to mobilise more than $100 billion by 2030 towards promoting solar power

---

Sustainable Development that if Russia and a few other countries ratify the Protocol, that will help its coming into force.

181 Bharat H. Desai, *Institutionalizing the Kyoto Climate Accord*, 29(4) Environmental Policy and Law 159 (1999).

182 Ritu Gupta, *India's First CDM Project,* Down to Earth (May 31, 2005), https://www.downtoearth.org.in/news/indias-first-cdm-project-9597.

globally. As of 2018, 70 countries have signed the ISA framework agreement, 47 of these have ratified, and more are set to join. The office of the ISA is in India, with an Indian bureaucrat as its current Director General. A target of achieving 100 GW power from solar energy alone by the year 2030 was set. Despite efforts to develop more renewables and change the energy mix ratio, the Paris-based International Energy Agency (IEA) in its 2018 Report titled *Global Trends in Energy 2018*[183] reported that owing to the impetus for economic growth and development, the consumption of energy in 2018 had doubled compared to estimates in 2010. The Report attributed this significant rise to the growing use of fossil fuels, especially coal. The Economic Survey of 2022–23 reported a drastic rise in coal production and estimated the same for 2023 to be around 911 million tonnes, which is 17% higher than the same in 2022. Further, the production capacity is expected to reach a billion tonnes by the year 2026.[184]

5.6.1.3 Actions to Stall Ozone Depletion

India is an emerging economic powerhouse. It is also the world's third-largest energy consumer and GHG emitter.[185] These emissions are the leading cause of the rapid depletion of the protective ozone layer in the Earth's upper atmosphere, which filters out the harmful ultraviolet rays of the sun before they reach the surface, thereby preventing harmful effects on humans, plants, and animals.

The problem of ozone depletion was first highlighted at the global level in 1970, when it was found that some chemicals cause damage to the Earth's protective ozone shield. The hole in the ozone layer peaked in 1998 at 2.6 billion hectares, more than 2.5 times the area of Europe, and even covered some populated areas of the southern hemisphere. However, the most disastrous impact of ozone depletion was feared to be on the north. The danger of cancer among the people was a significant factor in pushing governments of the industrialised nations into action against the use of ozone-depleting substances (ODS).

However, due to pressure from manufacturers of chlorofluorocarbons such as Du Pont,[186] the Vienna Convention for the Protection of the Ozone layers, signed in 1985,[187] did not even mention ODS, leave alone banning their use. It was merely an umbrella agreement to cooperate on relevant monitoring, research, and data exchanges. The Montreal Protocol on Substances that Deplete the Ozone Layer,

183 *International Energy Agency*, Global Energy and CO2 Status Report, (2019).

184 Ministry of Finance, Economic Survey 2022–23, https://www.indiabudget.gov.in/economicsurvey/doc/eschapter/echap09.pdf 278.

185 Anjali Jaiswal, *The Road from Paris: Progress on India's Climate Pledge,* NRDC, https://www.nrdc.org/experts/anjali-jaiswal/road-paris-indias-advancement-its-climate-pled (last visited June 12, 2024).

186 Montreal Protocol, *Du Pont: A Case Study in the 3D Corporate Strategy,* 9th Meeting of the Parties to the Montreal Protocol, https://courses.seas.harvard.edu/climate/eli/Courses/EPS281r/Sources/Ozone-hole/more/Greenpeace-on-DuPont.pdf (last visited June 12, 2024).

187 In force from Jan 1, 1989, ratified by 178 countries.

signed in 1987, set reduction targets for eight ODS. The Protocol has undergone four amendments, to include other substances.[188] However, many countries of the South were not involved in the initial negotiations, but were pressured to join the Protocol after agreement was reached among the industrialised countries. There were discriminatory provisions in the Protocol, but the developing countries had to satisfy themselves with a few amendments, and a 'Multilateral Fund' to help them meet their commitments.

Some countries recommended deciding on an upper limit for CFC use and dividing equal use allocations among all nations based on population. But this was not followed. Instead, the Protocol took existing levels of use as the basis for future reductions, and reduction timetables were based on percentages rather than absolute levels. This system of 'grandfathering', i.e. taking the already higher consumption of the North as a basis for negotiating future use, was also followed in the Kyoto Protocol.[189]

Yet another problem is that the Montreal Protocol sets no precedent for holding companies responsible for their products and does not follow the polluter-pays principle. Companies could go scot-free and actually benefit from the Montreal Protocol. They were allowed to market their dangerous products, even after it was established that CFCs were harmful to the ozone layer. Once the technology shift to hydro-chlorofluorocarbons (HCFCs) was promoted, it was often the same companies that made a profit. As new PDS are discovered, governments have to once again face industry opposition to phase out schedules.[190]

It is pointed out that the Montreal Protocol does not help developing countries to 'leapfrog' technology. In the alternate, it ensures profit for Northern companies by encouraging the dependence of Southern countries on interim ODS alternatives like HCFCs,[191] hydro-fluorocarbons, and perfluorocarbons. While the former depletes the ozone, the latter causes global warming. However, they may be required to be phased out.[192]

India responded to the issue of ozone depletion by passing the Ozone Depleting Substances (Regulation and Control) Rules, 2000, under Section 3 of the EPA, which seeks to eliminate ODS in a phased manner, and regulate production, trade, import, and export. The Ministry of Environment Forest and Climate Change also established an Ozone Cell. The planned phase-out dates are as follows:

188 London Amendment [1990], ratified by 148 countries; Copenhagen Amendment [1992], ratified by 125 countries; Montreal Amendment [1997], ratified by 58 countries; Beijing Amendment [1999], ratified by 8 countries [as on June 2001].

189 Gunther Handl, *Environmental Protection and Development in Third World Countries: Common Destiny-Common Responsibility,* 20 New York University Journal of International Law and Politics (1988).

190 Anil Agarwal, *Global Environmental Negotiation; Poles Apart*, Centre for Science and Environment (2001).

191 According to the Montreal Protocol, HCFC shall be phased out by the year 2040.

192 The Protocol fails as a model for other environmental treaties, since it does not assign any penalties for the overuse or abuse of the Earth's common resources.

(a) Chlorofluorocarbons (CFCs) may not be used in manufacture beyond January 2003, except for medical purposes and metered dose inhalers for which affordable replacements are not readily available.
(b) The use of halons is generally prohibited after January 2001.
(c) Methyl bromide, used in limited quantities for pre-shipment and quarantine, was to be phased out by the year 2005.
(d) Hydrochlorofluorocarbons may be used until 2040.

The Rules also specify compulsory registration of ODS producers, manufacturers of ODS-based products, importers, exporters, and stockists. They are required to maintain records and file periodic reports on the production and use of ODS. Moreover, licences are required for all imports and exports of ODS and products containing ODS.

5.6.1.4 Developments in Law and Policy[193]

India has ratified the Kigali Amendment, which was signed in 2016. It came into force in 2019, after more than 60 countries signed the Amendment. As a result, a number of reiterations have taken place in various environmental law and policy journals and magazines in India. The Kigali Amendment is legally binding and contains non-compliance measures. It divides the signatory parties into three new groups. The First Group comprises the rich and developed economies who will be required to phase down HFCs by 2019 or reduce it to 15% of 2012 levels by 2036. The Second Group consists of emerging economies like China, Brazil, and the African countries which will phase down by 2024 and reduce it to 20% of 2021 levels by 2045. The Third Group comprises developing economies and some of the hottest climate countries like India, Pakistan, Iran, Saudi Arabia, etc., which will phase down HFC by 2028 and reduce it to 15% of 2024–26 levels by the year 2047.

Since India played a flexible and cooperative role during the negotiations, it has agreed to a lenient schedule as it consumes only 3% of HFCs as compared to the USA (37%) and China (25%). However, it is quite difficult for India to fulfil its commitments, along with the Paris Agreement and its ambitious 'Make In India' programme aimed at increasing industrial production. The Indian Government has agreed to pass an order to stop the production of HFC-23, a by-product of commonly used refrigerant. This will reduce emissions by 100 million tons, an equivalent of carbon dioxide, in the next 15 years.

Implications of Kigali Amendment for India: the Amendment will have some serious consequences for the Indian air conditioning and automatic industry, which

193 Sairam Bhat & Aparna Sojan, *Ozone Layer*, 33(1) YEARBOOK OF INTERNATIONAL ENVIRONMENTAL LAW 51 (2022).

are mostly financial and technological in nature.[194] Industries will have to invest either in research and development to find substitutes for HFCs or buy patented substances and technologies from multinational companies. The cost of production will increase and may reduce the buyer base for their products. Moreover, some developed nations have already started using HFC substitutes and have sound technological know-how. Thus, without technology transfer or research, it will be difficult for domestic industries to compete with them in the global as well as domestic market.

Indian negotiators had two objectives with respect to the Kigali Amendment – securing an ambitious global HFC phase-down and ensuring that the Indian market doesn't bear disproportionate costs for it. The Indian Government utilised India-specific research and stakeholder interaction to better understand the implications of the different amendment proposals for the country. The issue of economy-wide costs was highlighted by the Indian negotiators during a multilateral meeting in Vienna in July 2016. This intervention widened the narrative to include trade-offs between economic burden and climate benefits.

In the year 2016, via the Amendment, India was set to prepare a specific policy directive, followed by a specific legislation to kerb HFC-23 emissions. However, there was no update as to the time frame for the same. Five fluoro-chemical companies manufacturing HCFC-22 have been shut down in India, and the remaining HFC-23 found in the manufacturing units is to be incinerated. A statement has been issued that efforts are going to be made to eliminate the use of HFC-23, a greenhouse gas that harms the ozone layer.[195] Thus, India shall take the lead on tackling climate change.

Another effort in this direction on the part of India deserves to be mentioned here. Under Article 4 of the Paris Agreement, India has committed itself to make certain Nationally Determined Contributions (NDCs) for the implementation of the Agreement. In its NDCs, India is committed to achieve about 40% cumulative electric power installed capacity from non-fossil-fuel energy resources by 2030.[196] India is also committed to reduce the emissions intensity of its GDP by 33% to 35% by 2030 from 2005 levels.[197] India's emission intensity has reduced by 21% over the period 2005–14, and by 2030, India's emission intensity is projected to be even lower – in the range of 35% to 50%. The above NDCs were updated before COP26, Glasgow. The main focus was on achieving net-zero emissions by

194 Sameer Kwatra & Alex Hillbrand, *Implementing the Kigali Agreement: Key Issues for India,* NDRC, https://www.nrdc.org/experts/sameer-kwatra/implementing-kigali-amendment-key-issues-india (last visited June 12, 2024).

195 PTI, *India to Eliminate Potent Greenhouse Gas HFC-23,* ECONOMIC TIMES (Oct. 13, 2016), https://economictimes.indiatimes.com/news/politics-and-nation/india-to-eliminate-potent-greenhouse-gas-hfc-23/articleshow/54834662.cms.

196 *India's Intended Nationally Determined Contribution*, UNFCCC, https://www4.unfccc.int/sites/ndcstaging/PublishedDocuments/India%20First/INDIA%20INDC%20TO%20UNFCCC.pdf (last visited June 12, 2024).

197 *Id.*

2070. To help with the same, India committed to improving energy efficiency and increasing its solar capacity. India also pledged to generate 50% of its cumulative electric power from non-fossil-fuel-based sources by 2030.[198]

Thus, India is on track to not only achieve but is likely to exceed its non-fossil fuel electricity capacity and its targeted reduction in emission intensity. India's third NDC commitment is to create an additional carbon sink of 2.5 to 3 billion tons of carbon dioxide equivalent through additional forest and tree cover by 2030.[199] However, the progress has been limited, and more work needs to be done in this direction.

An important case in this regard decided in the last decade by the National Green Tribunal is that of *Ridhima Pandey v. Union of India*.[200] In this case, a petition was seeking directions to assess climate-related issues, to prepare targets or a carbon budget for the total amount of CO_2 emissions that can be released until 2050 ensuring that India fulfils its responsibility to achieve climate stabilisation and reduce atmospheric CO_2, and to prepare a time-bound national climate recovery plan. However, the Court dismissed the petition stating that the authorities under the Environment (Protection) Act, 1986, have to perform their obligation of impact assessment and the issue of climate change is already covered within it. Thus, the Court did not consider it necessary to issue any direction under Sections 14 and 15 of the National Green Tribunal Act, 2010, and held that there is no reason to presume that the Paris Agreement and other international protocols are not reflected in the policies of the Government or are not taken into consideration in granting environment clearances.

5.7 Regulation of Noise Pollution

Another growing concern that has plagued the country is that of noise pollution. While the issue of noise pollution has not been one of much significance amidst other environmental problems, it has raised many concerns among the general public. Noise by its colloquial understanding may refer to any sound that is excessive or unwanted and which may have drastic effects on human health and the environment. It may be said that noise pollution emanates from man-made and natural sources. From erupting volcanoes and the sound of roaring thunder to excessive vehicular honking to noise emanating from equipment, noise pollution can be traced to an array of sources. While the law cannot possibly impose limitations or kerb the noise generated from natural causes, it can seek to regulate that emanating from man-made activities. As such, the law regulating noise pollution is aimed at

198 *India's Intended Nationally Determined Contribution*, UNFCCC, https://unfccc.int/sites/default/files/NDC/2022-08/India%20Updated%20First%20Nationally%20Determined%20Contrib.pdf (last visited June 12, 2024).

199 *National Green Aviation Policy - Presented by India* (International Civil Aviation Organization, Working Paper A40-WP/372 EX/151 15/8/19 presented at the 40th Assembly Session 2019).

200 Ridhima Pandey v. Union of India, App. No 187/2017, NGT, Decided on 15 January 2019.

regulating those unnecessary noises that can be limited or prohibited by virtue of some human intervention.

The issue of noise pollution was earlier remedied under the common law principle of nuisance. Nuisance, in its legal sense, refers to the unreasonable interference with a person's enjoyment of his or her property or life. Thus, any unwarranted disturbance or annoyance caused by excessive sound or noise was remedied under the common law of nuisance, whereby damages could be sought through the institution of a civil suit. In the landmark case of *Christie v. Davey*,[201] the facts involved Christie, who was a music teacher and took classes at her home. The defendant in the adjoining house, greatly disturbed by the sounds, maliciously interrupted and disturbed the Plaintiff by beating trays, whistling, and shouting during lessons. The Plaintiff claimed that these noise disturbed the comfort of her family. The defendant argued that the noise created by the Plaintiff's music constituted nuisance. The Court held that it was the defendant's actions that constituted nuisance, and injuncted the defendant from making unreasonable and deliberate noises to interrupt the claimant, because the defendant's malicious motives to cause the claimant discomfort meant that the actions were not legitimate. The Court did not, however, stop him from making noises that a reasonable household may make.

In the case of *Andreae v. Selfridge and Co. Ltd.*,[202] the Defendant owned the land surrounding the Plaintiff's land and carried out demolition work on this land for rebuilding purposes. The Plaintiff sued the Defendant for nuisance arising out of the dust and noise and claimed loss of business as a result. The Court held that since building operations necessarily involve a certain amount of noise and dust, neighbours have to put up with some amount of discomfort. If building works were reasonably carried on and all proper and reasonable steps were taken to ensure that no undue inconvenience was caused to neighbours, they would not be entitled to complain. However, the Defendant had caused noise at unreasonable hours and the quantity of dust and grit was insufferable. The Defendant had failed to fulfil his duty to take proper precautions, reasonable skill, and care and was thus held liable for causing nuisance.

In the case of *Halsey v. Esso Petroleum Co. Ltd.*,[203] the facts involved Halsey who lived down the road from an oil factory. Halsey claimed that the factory's emissions produced an offensive smell, and that the acidic residue from the factory's smoke damaged his linen and car paint. Halsey was also disturbed at night by the noise from the trucks moving in the area. The Court held that, 'Nuisance by smell or noise is something to which no absolute standard can be applied. It is always a question of degree whether the interference with comfort or convenience is sufficiently serious to constitute a nuisance'. Thus, the locality and character of the neighbourhood are important for determining whether nuisance is caused. The factory could operate without causing nuisance, and there was little noise pollution

201 Christie v. Davey, (1893) 1 Ch 316.
202 Andreae v. Selfridge and Co. Ltd., (1938) Ch 1.
203 Halsey v. Esso Petroleum Co. Ltd., [1961] 2 All ER 145.

during the day. Thus, the Court granted an injunction only at night, to prevent the noise from affecting the neighbourhood.

As India follows the common law system, the same principles were by and largely adopted in addressing the issue of noise pollution. In India, the act of public nuisance caused via noise pollution was also punishable under the Indian Penal Code, 1860.[204] Any person who commits an act of public nuisance thereby inflicting injury to any person is liable to be punished under the Code. As noise pollution, by implication, can amount to nuisance, the same is also punishable under the Code. Besides the Indian Penal Code, under Section 133 of the Code of Criminal Procedure, 1973, the Magistrate having the requisite jurisdiction may issue a conditional order requiring the removal of the nuisance which may include noise pollution.[205] There were a handful of legislations that *inter alia* addressed the issue of noise pollution, in reference to specific categories of activities. For instance, under Section 5 of the Aircrafts Act, 1934, the Central Government is empowered to make rules for the manufacture, possession, use, operation, sale, import, or export of any aircraft and this may cover the regulation of air transport services and the prohibition of the use of aircraft. Thus, in ensuring that aerodromes are constructed beyond the vicinity of any residential areas, so as to prevent excessive noise to local residents, the Government is authorised to frame rules. The Motor Vehicles Act, 1939, empowered the State Governments to frame rules for the upkeep of motor vehicles and control of noise produced by them in this jurisdiction. Specifically, under Section 70 of the Act, State Governments were empowered to prescribe rules for the reduction of noise emitted or caused by vehicles.[206] However, this Act was later replaced by the Motor Vehicles Act of 1988. Under the Act of 1988, the Central Government may make rules regulating the construction, equipment, and maintenance of motor vehicles and trailers with respect to the reduction of noise emitted by or caused by vehicles.[207] Furthermore, any person who drives or causes or allows to be driven, in any public place, a motor vehicle which violates the standards prescribed in relation to road safety, control of noise, and air pollution, shall be punishable under the Act.[208]

204 Section 268 penalises any person who is guilty of any public nuisance if that person commits an act which can cause injury to any person, which may irritate the general public or which can cause any general obstruction. Section 287 specifies that any person who irresponsibly handles any machinery which later causes injury or harm to someone is punishable under the Code. Section 290 provides that whoever commits a public nuisance in any case not otherwise punishable by this Code, shall be punished with a fine which may extend to 200 rupees.

205 Code of Criminal Procedure, 1973, § 133.

206 The Motor Vehicles Act, 1939, § 70.

207 The Motor Vehicles Act, 1988, § 110(1)(h).

208 Under Section 190 of the Act, such acts attract imprisonment for a term which may extend to three months, or with a fine which may extend to 10,000 rupees or with both, and he shall be disqualified for holding a license for a period of three months, and for any second or subsequent offence with imprisonment for a term which may extend to six months, or with a fine which may extend to 10,000 rupees or with both.

Although the above-mentioned legislations addressed noise pollution to a certain extent, they were limited in their scope and extent. Thus, a law for the prevention and regulation of noise pollution was framed in the year 2000, known as the Noise Pollution (Regulation and Control) Rules, 2000. Under Section 3 of the Environment (Protection) Act, 1986, the Central Government is authorised to make rules for the protection of the environment which includes the regulation of noise pollution. Keeping in view the serious health hazards due to noise, the Government thought it fit to enact a special law in regulation to the control of noise pollution in the country and thus, these Rules reflected a comprehensive law in controlling the increase of the noise level in industrial, commercial, residential, and silence zones. The Rules categorise these four categories or zones to delineate the maximum permissible limit of ambient air quality standards for noise.[209]

5.7.1 The Right to Freedom of Expression and Sound

Laws regulating the levels of noise pollution have often come under constitutional scrutiny as any attempt to regulate the expression of ideas through particular means will naturally invade the fundamental right to freedom of speech and expression. Article 19 of the Indian Constitution guarantees to every citizen the fundamental right to freedom of speech and expression, subject to reasonable restrictions of decency, morality, security of the State, defamation, incitement of offence, etc.[210] The use of loudspeakers as a means of expression is regulated by reasonable restrictions, to maintain public order and safety. A perusal of Article 19(1)(a) suggests that there are limitations on the power of the District Magistrate, Sub-Divisional Officer, and the Police authorities to grant at will, permission to use microphones, without having any regard to the fundamental rights of the fellow citizens. While citizens have a right to freedom of speech and expression, there is also a parallel right of other citizens to sleep and a right to leisure. The use of microphones as a means to express one's right therefore involves limitations as it is subject to the parallel rights of other citizens.[211] In other words, the expression of one's right ends where the exercise of another's right begins.

In India, however, the use of loudspeakers assumes the status of a fundamental right by virtue of Article 19(1) and Article 25 of the Constitution. A by-law of a municipality requiring permission for using a loudspeaker does not infringe Article 19(1)(a).[212] The State can regulate the use of loudspeakers and mechanical or other contrivances to amplify sound, without amounting to an infringement of the right under Article 19(1)(a).[213] Similar is the case with explosives, firecrackers, etc. Further, Clause (1) of Article 25 of the Constitution protecting the freedom,

209 *See* Rule 3 and the Schedule of the Rules.

210 India Const. Art. 19(1)(a).

211 Birangana Religious Society v State of Orissa, [1996] 100 cal WN 617.

212 Free Legal Aid Cell v. Government of NCT of Delhi, AIR 2001 Delhi 455: Ahmad Koya v. Rajan, 2002 (2) KLT 335.

213 Mazdoor Kisan Shakti Sangathan v. Union of India, AIR 2018, SC 3476.

conscience, and free profession, practice, and propagation of religion, states: 'Subject to public order, morality and health and to the other provisions of this Part, all persons are equally entitled to freedom of conscience and the right freely to profess, practice and propagate religion'.

In *P.A. Jacob v. Superintendent of Police, Kottayam*,[214] the Petitioner, who was a Christian, wanted to use sound amplifiers to propagate his faith and belief.[215] This was not permitted by the Superintendent of Police, on the ground that this might incite violence. So, he claimed violation of his fundamental right to use a loudspeaker at public meeting to voice his views. The petitioner relied on the case decided by the Gujarat High Court in *Indulal v. State*,[216] where it was held that freedom of speech includes freedom to use sound amplifiers. The Gujarat High Court had in turn relied on *Francis v. Chief of Police*,[217] where it was pointed out that there should be some regulation in the use of the loudspeaker in order that the citizens who do not wish to hear what is being said may be protected. Thus, the Kerala High Court held that free speech does not protect sedition, libel, or obscenity. It also does not sanction intrusion into the rights of others. To be let alone is as much a freedom as the right to be heard. Right to silence or solitude is as much a right as the right to expression is. What is negatively the right to silence is positively the freedom from injury by noise. Therefore, the Court held that there was no fundamental right to use a loudspeaker. The approach of the Kerala High Court to loudspeakers has varied from case to case, with permission being granted to the Guruvayur Temple management[218] to use loudspeakers but a prohibition being imposed in respect of loudspeaker use at a congested junction.[219]

In *Mulana Mufti Syed Barkati v. State of West Bengal*,[220] the Calcutta High Court rejected a petition to change the restriction on loudspeakers imposed by the State between 9.00 pm and 7.00 am. The petitioners assailed the restrictions on the ground of violation of their fundamental right to freedom of religion guaranteed under Article 25 of the Constitution. They claimed that Azan was integral to Islam, and was required to be called five times a day through loudspeakers. Without loudspeakers, it was not possible for the voice of Azan to reach the believers of Islam. Dismissing the petition, the Court held that the use of loudspeakers was a technological development and was not a part of Islam.

This right is made subject only to public order, morality, and health. Since this right is subject to health, the noise caused by the use of loudspeakers, firecrackers, and explosives can be prohibited in the interest of health, but the nexus between

214 P.A. Jacob v. Superintendent of Police, Kottayam, AIR 1993 Ker. 1.

215 Members of the 'Knanaya' Community did not marry outside the community with a view to preserve the purity of stock, and this practice is criticised by the petitioner.

216 Indulal v. State, AIR 1963 Guj. 259.

217 Francis v. Chief of Police, [1973] 2 ALL E R 251.

218 Chairman, Guruvayur D. M .C v Superintendent of Police, AIR 1998 Ker. 122.

219 New Road Brothers v. Commissioner of Police, AIR 1999 Ker. 262.

220 Mulana Mufti Syed Barkati v. State of West Bengal, AIR 1999 Cal. 15

noise and health will have to be judicially established.[221] There are various other sources of noise pollution, including aeroplanes, trains, cars, automobiles, and radio and television sets. All of them produce noise, now considered to be the most dangerous pollutant of man's environment. The judiciary has come up with some interesting observations, in relation to the intersection between the freedom of expression, the right to religious practice, and the right to a pollution-free environment. It has sought to create a balance between the needs of development and the health of citizens.

5.7.2 The Response of the Judiciary

The adverse effects of noise on health deserve the attention of the judiciary but have failed to gain the same. Since pollution is referred to as the wrongful contamination of the environment which causes material injury to the right of an individual, noise can well be regarded as a pollutant because it contaminates the environment, causes nuisance, and affects the health of a person. Thus, noise beyond reasonable levels would result in the violation of Article 21.

As early as in 1952, the Bombay High Court in *State of Bombay v. Narasu Appa Mali*[222] directed the authorities to regulate the use of loudspeakers at night when *Ganesh Chaturthi* and *Navratri* festivals were celebrated. The Court held that although nobody can object to the celebration of festivals, the means of celebration must not disturb the peace and tranquillity of the neighbourhood.

When noise amounts to nuisance, a person causing noise can be restrained by injunction, even though that person was causing noise in the course of conducting his business. In *Godham Construction Co. v. Amulya Krishna Ghose*,[223] the nuisance complained of was noise generated by the hammering of steel sheets with hammers varying in weight from half a pound to four pounds. The Court held that no money could afford adequate relief to the plaintiff and his neighbours who were discomforted. It was observed that in determining whether such noise was actual discomfort, the Court as an expert can need no opinion evidence of an expert in order to determine whether the hammering of steel plates by hammers up to four pounds in weight would create a terrific noise or not and whether such nuisance could be wholly abated or not by treating the workshop with the well-known methods of acoustics.

In the case of the *GIDC Housing Association*,[224] a writ petition was filed by the residents of the housing association complaining about noise pollution caused by an iron and steel factory. The Gujarat High Court applied the 'who came first' rule, as per which, a person who goes to a place of nuisance cannot complain unless the nuisance began after the resident colony was established. Since the housing

221 State of Bombay v. Narasu Appa Mali, AIR 1952 Bom. 82.

222 *Id.*

223 Godham Construction Co. v. Amulya Krishna Ghose, AIR 968 Cal. 91.

224 GIDC Housing Association v. State of Gujarat, 1997 Guj. 221.

colony was within the industrial estate and was established after the factory was functioning, the court held that the residents had come to the place of nuisance; hence, they could not complain. The Court asked the company, on the other hand, to stick to the standards for noise emission under the Environmental Protection Act.

On the use of multi-toned electric horns which produce a shrill discomforting sound, the Calcutta High Court in the *Rabin Mukherjee*[225] case held that the State authorities should strictly implement the Motor Vehicles Act 1988, ban the use of such horns, and impose fines wherever necessary.

The noise from the use and bursting of firecrackers came up before the Calcutta High Court in the *Burrabazar*[226] case. Taking a highly activist stand, the Court put severe restrictions on the manufacture, storage, and selling of fireworks, even in the absence of specific legislation for controlling noise creators. The High Court relied on Art. 19(1)(a) read with Art. 21, to hold that citizens have a right to a decent environment, a right to live peacefully, a right to sleep at night, and a right to leisure, which are all the necessary ingredients of the right to life. In *Free Legal Aid Cell v. Government of NCT of Delhi*,[227] the Court directed the establishment of separate courts to deal with the problem of noise pollution. Further, it held that all District Magistrates should be empowered to issue prohibitive orders under Sec. 144 of CrPC to limit the hours for the use of loudspeakers. The Court directed the Delhi Government to restrict the use of firecrackers in religious festivals, marriages, processions, etc. Moreover, it was stated that the SDMs had a duty to ensure that the Noise Control Rules are strictly adhered to and that any default in this regard was to be treated as misconduct, liable for disciplinary action besides action for disobeying the court's order.

In *Chikkarangappa v. Karnataka State Pollution Control Board*,[228] the Petitioners had installed power-looms within municipal limits of Nelamangala and also secured a licence from the Municipal Council for it. The residents of the surrounding locality complained to the Assistant Environmental Officer, Tumkur, with respect to the inconvenience and discomfort caused due to the noise pollution from the power-looms. It was found out that the noise levels emanating from the power-looms were in excess of the standards stipulated for residential areas. However, the Petitioners argued that they had taken the necessary precautions to reduce the noise levels by fixing irremovable glass shutters for the windows and metal shutters for the doors and also increased the height of the compound wall from 6 feet to 11 feet. The Court while dismissing the petition held that Section 22-A does not impinge the powers of State Boards under Section 17(1) and Section 31-A of the Air (Prevention and Control of Pollution) Act, 1981. A conjoint reading of these

225 Rabin Mukherjee v. State of West Bengal, AIR 1985 Cal 222.

226 Burrabazar Fire Works Dealers Association v. The Commissioner of Police, Calcutta 1997 (2) CLJ 468.

227 Free Legal Aid Cell v. Government of NCT of Delhi, AIR 2001 Delhi 455.

228 Chikkarangappa v. Karnataka State Pollution Control Board, 2002 (4) Kar. L.J. 196

Sections sufficiently empowers the Board to issue directions for the closure of an offending unit even without taking recourse to Section 22-A of the Act.

5.7.3 Religious Right to Means of Expression

After the case of *Narasu Appa Mali* was decided by the Bombay High Court, very little was said or done to regulate noise from religious establishments, due to the sensitive religious sentiments prevailing in India. Thus, Courts have dealt with this subject with caution and reverence, and the majority of the decisions have been based on the facts of the case, without discussing any aspect of religious practices.

In the *Birangana* case,[229] the Court upheld the power of the Sub-Divisional Magistrate to prevent a religious organisation from using microphones, if the same obstructs the right of citizens to lead a life of peace and tranquillity, under Sec. 34A of the Police Act, 1861.

In an organised society, rights are related with duties towards others including neighbours. This was reiterated in the *Church of God* case,[230] in which the Apex Court came down heavily on the practice of beating drums and use of loudspeakers early in the morning in places of worship. The Supreme Court ruled that no religion prescribes or preaches that prayers are required to be performed through voice amplifiers or by disturbing peace and tranquillity. The Court stated,

> In a civilized society in the name of religion, activities which disturb old or infirm persons, students or children having their sleep in the early hours or during day or other persons carrying on other activities cannot be permitted … Babies in the neighbourhood are also entitled to enjoy their natural right of sleeping in a peaceful atmosphere.

Rejecting the contention that this violated the Church's fundamental right under Art. 25, Justice Shah said that the fundamental right to preach religion was subject to public order, morality, and health.

An individual can also file a writ petition, complaining of noise pollution as a public nuisance.[231] Moreover, the fact that one individual approached the Court cannot be dismissed on the ground that only the petitioner was affected. In the case of *Sayeed Maqsood Ali v. State of M.P.*,[232] a cardiac patient, residing near a hospital, a *Dharamshala*, and an educational institution, complained to the Court that the State-run *Dharamshala* was given on rent for the purpose of holding marriages and other religious functions throughout the year, resulting in continuous noise at a high level. Loudspeakers were used and music was played at a very high pitch,

229 Birangana Religious Society v State of Orissa, [1996] 100 Cal WN 617.

230 Church of God [Full Gospel] in India v. KKR Majestic Colony Welfare Association, 2000 SCC 282.

231 The Court clarified that the effect of noise pollution was more important than the effect on one or many individuals.

232 Sayeed Maqsood Ali v. State of M.P., AIR 2001 MP 220.

creating disturbance to the petitioner and others residing in the locality. The Court upheld the complaint of the petitioner and ordered the restricted use of such public places.

5.7.4 The Noise Pollution (Regulation and Control) Rules, 2000

A comprehensive law regarding the prevention and regulation of noise pollution was framed only in the year 2000. The Noise Pollution (Regulation and Control) Rules, 2000, were framed with the objective of regulating and controlling noise-producing and generating sources – such as industries, generators, loudspeakers, vehicles, etc., with the aim of maintaining the ambient air quality standards in respect of noise.[233] Schedule III of the Environmental Protection Act prescribes the measure of noise pollution in a very crude form. Keeping in view the serious health hazard that can occur due to noise, the Government thought it fit to enact a comprehensive law for the regulation and control of noise pollution. The enactment of the Noise Pollution (Regulation and Control) Rules, 2000, under Section 3 of the Environmental Protection Act, 1986, was therefore a special step taken to control the increasing noise level in industrial (75 decibels), commercial (65 decibels), and residential zones (55 decibels).

The Rules prescribe different levels of noise in specifically identified areas, and provide for the appointment of the Deputy Commissioner of the District as the regulatory authority to ensure strict implementation. The Rules mention the creation of silence zones to define an area of 100 metres around schools, courts, educational institutions, and hospitals. The following are some of the main features of these Rules:

1. No permission can be granted by any authority for the use of public address systems in the open after 10:00 pm and before 6:00 am. No exception is possible. Any person or organisation making noise on an amplified system after 10:00 pm is in violation of the law and can be prosecuted under the EPA, 1986.
2. Sub-divisional Magistrates can only grant permission for the use of an amplified public address system in the open for the period between 6:00 am and 10:00 pm.
3. After permission has been procured, the sound must fall within the sound limits prescribed in the Noise Rules. This can be measured on a sound meter.
4. Any person violating the Rules is liable to be arrested under the EPA.
5. If the authorities do not act to stop violation of the Noise Rules, the citizen who has filed a complaint can approach the Court with his complaint after 60 days' notice and the Court can initiate prosecution.

233 Noise Pollution (Regulation and Control) Rules, 2000, Statement of Objects and Reasons.

6. The Rules also fix different ambient air quality levels for firecrackers and industrial activities.[234]

5.7.4.1 Recent Amendment to the Rules in 2017 and Its Effects

Prior to the Amendment, Rule 3(5) indicated an area comprising not less than 100 metres around hospitals, educational institutions, and courts as 'silence zones'. However, after the 2017 Amendment, an addition has been made to the existing rule which gives power to the State to notify a silence zone, in accordance with sub-rule (2).

Previously, Rule 5(3) dictated the usage of public speakers beyond 10 pm and up till 12 am on 'festive occasions' not more than 15 in a month. However, the amended rules now contain a specific definition of 'festive occasions', which is as follows:

i. 'Festive occasion' shall include any National function or State function as notified by the Central Government or State Government.
ii. 'National function or State function' shall include:
    (a) The Republic Day.
    (b) The Independence Day.
    (c) State Day.
    (d) Such other day as notified by the Central Government or the State Government.

The 2017 Amendment omitted Note (3) to the Schedule to the Principal Rules, which contained the definition of silence zone. After the Amendment, the scope of the silence zone has been broadened and now only the State Government can notify the silence area/zone.

In the past years, very few cases relating to noise pollution came before the National Green Tribunal, the High Courts, and the Apex Court. One of the cases was in 2017;[235] a petition was filed by three infants represented by their father, alleging that their health was being seriously compromised due to the indiscriminate use of firecrackers which not only resulted in severe degradation of the air quality but also caused noise pollution. The Supreme Court directed that only crackers with reduced emissions and green crackers should be permitted to be manufactured and sold. It also directed the Petroleum and Explosives Safety Organisation ('PESO') to review the composition of fireworks, reduce the aluminium content therein, and submit a report within two weeks. PESO also had to collaborate with the Fireworks

234 Regarding the use of loudspeakers, the rules stipulate that between 10:00 pm and 6:00 am there cannot be use of loudspeakers except in closed premises.
235 Arjun Gopal v. Union of India, AIR 2018 SC 5731.

Research and Development Centre ('FRDC') for the same.[236] Further, a two-hour window between 8 pm and 10 pm was granted by the Supreme Court to the citizens in New Delhi when they were allowed to burst crackers. The judgment was so significant that as a result of this, the air pollution levels that year were significantly lower than the preceding years.

In other cases, as well, the Supreme Court has reiterated the importance of maintaining the ambient quality of noise under Article 21 of the Constitution of India, saying that a person wishing to live in peace and comfort in his house is entitled to a right to prevent noise pollution. One cannot be granted the right to make noise, even within his own premises that travels beyond it and causes nuisance to others. Any unwanted noise which materially interferes with the ordinary comforts of life and in violation of a reasonable man test, is a nuisance. Whether a nuisance becomes actionable is to be decided based on its degree, circumstances, place, and time.[237]

5.8 Conclusion

While attempting to create a robust legal framework, the compliance thereof is easier said than done. While India at the COP21 has updated its NDCs, it has to be seen how far the same are upgraded from time to time. With respect to air pollution, the Supreme Court has more or less maintained its activist role, for example, its pro-cracker ban stance in *Arjun Gopal's* case. The Government's efforts to reduce vehicular emissions are also laudable.

The Air Act has recently been amended by the Jan Vishwas (Amendment of Provisions) Act, 2023. The most notable change made is the decriminalisation of violations of provisions under the Act. The other changes are also quite significant. In Section 21, which provides for mandatory permission before establishing industrial plants in control areas, an exception has been added. The Amendment exempts the need for prior consent for 'certain categories' of industries, as notified in the Gazette from time to time. It may be noted that the addition of Section 21A further increases the Central Government's control of the process of regulation of air pollution, whereby the State Boards are mandated to comply with the guidelines issued by the Central Government with respect to the grant of approvals for the establishment or operation of industrial plants in an air pollution control area. Under the Jan Vishwas Act, penalties for certain actions have been amended; it may be observed that Sections 37 to 41 have been entirely substituted to decriminalise offences under Section 22 or 31A. Interestingly, the addition of Section 39A provides for the participation of an adjudicating officer in an inquiry to quantify the monetary penalty to be levied. A provision for appeal before the National Green Tribunal against an order passed by the said Adjudicating Officer

236 Bhumika Indulia, SC: *Blanket Ban on the Sale of Firecrackers*?, SCC Online (Aug. 02, 2018), https://www.scconline.com/blog/post/2018/08/02/sc-blanket-ban-on-the-sale-of-firecrackers/.

237 Dr. Mahesh Vijay Bedekar v. State of Maharashtra, 2016 (6) ABR 533.

has been provided for under Section 39B, to be filed within 60 days, provided that the person aggrieved deposits 10% of the amount of the penalty imposed by the Adjudicating Officer. While the criticism of the decriminalisation of the Air Act is at bay, it is pertinent to note that the amendments strengthen the mechanism of the Environmental Protection Fund established under Section 16 of the Environment (Protection) Act, 1986, as all monetary penalties are required to be credited to the said fund.

Although it is to be seen how the Amendment affects the levels of pollution, the same depends on the implementation of the scheme and the judiciary's interpretation of the amendments. Approvals to industries can be made more stringent; however, the Amendment also grants exemptions to certain categories as well. Therefore, the effect of the same is up in the 'air'. Even if approved, compliance with the conditions imposed is essential for maintaining the pollution levels. However, infringement of the same, under Section 21 of the Air Act, has been decriminalised.

Therefore, in order to manage air pollution levels effectively, the mere introduction of new schemes may not suffice. The Government has to follow them up with strict compliance. Economic development through industrialisation, though important, cannot be at the cost of clean air. While the Jan Vishwas Act will help propel economic growth and ease of doing business, it is important to protect clean air for the future generation. Even in the US, which is known for its business-friendly laws, environmental violation is categorised as a white-collar crime. Penalty includes both compensation and jail term.[238]

Thus, to conclude, the legal framework regulating air pollution in the country suggests that India has a comparatively extensive set of laws designed to improve and control air quality. Though the legal framework is rather complex and dispersed to certain extents, together, the rules and regulations are comprehensive enough to deal with and adequately address the emerging problems associated with air pollution. The comprehensive structure of the legal framework is evident from the fact that the laws not only incorporate general principles of environmental governance but are also streamlined to address the specific dimensions of sectoral air pollution. Given the alarming rate at which air quality declined since the dawn of industrialisation, one can say that the air regulations were in part responsible for observed improvements in the air quality and arguably, for preventing a turn for the worse. Having stated this, the present state of affairs calls for significant changes and improvements in the legal framework, especially in climate crisis.

Review Questions

- Trace the legislative developments in the prevention and control of air pollution.

238 *Basic Information on Enforcement*, United States Environmental Protection Agency, https://www.epa.gov/enforcement/basic-information-enforcement (last visited June 12, 2024).

- Analyse the functions of the Pollution Control Boards at the Central and State levels.
- Explain with the help of appropriate case laws how the Indian judiciary has addressed the issue of 'stubble burning'.
- Elaborate the judicial pronouncements on regulating air pollution.
- Discuss the various obligations of India in resolving air pollution under international law.
- Appreciate the right to the environment vis-à-vis the freedom of religion and the right to means of expression.

Index

FSC
www.fsc.org
MIX
Papier | Fördert
gute Waldnutzung
FSC® C083411

Kolibri 360 GmbH
Ferdinand-Jühlke-Straße 7
99095 Erfurt, Deutschland
produktsicherheit@kolibri360.de